Introduction to the course

Pacesetter

Pacesetter is a four-level course which takes teenage learners from beginner to intermediate level of English. It has been carefully written to build students' ability to communicate accurately, fluently and confidently in English.

The topics are chosen to keep teenagers' attention because students learn better if they are interested in the subject matter. New language is presented and practised via a mixture of familiar and new topics which will increase the students' general knowledge and interest in the world around them.

Pacesetter methodically introduces and practises study skills so teenage students can become more aware of how they learn, and can develop the learning strategies which suit them best.

Pacesetter is also designed for teachers. The logical progression of presentation and practice in each unit, within each book, and across the course as a whole, makes it straightforward to use. There are clear headings and instructions in all the components, showing how the materials are intended to be used. The Teacher's Books give a helpful description of the methodology of the course and thorough notes for lesson planning.

What is the methodology of *Pacesetter*?

This section of the introduction explains the methodology of the course. It will help you to use the materials in the way we intend.

Presenting new language

In *Pacesetter*, new grammatical structures and key words are introduced one by one, and the communicative use is always emphasized.

The topic of the unit is typically introduced with a warm-up activity which encourages the students to make predictions about the subject, or to say something about their own experience of it. This stage is vital as it mentally prepares the students for the unit, and gives the teacher an opportunity to generate interest in the lesson and to find out how much the students already know.

All new language – whether grammatical or functional – is presented in relevant and interesting contexts to ensure that the meaning and use is as clear as possible. A variety of presentation techniques are used, for example, listening to a dialogue, discussing pictures or looking at language in reading texts.

Practising new language

The presentation stage is immediately followed by contextualized, controlled practice activities which allow the students to become confident in using the new language.

This confidence-building stage is followed by freer practice activities which allow the students to use the language and to experiment with what they have learned.

Many of the practice activities provide opportunities for the students to talk about their own experiences. This stage is vital for learners to perceive the language as something they can really use to communicate their ideas. Students, like most people, enjoy talking about themselves, after all.

Grammar

New grammar is always presented in meaningful contexts that encourage the students to work out the use and construction of the grammar for themselves. In this way students develop the habit of thinking about language, which in turn helps their confidence and communicative use of the language.

The practice stage ensures that students have the opportunity to manipulate the structure in a controlled context before moving to more demanding free practice activities.

Vocabulary

New vocabulary is systematically presented in clear contexts so students can easily understand the new words and build up sets of vocabulary. By learning vocabulary in lexical sets, or groups of words, students will find it easier to remember the new items. Throughout the course, vocabulary is recycled and extended in the context of different topics.

To encourage personal development in vocabulary learning, students are taught how to start and build up a vocabulary book, using a variety of helpful methods of vocabulary recording. There are frequent reminders to the students to refer to and add to their vocabulary books.

To help teachers identify the active or key vocabulary in each unit, there is a list at the beginning of each unit in the Teacher's Book which divides the unit's vocabulary into Key (the words which should be actively used), and Other (the passive vocabulary which is for recognition only). This division means that development of vocabulary and the learning load is carefully controlled.

In later levels of the course, the Vocabulary sections in the Student's Book units are designed to build students' awareness of ways in which they can generate words and combinations for themselves through correct use of prefixes and suffixes, word families and their relationships of meaning, common phrasal verbs, and so on.

Presenting new vocabulary

There are detailed suggestions in the Teacher's Notes on how to teach students to work out the meanings of new words in topics and texts. Students are constantly encouraged to work out meanings for themselves from contextual and other clues, and to build up areas of vocabulary as they progress through *Pacesetter*.

They are also encouraged to use their growing vocabulary in confident self-expression in speaking and writing.

Skills

The aim of the speaking, listening, reading or writing parts of the work is to develop students' fluency and confidence in understanding and *using* English. Skills of any sort are best developed through regular coaching and practice, so every unit of *Pacesetter* contains some work on each of the main language skills. Each of the four main skills is divided into sub-skills, which are systematically taught and practised. Regular practice in using particular sub-skills takes place repeatedly in later units. For example, skimming (learning how to glance quickly through a text to find the gist of it) is a useful, basic reading sub-skill which is introduced in the Starter level. This basic skill is essential if students are to become efficient readers, and it is revisited later in the course so that students will be taught to use the sub-skill automatically when they come across a text in, for example, an examination.

When helping students with their skills work, it is important to focus on how effectively they communicate their ideas, and to respond genuinely to the content of what they say or write. With regular practice of skills, students develop their all-round communicative ability and confidence – this is a prime aim of *Pacesetter*.

Teaching skills and sub-skills

Reading

In addition to skimming, students are taught to scan a text for specific pieces of information, finding answers and possibly making simple notes in the process. They are introduced to ways of guessing meanings of unknown words from context or other non-verbal clues, such as pictures. They are taught to understand the way pronouns are used to make references, and to recognize how some words are used as links of structure and meaning between parts of texts. These reading sub-skills and others are introduced gradually and then practised throughout the whole course, with the aim of teaching students to be efficient readers of English from the start.

In every unit of *Pacesetter* there is at least one main reading text, and in many units there are two. With each text there are appropriate skills tasks to be done pre-, while- and/or after reading.

Listening

There is listening practice in every unit of *Pacesetter*. In the cassette recordings, students are presented with a wide range of types of spoken English: dialogues, mini-dramas, announcements, recorded messages, TV or radio programmes, phone calls, and so on. With all the *Pacesetter* recordings learners are helped by sound effects, pauses, repetitions or rephrasings (built-in redundancy), and by the clear delivery of all the language on the cassettes.

Students learn to listen to spoken English with confidence, to understand it accurately, and to develop specific sub-skills for effective listening such as understanding the gist of a conversation/ message, listening for detail, listening 'through' difficult or unknown language without panicking, understanding the speaker's mood or attitude, and so on. All these and other listening skills are presented and systematically developed in *Pacesetter* through pre-, while- and after-listening tasks.

Writing

The writing activities in *Pacesetter* are carefully structured so students are supported at each stage of the process. As with all skills activities, there is an emphasis on the communicative purpose, so students are encouraged to think about their reader while they are writing. For example, if they are writing a tourist guide for their town, their 'reader' will be someone with little or no knowledge of the area, so they would need to include basic information.

The writing activities help to build students' confidence to write a variety of types of text in accurate English, for example, notices, letters, posters, articles, stories and diary entries.

Pacesetter helps students to develop essential sub-skills of writing such as planning and organizing ideas, checking and editing so they can develop their confidence in – and enjoyment of – the written form. There are frequent opportunities in *Pacesetter* for students to write about their own ideas and experiences, using new language in personalized ways.

Speaking and pronunciation

In *Pacesetter Starter*, the aim is to encourage students to express themselves in a variety of practical situations. At this early stage it is essential to start developing students' confidence in speaking in English and being easily understood. Many speaking activities in the Starter level are necessarily controlled, with regular dialogues and role-plays being used to provide support and guidance. However, each unit also has freer discussion topics supported by cue questions and prompts so that students can start to express their own thoughts from the very beginning of the course.

English pronunciation is practised regularly and there is usually a listen and repeat drill to provide controlled practice of individual sounds, word and sentence stress and intonation patterns. The 'Useful English' sections in particular are designed to develop students' sensitivity to and use of natural stress and intonation.

What classroom procedures does *Pacesetter* use?

Pacesetter includes a range of different types of activities which are all fully explained in the Teacher's Books. In addition, there are alternative suggestions in the Teacher's Books so individual teachers can vary their lessons to suit the needs of their students. The varied activities mean that different learning styles are catered for and that all students will find tasks that interest and motivate them.

Whole class work

In presenting new language and initially practising it, the teacher usually works with the whole class. Some discussions and most checking of answers take place on a whole-class basis too.

Pair and group work

A lot of activities, such as dialogues, role-plays and discussions, are best done in pairs or groups so that as many students as possible have a chance to speak and listen to English. Don't correct your students while they are doing their pair and group work unless someone asks you a specific question. It is preferable simply to monitor students' work and make a note of common problems that can be dealt with later with the whole class.

In many schools the layout of desks and chairs may seem to be an obstacle to pair or group work, but there are simple solutions. Students who sit next to each other can easily work in pairs; students in front can turn to face those behind them for work in groups of four.

Noise is sometimes seen as a drawback in pair and group work also, but the moderate noise of students using English to carry out tasks is surely to be welcomed! Students can easily be trained, by regular reminders at the beginning of their course, to recognize when noise is too loud for neighbouring classes and to be considerate about it. A signal to lower the noise level, for example, switching the light on (or off), can be agreed with the students, and used as necessary.

Individual work in the classroom and homework

Many activities in the *Pacesetter* Student's Books are for students to do alone in class, for example, reading a text or planning a piece of writing.

Homework will also be done individually, often using the Workbook. In *Pacesetter* students are taught how to study independently. Features such as the 'Learn to learn' sections in the Student's Book and the 'Prepare for Unit X' (self-access) vocabulary preparation phase at the end of every Workbook unit are designed to teach students to study effectively on their own. Confidence in working well alone will help students with all aspects of working independently, such as more advanced study or revising for exams.

Learner training

Pacesetter introduces students to techniques for studying effectively and independently through the 'Learn to learn' sections that appear in many units throughout the course. The Starter level, for example, introduces dictionary skills, basic vocabulary recording methods and simple self-check methods. It encourages students to think about specific aspects of their own methods of language study.

Dictionaries are valuable language learners' tools but only if they are used properly. *Pacesetter* students are therefore taught good habits of dictionary use. For example, that they should first try to work out meanings for themselves before reaching for a dictionary.

Many students in the early stages of language study gain confidence from using a bilingual dictionary. Teachers can later encourage them to use an English/English (monolingual) student's dictionary, when they can understand the language used in the definitions of the dictionary. The most important consideration is to make sure that students use good quality dictionaries, such as those published by Oxford University Press, which contain useful information about grammar, pronunciation and American English variants.

Using the students' own language

Some teachers worry about occasionally explaining things in their own language, but there can be good reasons for sometimes doing so in monolingual classes. For example, explanations are possible which are beyond the level of the student's English or interesting cultural facts can be explained quickly. Occasionally it is more effective to check the meaning of an abstract or scientific concept by asking for the equivalent word in the student's own language. Obviously, use of the students' own language should be kept to a practical minimum, since the more English they are exposed to, the

quicker they will progress in the language. However, it is sometimes simply more efficient and effective to use the students' own language.

Project work

Pacesetter has projects in the Consolidation units at the end of every block of five units. These projects are carefully structured to revise the language and skills taught in the earlier units, while giving students motivating opportunities for more extended, personalized, creative pieces of writing.

Projects play a special role in activating the skills of organizing and planning, drafting and editing, and final presentation. The Teacher's Notes regularly suggest ways in which students' project work can be displayed once it is finished. When a project is displayed, it provides a real audience for students' writing, which is motivating and encourages greater care with presentation.

Songs

There are numerous songs in different musical styles in the 'Freewheeling' sections throughout *Pacesetter*, and they are all recorded on the cassettes.

The songs are there for enjoyment but there is always a teaching point behind them, either more informal exposure to the new language points or an extension of the topic and vocabulary through music.

Students are not expected to study the language of songs in any detail (it is often 'above level' in any case, so close study is not desirable), but rather to enjoy listening to and singing along with pop songs in English while doing a simple task.

Testing and assessment

Checking students' progress takes place regularly in the self assessment (Check yourself) sections in the Workbook. Students can see the areas they are strong or weak in, and teachers can then suggest ways of tackling individuals' problems.

In addition, regular and continuous assessment of individual students' progress in oral work in class is recommended. A basic aim should be to try to get every student in a class to say something in every lesson, so that continuous assessment can become automatic, and the teacher can take regular notes on individual students' progress and their problems in speaking English.

In this Teacher's Book there is a photocopiable progress test for each unit, which will provide you with a regular up-date of each student's development. Bear in mind that a progress test is a positive tool for both you and the student, and is designed so that the majority of students will do reasonably well. As well as monitoring progress on a regular basis, the test results should have the secondary benefit of motivating the students; a good mark is more likely to achieve this than one which is harsh.

What does *Pacesetter* consist of?

The Starter Student's Book contains:
- contents pages outlining what comes in each unit
- preliminary pages introducing classroom language and some international English words.

- 15 main units which include a photo-story, a language review section in each teaching unit and end-of-unit ('Freewheeling') activities, including songs, puzzles and games
- three Consolidation units including project work
- information gap activities for skills work

The Starter cassettes go with the Student's Book. They contain:

- recordings for listening activities
- the photo-story dialogues
- pronunciation models and activities
- songs
- recordings of many of the reading passages

The Workbook is linked closely with the Student's Book. It contains:

- a preliminary page introducing dictionary work and Workbook instructions
- 15 units which provide further practice on all aspects of the language in the Student's Book
- 3 Consolidation units which review and check the language and skills taught in the earlier units
- models of how to record and store vocabulary
- unit-by-unit word lists

The Starter Teacher's Book contains:

- this introduction to the methodology and procedures of *Pacesetter*
- step-by-step teaching notes, with answer keys, tapescripts and optional activities
- helpful background cultural notes
- a key to the Workbook exercises
- photocopiable, optional activities
- a photocopiable test for each unit

What are the features of the Student's Book?

Topics

The first four pages of every main unit of the Student's Book are devoted to two loosely linked aspects of a theme or topic. Topics are carefully selected to provide natural contexts for language presentation and to be of real interest to teenagers.

With two related topics in each unit, a good range of vocabulary from the overall topic area can be introduced and recycled. A further important aim is to build on students' own interests and experience, and to develop their understanding of the world around them.

Work it out

The 'Work it out' sections in every unit focus on particular grammatical structures and their uses, or on particular communicative functions. Students are guided to identify grammatical patterns and to work out for themselves the basic rules of formation and use.

Following the presentation of new language, initial practice exercises are always closely guided. Less guided practice in using new language then follows, sometimes written and sometimes oral.

Useful English

The regular 'Useful English' sections do not focus on grammatical structures, but rather on functional English. They bring together phrases and expressions in specific functional groups, for example, the language for agreeing/disagreeing or for complaining.

A valuable benefit of the 'Useful English' sections is that the students learn *when* to use the language. This focus on register will teach them if the phrase is, for example, formal or informal, polite or less polite, appropriate for friends, family or adults.

Each expression is recorded so the students practise saying the language with correct stress and intonation before using it in the oral task that follows.

Learn to learn

The 'Learn to learn' feature gives systematic guidance in basic language study skills: 'learner training'. Students do not instinctively have such disciplined skills, so teaching and then practising them is of both general and specific educational value to them.

In the Starter, for example, students are taught how to create a personal vocabulary book, when and how to use a dictionary correctly and how specific sub-skills can improve their reading or writing. Study skills are further developed and expanded in later levels of the course.

Vocabulary

There are regular 'Vocabulary' sections in *Pacesetter*. In the first two levels these focus mainly on specific sets or areas of vocabulary. In later levels they also focus on ways of recognizing and using patterns of vocabulary and word-formation, such as word families, collocations (words frequently used together like 'heavy + rain'), prefixes and suffixes. All such aspects are practised in Workbook exercises.

Photo-story

An episode of the photo-story telling the story of a group of typical British teenagers appears on the final spread of every unit of the first two levels. The story shows aspects of the everyday lives and speech of young British teenagers and the photos, action and language give insights into British life.

Each episode recycles examples of the target language of the unit so students see structures and key words re-used in the story setting. Before and after each episode of the story there are exercises focusing on language and content.

Below is a summary of the Starter photo-story.

A group of six 15–17 year old students meets regularly at a youth club in Oxford, the OK Club. One day there is a fire at the club and, after putting it out, the group decide to repair and redecorate the clubroom themselves. They devise various ways of raising money for the paint, etc. Then a TV company becomes interested in filming the group at work and agrees to help with money for the materials. Some money goes missing because of a mix-up and is gratefully recovered; three of the group play a little trick, to encourage a teenage romance that starts between two other members of the group. These two eventually start 'going out' together after a final big party to celebrate the success of 'Project OK', the redecorating project.

Set the pace

The 'Set the pace' exercises after the photo-story practise the everyday colloquial English used by British teenagers. Students are asked to work out the meanings of these pieces of language from their contexts in the story, and then to practise saying them, copying rhythm and intonation in particular.

Review

A grammar 'Review' section appears on the final page of every main unit. It provides students with a summary of new grammar in the form of clear tables, simple explanations of use, and examples. Some basic grammatical terms are used so that students can talk about language, using correct basic terminology such as the names of the main parts of speech.

Following the Review, there are two or three extra exercises on the main grammar points of the unit.

Freewheeling

When you are cycling down a hill and don't need to pedal, you are freewheeling. Used as an idiom, freewheeling means relaxing or not making unnecessary effort.

The 'Freewheeling' sections at the end of every main unit offer an enjoyable, freer activity. Typically, it will be a song, game or word puzzle.

Consolidation units

The three Consolidation units in each of the Student's Books revise and recycle the grammar, vocabulary and skills of the previous five units, combining these in fresh, interesting ways.

The Consolidation units all end with a project aimed at a systematic review and further practice of work recently done on specific sub-skills, especially those of reading and writing. The projects also aim to give students opportunities for self-expression and some creativity with the language they have learned.

What do the cassettes contain?

The cassettes contain all the listening texts, exercises and songs. You will need to use the cassette when you see this symbol: 📼 .

The voices on the cassette give examples of a normal range of slight British English accents and some examples of Australian, New Zealand and North American English.

The speed of speech is very slightly slower than that of a native speaker to compensate for the limitations of the classroom environment. However, the rhythm, stress and intonation are all natural.

Some background sound effects are used to establish the context of the recorded material but these do not interfere with the clarity of the speech.

What does the Workbook contain?

Main units

The main units of the Workbook mirror and support all aspects of Student's Book work on grammar, vocabulary and skills. In the Starter and Elementary Workbooks there is additional work on basic writing techniques and skills of accurate writing, for example, practice of sentence formation, punctuation, and linking ideas.

'Prepare for Unit X' at the end of each main Workbook unit is designed to train students in simple aspects of self-access learning: researching and preparing areas of new vocabulary for the next unit of the Student's Book. Taking personal responsibility for such aspects of self-preparation noticeably raises most teenage students' sense of responsibility for their own learning, as well as their motivation.

Consolidation units

The Consolidation units in the Workbook provide review of the language and skills work recently introduced.

There is a 'Check yourself' section where students can assess how well they have learned the language and skills taught in the previous five units. It is an important aspect of learner training to encourage students to analyse their own progress at regular stages in the course, and to identify areas where they need to study further for a full grasp of the language.

This is a progress test designed to show the students how much they have learned (or not!), so most students should get good marks.

The Review section of the Consolidation unit is used to record the marks from the test section. This provides an opportunity for students to assess for themselves how much they have remembered.

A useful feature of the Workbook is the Vocabulary section. This is a unique developmental tool designed to help students build a personal record of the vocabulary they have learned and to encourage a variety of storage techniques.

At the back of each Workbook there is a wordlist containing all the key vocabulary for that level of the course. This can be used in a variety of ways, for example, as a reference or to guide students in techniques of vocabulary storage and study.

What does this Teacher's Book contain?

The Teacher's Book is the coordinating book in the *Pacesetter* series at each of the four levels.

It contains the full introduction you are now reading, with general notes to help you use *Pacesetter* effectively. Following the introduction are unit-by-unit teaching notes, with tapescripts and answer keys. Where necessary, there are notes on cultural or other specific factual details, so that teachers can prepare themselves with extra information on some topics. Basic lesson planning is reliably done for you in this book.

Enjoy using the course!

Introduction

Syllabus

Topic
English in Class
English you know

Grammar
Imperatives

Function
Classroom language

Vocabulary
International words

Learn to learn
Using a vocabulary book

Vocabulary

Key vocabulary

a	I	that's right
again	it	the
at	Japan	this
Australia	listen	understand
Britain	look at	use
Canada	mean	what
Do	no	write
example	please	wrong
excuse me	read	yes
good morning	say	you
goodbye	thank you	

Other vocabulary

bank	hotel	taxi
basketball	lemonade	telephone (n)
cafe	museum	television
cassette	park	tennis
cinema	partner	train (n)
coffee	picture	university
cola	pizza	video
computer	policeman	volleyball
doctor	restaurant	work with
football	sandwich	yacht
hamburger	secretary	

Materials preparation

1 Beginner or elementary dictionaries for Student's Book page 7, Exercise 3 and Workbook page 3, Exercises 1 and 2.
2 Notebooks for Student's Book page 7, Exercise 2, for each student to record new vocabulary.

English in class

Aims

This section introduces basic classroom language, including commands, so that English can be used from the start of the course. The language is presented through pictures and listening activities, and practised orally.

1

Background information

In Britain school starts at nine o'clock, so the clock on the wall in picture 1 is intended as a clue to the meaning of the phrase *Good morning*.

● Use the mother tongue for explanations and discussion in Exercises 1–4.

● Explain that the aim of the exercises on this page is to help you all to use English in class as much as possible. As an example, tell students that you and they can already greet each other in English at the beginning of class by saying *Hello*.

● Students suggest other common classroom language (in the mother tongue). If necessary, prompt them with mime, but do not teach the English expressions yet. For example:
Point to the cassette recorder and bring your hand to your ear for *Listen*. Walk to the door, waving for *Goodbye*. Open or close a book.

● Students look quickly at the pictures on page 6 and guess who is speaking: the teacher or a student. Do not give answers yet.

● Put students into groups of 3 or 4 to guess what the teacher or student is saying in each picture. Allow about 5 minutes for this. Groups then choose a representative to speak for them. Each representative in turn states their group's guess about each picture. In this way they compare their ideas with those of other groups.

● ▣ When you feel students have understood the general idea of what is being said in each picture, explain that they are going to hear the English for each picture in turn. They must listen and follow the pictures. Play the cassette and check that students are looking at the right picture for each speech.

Option

● If students have difficulty interpreting a picture, ask questions to guide them. For example, for picture 1: *Where is the teacher?* (at the door). *Is the door open or closed?* (open). *Is she coming in or going out?* (coming in). *What time is it?* (nine o'clock). *If she is coming in, is nine o'clock the start or end of the class?* (the start). *So, if she is coming in to start the lesson, what does she say to the class?* (Good morning).

2

● ▣ Play the cassette for picture 1 again.

● Ask students how they would say *Good morning* in their language. Most should be confident of the correct translation by now.

● Continue with the other pictures, playing the cassette for each picture in turn. At this stage, do not try to teach any grammar structures or individual words of English.

Option

● Students write a translation of each phrase in Exercise 1.

3a

● By this time, students should be familiar with the recorded phrases. Explain that they are going to hear six of the phrases again: they match each of the phrases with the correct picture.

● Students write the letters A–F in their notebooks.

● ▣ Play the cassette. Students write the picture number next to each letter.

● Check the answers.

Tapescript

A **Boy** Excuse me. I don't understand.
B **Girl** What does this mean?
C **Teacher** Good morning.
D **Boy** Thank you.
E **Teacher** Goodbye!
F **Boy** Say it again, please.

Answer key

B *7* C *1* D *6* E *11* F *5*

3b

● ▣ Play the cassette again. Stop or pause after each phrase and, with gestures, encourage the class to repeat it.

● Play each phrase again for students to repeat, but this time with books closed so that students can concentrate on listening to the sounds, rather than reading the words. Give encouragement in English: *Well done! That's good.*

Option

● Students practise saying all the phrases in Exercise 1, using the procedure for Exercise 3b.

Tip 1 ★

Techniques for further speaking practice

● The following techniques allow you to extend 'Listen and repeat' exercises. Their aim is to provide variety, to keep students alert, and to help you assess how individual students are performing. For each step, you will need to play the cassette.

  1 Divide the class into two sections, for example, down the middle of the class. Gesture to each half to repeat the phrase, one group after the other.

  2 Divide the class into four sections, for example, front left, front right, back left, back right, and repeat the procedure.

  3 Gesture to 4 or 5 individual students, one after the other, to repeat each phrase. Choose students at random. This will keep students alert in case their turn comes next.

4

- Explain that the symbols a–d are ones used in the Student's Book. Students find examples of each symbol in Units 1–3.
- In the mother tongue, ask the class to say what the symbols might mean. Then ask if any student knows the English phrase for any of them. Try to use some of the phrases in Exercise 1 when responding, for example: *Yes, that's right. Say it again, please.*
- Students match each symbol with an instruction. If they do not understand *Work with a partner*, they should be able to work out the answer by doing the other three first.
- To check students' answers, draw each of the symbols on the board. Write a number next to each. Say the four instructions at random. Students call out (in the mother tongue) the number of the right picture on the board. Say each phrase several times. Begin slowly and clearly, then say the phrases slightly faster as they become more confident in understanding you.

Answer key
1 *c* 2 *d* 3 *a* 4 *b*

Suggested Workbook practice
Page 3, Exercise 2

English you know

Aims
In this section, students are presented with some English words that they probably already know to give them confidence that they can learn English. The words are presented through pictures and text, and practised in a listening activity. The 'Learn to learn' activities present ways for students to record new words.

Option
- Write the heading *International English* on the board. Write a list of two or three words under the title, such as *taxi*, *cola*, *football*. Point to the heading, say it aloud, and ask in English, *What does this mean?* Students offer suggestions of what it means. To find out how much English students already know, ask them to suggest other words to add to the list on the board, and to tell you what they mean.

1a

- Tell students: *Look at the pictures. Now look at the words*. Point to the page to show your meaning. Then say: *Match the pictures and the words*. Use gestures and the example (*cafe* and picture 1) to show your meaning.
- Say: *Work with a partner*, at the same time gesturing to students that they should work in pairs. Move around the class repeating the instruction, and using gestures to show students who they should work with.
- Students write the correct number in the box next to each word. Walk round the class and check that all students have understood what to do.
- Hold up your book and point to the first picture. Say the picture number. Students call out the corresponding word. Continue with the other pictures.

Answer key
coffee 8 *cola* 15 *computer* 16 *doctor* 4 *football* 18 *hamburger* 5
pizza 6 *policeman* 10 *restaurant* 12 *sandwich* 11 *taxi* 17
telephone 14 *television* 3 *tennis* 2 *train* 13 *video* 9 *yacht* 7

Option
- Pairs who finish early can cover the list of words and use the illustrations to test each other.

1b

- ▣ Play the cassette twice, pausing after each word to allow students time to repeat.
- To assess how well individual students are pronouncing English words, call out picture numbers (in the mother tongue) at random, gesturing to individual students to answer with the right word.

Option
- Ask students which of the words they think are the most difficult to pronounce. They may mention words where spelling and pronunciation are different, such as *restaurant*, or words that are used in both English and the mother tongue, but which are pronounced differently. Give extra practice in saying these words but do not expect perfection, so do not ask a student to repeat a word more than once or twice.

Learn to learn: using a vocabulary book

Option
- Students close their books. In the mother tongue, ask: *How do you learn new vocabulary? If you write it in a book, how do you organize it?* Start them off with a suggestion, such as having a page for each letter of the alphabet and writing each new word on the relevant page. Get as many ideas as possible.
  Along the top of the board, write *cafe*, *cola*, *football*, *pizza*, *sandwich*, *tennis*. The students who gave ideas on recording vocabulary come to the board in turn and show how they would record the words you have written.
  Discuss with the class, in the mother tongue, which method they think is best for the words on the board, and why.

2

- Tell students that they will need to keep a record of all new vocabulary, and either distribute vocabulary notebooks or ask students to get them out.
- Point to the three examples of ways of recording vocabulary in Exercise 2. Ask students, in the mother tongue: *What is the name of the first method?* (Picture dictionary). *What category of vocabulary is it recording?* (Food and drink). Ask about the other two methods in the same way.
- Tell students to look at pages 73–76 of their Workbooks and find other ways of recording vocabulary. Explain that they can also use these pages to store vocabulary as well as, or instead of, in a vocabulary book.
- Briefly discuss with the class which method they think is best for the category 'Food and drink', and why.

- Students, in pairs, look at the other words in Exercise 1 and group them into categories. Possible categories are *Equipment*, *Jobs*, *Sport* and *Transport*. Pairs work out categories, then decide which of the three methods is best for recording each category. For instance, they may decide that transport and equipment words are too difficult or take too long to draw, so one of the other methods would be better.
- Get individual students to name their categories. As they name them, tell the class the English for each, and write it on the board.
- Students record the various category words in their notebooks.

Option
- If there is not enough time to record vocabulary in class, students could write just the topic headings now, and record the vocabulary at home.

3
- Students look up the words in dictionaries, if necessary.
- Get students to put the words in the box into categories. For example, in the mother tongue ask: *Which words belong to the topic 'Food'?* (lemonade). *Which words belong to the topic 'Sport'?* (basketball, volleyball). *What new topics are there?* (*Countries* and *Buildings* or *Places*).
- Students suggest the most suitable method of recording the new categories. For example, they could draw a flag next to each country, and do a word map for *Buildings/Places*.
- Students record all the words in their notebooks, starting new pages for the new categories. Explain that they will be adding further words for these topics in later lessons.

Option
- To save time, allow students to work in pairs for the dictionary phase. Each partner looks up half the words. When they have finished, they share their answers.

Suggested Workbook practice
Page 3, Exercises 1, 3 and 4

Preparation for Unit 1
- This activity allows students to explore the content and layout of the Student's Book and Workbook. Make sure students have both books with them. Write a list of questions on the board, in the mother tongue, for students to answer either in class or at home:
  Student's Book and Workbook
  1   How many units do they have?
  2   Where is the Contents page?
  3   Where is the grammar summary for each unit? What is it called?
  4   Which of the books has fewer pages?
  5   Find the photo-story. Where do the episodes appear?
  6   Which book has exercises to prepare for the next unit?

Answers
1   *Both have 15 units and 3 consolidation units.*
2   *At the beginning of the Student's Book.*
3   *At the end of each Student's Book unit. It's called Review.*
4   *The Workbook.*
5   *On the fifth page of each unit.*
6   *The Workbook.*

Workbook answer key
English you know
1a 2 computer   3 doctor   4 football   5 hamburger
6 lemonade   7 museum   8 secretary   9 video   10 yacht
1b 1 cafe   2 Canada   3 cassette   4 cinema   5 coffee
6 cola   7 computer
2 Student's own answers
3 1 page 75   3 page 74   4 page 74   5 pages 76-80
6 page 76   7 page 73   8 page 76
4 1 basketball   2 hamburger   3 train   4 doctor   5 cassette
6 cola   7 video   8 television   9 taxi   10 football

Unit 1

Syllabus

Topic
New friends
Countdown: *numbers*
The OK Club

Grammar
Imperatives
The verb *be* (singular)
my, your

Function
Introductions

Vocabulary
Countries
Numbers 0–10
Phrases for warning and apologizing

Reading
Reading messages

Listening
Identifying countries, phone numbers

Writing
Writing about yourself
Writing messages

Speaking
Introducing yourself

Pronunciation
Saying phone numbers
Sentence stress in greetings
/i:/ and /ɪ/

Vocabulary
Key vocabulary

address	her	she
and	hi	six
Argentina	his	sorry
be	how	Spain
Brazil	Hungary	ten
brother	Me	thanks
eight	Mexico	three
England	my	to
family	name	Turkey
fine	number	two
five	OK	United States
four	one	very
from	phone (v)	we
Greece	pleased	well
he	Poland	where
hello	seven	your

Other vocabulary

careful	in	new
club	later	nine
fax	Look out!	really
for	meet	
here	message	

Materials preparation

1   For Student's Book page 10, Exercises 1 and 2: prepare sets of 10 squares of card with the numbers 1–10 written in numerals. Prepare enough sets for one for each group of 4 or 5 students, and a larger set for yourself.

2   For page 10, Exercise 2 Option: a sheet of paper for each student.

3   A small prize for the students who complete the Freewheeling wordsquare fastest.

New friends
Introductions

Aims
In this section, students learn how to greet people they are meeting for the first time.

Option
- Greet several students by name, for example, *Hello, Demet! Hello, Carla!* Get students to respond with *Hello!* Introduce yourself by your title and name, for example, *Hello. I'm (Mr Lake).* Point to yourself as you say it, then write the sentence on the board. Ask a student: *What's your name? (Sam)? (Donald)?* Point to the sentence on the board to show that the student should reply *I'm ...* and his or her name. Write *What's your name?* on the board. Choose a student to ask the question and another to reply. Do this with several pairs. Call two confident students to the front and introduce them, for example, *This is (Paul).* Show that the class should reply, *Hello, (Paul).* Introduce the two students to each other, for example, *(Paul), this is (Kate).* Show that 'Paul' should say *Hello.* Then, *(Kate), this is (Paul).* 'Kate' says *Hello.*

1a

Background information
***Hello* and *Hi*.** Note that Kerry, who speaks first, says *Hello*, a neutral greeting. Dave answers *Hi*, which is slightly more friendly and informal.

- In the mother tongue, ask about the picture: *Where are they?* (in a cafe). *Why are they there?* (for a coffee/to talk together). *Which two do you think are brother and sister?*
- Still in the mother tongue, ask questions about the dialogue: *What is the blond girl's name?* (Kerry Walker). *What is the other girl's name?* (Carol). *What is the boy's name?* (Dave). *Where is Kerry from?* (Australia). *What does 'I'm from ...' mean? What does 'Where are you from?' mean? What is another word for 'Hello'?* (Hi).
- Students quickly number the four speeches in the order in which they think they will hear them.
- 📼 Play the cassette. Students listen and check if their guesses were right.

1b
- Read the instruction and check that students understand what to do.
- 📼 Play the cassette again, pausing after each phrase for students to repeat.

2
- Write the name of the students' country in English on the board, and say: *I'm from (name of country).* Ask a student: *Where are you from?* The student replies: *I'm from ...*
- Explain that the voice on the cassette will ask questions, and that they must answer.
- Point to the prompts (*My name's ... I'm from ...*). Explain that they must use these words to reply to the questions. Ask the class to guess the questions (*What's your name?* and *Where are you from?*).

- 📼 Play the cassette, pausing after each question for the class to answer.

Tapescript
Carol   Hello. My name's Carol. Carol Hill. What's your name? I'm from Britain. Where are you from?

3
- Make sure that students understand the use of full names. For example, in the mother tongue, ask: *What is Kerry's family name?* (Walker). *What is Dave's family name?* (Hill, like his sister's).
- Practise the dialogue with the whole class listening and repeating. (See Tip 2 below.)
- Write the dialogue in Exercise 3 on the board. Call two students to the front of the class, and help them to act it out. They should use their real names and act the situation by smiling and shaking hands as if they were meeting for the first time.
- In pairs, students practise the dialogue in the same way, taking turns to play A and B.

Option
- Students each choose a famous person, such as a pop star, film star or sports personality, and become that person. They have five minutes in which to meet and introduce themselves to as many people as possible, saying who they are and where they come from. When they have finished, ask some students, in the mother tongue, who they met.

  If it is not possible for students to move round the classroom, arrange students in groups of four:

Tip 2 ★
Back-chaining
- The technique of 'back-chaining' helps students build up longer sentences in short steps, starting with words from the end of the phrase.

  On the board, write: *Carol Hill.* Then say the words in each step for students to repeat. Make sure they have mastered each phrase in the sequence before going on to the next one. Get students to repeat as a class, in groups or individually.

Step 1	Hill.
Step 2	Carol Hill.
Step 3	My name's Carol Hill.
Step 4	Hello! My name's Carol. Carol Hill.
Step 5	Hello! My name's Carol. Carol Hill. What's your name?

4
- Students write answers to the questions using information about themselves.

- Walk around checking that students are writing the apostrophe in *My name's ...* . Tell students that you will explain the apostrophe later (in Exercise 5 on Student's Book page 9).

Where are you from?

Aims

In this section students learn to ask and give simple information about a person's country of origin, and to use singular forms of the verb *be*. The language is presented through pictures and dialogue and practised in a guessing game, writing and a chant.

1

Option

- In the mother tongue, ask questions about the picture on page 9. For example, *How old are the people?* (teenagers, students). *Are they from the same country or different countries?* (different countries, each one has their country's flag in front of them). *Do you recognize any of the flags?*

- Explain the exercise and do the first one with the class. Tell students: *Find Steve*. Ask if anyone recognizes the flag. When someone does, ask the class to look at the globe, locate the country, and tell you the name of the country in English. Students write *Britain* next to Steve's name.

- In pairs, students work out the answers to 2–7 in the same way.

- To check answers, write the following table on the board. Point to the names column and say: *Steve is from Britain. Who is from Poland?* Ask a student to write the answer on the board. Continue in the same way for the other countries.

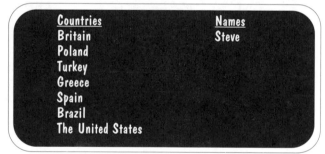

Countries	Names
Britain	Steve
Poland	
Turkey	
Greece	
Spain	
Brazil	
The United States	

Answer key
1 *Britain* 2 *The United States* 3 *Turkey* 4 *Poland*
5 *Greece* 6 *Brazil* 7 *Spain*

2

- Tell students to read the list and underline any countries not mentioned in Exercise 1 (*Argentina*, *Canada*, *Hungary*, *Japan* and *Mexico*).

- Read the instruction aloud. Make sure students understand the meaning by asking questions, for example, *Will you hear all the countries?* (No, only some of them). Tell students that the names of the countries on the cassette are in the same order as in the exercise.

- 🔲 Play the cassette. Students listen and tick the correct boxes.

- In the mother tongue, ask: *What countries didn't you hear?* (*Britain* and *Japan*).

Tapescript / Answer key
Presenter Argentina, Brazil, Canada, Greece, Hungary, Mexico, Poland, Spain, Turkey, The United States

Option

- 🔲 Students practise saying the names of the countries, paying special attention to word stress. (See Tip 3 below.)

Tip 3 ★
Marking word stress

- Write *Japan* twice on the board, underlining the first and then the second syllable: 1 <u>Ja</u>pan 2 Ja<u>pan</u>. Say the word, clapping your hands as you say the second syllable. Ask a student to repeat the word and then point to the correct word on the board. Play the cassette to confirm it. Students then work in pairs, saying aloud the countries in Exercise 2 to decide which syllable is stressed. Ask different students in the class to say a country and to clap their hands to indicate the stressed syllable. Confirm answers by playing the cassette.

3

- Read the dialogue aloud. Check that students understand *Are you from Poland?*

- Explain and demonstrate the guessing game. Show a blank piece of paper to the class. Write a name from Exercise 1 on it, for example, *Eleni*. Fold the paper so students do not see what you have written. On the board write: *Are you from Britain? Are you from Brazil?* and gesture that students should ask similar questions. Answer each question with *No* until a student guesses correctly, then say: *Yes!* Write on the board: *You're Steve. You're Tina*, and look questioningly at the class as you write each to get students to guess the name on your paper. When a student correctly answers *You're Eleni!* open up the piece of paper, show it to the class, and say: *Yes, that's right!*

- Put students into pairs to play the game, taking turns to choose a name or guess. As students play, walk around to make sure that they have understood what to do, and that they are talking in English.

- Let pairs play about four games, then play one last game with one student at the front and the rest of the class guessing who he or she is.

4a

- Read the example to the class. Ask a confident student to finish the sentence (*Britain*).

- Write the names from Exercise 1 on the board. Point to each of the boys' names and say: *He ... He's from ...* Point to each girl's name and say: *She ... She's from ...*

- Write *He's from* and *She's from* on the board. Point to each and ask: *What does 'He's from ...' mean? What does 'She's from ...' mean?*

- Write the example on the board and ask a student to come and complete the sentence. Do the same with *This is Shannon. She's from ...* .

- Students write introductions for the other people in Exercise 1.

4b

- Explain the instructions in the mother tongue.
- Students write the two introductions. Move around checking that students are using *He's/She's* ... correctly.

4c

- Ask three or four students in turn to stand up and read their introductions. Encourage students to act them out in a lively way, gesturing to their friends as their names are mentioned. The friends bow or wave as they are introduced.

Work it out: the verb *be* (singular)

5

- Read out the headings *Short forms* and *Long forms*, showing the meaning of long and short as you do so, by holding your hands close together for *short*, and further apart for *long*.
- In the mother tongue, ask students to find a short form in Exercise 2 (*You're*). Ask if *you're* and *you are* have the same meaning (Yes, but in speaking, and sometimes in writing, we often use the quicker short form).
- Tell students to look through pages 8 and 9 to find the other short forms.
- Students complete the chart. Walk round checking that they have understood what to do and that they are using the apostrophe.
- Students check answers with a partner. Give extra help to students who have different answers.
- Write the short forms on the board or call individual students to the front to write them.

Answer key

I'm   You're   He's   She's

6a

- Explain that students are going to hear a chant about some young people from different countries. Tell them to listen and note where the people are from.
- 🔲 Play the cassette. Students listen and note the countries.
- Check answers with the class.

Tapescript

Kazia is from Poland
Paco is from Spain
William is from Britain
Now say it all again.
Callum is from Canada
Marta is from Spain
Judit is from Hungary
Now say it all again.

Answer key

Poland   Spain   Britain   Canada   Spain   Hungary

6b

- 🔲 Play the cassette again, pausing after each line of the tapescript. Students repeat the chant line by line. The chant is meant to be fun, so encourage students to clap hands or snap fingers, and sway their bodies in time to it.

Suggested Workbook practice

Page 4, Exercises 1–4

Countdown!
Numbers 0–10

Aims

In this section, students learn and practise numbers 1–10 and how to begin and end telephone calls.

1a

Background information

A countdown is when you count backwards to zero, such as when launching a spaceship.

Option

- Find out if students already know the numbers 1–10. One by one, hold up the large number cards (see Materials preparation 1), and ask students: *What number is this?*

- 🔲 Say: *Listen and repeat*. Play the cassette, pausing for students to repeat each number.

Tapescript

Presenter   one, two, three, four, five, six, seven, eight, nine, ten

1b

- One by one, show the large number cards in 1–10 order. Students look and say the numbers.
- The class counts to ten. Then ask individuals to count.

1c

- Tell students to listen and decide what is happening.
- 🔲 Play the cassette. Students listen and decide the context (a spaceship is about to be launched). Explain that this sequence is called a *countdown*. Point to the title of the page.
- Play the cassette again. Students listen and repeat.

Tapescript

Presenter   ten, nine, eight, seven, six, five, four, three, two, one

2a

Background information

Bingo is the name of a game played with cards on which numbers are printed. A caller calls out random numbers, and the winner is whoever's numbers are all called first. Bingo is very popular in Britain: people go to 'Bingo Halls' for afternoon or evening sessions and can win big cash prizes.

- Explain that students are going to play a numbers game called *Bingo*.
- Each student writes five numbers between 1 and 10 in their notebooks, for example: 1, 5, 9, 4, 6 or 2, 7, 9, 1, 4. (See Option below.)
- In the mother tongue, explain that students will hear random numbers. If they hear one of the numbers they have written down, they should tick that number. If they tick all their numbers, they raise a hand.
- 🔲 Play the cassette. Students listen and tick any numbers on their list that they hear.

- Check the cards of students who put up their hands. If they are correct, hold up the cards and say: *Well done! Bingo!* If no student has all five numbers, ask who has ticked 4 of their 5 numbers.

Tapescript

A four ... seven ... one ... nine ... three ... six ... eight ... ten
B Yes! ... Bingo!

Option

- Give out a sheet of paper which can be used and re-used as the Bingo card. Students use *pen* to divide the paper into 10 squares. They use *pencil* to write a number in five of the squares.

2b

- Put the class into groups of 4 or 5. Explain that they are going to play Bingo.
- Give each group a set of number cards (see Materials preparation 1), or give out sheets of card, and ask each group to make their own set.
- Tell groups to choose one student to call out the numbers. This 'caller' shuffles the number cards while the other students erase the numbers from their cards, and write five new ones.
- When the group is ready, the caller reads out numbers, placing the used cards on the table (to keep a check on numbers that have been called). The player who first hears all five of his or her numbers calls out *Bingo!*
- Let groups play 3 or 4 games, changing the caller for each game. They erase and write new numbers each time.

3

Option

- Write an invented phone number on the board, for example: 905 4453. Make sure it has a zero and a double number in it. Read out the numbers: *nine, oh, five ... four four, five, three*. Explain that zero is said as *oh* and 44 can be said as *double four*.

- Explain that students are going to hear a recorded telephone message. Give them time to read the text, and then check understanding in the mother tongue: *Who is speaking?* (Kerry). *Who is she calling?* (Steve). *Where does Steve come from?* (Britain). *Is Kelly from Britain, too?* (No, she's from Australia). *Where is she at the moment?* (in a London hotel). *Who is she with?* (her family). *What sort of information is needed in the gap in the text?* (the hotel phone number).
- 🔊 Play the tape. Students listen and write the missing number.

Answer key
625 3908

Useful English

- On the board, write *6482350*. Students close their books. Ask them to listen and tell you how the numbers are divided when speaking.
- 🔊 Play the cassette. Students listen.
- Ask the class, in the mother tongue, how to say the number. (Say the first three as a group, then the other four numbers.)

- Explain that British people often say their telephone number when they answer the phone. They may just give their number, or they may say *Hello. This is ...* before they say their number. *Goodbye* or *Bye!* ends the conversation.

4

- Give instructions in English: *Look at Exercise 4. Listen, and repeat the phone numbers*.
- 🔊 Play the cassette, pausing after each number. Let students read the numbers in the exercise as they listen and repeat.
- Play the cassette again, this time with books closed so students concentrate on listening rather than reading.

5a

- In English, ask questions about telephone numbers in Exercise 4, for example, *My name's Levent. What's my phone number? My name's Eleni. What's my phone number?*
- Now ask about people, for example, *My number's 917 8532. What's my name?*
- Two students read out the example dialogue.
- Two other students read out the same dialogue but change the number and name.
- Put the class into pairs to practise the dialogue, using different names, and changing roles after each turn.

5b

- Read out and explain the instructions.
- Give students a minute to write phone numbers.
- Call one student to the front. Another student reads one of his or her phone numbers. The student at the front writes the number on the board.
- Tell students: *Work with your partner again*. Give pairs enough time to say and write all of each other's numbers.

6

- Students write the title *Numbers* on a new page in their vocabulary books. They copy the three numbers, then write them in words.

Suggested Workbook practice
Page 5, Exercises 1 and 2

How are you?

Aims
In this section, students learn how to greet friends and write simple messages. Through listening and speaking activities, they start to become aware of sentence stress and, through the letters of the alphabet, the pronunciation of individual sounds.

Useful English

- Ask students to look at the phrases in the box. At this point, do not explain meaning.
- Tell students they are going to listen carefully to each phrase and underline the word in each that is stressed most strongly. Give an example. Write on the board: *My name's Steve*, and *Where are you from?* Say the sentences, exaggerating the stress on the words *Steve* and *from*. Students tell you which word to underline in each sentence.

- 🔊 Play the cassette. Students listen and mark the stressed word in each phrase.
- Check answers. Then play the cassette again, pausing between each phrase for students to repeat.

Answer key

How <u>are</u> you?
I'm <u>fine</u>, thanks.
I'm very <u>well</u>, thanks.

1

Option

- Revise the names of the students on page 9. Students look quickly at the picture on page 9, then turn back to page 11. Ask questions about the characters, for example, *Where is Carlos from? Where is Eleni from?*

- Explain to students that they are going to hear a telephone conversation between two of the people named in the box. They must understand <u>which</u> two people are speaking, but they do not need to understand every word.
- 🔊 Play the cassette. Students listen and write their answers.

Tapescript

Steve Hello? 648 2350.
Shannon Hi, Steve. This is Shannon here.
Steve Oh, hi, Shannon! Thanks for your message. How are you?
Shannon I'm fine, thanks. How are you?
Steve I'm very well.

Answer key

Steve and Shannon

2

- Give students time to read the dialogue.
- Students work with a partner and remember or guess some of the missing words. This should be done as an oral exercise only.
- 🔊 Play the cassette again. Students listen and write the missing words. Check answers by asking individual students to read a line of the dialogue each.

Answer key

See Exercise 1 tapescript.

Option

- Write the following on the board, underlining the sentence stress:
    <u>Hi</u>! How <u>are</u> you?
    I'm <u>fine</u>, thanks. How are <u>you</u>?
    I'm very <u>well</u>, thanks.
  Read out the dialogue line by line, clapping to show rhythm and stress. Students listen and repeat. Point out that *How are you?* has a different stress in the second line because the question is being repeated to the first speaker. Then walk around the class greeting students, as in the dialogue on the board.

3

- Explain that students should practise the dialogue, using their own names and phone numbers. Give students a few moments

to write down their numbers and practise them in English before they start.
- Students practise the dialogue in pairs, taking turns as A or B.
- Two students on opposite sides of the class say the dialogue. They will need to speak clearly so that the other students can hear them.

Tip 4 ★
Reverse dialogue-building

1 This activity is a way of helping students learn useful dialogues. Write the dialogue from Exercise 1 on the board. Students read and say each line. Erase one word from each line of the dialogue, and replace it with a dash, for example:
I'm fine, thanks. How ___ you?
I'm ___ well, thanks.
Students say the dialogue again, adding the missing words from memory.
Erase more words, for example:
I'm ___, thanks. How ___ you?
I'm ___ well, _____.
Continue erasing words until just a few or no words remain.

4

- Students read the fax carefully, and underline any words or phrases they do not understand.
- Explain, or get students to explain, any new vocabulary.
- Read the first incomplete sentence. Get the class to tell you the missing information.
- Give students a few minutes to find the other answers individually.
- Check answers by asking questions, for example, *Who is the message from? What's Steve's fax number?*

Answer key

1 *Steve Benson*   2 *01865 735 0188*
3 *Tina Canto*   4 *638 0759*

5

- Write Steve's postal address from the fax in Exercise 4 on the board. In the mother tongue, ask the class to explain each section of the address. For example, *What is 7?* (the house number). *What is Park Road?* (the street Steve lives in).
- Give students a minute or two to read the text.
- Read out the instruction. Ask questions to check that students understand what to write, for example, *Who are you writing to? Where can you find information about him? What address are you going to write? What does 'Please write to me' mean?*
- Students complete the fax individually. As they write, walk around the class checking answers.

Pronunciation: /iː/ and /ɪ/

6a

- Say the sound /iː/ to the class. Students repeat it. Then say: *Listen and repeat*.
- 🔊 Play the cassette. Students listen and repeat the words.
- Repeat the task, this time with books closed so that students can concentrate on listening rather than reading.

6b

- Say the sound /i:/ to the class to show what the phonetic symbol represents.
- Put students into pairs. Partners say the words to each other to see if they can guess which ones contain the sound /i:/.
- 📼 Play the cassette. Students tick the /i:/ words, or check their answers.

Answer key

read, three, me

6c

- Repeat the procedure for 6a above, this time for the sound /ɪ/.

Tapescript

Presenter with … listen … is

Option

- Demonstrate the difference in mouth shape when making the two sounds. Use two similar words to do this, for example, *he's* (for /i:/) and *his* (for /ɪ/). Make sure students can see the shape of your mouth and lips as you contrast the two sounds.

6d

- Students close their books. Explain that they will hear some letters of the alphabet which all contain the same sound, either /i:/ or /ɪ/. They must listen and tell you which sound it is.
- 📼 Play the cassette. Students listen and identify the sound (the /i:/ sound).
- Students look at the letters in the exercise, all of which appear in red in the alphabet at the foot of the page. Tell them: *Listen and repeat*.
- Play the cassette again. Students repeat each letter.

6e

- Students work in pairs and say the letters to each other. One partner points to a letter group, the other says it as quickly as possible. They then change roles.

Suggested Workbook practice

Page 5, Exercises 3, 4 and 5
Page 6, Exercise 1
Page 7, Exercises 1 and 2

The OK Club
Pleased to meet you

Aims

This section is the first episode in the photo-story. It introduces the main characters, presents informal English in a lively context, and brings together the language students have been practising in the unit. In this episode, the focus is on introductions and greetings.

1a

Background information

Youth clubs are local organizations which are set up by voluntary groups. Clubs may be attached to schools, local councils, religious establishments, or other concerned groups. They provide a place where teenagers can meet together and share interests and hobbies.

Option

- Ask students if they belong to any clubs and, if so, how often they meet and what they do there. If they are unfamiliar with the idea of youth clubs, explain their general purpose, then ask, in the mother tongue: *Do you think youth clubs are a good idea? If a club was organized in this school, what would you like to do there? What time would you meet? How often would you meet?*

- Explain that students should look quickly through the story in order to find the names of the five people. They do not need to understand every word of the dialogue.
- Students complete an introduction (*This is …*) under each picture.

1b

- 📼 Play the cassette. Students listen and read to check their answers.

Answer key

1 *Carol Hill*   2 *This is Dave Hill.*   3 *This is Emma Starr.*
4 *This is Ricky Sinclair.*   5 *This is Jack Morris.*

Set the pace

2a

- Write the four expressions on the board. Say: *Close your books and listen again.*
- 📼 Play the cassette again up to the point where Dave says *Hey, be careful! Look out!* Stop the cassette before the accident. Ask: *What happens next?* (Ricky crashes into Dave). *What does Ricky say next?* (*I'm sorry*). Continue playing the cassette to the end of picture 4. Ask in the mother tongue: *What are they doing?* (introducing themselves). *What do you say in English when you are introduced to someone for the first time?* (*Pleased to meet you*).
- Students open their books again, look back through the pictures to check the story, and individually write what they think the four phrases mean. Check answers with the class.

2b

- 📼 Play the cassette. Students listen and repeat. Encourage them to repeat the phrases with a lively intonation.

3

- Put students into groups of four. Tell them that each person in their group will take the part of one character. To check that students have done this, call out: *Who is Emma? Who is Jack?* and so on. For each name, one person in each group should raise their hand.

- Tell students to look at picture 4. Ask one group to read their parts to the class. If they do not automatically gesture, shake hands or wave, suggest they read the dialogue again, but this time with actions too.
- Groups practise the dialogue.

Review

Aims
The Review section summarizes and briefly revises the key language features of Unit 1: commands, and the verb *be* (singular).

Commands

- The use of the imperative for commands has not been taught explicitly, though both negative and positive forms have been used in instructions, for instance on Student's Book page 6, Exercise 1: *Say it again, please. Don't look at the picture.*
- Write a list of commands on the board, for example:
  Listen to me. Write your name. Read the text. Work with a partner.
- Students say the negative forms of the commands.

The verb *be* (singular)

- Point out that we do not say *This's … .*

1

- Students look through the dialogue to see what it is about (Introductions).
- Ask, in the mother tongue: *How many people are meeting together? What are their names?*
- Do the exercise orally with the whole class. Students can write the answers individually in class or for homework.

Answer key
A   Hello. **I'm** Magda. What**'s** your name?
B   Hi, **Magda**. My name's Mary Lou. **I'm from** the United States. Where **are you** from?
A   **I'm** from Poland. Oh, this **is** Carlos. He's from Spain.

2a

- This exercise practises greetings. Students work in pairs, using their own names in the dialogue. They check their dialogues with the one on page 11, Exercise 1.

2b

- Put students into pairs to practise the dialogue. They take turns to play the roles. Walk round the class listening to pairs.

Vocabulary

- *Countries.* Students record new countries on the relevant page in their Vocabulary notebook. Remind students to make a note of the stressed syllable where appropriate, for example, Bra<u>zil</u>, <u>Hol</u>land.
- *Numbers.* Students have already written telephone numbers. They can also write numbers 1–10 in ascending or descending order, or write their parents' car number. Tell them to leave space on the page for higher numbers, which they will be learning later.

Suggested Workbook practice
Page 6, Exercises 2, 3 and 4
Page 7, Exercise 3

Freewheeling

- Make this into a competition between students, who put up a hand as soon as they've finished. Give students enough time to finish, then give a small prize to the students who completed the exercise first.

Answer key
Horizontal: England   Spain   Brazil   Argentina
Vertical: Greece   Turkey   Canada   Hungary   Poland   Australia

Preparation for Unit 2
Workbook page 7, Exercise 4

Workbook answer key

New friends

1   2 *What's your name?*   3 *He's from England.*
   4 *She's a doctor.*   5 *It's a hamburger.*
   6 *The book's from Poland.*   7 *I'm from Australia.*
   8 *My name's Kerry.*

2a   2 *This is Kate.*   3 *This is Leonardo.*
   4 *This is Ronaldo.*

b   2 *She's from Britain.*   3 *He's from the USA.*
   4 *He's from Brazil.*

3   *Britain Australia America Greece Japan Canada Hungary Turkey Poland Spain Mexico Brazil Switzerland*

4   2 *the USA*   3 *Mexico*   4 *Brazil*   5 *Britain*
   6 *Poland*   7 *Hungary*   8 *Spain*   9 *Greece*
   10 *Turkey*

Countdown

1   2 *She's from Japan.*   4 *I'm from Italy.*
   3 *308732*   5 *23 London Road*

2   1 *Helen she Her*   3 *Her she Her*
   2 *His Tim he His*

3   *Hello, 64309.*
   Hi, Adam, it's Helen here.
   Helen, hi! How are you?
   I'm fine. How are you?
   Very well, thanks. Where are you?
   I'm at the hotel.

4 1 *six five four three*
    2 *eight ten*
    3 *five three one*
    4 *three six four seven five eight*

5 2 *Louise*   5 *Michael*
    3 *Paul*   6 *Lidia*
    4 *Janet*

Pleased to meet you

1b *meet   this*
     people practise
     please six

2 2 *What's* 3 *meet* 4 *I'm* 5 *Where* 6 *from*
    7 *your* 8 *phone*

3 *My your*
    (Student's own answer)
    meet
    from
    Where
    (Student's own answers)

4a 1 *I'm sorry!*   3 *Look out!*
     2 *Phone me later.*   4 *Pleased to meet you.*

b *a 2 b 3 c 4 d 1*

Skills: a fax message

1a 1 *FAX* 2 *To* 3 *From* 4 *Date* 5 *Dear* 6 *fine*
     7 *hotel* 8 *brother* 9 *Restaurant* 10 *phone number*
     11 *Bye*

b *2 a 3 c 4 b 5 f 6 e*

2 *Student's own answers except:*
    Dear
    fine
    New York
    my brother
    Smith's Hotel
    later at Dino's Restaurant
    The phone number of the hotel is 02134 700 1689

3 *Countries: Brazil Britain Hungary Mexico Poland Spain*
    Turkey
    People: brother family friend student
    Numbers: eight five four one six ten three

Prepare for Unit 2

4 bird   man   fifteen
    elephant   sister   nineteen
    fish   woman   thirteen

Unit 2

Syllabus

Topic
Looking around: *countries*, *classroom objects*
The Top Twenty
The OK Club

Grammar
The verb be (plural)
Who? What?
Indefinite article: *a/an*
Demonstratives: *this/that*

Function
Asking about people and objects
Asking about meanings of words

Vocabulary
Classroom furniture and objects
Numbers 11–20

Reading
Checking statements

Listening
Identifying objects

Speaking
Asking about age

Pronunciation
Sentence stress in questions
/e/ and /i:/

Learn to learn
Using a dictionary (1)

Vocabulary

Key vocabulary

Africa	eleven	see (you)
America	fifteen	seventeen
an	fish	shark
animal	fourteen	sister
ant	France	sixteen
bag	girl	table
bird	How old ...?	they
book (n)	insect	thirteen
boy	nineteen	too
chair	not	twelve
country	old	twenty
desk	pen	who
eighteen	pencil	woman
elephant	Scotland	

Other vocabulary

about	help	smile
agent	kettle	story
city	know	student
come	man	together
evening	member	welcome
(on) fire	operation	Well done!
friend	people	worry
great	poster	young

Materials preparation

1   For page 14, Exercise 1 Options and page 15, Work it out:
    Make a set of at least 6 flashcards using pictures of famous
    characters, such as Indiana Jones, Rose from the film *Titanic*.
    Make sure they include individual males and females, and some
    with more than one person, such as The Flintstones.

2   Dictionaries for page 15, Exercise 1 and page 17, Exercise 4c.

3   For page 16, Exercise 1 Options: prepare a set of 10 large
    squares of card with the numbers 11–20, written in numerals.
    Bring in the large set of cards for numbers 1–10 used in Unit 1.

4   For page 17, Exercise 1 Option 1: make two cards. In large
    letters, write *this* on one, and *that* on the other.

Looking around
Where are they from?

Aims

Students learn to ask and answer simple questions about other people, using *Who is/are …?*, and the plural pronouns *we*, *you* and *they*. The section also extends and gives further practice in talking about country of origin.

1

Background information

1 **The characters in Exercise 1**

1 **James Bond** (actor Pierce Brosnan in the photo) is a fictional secret agent, created by Ian Fleming, with the code name 007. Students probably know some of his films, such as *Dr No*, *Live and Let Die*, *The World is not Enough*.

2 **Catwoman** appears in the *Batman* comic books. She is Batman's enemy, but they quite like each other.

3 **Braveheart** was the nickname of William Wallace, a Scottish lord who lived at the end of the 13th century, and who fought to free his land from English rule. The photo is from the recent film *Braveheart* showing actor Mel Gibson as Wallace.

4 **The Simpsons** – Homer and Marge and their children Bart, Lisa and baby Maggie – is a popular American cartoon series.

5 **Sherlock Holmes** is the famous London detective created by Sir Arthur Conan Doyle. The stories are narrated by **Dr Watson**, Holmes' friend and assistant.

6 **The Three Musketeers** – Athos, Porthos and Aramis – are from the famous novel by the French author Alexandre Dumas. The story is set in 17th-century France.

2 **Countries of the British Isles**. A distinction should be made between Britain (England and Wales), Great Britain (England, Scotland and Wales), and the United Kingdom (Great Britain and Northern Ireland). The Republic of Ireland (southern Ireland) is a separate sovereign state.

3 **America** and **the United States of America**. *America* is used to describe the geographic regions of the Americas (North, Central and South America). *The United States* is often shortened to *the USA* or simply *America*.

Options

- Using the flashcards of characters (see Materials preparation 1), hold up the pictures of single characters and ask, as appropriate, *What's his name? What's her name?* Students answer with *His name's …* or *Her name's …*. Say: *Listen!* and hold up the pictures again, saying sentences with *He's …* / *She's …* twice for each picture, for example: *He's Indiana Jones. She's Rose.* Write the sentences on the board.

- To introduce *They're …*, repeat the procedure for *He's …* / *She's …* with the other flashcards.

- Mix up the flashcards and hold them up one at a time. For each ask, as appropriate, *Who is he?*, *Who is she?* or *Who are they?* Gesture to the sentences on the board for students to respond *He/She's …* or *They're …* . (For further practice see Tip 1, page 9.)

- Point to picture 1 and ask: *Who is he?* When a student correctly identifies him with *He's James Bond*, ask first that student, then the whole class to repeat the sentence.

- Put students in pairs and check they understand the task. In the mother tongue, ask: *What questions are you going to ask your partner?* (who the people in the pictures are). *How do you begin each question?* (with *Who*). *How do you answer the questions?* (with *He's*, *She's* or *They're*). Do not confirm the answers yet.

2

- Point to the picture of James Bond and ask: *Where's he from? America? Britain? France?* Students guess, for example, *America*. Point to the examples in Exercise 2 and say: *He's from Britain.* Do the same for picture 4 (*They're from America*).

- Point to picture 3 and ask, with a puzzled expression: *Where's he from?* and quickly reply: *I don't know*, making 'I don't know' gestures.

- In the same pairs, students ask and answer about where the characters are from. Do not confirm answers yet.

3a

- Tell students they are now going to find out if they were right about who the characters are and where they come from. Tell them to put up their hand afterwards if they had all the information right.

- 📼 Play the cassette. Students listen to confirm their answers.

- Note students who put up their hands and ask them, two at a time, to go through the pictures asking and answering as in Exercises 1 and 2. Write the names on the board as each character is named.

....

Tapescript / Answer key

1
A Who's he?
B He's James Bond.
A Where's he from?
B He's from Britain.
2
A Who's she?
B She's Catwoman.
A Where's she from?
B She's from America.
3
A Who's he?
B He's Braveheart.
A Where's he from?
B He's from Britain.
4
A Who are they?
B They're the Simpsons.
A Where are they from?
B They're from America.
5
A Who are they?
B They're Sherlock Holmes and Doctor Watson.
A Where are they from?
B They're from Britain.
6
A Who are they?
B The Three Musketeers.
A Where are they from?
B They're from France.

....

3b

- On the board, write *Where's he from? He's from Britain*.
- Tell students to listen carefully and to tell you if they can hear any difference in the way the word *from* is said. Say the question and answer, with the strong form /frɒm/ in the question, and the weak, unstressed form /frəm/ in the answer. Repeat the sentences until students hear the difference.
- Say the strong form. Students repeat it. Do the same with the weak form.
- Explain that students are going to listen to and repeat some sentences with the weak form.
- 📼 Play the cassette. Students listen and repeat.

Tapescript
1 He's from Britain.
2 She's from America.
3 He's from Britain.
4 They're from America.
5 They're from Britain.
6 They're from France.

4

- Students write two sentences about each character in Exercise 1, one about *who*, the other about *where*, as in the example.

Option
- Ask students to write similar sentences about all or some of the people on the flashcards.

5

- Introduce *We're …*, using the same flashcards you used for *They're …* . Bring a student to the front of the class, point to both of you and say, for example, *We're Tarzan and Jane*.
- For guidance on how to introduce and play this guessing game, see the teaching notes for Unit 1, page 9, Exercise 3.

Option
- Students can also play the guessing game with the characters on the flashcards.

Work it out: the verb *be* (plural)

6a
- Let students complete this exercise by themselves. They can look back through Exercises 1–5 to check their ideas.

Answer key
1 *They're/They are*   2 *We're/We are*

6b
- Students can complete this exercise for themselves, and then look back through Exercises 1–5 to check their ideas.

Answer key
We're/We are   You're/You are   They're/They are

Option
- When students have completed the chart, call individual students to the board to help you write all the present forms, both long and short, of the verb *be*. Point out that *You are* is both a singular and a plural form.

6c
- Write the example wrong sentence on the board: *She from Japan.* Ask: *Is this right?*
- Choose a student who has said *No* to come to the board and correct the sentence. If that student makes the wrong correction, choose another student.
- Tell the class to work individually and correct sentences 1–5. Let them check their answers in pairs before you check with the whole class.

Answer key
1 *We're from the United States.*
2 *She's from Hungary.*
3 *They're from Poland.*
4 *Who's this?*
5 *What's that?*

6d
- Repeat the procedure for Exercise 6c, using *She's from America* as the example. Students do 2–5 individually.

Answer key
2 *I'm from England.*
3 *What's that?*
4 *Who's she?*
5 *They're from France.*

Suggested Workbook practice
Page 8, Exercises 2 and 3

Your classroom

Aims
In this section, students learn the names of common classroom objects, and how to ask about unknown objects using *What's this?* They differentiate between asking about the identification of people (*Who's …? He's/She's …*) and objects (*What's this? It's a …*). They start to use a dictionary on a regular basis.

Learn to learn: using a dictionary (1)

1
- Check first that students recognize what each object is. Ask: *What's this in (student's language)?*
- Put students in pairs. This series of exercises works best if all the As are on the left and all the Bs on the right of their partner.
- Read the instructions aloud and check they understand them. Ask in the mother tongue: *Who is A? Which four pictures do you look at?* Repeat for B. Then ask: *Do you talk with your partner about the words?* (no). *How will you find the meaning of the words?* (in a dictionary). *Where do you write the words?* (under the pictures).

- Students work individually, looking up and writing words. Walk round checking, and helping with using a dictionary if necessary. Do not check the answers or it will spoil Exercise 3.

Answer key

Box A: book, pen, pencil, poster
Box B: bag, chair, desk, table

2a

- This is a 'Listen and do' task. Students listen to all the words from Exercise 1 in random order, and point only to those words that they have looked up. If As are all in the same position in each pair, it is easier to identify those students who are having difficulties.
- Explain the task and check students understand it.
- 🔲 Play the cassette. Students listen and point to the things in their box only.

....

Tapescript

A a chair
B a pencil
A a desk
B a book
A a bag
B a poster
A a pen
B a table

....

Option

- 🔲 Play the cassette again. This time, students raise a hand when they hear a word from their box.

2b

- Read the instructions to the class. Ask in the mother tongue: *What are you going to do this time?* (listen and repeat). *Which words will you repeat?* (only their own four words).
- 🔲 Play the cassette again. Students listen and repeat.

Useful English

- Point to one or two pictures in Exercise 1, and ask: *What's this in English?* Students answer if it is a word from their box.
- Point to the title *Your classroom* at the top of Student's Book page 15, and ask: *What does this mean?* Choose a student to respond.
- Write *jack-in-the-box* on the board, and ask: *What does this mean?* Encourage students to say *I don't know*.
- 🔲 Play the cassette. Students listen and underline the word in each sentence that has the strongest stress. Check the answers.
- Play the cassette again. Students listen and repeat.

Answer key

What's <u>this</u> in English?
What does <u>this</u> mean?
Sorry, I don't <u>know</u>.

Option

- At the end of the lesson, draw a jack-in-the-box like the one on the right on the board to explain what it is.

3a

- Put students in the same pairs as in Exercise 1. Tell them they are going to teach each other the words from their box.
- Take the part of B and demonstrate the task with a student who knows the words in box A. Point to the pencil and read the first line of the dialogue. The student continues, pointing to a word in box B when asking the question. Answer the question.
- Point out to the class that they must say *It's a …* not just *It's …*, then let pairs practise on their own. Walk round listening, and encouraging students to help their partners with pronunciation.

3b

- Students write the new words in either box A or box B. They can check their partner's book for spelling.

3c

- Students turn to page 73 of the Workbook and look at *List and translation*.
- In the mother tongue, ask: *What is special about the order of the words already in the list?* (they are in alphabetical order).
- Students write the remaining four classroom words in alphabetical order, then translate all eight words.

Answer key

pen   pencil   poster   table

4

- Move around the classroom, pointing to a book, chair or pencil, and ask the owner of each: *What's this in English?* Only accept answers that begin with *It's a … .*
- After two or three known objects, point to an unknown one, such as a pencil case, and ask: *What's this in English?* The student should answer *I don't know*.
- Put students into pairs, if possible with new partners. Explain that they are going to ask each other about the English for things in the classroom, or things pictured in their books, such as a flag.
- Students take turns asking and answering about real or pictured objects.

Option

- In the mother tongue, tell students to look round the classroom and think of one object they would like to know the English for. One-by-one students walk to their chosen object and ask *What's this in English?* Write the mother tongue words on the board, but do not translate them. When the list is complete, students copy it into their notebooks. They look up the words in a dictionary for homework. You may prefer to divide the list, with each partner in a pair looking up half of the list.

Work it out: *Who ...?* or *What ...?*

5a

> **Option**
> - To explain the meaning of *people* and *things*, write two lists on the board:
>
> | People | Things |
> | --- | --- |
> | teacher | chair |
> | Jack | sandwich |
> | Catwoman | yacht |
>
>   Point to the headings and ask: *What does 'people' mean? What does 'things' mean?* The class suggests meanings in the mother tongue. Ask students to suggest more words for each heading.

- Ask students to look again at Exercise 1 on Student's Book page 14 and Exercise 3 on page 15.
- Write *Who?* and *What?* on the board. Say: *Teacher*, and point to the two question words on the board. Students respond with *Who*. Say: *computer*. Students respond with *What*. Continue with other people and objects.
- Using the flashcards (see Materials preparation 1) and objects in the classroom, ask *Who's this?* or *What's this?*, either holding up a flashcard or pointing to an object.
- Tell students to look at pictures 1–4 and write either *Who's* or *What's*. Do not check answers yet.

Answer key
1 *Who's*   2 *What's*   3 *What's*   4 *Who's*

5b

- On the board, write:
  a) <u>Who</u> is for people   b) <u>Who</u> is for things.
  c) <u>What</u> is for people   d) <u>What</u> is for things.
- Students discuss briefly with a partner which two statements are right.
- Invite a student to the board to point to the two correct statements.
- Students complete the grammar rule. Check they have all got the same rule, then check the answers to 5a.

Answer key
<u>Who</u> is for people. <u>What</u> is for things.

6

- Demonstrate the task with a confident student. Take A's role and ask about people or objects in the classroom or in the Student's Book. For example, point to picture 3 on page 14 and ask *Who's this?* Tap the desk and ask *What's this?* The student responds.
- Put students into pairs to take turns asking and answering.

Suggested Workbook practice

Page 8, Exercises 1 and 4

The Top Twenty
Numbers 1–20

Aims
This section revises the numbers 1–10, and introduces numbers 11–20.

1a

Background information
The Top Twenty. Newspapers and radio programmes often conduct surveys to find out the current 10, 20 or even 100 most popular pop songs, books, films, TV programmes, videos, and so on. The list is often given as a countdown from Number 20 (least popular) to Number 1 (most popular).

> **Options**
> - Write *The Top 20* on the board, and draw some music notes next to it. Ask in the mother tongue: *What's Number 1 in the pop charts this week?* If some students know and are able to answer, let them explain to the rest of the class what the Top Twenty is. If not, explain it yourself. Divide the class into groups of 4 or 5, and tell each group to make a list of their 5 favourite songs, in order of popularity. Allow 3–4 minutes for this. While groups are discussing songs, write on the board: *Number 5 is [My heart will go on] by [Céline Dion].* (Substitute whatever song and singer is most relevant to your class.) Ask each group to appoint a representative. Representatives stand up in turn and give their group's top five, using the example on the board as a model.
> - Revise numbers 1–10, using the number cards from Unit 1. Get students to say the numbers in order, forwards and backwards, then shuffle the cards and have individual students say numbers.
> - Hold up cards for numbers 11–20 (see Materials preparation 3) and ask *What's this in English?* to find out if students already know some of the numbers.

- Say: *Open your books. Look at Exercise 1.* Read out the instruction, and say: *Listen and repeat.*
- 📼 Play the cassette for numbers 1–10, pausing after each for students to repeat.
- In the mother tongue, tell students to listen to numbers 11–20 and underline the stressed syllable in each number except twelve. (See Tip 3, page 14.)
- Say: *Listen. Do not repeat.* Play the cassette for numbers 11–20.
- Individual students write the numbers on the board and underline the stressed syllable.
- Play the cassette for 11–20 again. Students listen and repeat.

Answer key
el<u>e</u>ven ... thir<u>teen</u> ... four<u>teen</u> ... fif<u>teen</u> ... six<u>teen</u> ... seven<u>teen</u> ... eigh<u>teen</u> ... nine<u>teen</u> ... <u>twen</u>ty

> **Option**
> - Give further practice in numbers 11–20, using the number cards. (See Tip 1, page 9.)

1b

- In this exercise, some numbers (and video names) are deliberately omitted on the cassette. Students must listen and write the missing numbers only.
- Tell students to look at the videos at the top of the page, and explain that these are the top twenty videos of the week. To familiarize students with the names of the videos, ask individual students questions, for example: *What number is 'Operation X'? What number is 'My Friends'? What number is 'The Game'?* and so on.
- Explain the task and check that everyone understands what to do.
- 📼 Play the cassette. Students listen and write down the missing numbers in numerals.

....

Tapescript

Twenty … James Bland – agent…
Nineteen … The Bird …
Eighteen … My friends …
Sixteen … Python …
Fifteen … My Africa …
Thirteen … Two Brothers …
Twelve … Two - One - Zero! …
Ten … Messages …
Nine … The Game …
Eight … Goal! …
Seven … Yes or No? …
Six … The English Doctor …
Five … Insect Man …
Four … London Story …
Three … Operation X …
Two … The Mexico Game …
One … The Simpsons.

....

Answer key

17   14   11

2a

- Say the video titles one by one. Students repeat. Explain the meaning of any titles that contain words they do not know.
- Taking the role of A, read the example with a confident student as B. Then repeat the dialogue using another number.
- Put students into pairs. As they work, walk round checking that As are asking questions using numbers in random order. After a few minutes, tell students to change roles so that B asks the questions.

2b

- This activity is the same as 2a, but this time students ask about the title and answer with the number. Point out the extra line in the dialogue in which A praises B. Ask students, in the mother tongue: *What will you say if B gets the answer wrong? (No, that's wrong.)*

Option

- To make the activity more challenging, turn it into a memory game. Student A studies the video titles for one minute, then covers the page. Student B looks at the page and asks *What number is …?* Student A tries to answer from memory. Students change roles after a few minutes.

How old are you?

Aims

In this section, students have further number practice and learn to ask and answer questions about age.

1

Background information

Film classification. All films are reviewed and classified by the British Board of Film (BBF). The classifications are: U = Universal – suitable for all; PG = Parental Guidance – general viewing, but some scenes may be frightening for very young children; 12 = suitable for people over 12 years old; 15 = suitable for people over 15 years old – themes requiring a more mature understanding; 18 = suitable for people over 18 years old – themes requiring an adult understanding.

Option

- Ask a student: *Are you 13? 14? 15? 16?* The student replies, for example, *15*. Then ask the same student: *How old are you?* Ask several other students: *How old are you?* Write the question on the board, then demonstrate how to say it. Link the words when the last letter of the first word is a consonant and the next word begins with a vowel:

  How old are you?

  Students repeat. Say it again, and ask a student to underline the stressed word on the board (*old*). Have the students ask the question once more, and answer (made-up answers are permitted!): *I'm 20*. Write it on the board. Choose several pairs of students to ask and answer the question.

- Read out the instructions and ask questions to check if they understand what to do: *Do you work alone or with a partner?* (with a partner). *What do you write in the first gap?* (the partner's age). *What do you write in the second gap?* (student's own age).
- In pairs, students read the dialogue aloud, adding the answers as they go. They then change roles. Finally, they write the answers in the gaps. If they are different ages, tell them to cross out the word *too*.

2

- Ask students to write the names of 5 other students sitting nearby.
- Read the instruction and examples. Check in the usual way that they understand what to do.
- Students ask 5 other students *How old are you?* and note the answers. They then write sentences like those in the examples. Ask a few students to each read out one of their sentences.

3

- Students look at the two videos next to Exercise 3. Ask in the mother tongue: *Why are they labelled 18 and 12?* If students cannot answer, explain the classification system. Then ask in the mother tongue: *Why are some films not suitable for younger people?* (See Background information above.)
- Students read the instructions and dialogues. Ask questions in the mother tongue to check understanding. For example: *Where do the conversations take place? What video do you both want to hire in dialogue 1? Are you allowed to hire it? Why not?* (it's a

category 18 film and students are too young). *What film do you want to hire in dialogue 2? Can you hire it? Why?* (because it's a category 12 film and they are older than 12).

- Students work in pairs to complete the dialogues. Move round, checking pairs. Ask two pairs with the right answers to read out the dialogues.

Answer key

1 *How   old   We   You're*
2 *old   are   're/are [age of students]*

Suggested Workbook practice

Page 11, Exercise 1

a/an

Aims

This section gives further practice of numbers 11–20, and students learn the indefinite articles *a* and *an*.

1

- Read out sentences 1–4, emphasizing the words *a* /ə/ and *an* /ən/.
- On the board write:

1	2
an insect	a fish
an animal	a bird

- Tell students to think about the difference between the two groups, but not to say anything. Meanwhile, write the words *agent*, *city*, *English woman*, *country* and *game* on another part of the board.
- Ask students to add the new group of words to the two lists. Following students' suggestions, add the words to the lists but do not comment on them.

Option

- If students seem confident about their choices in the lists, leave the grammar explanation until Exercise 4 on page 17. If not, do Exercise 4 now.

2

- Students read the instructions. Ask questions to check understanding.
- Students work individually, matching the topics with the four videos.
- On the board write: *What is number 6 about?* Have one student ask and another answer the question. Check the other answers in the same way.

Answer key

1 *an English woman*   2 *a city*   3 *a country*   4 *an agent*

3

- Use the question on the board to ask about one or two other videos. Students answer.
- In pairs, students continue, taking turns to ask and answer. Help them find singular words for plural titles, for example, (number 12) *It's about a family*.

Answer key

1 *a boy/a family*   2 *a country/a game*   3 *an operation*
4 *a city*   5 *an insect man*   6 *an English woman/an English doctor*
7 *a game/a question*   8 *a goal/a football game*   9 *a game*
10 *a message*   11 *a captain*   12 *an operation/an agent/a bomb*
13 *a family/two brothers*   14 *an animal/a bird*   15 *a continent /a story in Africa*   16 *an animal*   17 *a fish/a shark*   18 *a group of friends*   19 *a bird*   20 *an agent*

Work it out: *a* and *an*

4a

- Tell students to underline all the words in Exercises 1–3 that have the word *a* before them. Allow 1–2 minutes for this, then have students tell you these words. List them on the board as *List A*.
- Repeat the procedure for *an*, and list the words as *List B*. Lists should be:
     List A: *a fish, a bird, a city, a country*
     List B: *an insect, an animal, an agent, an English woman*
- Put students into pairs. Ask them: *When do we use 'a'? When do we use 'an'?*
- Give students a short time to discuss their answer, in the mother tongue. Check answers with the class.

Answer key

The word a *is used before words (a noun or noun phrase) beginning with consonant sounds.*
The word an *is used before words (a noun or noun phrase) beginning with a vowel sound.*
Note: It is the sound *that is important, not the letter. For example, we say* **an** *unusual book (where* u *is pronounced as a vowel), but* **a** *useful book (where* u *is pronounced as a* y*). The same applies to the letter* h*:* **a** *happy man (the consonant* h *is pronounced),* **an** *honest man (the* h *is not pronounced, so the first sound is a vowel sound,* /ɒ/*).*

4b

- Explain the task and tell students not to worry about new words.
- Students work in pairs and write answers in their notebooks.

Answer key

a: *bag   book   boy   girl   pen   student   table*
an: *animal   ant   elephant   operation*

4c

- Students tell you any words that are new to them. Write them on the board.
- Students look up the words in a dictionary. When they have finished, ask individual students to tell you what the words mean, and write the translations on the board.
- Ask students to name the animals in the list (*ant, elephant, insect*). Then ask them to look again at page 16 and find any other animals (*penguin, python, fish, bird*). Tell students to write the heading *Animals* in their vocabulary books, then discuss ways of recording the words. Word-maps are probably the best, with animals grouped as *Fish, Insect, Bird,* or *Other animal* but students may prefer to draw the animals. Students record the words, leaving room for more animals later.

this and *that*

Aims

In this section, students learn to refer to objects that are nearby and further away, work out how questions and short answers are formed with the verb *be*, revise vocabulary, and differentiate between the sounds /e/ and /i:/.

1

Options

- To present *this* and *that*, hold up the *this* card (see Materials preparation 4) and say: *This*. Walk round the class, stand next to students and introduce them, for example: *This is Anna*. Do the same with *that*, but point to students from a distance. Alternate the two: *This is Anna* (stand next to the student). *That is Meltem* (point from a distance). Have a few students take the cards and introduce people in a similar way.

- To present short answers, walk round the class and pick up or point to objects. As you do this, say, e.g. *Is this your pen? Is that your table?* Students answer *Yes* or *No*. Nod your head to show you accept their answers, but say after their answers: *Yes, it is* or *No, it isn't*. Gesture to the student to repeat the short form answer. Say each answer for the whole class to repeat. Make sure they link the last consonant sound of one word with the next word if it begins with a vowel:

    Yes, it is.   *No, it isn't.*

Background information

Gulliver's Travels. In this novel by Jonathan Swift, Gulliver is a sailor who has many adventures in strange, faraway lands. In one country, the people are as small as insects, while in another the people are giants, so Gulliver himself appears to them to be the size of an insect.

- Ask four students to describe a picture each in the mother tongue. Find out if anyone knows the story of Gulliver. If not, give a brief summary. Ask students to guess which country Gulliver is in in pictures 1, 3 and 4 (the land of giants).

- Explain that students must listen to each question and answer it orally. Give students a minute to read the questions and think of their answers.

- 📟 Play the cassette, pausing after each question for students to answer either *Yes, it is* or *No, it isn't*.

Answer key

1 *No, it isn't.*   2 *No, it isn't.*   3 *Yes, it is.*   4 *No, it isn't.*

Option

- Put students into groups of four. One student in each group asks questions about objects in the classroom, using *Is this a ...?* or *Is that a ...?* The other students answer the questions together. Questions should be mixed so that answers vary, for example: *Is that a pen? Yes, it is. Is this a pen? No, it isn't. It's a pencil.* This activity is more fun if some questions are absurd, for example, *Is that a penguin? No, it isn't. It's a boy!* After a few minutes, a different member of the group asks the questions.

Work it out: questions and short answers with *be*

2a

- Students read the examples. As they read, write on the board: *That's a bird.* and *He's from Poland.*

- Point to the sentences and ask: *What is the long form?* (*That is, He is*). Write, or get a student to write, the long form sentences on the board.

- Write the question forms under each long form sentence, with arrows as in the Student's Book. Pointing to the sentence or question, say: *That is ... Is that ...? He is ... Is he ...?*

- Erase the examples and replace them with two new examples, for example: *This is your bag.* and *You're fifteen.*

- Students work with a partner, and decide what the question is for each sentence. Give them time to do this, then choose two students to write the question forms on the board, with arrows to show how it's done: *Is this your bag? Are you fifteen?*

2b

- Read the instruction and example. Check that students understand the task by doing the first question with them orally.

- Students work individually, writing the question forms.

- Divide the board in two, and ask 5 students in turn to write the questions down the left half of the board. Leave the questions on the board for Exercises 2c and 3.

Answer key

1 *Are we*   2 *Are you*   3 *Are they*   4 *Is he*   5 *Is she*

2c

- In groups of 4 or 5, students work together to formulate a rule, in the mother tongue, that must mention the position of *be* in the sentence.

- A representative from each group tells the class their group's rule and writes it on the right-hand side of the board. Students vote for the version they think is the most accurate and well-written, and copy it into their notebooks.

Answer key

In questions, forms of the verb be *are placed before the subject.*

3

- Use the questions from Exercise 2b on the board to show how other short answers are formed. Write the two possible answers to *Are we right?* on the right of the board: *Yes, we are. No, we aren't.* Then ask different students to write positive and negative short answers to the other questions. Correct any mistakes.

- Tell students to read the instruction and look at pictures 1–4. Check they understand that the pictures are clues to the answers. Do the exercise orally with the class, then students ask and answer in pairs before writing answers.

Answer key

1 *Yes, she is.*   2 *No, they aren't.*   3 *No, he isn't.*
4 *No, they aren't.*

4

- Tell students they are going to play a memory game. Explain the task and demonstrate it with one student, using the example and taking the part of B.

- Put students into pairs and let them decide who is A or B. Say: *Look at the pictures for 20 seconds. Start now.* Time them, then say: *Student B, close your book.* Pairs play the game, changing roles after 2–3 minutes.

Option

- Students could play the game with other groups of pictures in the unit, such as page 15, Exercise 5.

Pronunciation: /e/ and /i:/

5a

- Follow the procedure for Unit 1 Pronunciation, Exercise 6a, but for the sound /e/.

5b

- Follow the procedure for Unit 1 Pronunciation, Exercise 6b.

Answer key

desk   pen   twelve   friend

5c

- Follow the procedure for Unit 1 Pronunciation, Exercise 6a, but for the sound /i:/.

Tapescript

coffee … he … three … me …

Option

- Demonstrate the difference in mouth shape when making the two sounds. Use two similar words to do this, for example, *men* (for /e/) and *mean* (for /i:/). Make sure students can see the shape of your mouth and lips as you contrast the two sounds.

5d

- Follow the procedure for Unit 1 Pronunciation, Exercise 6d, but for the sounds /e/ and /i:/.

Suggested Workbook practice

Page 9, Exercises 1–4

The OK Club
Help! Fire!

Aims

This section continues the photo-story. It presents informal English in a lively context, and brings together the language students have been practising in the unit. In this episode, Carol and Dave meet another member of the club, Jane.

1

- Students look up *kettle* in a dictionary, then find the one in the story. By looking at the pictures, they should get the gist of the story. Make sure they are not reading the dialogue while they are doing this.

Answer key

The kettle is in pictures 3, 4 and 5.

2

- Revise the names of the characters. Say: *Look at picture 1. Who is she? Look at picture 2. Who are they?* Students respond with the names.
- Tell students: *Read Exercise 2.* Ask questions to check they understand the task.
- Say: *Listen and read.* Play the cassette. Students listen, read and note answers. Ask individual students for the answers.
- Play the cassette again. Ask questions in the mother tongue to check comprehension: *Who is the girl who phones Carol?* (Emma). *Why does she phone her?* (To invite her and Dave to the club that evening). *In picture 2, why has Jack arrived early?* (It's his turn, with Jane, to work in the Coffee Corner). *Who introduces Jane to Carol and Dave?* (Jack). *Which boy is Jane smiling at?* (Dave). *How do you think Jack feels about this?* (jealous). *Why do you think the kettle catches fire?* (Either because it's faulty, or because Jane and Jack aren't paying attention to it).

Option

- Students can attempt the exercise before they listen, then listen to check their answers.

Answer key

1 *Jane*   2 *Dave*   3 *Carol*

Set the pace

3a

- Tell students to read the exercise. Explain that this time they work individually, then compare answers with a partner. Tell them you will play the cassette again if they feel it will help them.

Option

- If students find the task difficult, ask them to imagine each situation. For example, in the mother tongue, ask: *What do you say at the end of a phone call when you are going to see the person in the evening?* (*See you later!*). *What do you say to a new visitor to your house?* (*Welcome!*), *What do you say when you think you are in danger?* (*Help!*), *What do you say to reassure someone?* (*Don't worry!*).

3b

- Tell students to look at the story pictures again and imagine the characters' feelings as they say the four phrases (1 enthusiastic, happy; 2 proud, welcoming; 3 afraid; 4 reassuring).
- Play the cassette. Students listen only, noting the way the phrases are said.
- Play the cassette again. Students repeat each phrase, trying to imitate tone as well as pronunciation.

4

- Read and explain the instruction. Tell students to cover page 18.
- Ask a student to read the first phrase, and anyone who can remember the answer to raise a hand afterwards. When the phrase has been read, choose a student with a hand up to respond. Do not confirm the response yet. Do the same with the other phrases.
- Tell students to read the story again, and check their answers.

Answer key

1 *Yes, great!*   2 *Pleased to meet you, Carol.*   3 *Yes, please.*
4 *It's OK! Don't worry!*

Suggested Workbook practice

Page 10, Exercises 3 and 4

Review

Aims

The Review section summarizes and briefly revises the key language features of Unit 2: subject pronouns, the verb be, a or an, and this or that.

Subject pronouns; the verb *be*

- In pairs, students study the table carefully for a minute. Student A then covers the negative and question forms and tries to say all the missing forms to student B, who corrects any mistakes. They then change roles.

Tip 5 ★
Using tables to review grammatical forms

- To see how well students have learned the grammar, copy the table in the Student's Book onto the board, omitting much of the information. For example:

Positive	Negative	Questions
I'm (I am)	_____	_____
_____	You aren't	_____
He's (He is)	_____	Is she ...?

Get students, with books closed, to help you complete the table. Students can either call out answers, or individuals come to the board and write in an answer each.

a or *an*?

- Get students to look at the examples and tell you again when to use *a* or *an*.

this or *that*?

- Get students to look at the picture and explain why the example uses *This* for Jane, but *That* for Jack.

1–3

- These exercises can be done individually in class or set for homework.

Answer keys

1 1 *I* *you* 2 *She* 3 *it* 4 *you* 5 *you*
2 1 *an* 2 *a* 3 *an* 4 *a*
3 1 *What's that?* 2 *What's this?*

Vocabulary

- *Classoom objects*. Students can record these words by the List and translation method.
- *Numbers 11–20*. Students add these to the Numbers page, leaving space for higher numbers.

Freewheeling

- Explain the task carefully, making sure students understand that each horizontal, vertical and diagonal line must add up to 15, and that they can only use the numbers in the box to do this. Students work individually or in pairs to complete the puzzle. If necessary give them the position of number five.

Answer key

six	zero	nine
eight	five	two
one	ten	four

Suggested Workbook practice

Page 10, Exercises 1 and 2
Page 11, Exercise 2

Preparation for Unit 3

Workbook page 11, Exercise 3

Workbook answer key

Looking around

1a *Who are they?*   *Who is he?*   *What are they?*   *What is this?*
Who is she?

b 2 *Who are they?*   5 *What is this?*
   3 *Who is he?*   6 *What are they?*
   4 *Who is she?*

c 2 *They are members of the OK Club.*
   3 *He's James's Bond.*
   4 *She's Lisa Simpson.*
   5 *It's a pen.*
   6 *They're videos.*

2 2 *They're in the classroom.*   4 *We're at the OK Club.*
   3 *They're in Australia.*   5 *They're in her bag.*

3 2 *I'm from Portugal.*
   3 *We're in this group.*
   4 *You're a good student.*
   5 *Emma and Jack are at the OK Club.*
   6 *My phone number's 701 5763.*

4 1 *f* 2 *c* 3 *d* 4 *a* 5 *e* 6 *b*

The Top Twenty

1 2 *Is that a bird? it isn't.*
   3 *Is this an insect? it is.*
   4 *Is that a hamburger? it isn't.*

2a *video poster animal example shop insect question address fish elephant*

b
a	an
poster	animal
shop	example
question	insect
fish	address
	elephant

3a *eighteen   fourteen   twenty   seventeen   eleven   thirteen nineteen   fifteen   twelve   sixteen*

b *eighteen 18   fourteen 14   twenty 20   seventeen 17   eleven 11   thirteen 13   nineteen 19   fifteen 15   twelve 12   sixteen 16*

4b /e/   /iː/
guess   *me*
pen   *mean*
ten   *she*
well   *three*
yes   *we*

Help! Fire!

1   2 *We're fourteen.*   3 *She's my sister, Anna.*
    4 *They're from Scotland.*   5 *Pleased to meet you, Anna.*
    6 *Sorry, I don't know.*

2a *a 3   b 5   c 2   e 6   f 4*

b   2   *Pleased to meet you, Fran.*
    3   *We're fifteen.*
    4   *It's a picture.*
    5   *Sorry, I don't know.*
    6   *They're from France.*

3 1 *girl* 2 *smile* 3 *kettle* 4 *fire*

4

Animals	People	Countries
ant	*Carol*	*France*
bird	*Emma*	*Scotland*
shark	*Dave*	
insect	*Jane*	
fish	*Ricky*	
elephant		

Skills: videos

1a 1 *The Johnsons* 2 *Australian Game*
     3 *Friends and Family* 4 *Black Shark* 5 *Three Sisters*

b 1 *b* 2 *c* 3 *c* 4 *a* 5 *c*

2a *fire   kettle   poster   question   smile*
b *second   seventeen   shop   sister   sixteen   story*

Prepare for Unit 3

3a *Suggested answers:*

Pets	Wild animals
dog	*dog*
lizard	*fox*
snake	*frog*
stick insect	*giraffe*
	lizard
	snake
	spider
	stick insect
b *brother*	*sister*
father	*mother*
grandfather	*grandmother*

Unit 3

3

Syllabus

Topic
The living world
Families
The OK Club

Grammar
have got
Plural nouns
Adjectives

Function
Describing people and animals

Vocabulary
Colours
Animals
Family members
Parts of the body

Reading
Checking statements
Matching texts and pictures
Finding information

Listening
Completing information
Identifying family members

Writing
Writing descriptions of animals
Writing a personal description

Speaking
Describing your family
Discussing a problem

Pronunciation
Intonation in questions and answers
/ə/ in *have*
/eɪ/ and /aɪ/

Vocabulary

Key vocabulary

arm	frog	mouth
Asia	glass lizard	neck
big	giraffe	north
black	good	nose
blue	grandfather	orange
body	grandmother	paint
brain	green	problem
brown	grey	red
but	hair	short
cat	has	small
Central America	head	snake
colour	him	spider
curly	idea	straight
dark	leg	summer
dog	like (what's he …)	tail
ear	long	tall
Europe	maybe	their
eye	mess	white
fair	money	winter
father	mother	yellow
fox	moustache	

Other vocabulary

awful	guess (n)	same
bus	living	school
chance	lucky	so
change	now	think
different	pence	time
dream	penny	tree
false	pet	true
fantastic	place	wall
forest		

Materials preparation

1   For page 20, Exercise 1 Option: make enough cards for the class, each with one of the following colours on it: black, blue, brown, green, orange, red, white and yellow. Alternatively, use pens of those colours.

2   Dictionaries for page 21, Exercise 5b and page 22, Exercise 1.

3   For page 23, Exercise 4 Option: prepare a set of 26 cards with the letters of the alphabet.

The living world
Colours

Aims
In this section, students learn adjectives of colour through listening and speaking activities.

1

Option
- Write on the board: *What colour is the flag of Britain? It's red, white and blue.* Students work in pairs. Student A looks at the flags on page 9, and asks questions like the one in the example. Student B, with book closed, tries to remember. Now write on the board: *The flag is blue and white. What country is it?* Student B tests Student A.

Option
- Hold up each colour card in turn (see Materials preparation 1). Say the colour. Students listen and repeat. Go round the class offering the cards. As each student takes one, greet them according to the colour they have picked, for example: *Hello, Mr Green! Hello, Miss Black!* As you continue round the class, begin to introduce students to each other, revising the language of introductions. For example,
Mr Blue, this is Mr Yellow.
Hello, Mr Yellow.
Hello, Mr Blue. Pleased to meet you.
Remind students how to introduce themselves. For example,
Hello. I'm Miss White.
Hi, Miss White. I'm Mr Yellow. Pleased to meet you.
Students continue to practise colours and introductions in groups. They could stand up and walk around the class, greeting as many different people as they can in 3 minutes.

- Students match the colours in the box with the numbered fish in the picture. Do the first one with the class: *What colour is fish number 1? It's green.* Students write 1 by *green*.
- Students complete the exercise individually. Do not check answers until Exercise 2b (see Tapescript for 2b).

2a
- 📼 Play the cassette. Students listen and repeat the colours.

Tapescript
Black…blue…brown…green…orange…red…white…yellow

2b
- Tell students to listen and check their answers to Exercise 1, and to tick the colours as they hear them.
- 📼 Play the cassette. Students tick colours, and check that they have matched colours and numbers correctly.

Tapescript
A The blue fish is number five.
B The white fish is number six.
A The black fish is number four.
B The yellow fish is number seven.
A The red fish is number three.
B The brown fish is number eight.
A The green fish is number one.

Answer key
The orange fish, number 2.

have got

Aims
In this section, students learn to talk about personal possessions, and to describe animals, using positive and negative forms of the verb *have got*. They learn parts of the body and how to form plural nouns, as well as revising colours.

1
- Get pairs of students to ask and answer questions about the remaining fish. For example, Student A: *What colour is this fish?* Student B: *It's blue.*
- 📼 Play the cassette. Students listen and write numbers in the boxes.
- In English, check students' answers, for example: *What colour is fish number 9?*

Tapescript / Answer key
A The brown fish is number nine.
B The blue fish is number ten.
A The red fish is number eleven.
B The yellow fish is number twelve.
A The green fish is number thirteen.
B The orange fish is number fourteen.
A The black fish is number fifteen.

2
- Teach the words *aquarium*, *head*, *eye*, *tail*, *big* and *small*. Make sure students understand the meaning of *has/have got*, but do not teach it as a grammar point yet.
- Students read the instructions. Check that they understand what to do.
- Students scan the text (read quickly for specific information) to check if the sentences are true or false. They will read the text in more detail later. Give a time limit of one minute.

Answer key
I've got four red fish and three blue fish. ✗
The two blue fish have got green heads and orange tails. ✗
All the other sentences are true.

Option

- To teach the vocabulary for Exercise 2, draw two fish on the board:

Say the following sentences, pointing to the underlined features as you speak: *This is my aquarium. I've got a big fish. It's got a small tail … and a big eye. And I've got a small fish. It's got a big tail … and no eyes!*

Work it out: *have got* (1)

3a

- On the board, write an example with the short form *'ve: I've got four red fish.*
- In English, say: *This is the short form. What's the long form? (I have got four red fish).*
- Read the instructions, and explain that they are going to read the text in Exercise 2, and look for and underline all the sentences with *have got*. Make it clear that students must find <u>all</u> forms of *have got* (long forms, short forms and negative forms of *have/has got*).
- When students have finished, ask how many examples of *have got* they could find. Individual students read out the form of *have got* in each sentence.

Answer key

Every sentence has got at least one form of have got.

3b

- Students use the examples they have underlined to complete the chart. They should complete the positive sentences with long forms, and the negative sentences with the short forms *haven't* and *hasn't*.
- To check answers, have one student write the positive forms on the board, while another writes the negative forms.
- Get the class to tell you the correct form after *He/She* (*He's got, She's got*), and the short forms for positive sentences (*I've got …, You've got …*, etc.).

Answer key

Positive: I have got   It has got   We have got   They have got
Negative: You haven't got   It hasn't got   They haven't got

4

- Ask questions in English to get students thinking about the pictures before they read. For example: *What colour is the animal in picture 1? What country is picture 5?*
- Explain the task, and make sure they understand what to do. They need only understand the gist (general meaning), not every word of the texts.

- Students work individually, matching the texts with pictures. Check answers, then ask: *What words helped you to do this exercise?* (colours, countries).

Answer key

The Arctic Fox: picture 3   The tree frog: picture 2

Vocabulary: parts of the body

5a

- Help students to notice the word order of adjectives and nouns in English, so that they can work out which words in the text are body words. Write on the board: *big   eye   a*   and: *and   white   a   tail   red.* Students put the two sets of words in the right order (*A big eye. A red and white tail*). Ask students which words are parts of the body (*eye, tail*), and whether they come before or after adjectives (after).
- Students use sentences in the text to decide which words are parts of the body, then tick the right boxes. Do not confirm the answers yet.

Answer key

ears   eyes   head   legs   mouth   nose

5b

- Students work in pairs, looking up half the words each, then sharing their answers.

Option

- In groups, students look at the words in the boxes and find all the possible combinations, for example: *long nose, small eyes, small ears*. Each student then draws a face that includes a noticeable feature, such as a big mouth or a small nose, and in turn shows it to the rest of the group, who say what the feature is.

Tip 6 ★
Text completion tasks

- Before students attempt a text completion task individually, get them to cover the words in the box, and ask, in the mother tongue: *What kind of word is missing in each sentence? For example, is it a (part of the body)? a (place)? a (colour)?*

6

- Students read the gapped text quickly, and match it with the right picture.
- Check that they know the meaning of all the words in the box. Teach *summer* and *winter* by getting students to guess the meaning from: *The Arctic fox is white in winter and brown in summer.*
- Students complete the text, using the picture and the words in the box to help them.

Answer key

Picture 4 (clue: It's got no legs).
Europe   ears   tail   grey

7a

- Teach *arms, body, neck*.
- Students read the texts in Exercise 4 again before they start writing.

- Students work individually, and write a short paragraph about one of the other animals on page 21. Students sitting near each other should write about different pictures.

7b

- Put students into pairs. The pairs swap their descriptions, and look on page 110 for the name of the animal their partner has described.

Option

- Working together, pairs write a description for the final picture.

7c

- Tell students to help you write a list of all the parts of the body that they have learned in this unit. There are nine – *eyes, tail, ears, head, legs, mouth, nose, body, neck*.
- Students turn to page 73 of the Workbook, and complete the labels for those parts of the body that they have learned so far, on both the boy and the dog.

Suggested Workbook practice

Page 12, Exercises 1–3

Work it out: plural nouns

8a

- Students look for plural noun forms in the texts in Exercise 4, then fill in the gaps.

Answer key

1 *ears* 2 *forests* 3 *legs* 4 *countries*.

Option

- Students guess the plural forms, check their ideas with a partner, and then look through Exercise 4 to check their answers.

8b

- Students formulate a rule in the mother tongue. Help them to understand the question, but let <u>them</u> tell <u>you</u> the rule.

Answer key

You usually make the plural by adding -s.
The -y *ending usually changes to* -ies *in the plural.*

8c

- Before they begin the exercise, check that students remember the rule they have made for the use of *a* and *an*.
- Give one example for the right-hand column in the table: *two eyes*.
- Students complete the exercise individually, then check their answers with a partner.

Answer key

1 *two eyes* 2 *a bird   five birds* 3 *a family   three families*
4 *an insect   four insects*

Suggested Workbook practice

Page 12, Exercise 4

Families

Aims

In this section, students learn to talk about family members, using *have got* in positive, negative, question and short answer forms. Pronunciation practice focuses on the use of weak and strong forms of *have*.

1

- Students try to guess the meanings from the picture. Say, for example: *Look at the picture of the family. What does 'father' mean? What does 'grandfather' mean?*
- Students check their guesses in a dictionary.
- Put students in pairs. Partners ask each other about their family members, using *Have you got a …?*

2a

- Get students to guess which are boys' names, which are girls' names, and which might be the cat's name.
- Tell students that they will hear the cassette twice, so they shouldn't worry if they are unable to write all the numbers during the first listening.
- 📼 Play the cassette twice. Students listen and write the numbers next to the names.

2b

- Students compare answers with a partner before listening again.
- 📼 Play the cassette again. Students check or complete their answers.

Tapescript
Interviewer Hello, Diana. Tell me about your family. Have you got a brother?
Diana Yes, I have. My brother is called John. He's twenty. He's a student.
Interviewer And have you got a sister?
Diana Yes, I have. She's at our school. She's 13.
Interviewer What's her name?
Diana Monica. And my father's name is David. He's a doctor. Doctor David King.
Interviewer And your mother?
Diana Her name's Sonia.
Interviewer Has she got a job?
Diana Well … er … yes, she has. She's our mother! That's her job – and it's very hard work!
Interviewer And what about pets – have you got a dog or a cat?
Diana Well, we haven't got a dog. But we've got a cat. Its name is Shakespeare.
Interviewer That's a good name for a cat! And have you got a grandmother … or grandfather?
Diana Yes, I have. My grandmother is called Hanna and my grandfather is called William.

Answer key
*David 1   Hanna 5   John 3   Monica 6   Shakespeare (the cat) 7
Sonia 2   William 4*

3

- Check that students understand what to do. Ask, in the mother tongue: *What information is missing from the family tree?* (names and words for family members).
- Students use information from Exercises 1 and 2 to complete Diana's family tree.

- To check answers, draw a blank version of the family tree on the board. Ask three students to come and write in names. Another three students come and write the words for family members.

Answer key

grandmother (Hanna)   (grandfather) William   mother Sonia
father (David)   brother John   (Diana)   sister Monica

Work it out: *have got* (2)

4a

- Get students to tell you the long form for *You've got a brother*.
- To provide extra help with question forms, remind them that they have used the form in Exercise 1, and that the word order changes.
- Students complete the sentences individually, then check their answers in pairs.

Answer key

Have you got   have you got

Option

- To highlight the change in word order and revise *is/are* questions, write on the board one of the examples showing the word order for questions with *be* on page 17, Exercise 2a. Next to it, write: *You've got a sister. You've got a brother.* Ask for volunteers to come to the board and write the question forms underneath, using arrows to show the change in word order, as in the example for questions with *be*.

4b

- Students read the instructions. Check that they understand the task. For example, say: *Look at number 1. Is it a positive sentence, a negative sentence, or a question? What is the first word?*
- Students complete the exercise, then check their answers in pairs.

Answer key

1 *Have you got a red pen?*   2 *Has she got a grandmother?*
3 *Has it got a long tail?*

Tip 7 ★
Working out short answers

- To draw attention to correct short answer forms, tell students to close their books. Write a question on the board followed by a number of answers. Ask students to pick the two possible right answers. For example, for the question *Has Diana got a grandfather?*:

Yes,	a	she's got	No, she	a	hasn't got.
	b	she has got		b	not got.
	c	she's		c	hasn't.
	d	she has.		d	haven't.

When checking their answers, make them explain why the others are wrong before you confirm the correct answers *Yes, she has* and *No, she hasn't*.

5

- Students read the phrases in the box, and questions 1–7. Ask them to guess the meaning of any new vocabulary.
- Do the exercise orally with the whole class.

Pronunciation: *have*

6a

- The purpose of this exercise is to focus students' attention on the changing pronunciation of *have*: the (weak) unstressed forms /həv/ and /həz/ in questions, and the (strong) stressed forms /hæv/ and /hæz/ in short forms.
- Explain that the pronunciation of words sometimes depends on whether they are stressed or not. Illustrate this point by writing two sentences on the board:
  A: *I've got 3 fish and 2 cats.*
  B: *I've got 5 fish, 4 cats **and** a python!*
  Say the sentences out loud: *I've got 3 fish 'n (/ən/) 2 cats. I've got 5 fish, 4 cats and (/ænd/) a python!*
- Tell students to listen carefully and decide if the word *have* sounds the same or different in each set of questions and answers.
- 🔲 Play the cassette. Students write *S* or *D* for each pair of questions and answers.

Tapescript

Interviewer Sue, have you got a brother?
Sue Yes, I have.
Interviewer Have you got a sister?
Sue Yes, I have.
Interviewer Have you got grandparents?
Sue Yes, I have.
Interviewer Have you got short hair?
Sue Yes, I have.
Interviewer Have you got brown eyes?
Sue Yes, I have.

Answer key

The pronunciation is different in each case. The questions use the weak, unstressed form; the short answers use the strong, stressed form.

6b

- Write the first question on the board: *Have you got a brother?*
- Ask students: *Is this a question or a short answer?* (a question). *How do you say 'have' in a question – /hæv/ or /həv/?* (/həv/). Say the question aloud, exaggerating the weak form of *have*.
- Tell students to listen and repeat the questions, taking care to say *have* correctly.
- 🔲 Play the cassette, pausing after each question for students to repeat.

Tapescript

Have you got a brother?
Have you got a sister?
Have you got grandparents?
Have you got short hair?
Have you got brown eyes?

6c

- Help students to say *moustache*: /mə'stɑːʃ/.
- Say the questions in Exercise 5, taking care to use the weak form of *has*, /həz/. Students repeat.
- Put students into pairs to take turns asking and answering the questions in Exercise 5.

Tip 8 ★
Pair work partners

- To practise an activity more than once, get students to work with new partners. This can be done without students moving out of their seats. For example:

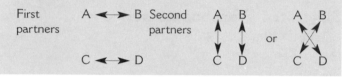

6d

- Students look at the questions in Exercise 5 again. Tell them they are going to ask the same questions about each other.
- Ask the first question: *Have you got a grandfather?* Point to a student and help him/her respond with *Yes, I have* or *No, I haven't*.
- Choose individual students to ask and answer the other questions in the same way. Help with forms and pronunciation.
- In pairs (see Tip 8 above), students take turns to ask and answer the questions about each other. Walk round, checking their pronunciation of *have*.

7a

- Students do this task in their vocabulary notebooks. Students work individually, drawing their own family tree.

Option

- If students have already completed Workbook page 13 Exercise 3, they can use that and go straight to 7b.

7b

- Ask one student to come to the front with his or her family tree. The rest of the class asks questions, using the language they have learned so far, for example: *Have you got a sister? Has she got long hair? Has your father got a moustache?* The student replies with short answers.
- In pairs, students ask and answer questions about each other's family.

Option

- On the board, write words for family members, including *cat* and *dog*. Underneath these, write: *hair, moustache, white, brown, long*. For more choice, you can add to these two lists, for example, *cousin, aunt, tail, short, glasses*. Working in pairs, students use the words prompts on the board to ask and answer more questions about each others' families, for example: *Have you got an aunt? Has she got glasses? Have you got a dog? Has it got a long tail?*

Suggested Workbook practice
Page 13, Exercise 3

Describing people
Aims
In this section, students learn more vocabulary for describing people. The language is presented through a listening activity, and practised through speaking and writing a personal description. Students revise the sounds /iː/ and /e/ and differentiate between the sounds /eɪ/ and /aɪ/.

1

- Explain the meaning of *What's he/she like?* Get individual students to describe each picture to the class, using the language they have learned, for example: *He's got a moustache.* Use the pictures to teach *beard* and *dark, light, blond, straight* and *curly hair*.
- Get students to identify pictures. For example, ask: *Who has got blond hair? Who has dark eyes?*
- Explain that students do not need to understand every word, just enough to decide which pictures are Dan and Tony.
- 📼 Play the cassette. Students listen and choose two pictures.

....

Tapescript
A I don't know Dan. What's he like?
B Well, he's got blue eyes … he's got curly hair … er, his hair's light brown, and, um …he's got a moustache and a beard.
A I don't know Tony. What's he like?
B He's young – about 17 or 18, I think. … He's got short, dark hair. It isn't straight. It's curly… um …he's got nice brown eyes.

....

Answer key
Dan 3   Tony 4

Useful English

- Students read the phrases in the box and guess the long form of *What's* (*What is …?*)
- 📼 Play the cassette. Students listen and and underline the stressed words.
- Play the cassette again. Students listen and repeat.

Answer key
What's she <u>like</u>?
She's got <u>straight</u>, <u>fair hair</u>.
What's he <u>like</u>?
He's got <u>curly</u>, <u>dark</u>, <u>hair</u>.

2

- Tell students to find the family trees that they made in Exercise 7 of the last section.
- Ask a student to draw their tree on the board. Encourage the rest of the class to use the new vocabulary to ask questions about family members, for example: *What's your father like? Has your mother got dark hair? Has your sister got blue eyes?*
- In pairs, students ask and answer questions about each other's family.

3

- Make sure students understand the instructions. They use the questions, and any other information they can think of, to build a description of themselves.
- Students 'brainstorm' for ideas (think and discuss together) of other details that they could include.
- Ask and answer the questions with the whole class. Students suggest a title for their paragraph, such as *All about me*.
- Students are now ready to write the answers as a paragraph.

Options

- Teach *quite* and *very* to help produce more accurate descriptions, for example: *I'm quite tall. I've got very straight hair.*
- For further writing practice, students can produce a similar paragraph for another member of their family. Remind them to use *has got* when writing about a third person, e.g. *He is 13. He's got quite short hair.*

Pronunciation: /eɪ/ and /aɪ/

4a

- 📼 Students close their books and listen to and repeat the two sounds. Demonstrate the sounds in the usual way.

Tapescript

/eɪ/, /aɪ/

4b

- Ask the class to look at the list of words and find one with the sound /iː/ in it, and one with the sound /e/. Do the same for /eɪ/ and /aɪ/.
- Students organize the words into 4 groups according to vowel sound.
- Write the words on the board, with a number below each letter:

He	head	hi	eat	eye	read	red	write	game
1	2	3	4	5	6	7	8	9

these	friend	they
10	11	12

- Call out the words in random order. Students call out the corresponding number.
- Ask a student to come to the front and call out the words in random order. The class calls out the numbers.
- Students work in pairs: A says a word, B points to it. They then change roles.

4c

- 📼 Students listen and repeat the letters in the usual way.

4d

- In pairs, students say the letters to each other in the usual way.

4e

- This is a spelling dictation game. To demonstrate the game, dictate the following example, explaining that the letters make a sentence.

  S–E–V–E–N–A–N–D–E–L–E–V–E–N–I–S …

- When students have written the letters, tell them that the final word is missing. Ask them to guess what it is (eighteen).

- Put students into pairs. Tell all the B partners to close their books, and to have a pen and notebook ready. Tell As to dictate the letters in message 1 to their partner. When they have finished, B should read out the sentence (not the individual letters).
- A and B change roles for Message 2.

Option

- From your set of alphabet cards (see Materials preparation 3), remove the letters O, Q, R, U and W. Shuffle the remaining cards and use them to test students on the pronunciation of the letters they have learned so far.

Suggested Workbook practice

Page 13, Exercises 1, 2, 4 and 5
Page 14, Exercise 1

The OK Club
What a mess!

Aims

This section continues the photo-story. Students learn how to discuss problems and opportunities using everyday expressions such as *What a mess!* and *Any ideas?*, and common expressions with *have got* (*a chance, an idea*).

1

Background information

British currency. Students may ask about the value of the sums of money mentioned in this episode. Explain that there are 100p (pronounced '*p*' or *pence*) to the pound (£). The text mentions two amounts of money: £1.15 (about the price of a sandwich), and 20 pence (enough to make two local calls from a phone box).

Option

- Ask questions to remind students of the story so far. For example: *Who are Carol and Dave? Who are members of the OK Club? What is the problem in the Coffee Corner?* (a fire).

- Ask questions in the mother tongue about the story pictures. For example: *Look at picture 2. What are the club members thinking about?* (the damage to the Coffee Corner). *How are they feeling?* (depressed, shocked). *Look at picture 3. What are the club members showing each other?* (money, other small objects, or empty hands). *Why?* (they want to repair the Coffee Corner but they have no money). *What do you think the group wants to buy?*
- Students look at the small pictures at the top of the page. They guess how these things might come into the story.
- Explain that students need only understand the main events in the story, not every word.
- 📼 Play the cassette. Students follow the story in their books, and see if their ideas were right.

Answer key

1 paint   4 money

2

- Check that students understand the questions.
- Encourage students to scan (read quickly for specific information) the text for the necessary information. Again, they do not need to understand every word. Students answer the questions individually, then compare their answers with a partner.
- To check answers, get different students to ask students at a distance from them. This ensures that questions and answers are spoken loudly enough for the rest of the class to hear.

Answer key

1 Dave   2 Jane and Emma   3 Carol   4 Emma

3

- This discussion will need to be in the mother tongue. Remind students that the idea is to redecorate the club, then ask them what the problem is with that idea (how to get the money to do it). Explain that their task is to guess and explain to the class how Emma will solve the problem.
- Students work in groups of 5 or 6, then compare their guesses with other groups' guesses.

4a

- Check they understand all the dialogue, and the situation in the picture. Ask: *What's the problem?* (they haven't got any money). *Why didn't they bring money?* (they didn't plan to catch the bus, but it started to rain).
- Students work with a partner to complete the dialogue.

Answer key

A got   B 've (20)p   A haven't got   B haven't   got   ideas

4b

- Students try out their dialogues with a new partner (see Tip 8, page 37).
- Allow students 2–3 minutes to practise reading the dialogue. Walk around the class, checking that students are pronouncing the short forms *'ve got* and *haven't got* correctly.
- Choose students from opposite sides of the room to act out the dialogue for the class.

Option

- Use the reverse dialogue-building technique to help students learn the dialogue (see Tip 4, page 17).

Suggested Workbook practice

Page 14, Exercise 3

Review

Aims

The Review section summarizes and briefly revises the key language features of Unit 3: *have got*, plural nouns, and adjectives.

have got

- See Tip 5, page 30, and revise the forms of *have got*.

Plural nouns

- Tell students to look at the table quickly, then close their books. Write *tree*, *country*, *insect*, *leg*, *story* on the board. Ask individual students to come and write the plural form next to each.

Adjectives

- Tell students to close their books. Write and draw on the board:

A large cat   _____

- Alternatively draw trees or houses.
- Ask students *What word doesn't change for picture two?* (large) *Why not?* (because adjectives stay the same for singular and plural nouns). Have a student label picture two (two large cats).

1

- Use the questions for a class speaking activity. Question 1, in particular, can be used as a question-and-answer chain activity (see Tip 9 below for instructions and example).

Tip 9 ★
Question-and-answer chains

- This activity involves the whole class asking and answering questions at speed. The teacher starts off the chain with the sort of question he or she wants to practise, for example questions with *have got*, questions about location. At the end of the question, name a student to answer. That student answers the question, then asks another student a similar question. The chain continues round the class. Allow each student in the chain to choose the next speaker (though this should not be a student sitting nearby). For example:
  A *What have you got in your schoolbag, B?*
  B (showing items from his/her bag) *I've got a dictionary, and two blue books. What have you got in your schoolbag, C?*
  C *I've got three red pens and two big sandwiches. What …*

2

- Students work individually, finding the plural words, then writing the singular form.
- Point out that the plural of *fish* (page 20 Exercise 2,) is irregular.

Answer key

Exercise 4: countries – country   ears – ear   eyes – eye   trees – tree forests – forest   legs – leg. Exercise 6: colours – colour

Vocabulary

- *Animals.* Students add the animals from this unit to the page they started in Unit 2. Encourage them to make drawings next to each word.

- *Colours.* The words will be more memorable if students write each word in the appropriate colour, again with a little picture next to each, for example, the sun for *yellow*, the sea for *blue*.
- *Continents.* Students add these words to the page for Countries.
- *Parts of the body.* Students can either label sketches of a person and an animal, as on Workbook page 73, or they can cut out, glue and label pictures from a magazine.

Suggested Workbook practice

Page 14, Exercise 2
Page 15, Exercises 1 and 2

Freewheeling

a

- Tell students they are going to listen to a song. They have to listen to the words and music to decide if the song is sad or happy.
- 📼 Play the cassette. Students listen, with books closed, and decide the mood of the song.
- Play the cassette again. Students listen and read.
- Tell students to think of a title for the song. List their ideas on the board. Discuss in the mother tongue which is the best title and why.

b

- 📼 Play the cassette again. Students listen to the rhythm of the music and familiarize themselves with the tune.
- Play the cassette a last time, encouraging students to sing along to the music.

Preparation for Unit 4

Workbook page 15, Exercises 3 and 4

Workbook answer key

The living world

1 2 *Mark has got a dog and a lizard. He hasn't got a cat or a bird.*
  3 *Tim and Louise have got a cat and a bird. They haven't got a dog or a lizard.*
  4 *Graham and Jill have got a lizard and a bird. They haven't got a cat or a dog.*

2 *Student's own answers*

3 2 *neck* 3 *head* 4 *ears* 5 *eyes* 6 *mouth*
  7 *leg* 8 *tail*

4a Singular: *a frog an elephant an ant*
  Plural: *cats girls birds*

b 2 *families* 3 *secretaries* 4 *countries* 5 *dictionaries*
  6 *universities*

Families

1 2 *Has Dave got curly hair? No, he hasn't. He's got straight hair.*
  3 *Has Ricky got hair fair? No, he hasn't. He's got dark hair.*
  4 *Has Carol got black hair? No, she hasn't. She's got brown hair.*
  5 *Has Emma got light brown hair? No, she hasn't. She's got dark brown hair.*

2 *Student's own answers*

3 *Student's own answers*

4 1 *eyes* 2 *grey* 3 *eyes* 4 *grey* 5 *brown* 6 *eyes*

5b /eɪ/   /aɪ/
  eight   *eye*
  grey   *hi!*
  OK   *my*
  say   *nine*
  snake   *smile*

What a mess!

1 2 *I have got straight hair.*
  3 *My sister and brother have got fair hair.*
  4 *It has got a long tail and curly hair.*
  5 *My father has got brown hair and a moustache.*

2a 1 *He's sixteen.*
  2 *It's dark brown.*
  3 *It's short and very curly.*
  4 *No, they're blue.*
  5 *No, he hasn't.*
  6 *Yes, he is. Come to the club and meet him.*

b *c*

c 1 *d* 2 *a* 3 *b*

3 1 *idea* 2 *ears* 3 *money* 4 *sisters* 5 *teacher* 6 *pence*

Skills: descriptions

1 *He's got short dark hair. He's got a small nose and he's only got one eye; it's very small. He's got a big mouth and a long moustache.*

2 *He's got long fair hair.*
  He's got a big nose.
  He's got big eyes.
  He's got a large mouth and a short moustache (and beard).

Prepare for Unit 4

3b *Student's own answers*

4 2 *shirt* 3 *shoes* 4 *T-shirt* 5 *socks* 6 *jumper*

Unit 4

Syllabus

Topic
At home
Shirts and skirts: *clothes*
The OK Club

Grammar
there is, *there are*
Prepositions of place
Possessive *'s*
Possessive adjectives

Function
Describing a house/rooms
Expressing opinions

Vocabulary
Rooms
Furniture
Clothes

Reading
Checking information and details

Listening
Understanding a description
Identifying key information

Writing
Writing a description of your home

Speaking
Giving opinions
Describing rooms

Pronunciation
Word stress in questions and answers
/uː/, /ɑː/ and /əʊ/

Learn to learn
Using a dictionary (2)

Vocabulary

Key vocabulary

apartment	large	some
armchair	living-room	sometimes
bad	loud	sweatshirt
basin	millionaire	swim
bathroom	near	swimming pool
bed	next to	team
bedroom	on	then
car	our	there is
clothes	plant	thing
dining-room	player	toilet
door	radio	trainers
favourite	Saturday	trousers
fridge	shirt	T-shirt
garage	shoes	tomorrow
home	shower	under
house	sink (n)	up
jeans	skirt	watch (v)
jumper	socks	window
kitchen	sofa	

Other vocabulary

also	film	person
all	gold	plan (n)
all right	hand	room
amazing	happy	save
ball	helmet	sell
boring	holidays	street
cooker	lake	town
date (appointment)	modern	usual
excuse (n)	outside	visitor
fan	pair	

Materials preparation

1 Dictionaries for page 26 Exercise 2, page 28 Exercise 1, and page 31 Exercise 3b.

2 For page 28, Exercise 4d Option: make one photocopy of Worksheet 1 on Teacher's Book page 146 for each pair of students. Cut each worksheet in half. Study the pictures and make a list of any useful new vocabulary.

3 For page 29, Exercise 2 Option 2: bring in pictures from clothes catalogues or fashion magazines.

4 For page 29, Exercise 3 Option 1: the alphabet cards from Unit 3.

5 A small prize for the first student to complete the Freewheeling crossword.

At home
there is, *there are*

Aims

In this section, students learn to describe rooms and furniture in homes, and to talk about location. The language is presented through reading texts, and practised through listening and speaking activities.

1

Background information

Bill Gates is a founder of the computer software company Microsoft, and one of the richest men in the world. Students may know some of the *Microsoft* products such as *Microsoft Windows* (the main operating system for most office and home computers).

Option

- To find out what students know about *Microsoft* and its owner, Bill Gates, write key words on the board: *PC   Microsoft   Windows   Bill Gates.*
  Ask: *What is a pc?* (a personal computer). *What is 'Microsoft'?* (a computer company). *What is Windows 98?* (a computer programme). *Who is Bill Gates?* (the founder of the Microsoft company). *Where is he from?* (America). *Is he rich?* (extremely rich!). In the mother tongue, ask students if they know anything else about Bill Gates.

- Students look at the picture and predict the text topic.

Answer key
3 *a house*

Option

- If students all immediately guess 'house', ask in the mother tongue *Whose house it? What do you think it is like inside?*

Learn to learn: using a dictionary (2)

2

- Students work in pairs to find the meaning of the words in the box. One student looks up the top row of words, the other looks up the bottom row. They then share their answers. Check answers in the usual way.

- Students turn to Workbook page 74. Show them where to write their chosen head-word.

Option

- If your students have completed Workbook page 15, Exercise 3, they need only look up *garage* and move directly to the word-map activity.

3

- The 'true/false' sentences contain new vocabulary from the text including *next to, lake, visitors, watch, films, private* and *swimming pool*. Make sure that students understand all the sentences before they begin to read the text.

- Students read the text and decide if sentences 1–5 are true or false. Remind them that they do not need to understand every word at this stage. They should skim (read quickly for gist) to find the information they need.

- As you check answers, get students to correct the false sentences.

Answer key
1 *True*
2 *False. There are sofas and chairs for 150 people in the large living-room.*
3 *False. There are 12 bathrooms.*
4 *False. They watch films in their private cinema.*
5 *True*

4

- Check that students understand the meaning of the four words or phrases.

- As this is the first time students have done an exercise in identifying equivalent words or phrases, you may prefer to do this as a whole class activity. Help students to locate the answers by giving clues in the mother tongue for each item: *Number 1 – the word is in the title. Number 2 – look for a noun in paragraph 1 (follow-up clue – the word is in the first line). Number 3 – look for an adjective in the next paragraph (follow-up clue – the word is in the 2nd line). Number 4 – look near the end of the first paragraph.*

Answer key
1 *home*   2 *millionaire*   3 *large*   4 *TV*

Option

- 🔲 This text is recorded. Play the cassette. Students listen again, underlining any unknown words. Help students to guess the meaning of these words. For example, *Modern – is it an adjective or a noun?* (adjective). *What does it describe?* (the house). *How would you describe the house – old or new?* (new).

Useful English

- Explain that these phrases are useful for expressing positive and negative opinions. Do not give exact meanings yet.

- 🔲 Play the cassette. Students listen to the speakers' intonation, and look at the list in the box to decide the meaning (the phrases are listed from the most positive to the most negative).

- Write on the board: *What do you think?* and help students to link the sounds of the words.

- Play the cassette again. Students listen and repeat. Encourage them to imitate the speakers' intonation, to express enthusiasm, neutral feelings, and disapproval.

Option

- For further practice, get students to tell you the titles of 6 popular TV programmes. Write them on the board. Do a quick question-and-answer chain round the class (see Tip 9, page 39), using the question *What do you think of (name of the programme)?* Students then work in pairs or groups, asking for and giving opinions about the programmes.

5

- Students in groups of 4 ask and answer the question *What do you think of this dream home?*

Option

- Students work in pairs or small groups to ask and answer questions with *What do you think of …?* about the holiday pictures on Student's Book page 62.

6

- The picture shows the floor plan of a house, drawn from above, with the front door opening onto a corridor. Check that students understand the layout and basic details of the plan. For example, in the mother tongue, ask: *Which room has the biggest window?* (room 4). *What room is at the end of the corridor?* (a bathroom).If students are having difficulty with vocabulary, use gesture (pointing to a *wall*, *corner*, *window*, or mime (for *shower*, *basin*) to explain them.
- Students read the text silently, and decide which room it describes. To check the answer, ask in English: *Is it room 3?* (No). *Is it room 4?* (No). *What room is it?*

Answer key

Room 1

7

- Tell students to look at the pictures and guess where they would fit best in the plan. Ask questions to help, for example: *What do you think? Where are the armchairs? Are they in room 1 or room 4? Are they next to the window? Or next to the door?*
- Students will have to draw objects quickly as they listen, so first get them to devise simple ways to represent each object.
- ▭ Play the cassette. Students listen and draw the objects on the plan.
- Students check their answers with a partner. If necessary, play the cassette again.

Tapescript/Answer key

A There are two armchairs in the living-room. One armchair is in the corner, next to the small table. The other armchair is in the corner near the door.
B There's a sofa in the living-room – it's near the wall, next to the door.
A There's a television in the other corner of the living-room, near the window.
B There are two beds in the big bedroom. They're next to the door, near the wall.
A There's a desk in the big bedroom. It's next to the window.

Option

- If you think students will find Exercise 7 difficult, let them work in pairs. For example, student A draws the TV, beds and sofa, while student B draws the desk and armchairs. They then share answers, and listen again to confirm them.

8

- Now that students have completed the floor plan, they identify individually the four rooms.

Answer key

living-room 4   kitchen 2   big bedroom 3   small bedroom 1

Option

- Once you have checked the answers, ask questions in English about the location of different objects. For example: *Where is the plant?* (in the living-room). *Where is the cooker?* (in the kitchen). *What is in the corner of the small bedroom?* (an armchair). *Where is the shower?* (in the small bathroom). *Where is the bath?* (in the big bathroom).

9

- Read the example dialogue with the class. Then demonstrate the game with the class. Taking A's role, think of a place for the computer, for example, near the plant in the living-room. Students take turns to ask questions as in the example dialogue.
- Put students into pairs. They decide who takes which role.
- Students read the instructions. Then ask questions to check that they have understood what to do.
- Students play the game. Go round the room, helping students with their questions. After ten questions, pairs change roles.

Work it out: *there is/there are*

10a

- Students use the examples to complete the rules for themselves in the usual way.

Answer key

there is   there are

10b

- Check that students remember the meaning of 'short answer'. Tell them to find two short answers in Exercise 9 (*No, there isn't. Yes, there is*). Then ask them to work out the plural forms (see Tip 7, page 36).
- Write the negative form on the board without the apostrophe: *No, there arent*. Ask a student to put the apostrophe in the correct place (*No, there aren't*).
- Students use the plan in Exercise 6 to answer the two questions.

Answer key

1 *Yes, there is.*   2 *No, there aren't.*

10c

- Tell students to look again at Student's Book page 17 Exercise 2a, and study the examples. They make similar examples for *there is/there are* questions.

11a

- This task focuses on the need for capital letters at the beginning of every sentence. The text also provides a model for the writing task in 11b.
- Students look again at the second paragraph of the text on Student's Book page 26, and underline every word that begins with a capital letter. Then get them to explain, in the mother tongue, why the capital letter is necessary in each case.
- Students work individually to correct the text in 11a, then check their corrections with a partner.

Answer key

A capital letter is needed at the beginning of every sentence.

11b

- Students make a simple drawing of their own home (like the plan in Exercise 6, but without furniture).
- Choose a student to draw their house plan on the board. In English, ask questions about furniture, for example: *Where is your bedroom? Where is the bed? What is this room? Is there a television? Where is it? Are there chairs in the dining-room? What is in this room?* The student draws in items of furniture as you ask about them.
- Give the rest of the class a few minutes to draw furniture in their plans. Then put students into pairs to ask and answer about each other's plans.
- Students use their plans, and the model text in Exercise 11a to write a description of their own home.

Suggested Workbook practice

Page 16, Exercises 1–4

Shirts and skirts
Prepositions of place

Aims

In this section, students learn to talk about where things are, and to describe belongings, especially clothes. The language, which includes prepositions of place and possessive *'s*, is presented through listening and reading tasks, and practised through speaking and writing.

1

Options

- Students look at the pictures in Exercise 1. Ask: *What do you think of these rooms?* Students respond with phrases from the Useful English section. Agree with any student who says *They're awful,* and say: *Yes, they're a mess!* Write the phrase on the board and ask students to guess the meaning.
- Discuss the two pictures in the mother tongue. Ask: *Whose rooms are they?* (Carol's and Dave's rooms). *What do you think their mother will say to Dave and Carol?* (that they must tidy their rooms). Write *Tidy up your room!* on the board and ask students to guess the meaning.

- In pairs, students look up the words in the box, each student looking up half the words. (If students have completed Workbook page 15, Exercise 4, they will know many of these words already.)
- In the mother tongue, ask questions about the words: *Which words are plural? Which clothes do you wear on your legs? On your body? On your feet? Which one is worn only by females?*
- Students look at the pictures and note which clothes are in the rooms. They compare answers with a partner.
- Students turn to Workbook page 74 and complete word-map 2.

Answer key

jeans   jumper   shirt   shoes   socks   T-shirt   sweatshirt   trainers

2a

- Students read the instructions. Check, in the mother tongue, that they understand what they are going to hear. Ask: *Who are*

you going to hear?* (Carol and Dave's mother). *What do you have to guess?* (who she is talking to). *What do you think she will be talking about?* (the mess in the room). *Will she be happy?* (no – angry). *How can you guess who she is talking to?* (from the description of what's in the room.

- 🔲 Play the cassette twice. Students listen and choose the right room. If they are still unsure of the answer, let them discuss their ideas in pairs, then play the cassette again.

Tapescript

Your room's a real mess! There are trainers and T-shirts on the desk. There's paper under the desk. There are three shoes near the door … Where's the other shoe? There are jeans and sweatshirts on the chair! Your schoolbag is next to the bed, and it's got socks in it! And there are books and shirts on your bed… And look at your CDs and cassettes! It's terrible! Please tidy it up.

Answer key

Carol

2b

- Tell students to look at the pictures, which illustrate prepositions of place. Use the picture of Carol's room to practise the prepositions with the class. For example, ask: *Where are her trainers?* (on the desk). *Where are her shoes?* (near the door). *Where are her socks?* (in her school bag).
- Read the instructions, then check that they understand what to do.
- Students read the text, check it against the picture, and underline the three mistakes.

Answer key

The trainers and T-shirts are on the desk.
There are two pairs of shoes near the door.
There are jeans and sweatshirts on the chair.

Options

- To provide further practice of prepositions, students do a question-and-answer chain round the class (see Tip 9, page 39), asking about objects in their classroom. For example: David *Jan, where's your bag?* Jan *It's under my desk. Emmet, where are your books?*
- Play *I spy.* (See Game 1 below.)

Game 1 ▼
I spy

- This is a traditional children's game, with *spy* here meaning *see*. One person chooses an object that everyone can see, for example, a clock, but does not say what the object is. He or she says: *I spy with my little eye something beginning with …* and gives the first letter of the word, in this case *C.* Everyone else looks around and tries to guess the object, using *Yes/No* questions, for example, about colour: *Is it red?* or location: *Is it near me?* They then try to guess the object itself. Whoever guesses correctly thinks of another object.
  Example: *Is it green?* (No, it isn't.) *Is it brown?* (Yes, it is.) *Is it on a desk?* (No, it isn't.) *Is it near the door?* (No, it isn't.) *Is it on the wall?* (Yes, it is.) *Is it a clock?* (Yes, it is!)

3a

- Ask a few students to describe what is on their desks, using *There is* and *There are*. Give examples first: *There are two books on my desk. There is a pen on the book. There is a blue dictionary.*
- Put students into pairs, and tell them to decide who will describe which room.
- Make sure students understand the task.
- Give students one minute to look at the pictures, then tell them to close their books and write 5 sentences describing objects in the room. Go round the class, checking that they are using *There is/are* correctly.

3b

- Ask two students, from different pairs, to demonstrate the activity. In turns they read a sentence, and the other checks the sentence by looking at the picture and confirming or disputing the sentence using *Yes, there is/are* or *No, there isn't/aren't*. To make sure students listen to their partners' sentences, not read them, have students turn to face their partner.
- Allow 3–4 minutes, then ask the class, in the mother tongue: *Did anyone write five correct sentences? Did anyone find a mistake in their partner's descriptions?*

Work it out: possessive *'s*

4a

- Students look at the examples to work out the correct form to use in 4b.
- Point out that this form is also used in the pictures: *Carol's room, Dave's room*.

4b

- Students complete the two captions.

Answer key

Emma's   Carol's

4c

- Put students into pairs or small groups to discuss, in the mother tongue, the meaning and sentence structure of possessive *'s* sentences.
- Allow students 3–4 minutes to write down their ideas. Each group then chooses a representative to read out their group's ideas to the class.

Answer key

Name + 's (apostrophe -s) + singular or plural noun shows that the object belongs to the person.

4d

- This is a reversal of the memory game in Exercise 3b, and provides controlled practice of possessive *'s*.
- Demonstrate the activity by playing the game with the class first. Tell students to close their books, and say whose room. Say: *There's a bag under the bed.* (It's Dave's room.) *There are three shoes near the door.* (It's Carol's room.)
- Put students into pairs to play the game. After one or two minutes, pairs change roles.

Option

- To practise prepositions and questions with *there*, play *Find the differences* (see Game 2 below). You will need one copy of Worksheet 1 for each pair of students (see Materials preparation 2). Student A and Student B take turns to ask each other questions about their pictures to find out what the differences are.

Answer key

In Student B's picture …
1 *there are two plants in the corner, not one.*   2 *there are pictures of animals on the wall, not people*   3 *there aren't any pencils on the desk next to the door.*   4 *there isn't a pen on the desk next to the door.*   5 *there are two books on the desk next to the door.*   6 *the bin is under the desk, not next to it.*   7 *the basket is near the table next to the window, not next to the door.*   8 *there is a computer on the desk near the window.*   9 *there isn't a jumper on the chair near the window.*   10 *there are four fish in the aquarium, not three.*

Game 2 ▼
Find the differences

- This activity uses two similar, but not quite identical pictures. Each student in a pair has one of the pictures. By asking each other questions, they discover what the differences are. Teach any new words that students will need before they play. Put students into pairs, with partners facing each other in such a way that neither can see the other's picture. Explain how to play, and get students to suggest some example questions, such as *Is there a televison near the sofa? (Yes, there is. / No, there isn't.) Has the girl got a small dog? (Yes, she has. / No, she hasn't.) Is the sofa green? (Yes, it is. / No, it isn't.) Are there two plants in the corner? (Yes, there are. / No, there's one plant in the corner.)* Pairs continue the game on their own until one pair thinks they have found all the differences.

Suggested Workbook practice

Page 17, Exercise 1
Page 18, Exercises 3–5
Page 19, Exercise 1

What's your favourite team?

Aims

In this section, students learn the remaining possessive adjectives, and have further practice of *have got*. They also learn and practise more vocabulary for colour and clothes. In the pronunciation section, students differentiate between the sounds /uː/, /ɑː/ and /əʊ/, and learn the final letters of the alphabet.

1

Options

- Students look at the row of small pictures. Ask *Who are these people?* (American baseball players). *What are the London Monarchs and the Chicago Bears?* (the names of American baseball teams).
- Explain new vocabulary: *favourite*, *team*, *player* and *fan*. Ask students about their own interests, for example: *Do you like football? Have you got a favourite team? So you are a (Real Madrid) fan! Who's your favourite player?*

- Students read the instructions.
- Help students to guess the meaning of new vocabulary, such as *helmet, gold, our, their*, by using the pictures.
- Do the first match with the class to make sure students understand what to do. Tell them to underline any unfamiliar words as they read, but not to look them up at this stage.
- Students quickly match the texts. To check answers, ask in English: *Who is a London Monarch fan?* (number 4) *Who is a Chicago Bears fan?* (number 3) and so on.

Answer key

1 *Denver Broncos*   2 *Barcelona Dragons*   3 *Chicago Bears*
4 *London Monarchs* /ˈmɒnəks/   5 *San Francisco 49ers*

Work it out: possessive adjectives

2a

- Students underline all the possessive adjectives (for example, *my, your*) they can find in Exercise 1. With a partner, they check underlined words, and complete the chart.
- Walk round, checking that students have identified the right words, and are completing the chart correctly.

Answer key

your   his   her   our   their

2b

- Students read the example. Check that they understand the task by writing the example sentences on the board, one under the other, and underlining *He* and *socks* in the first sentence, and *his socks* in the second. Draw arrows from *he* and *socks* to *his socks* to show how the word order is changed.
- Do sentence 1 with the whole class in the same way. Students complete the exercise individually.

Answer key

1 *Our trousers are white.*   2 *Your socks are blue and red.*
3 *Her skirt is red and white.*   4 *My football shirt is green and white.*
5 *Their helmets are gold.*

Pronunciation: /uː/, /ɑː/ and /əʊ/

3a

- Before playing the cassette, demonstrate the difference between the sounds /uː/ (*oooh!*), /ɑː/ (*ah!*), and /əʊ/ (*oh!*) in the usual way.
- 🔲 Play the cassette. Students listen and repeat the letters.

3b

- Make this a 'Say and Point' pairwork activity. Student A spells the words, student B points to the right word. They then change roles.

3c

- 🔲 Play the cassette. Students listen and repeat the sounds of the letters.

Tapescript

A, B, C, D, E, F, G, H, I, J, K, L, M, N, O, P, Q, R, S, T, U, V, W, X, Y, Z

Suggested Workbook practice

Page 17, Exercise 2

The OK Club
Emma's idea

Aims

This section continues the photo-story. It presents informal English in a lively context, and brings together the language students have been practising in the unit. This episode practises the language of suggestions and opinions, and extends language for saying goodbye.

1a

- Students try to guess Emma's idea from pictures 1 and 2.

1b

- 🔲 Play the cassette. Students listen and check their guesses about Emma's plan.
- Ask students to explain their ideas in the mother tongue. If they have not guessed correctly, tell them to read the dialogue for pictures 1 and 2 again, and to underline any words they do not know, such as *sell, buy*. Help students to guess the meaning of these words.

Answer key

Emma's idea is to sell hamburgers to make money for the club.

2

- This exercise focuses on language for saying goodbye. Students should be able to remember the missing words. If not, play this section of the cassette again.

Answer key

See   Good

3a

- Students look back at the story, using the pictures to help them guess the meaning of the phrases.

3b

- Ask students whether each word is an adjective, noun or verb (this will help them in their vocabulary task).
- Students check their guesses in a dictionary. Warn them that *date* has more than one meaning, and they must choose the best one (here it means *a meeting, an appointment*).

Set the pace

4a

- Again, students should use the context of the story to work out the meaning of these expressions.

Answer key

1 *understand?*   2 *very good / great!*   3 *Goodbye (implying 'until I see you again')*

4b

- Help students to repeat both intonation and stress patterns correctly.

4c

- Make sure students understand the drama in pictures 3 and 4. in the mother tongue ask: *Why is Jack in a bad mood?* (he thinks that Jane likes Dave, and he is jealous). *Who understands this – Jane? Ricky? Emma?* (Only Emma).
- Put students into groups of 5 to practise the dialogue for pictures 1–4. Tell them that you will go round and listen to the best actors. Choose the group which practises the dialogue in the most lively way to come to the front of the class and act out the dialogue again.

5

- Do this exercise orally with the class first. Students then write the corrected sentences in their notebooks.

Answer key

1 *Ricky has got a loud voice.*   2 *Carol thinks that Emma's idea is fantastic.*   3 *Jack has got a date with a friend on Saturday.*

Option

- Students think of more words that can be used in the same place in each sentence. Teach some extra words if students suggest them in the mother tongue. For example: 1 *quiet, interesting, boring (high, low)*, 2 *amazing, all right, not bad (stupid, clever)*, 3 *with his sister, his father (his girlfriend)*.

6

- Do this as a final class activity to bring the discussion back to the story. Students can give their opinions using the language they learned in the *Useful English* section on page 27.

Suggested Workbook practice

Page 18, Exercise 1
Page 19, Exercise 2

Review

Aims

The Review section summarizes and briefly revises the key language features of Unit 4: prepositions of place, and possessive *'s*.

there is/there are

- See Tip 5, page 30, and revise the forms of *there is/there are*.

Prepositions of place

- Read the rule and the examples. Revise the prepositions with a quick question-and-answer chain (see Tip 9, page 39), for example: *Where's (Jack's pen)? It's (under his desk)*.

Possessive *'s*

- Students add here the rule they wrote themselves.

1

- Point out that students can only use each phrase once, then let them work individually.

Answer key

1 *are*   2 *is*   3 *aren't*   4 *isn't*

2

- Students do the exercise from memory, then turn back to page 28 to check their answers.

Answer key

Next to 5   under 4   in 1   on 2   near 3

3

- To avoid partners writing the same questions, write two lists on the board:
  List A – *armchairs, basin, bed, cooker, desk, fridge*
  List B – *plant, shower, sink, sofa, television, toilet.*
- Put students into pairs. Partners decide who will write questions about which list.
- Students work individually to write their three questions using *Where…?*
- Students exchange questions with their partner, and write answers to their partner's questions. Partners check their answers together.

Vocabulary

- *Rooms and furniture*. Tell students to study the word-map on page 74 of their Workbooks for 1 minute. They then try to reproduce the map from memory in their vocabulary books, adding any further words that they have learned for household objects and furniture.

- *Clothes*. Students draw pictures of people in various clothes and label the clothes.

- *Adjectives*. Make sure students are aware that adjectives come before the noun they describe. Have students look back through the unit and make a list of all new adjectives. They should write examples of adjectives in short sentences or noun phrases (article + adjective + noun), showing the position of the adjectives. Encourage students to use colour, underlining and shape to make the words eye-catching and therefore memorable. For example:

He's got a **LOUD** voice!

Freewheeling

- The crossword can be done either for homework or as an end-of-class competition. Tell students they should do the crossword as quickly as possible because there will be a prize for the first person to complete it.

Answer key

1 *sweatshirt* 2 *socks* 3 *shoes* 4 *trousers* 5 *jeans* 6 *skirt*
7 *jumper* 8 *T-shirt* 9 *trainers*

Preparation for Unit 5

Workbook page 19, Exercise 2

Workbook answer key

At home

1a A *garage* B *kitchen* C *bathroom* D *bedroom* E *living-room*

b 1 *car* 2 *sink* 3 *fridge* 4 *cooker* 5 *bath* 6 *toilet*
7 *basin* 8 *shower* 9 *bed* 10 *sofa* 11 *table* 12 *chair*

2 3 *There is*   6 *There are four*
   4 *There are two*   7 *There is one*
   5 *There isn't*

3 2 *No, there aren't. There's one bedroom in the house.*
   3 *No, there aren't. There's one car in the garage.*
   4 *No, there aren't. There are two armchairs in the living-room.*
   5 *No, there isn't. There are two TVs in the house.*

4b 1 *This house has got four rooms.*
   2 *a table and four chairs.*
   3 *it has got a shower.*

Shirts and skirts

1 2 *next to* 3 *in* 4 *in* 5 *near* 6 *near* 7 *on* 8 *on*
   9 *under* 10 *on* 11 *in*

2 2 *It's their house.* 3 *It's their computer.* 4 *It's her bag.*
   5 *They're her trainers.* 6 *They're his trainers.*

3 3 *has* 4 *Possessive* 5 *is* 6 *has* 7 *is*

4 *head: helmet*
   body: jumper shirt sweatshirt T-shirt

legs: jeans skirt trousers
feet: shoes socks trainers

5a *Here's Martin, with a black shirt, white trousers and black shoes.*
b *Here's Maria with a white jumper, black jeans and white trainers.*

Emma's idea

1 *Student's own answers*

2 1 A *What do you think of the house?*
      B *It's amazing!*
   2 A *This is the living-room. There's a sofa and two chairs.*
      B *It's not bad …*
   3 A *Your room is a real mess! Tidy it up!*
   4 A *This is my jumper!*
      B *No, it's not! It's my sister's jumper!*
   5 A *See you tomorrow!*
      B *Yes, see you!*

Skills: describing a room

1b *It's a big room with two windows. I've got a large sofa under one window and there are two armchairs next to the sofa. There's a small table in one corner with a plant on it. There's a TV and video near the door.*

Prepare for Unit 5

2a *Food: hamburger pizza sandwich apple bread chicken lamb lemon potato rice yoghurt*
   Drink: coffee cola lemonade milk tea

c *coffee tea*
   potato
   apple lemon
   chicken lamb
   cola lemonade milk

Unit 5

Syllabus

Topic
The best of British: *food*
What would you like?: *menus*
The OK Club

Grammar
The present simple
Countable and uncountable nouns
some and *any*

Function
Expressing likes/dislikes and preferences
Talking about and ordering food

Vocabulary
Food and drink
Ingredients
Prices
Numbers 21–100
Nationalities

Reading
Skimming a text to identify topic and content
Reading and using a menu

Listening
Checking specific and general information

Writing
Describing a drink

Speaking
Asking about cooking and eating
Ordering food in a cafe

Pronunciation
Word and sentence stress in simple dialogues
/s/, /z/, /ɪz/

Vocabulary

Key vocabulary

any	garlic	pie
apple	(a) hundred	pork
banana	ice	potatoes
beef	ice cream	pound
bread	juice	pudding
carrot	ketchup	recipe
cheese	lamb	rice
cherry	lemon	roast
chicken	lettuce	salt
chillies	like	sauce
chips	(a) lot (of)	sausage
chocolate	love	seventy
coconut	meal	sixty
cook	meat	strawberry
coriander	milk	sugar
dish	milkshake	tea
drink	mineral water	thirty
eat	mushroom	tomato
egg	mustard	tuna
eighty	ninety	vanilla
fifty	oil	vegetable
food	olive	water
forty	onion	would like
fruit	pear	yoghurt

Other vocabulary

another	famous	programme
ask	hot	secret
bike	important	sort
cent	information	spice, spicy
choose	international	teach
cold	list	these
cow	main	thick
count	only	thin
delicious	order (n & v)	today
enjoy	other	want
extra	pig	

Materials preparation

1 Dictionaries for page 32 Exercise 1a, and page 35 Exercise 1.
2 For page 32, Exercise 1 Option: make cards for teaching the vocabulary (see Tip 10, page 50).
3 For page 32, Exercise 3a Option: prepare a list of sentences and substitute words for practising the present simple (see Tip 11, page 51).
4 For page 34, Exercise 7a Option: make cards with numbers 1–30 and 40, 50, 60, 70, 80, 90,100. Bring in the number cards used in Units 1 and 2.
5 For page 34, Exercise 7c Option: prepare a list of simple addition questions and answers, using two-digit numbers, for example, 32 + 24 (= 56).

The Best of British
The present simple

Aims

In this section, students learn to talk about likes and dislikes, using the present simple. The language is presented through pictures, and listening and reading activities, and practised through guided discussion. The pronunciation section focuses on third person endings /s/, /z/ and /ɪz/.

1a

Background information

1 **Pies**. In Britain, pies can be savoury or sweet. They are made of pastry filled with meat, vegetables or fruit. They can be eaten hot or cold.

2 **Puddings**. Traditonal puddings are made of a steamed cake mixture with jam, syrup or a fruit or chocolate sauce as flavouring. Summer pudding, however, is made in a bowl lined with bread, and filled with a mixture of stewed fruit, then left to set. Some British people call any dessert a 'pudding'.

Option

- On the board, write a list of food words from Workbook page 19, Exercise 2. Teach the words (see Tip 10 below), or check that students understand them. Add the names of some local dishes that students know well. Read the list aloud, using *I like* and *I don't like*. Use tone of voice and facial expression to show the meaning. For example, say: *Mmm! I LIKE apples!* (look happy) or *I don't like milk very much* (shake your head). Ask students to guess what you mean, but do not give a grammar explanation yet. Point at the list and ask different students: *What do you like?* They reply with just the names of food.

- Write *pie* and *pudding* on the board, and explain what they are (see Background information). Say: *Look at the pictures*. Explain that most of the pictures show pies and their ingredients. In the mother tongue, ask: *What are the ingredients of the first pie?* They will probably say *meat* instead of *beef*, but that doesn't matter at this stage. Ask about the other pictures in the same way.

- Point to objects in the pictures and ask in English, for example: *What is an onion? What are meat pies? What is ...?* Students translate.

- Ask about food they already know: *What number is 'bread'?* (9). *What number is 'apple'?* (11). *What number is 'potato'?* (3). Show students where to write the numbers.

- Put students into pairs. Each partner looks up half of the remaining words. They both write the numbers by the right food. Check the answers. Ask: *Which words are fruit? Which words are meat? Which words are vegetables? What is number 4?*

Answer key

1 *beef* 2 *lamb* 3 *potatoes* 4 *cheese* 5 *carrots* 6 *olives*
7 *tuna* 8 *lettuce* 9 *bread* 10 *strawberries* 11 *apple*
12 *banana*

1b

- Tell students to turn to Workbook page 76. Explain that this is another way of recording vocabulary, connecting words like the branches of a tree – one part dividing into smaller parts, which themselves divide into still smaller parts. Explain this idea with a drawing on the board:

- Students either complete the word tree in the Workbook, or copy it into the Food and Drink section of their vocabulary notebooks. Tell them to leave space for more words later.

Tip 10 ★
Learning new vocabulary

- Make enough cards for each item, for example; all the food words from Exercise 1 of this unit. Write the word in English on one side and in the mother tongue on the other side. Show the English side of each card in turn and ask *What's this?* Students reply with a mother tongue translation. Turn the card around if they make a mistake to show the correct answer. Shuffle the cards and repeat until students can respond confidently.

  Now show the reverse side of each card and ask *What's this in English?* Go through the cards as many times as necessary, shuffling the cards each time. Start to put aside the cards that students remember easily, concentrating on cards that cause more difficulty, until students can remember all the words.

2

- Read the sentences, and make sure that students understand them.

- Tell students that the first dialogue is in a shop, the second at home. Students do not need to understand every word, just the general meaning.

- 🔊 Play the cassette. Students put a tick or cross in the boxes.

Option

- 🔊 Students listen to the cassette again for more detail. For example, using the list of words in Exercise 1, they tick all the food words that they hear mentioned in the two conversations (see tapescript).

Tapescript

1
Woman Good morning ... you've got all these different **pies** today, I see. What are they?
Shopkeeper Good morning ... er ... this is a **beef** and **onion** pie ... It's very popular – a lot of people buy it ...
Woman I'm afraid my family and I don't eat a lot of **meat** ...
Shopkeeper Well, there's a nice vegetable pie here. It's got onions, **carrots**, and **olives** in it ...

Woman Mmm, yes, please. One vegetable pie, please. We eat a lot of **vegetables**, and we all like olives.
2
Girl I'm hungry! What's for supper?
Mother Well, we've got two different pies … there's a **fish** pie – with **tuna** fish and **egg** – or **a cheese** and **potato** pie.
Girl Mmm. I like fish pie <u>and</u> cheese and potato …
Mother Me too!

....

Answer key
1 *True*　2 *True*　3 *True*　4 *False*

Work it out: the present simple (1)

3a

- Make sure students understand the positive column of the first chart. They then look back at the sentences in Exercise 2 to find the negative form of *like* and *eat*. Check understanding by saying, for example: *I like olives. I don't like fish. I eat vegetables.* Get a few students to tell the class some of their likes and dislikes in the same way.
- Students look at the other chart. In the mother tongue, ask: *Are these questions formed in the usual way?* (No). *What's different about them?* (They use *Do* to make the question). *Where does the word 'do' go?* (at the beginning). *What is between 'do' and the verb?* (*I, you, we* or *they*).
- Ask random students some quick *Yes/No* questions with *be* and *have got* that require short answers, for example: *Is an apple a fruit? Have you got a pen? Are you all boys?* Then ask: *Do you like fish?* If no one answers correctly, tell them to look at the chart, then ask the question again.
- Students complete the chart.

Answer key
I / You / We / They don't like
I / You / We / They don't eat

Option

- To familiarize students with the question form, do a substitution drill (see Tip 11 below). Say: *Do you like sugar?* Then substitute, in turn, *tomatoes, they, eggs, eat, bread,* and *I*.

3b

- Ask questions 1–4 round the class. Students respond with short answer forms.
- Use question-and-answer chains (see Tip 9, page 39) to practise questions and short answers.

4

- Students read the instructions. Check that they understand what to do.
- Teach *a lot of*.
- Students think of other questions they can ask, for example: *Do you eat (potatoes) at home? Do you eat (potatoes) with eggs? Do you like green bananas or yellow bananas? Do you like green apples or red apples?*
- Students work in pairs, taking turns to ask and answer questions about the pictures in Exercise 1.

5

Background information
Madhur Jaffrey /ˈmædʊə ˈdʒæfri/ is a popular Indian cook, well known in Britain for her recipe books and TV cookery programmes.

- Check that students understand the three titles before they begin to read. Explain that the correct title will describe the <u>main</u> idea of the text, not just parts of it. Tell students to read quickly, and that they do not need to understand every word.
- Ask students to guess the title before they read.
- Students skim the text for gist and decide which is the best title.

Answer key
2 *Britain's favourite food*

Option

- ▣ This text is recorded on the cassette. You may wish to play the cassette as students follow the text to encourage students to read quickly, and not pause for unfamiliar words.

6

- Students read the text again, scanning it for specific information.

Answer key
1 *roast beef, fish and chips, meat pie*　2 *Chinese, Italian, French*
3 *Indian*　4 *recipe book*　5 choose from: *onions, garlic, coriander, chillies, spices, oil, salt*

Tip 11 ★
Substitution drills

- Say a sentence and get the class to repeat it. Then call out a word, which could be a noun, a verb, a pronoun, an adjective, or even a plural noun to replace a singular noun. Students must repeat the basic sentence, but substitute the word you have called out for its corresponding word in the original sentence. Prepare the drill in advance. Examples:

1	**Teacher**		**Students**
	I like carrots.	→	I like carrots.
	We	→	*We* like carrots.
	eat	→	We *eat* carrots.
	bananas	→	We eat *bananas*.
	don't	→	We *don't* <u>eat</u> bananas.
	she	→	*She* <u>doesn't</u> eat bananas.
2	**Teacher**		**Students**
	My mother cooks lunch.	→	My mother cooks lunch.
	breakfast	→	My mother cooks *breakfast*.
	father	→	My *father* cooks breakfast.
	they	→	*They* cook breakfast.
	don't	→	They *don't* <u>cook</u> breakfast.
	eat	→	They don't *eat* breakfast
	I	→	*I* don't eat breakfast
	My brother	→	*My brother* <u>doesn't</u> eat breakfast

For a change, write the first sentence and list of substitution words on the board. Students do the drill in pairs or groups.

Work it out: the present simple (2)

7a

- Students look at the Positive section of the chart, and read the examples. In the mother tongue, ask: *What is the difference between the verbs here and the ones in the chart on page 32?* (the verbs have -s at the end). Repeat for the Negative, Questions and Short answers sections (the verbs use *does/doesn't* instead of *do/don't*).

- Students look at the text again and find an example like *He uses … (She teaches)*. They then find a negative example (*She doesn't use …*).

Answer key

Negative: doesn't   doesn't
Questions: Does   Does
Short answers: does   doesn't   does   doesn't

Option

- To check understanding, write some incorrect sentences on the board and ask students to correct them. For example:
  1 *My sister like fruit pie.*   2 *Does you like meat pie?*
  3 *Yes, I like.*   4 *My friends likes cherry pie.*

7b

- Students cover the text and answer the questions from memory. They then read the text to check their answers.

Answer key

1 *Yes, she does.*   2 *No, she doesn't.*   3 *Yes, she does.*
4 *No, she doesn't.*   5 *Yes, she does.*

8

- Explain the task by getting students to ask you the questions first. Give full answers. For example, for question 1: *I'm the main cook.* For question 2: *I make a lot of dishes with rice and meat. I use a lot of vegetables – tomatoes and onions and potatoes.*

- Students take turns asking and answering the questions in pairs.

Pronunciation: /s/, /z/, and /ɪz/

9a

Option

- On the board, write the phonetic symbols and some verbs with the sounds:

1	2	3
/s/	/z/	/ɪz/
it starts	she listens	he chooses

  Say the verb forms aloud, exaggerating the way the final -s is pronounced. Then ask students to decide which sound they hear in the words *buys* (2), *uses* (3), and *eats* (1).

- 📼 Play the cassette. Students write down the verbs they hear.

- Play the cassette again. Students decide which category each verb belongs to according to the pronunciation of the final -s.

Tapescript

/s/ eats
/z/ buys
/ɪz/ uses
loves, likes, writes, teaches, puts, makes, enjoys

Answer key

1 *likes   writes   puts   makes*   2 *loves   enjoys*   3 *teaches*

Options

- To save students writing the verbs twice, have them write just 1, 2, or 3 next to each. After you have checked answers, give them time to write each verb in the right list.

- 📼 If students find the task difficult, allow them to discuss their answers in pairs, then play the cassette one more time.

9b

- 📼 Students listen and repeat the words.

Option

- Get students to guess the pronunciation of more verbs, for example: *says, talks, guesses, sells, stops, repeats, opens, closes.*

Suggested Workbook practice

Page 20, Exercises 1–3
Page 21, Exercises 4 and 5

What would you like?
Ordering food

Aims

In this section, students learn how to order food in a cafe, using *would like*, and to identify countable and uncountable nouns. The pronunciation section introduces the numbers 21–100.

1

Option

- In the mother tongue, ask general questions about the topic. For example: *Where are pizzas from? Do you eat them sometimes, often or never? Where can you eat pizza in this town? What ingredients can you have on pizzas? What ingredients do you like on pizzas?*

- Get students to think about the menu before they read the text. For example, in the mother tongue, ask: *What is the name of the restaurant?* (Pizza Cafe). *How many types of pizza do they serve?* (four). *Look at the ingredients. What does 'extras' mean?*

- Students quickly read the menu to find which pizzas are spicy and which are thin.

- Check the answers. Students then read the descriptions again, and underline any words or phrases they do not understand. Help students to guess the meaning from context.

Answer key

1 *Mediterranean   Mexican*
2 *Italian   Mexican*

2

- Make sure students understand the situation in the dialogue. Ask: *Where do you think these people are?* (in the Pizza Cafe). *What are they going to order?* (the different types of pizza). *What else will they ask for?* (different 'extras').
- 📼 Play the cassette. Pause after each speaker's request to give students time to tick, on the menu, the pizzas and ingredients that the speakers ask for.
- Students write their answers in full.

....

Tapescript

Steve Right, Shannon. What would you like?
Shannon I'd like a big pizza.
Steve OK, …er…an Italian pizza?
Shannon Yeah, I'd like an Italian pizza, please … and I'd like some olives and some extra cheese, too, please.
Steve And you, Kerry? What would you like?
Kerry I'd like a spicy pizza, please … mmm …
Steve Do you want meat on it?
Kerry Yes, I do … I like meat. I'd like the Mediterranean pizza, please … with some spicy sausage on it.
Steve OK. Now … what do I want? … er …
Kerry Try the Mexican pizza, Steve. It's delicious!
Steve Good idea. A Mexican pizza … with … er … some chicken on it, I think.

....

Answer key

Shannon: an Italian pizza with olives and cheese
Kerry: Mediterranean pizza with spicy sausage
Steve: Mexican pizza with chicken

Option

- 📼 If you think students will have difficulty getting the information, play the cassette twice: the first time students listen for the types of pizza mentioned; the second time for extras.

3

- Write on the board: *restaurant   waiter   customer   menu.* Check that students understand the words.
- In English, say: *This room is a restaurant. I'm a waiter. You are customers.* Say to three or four students: *Good evening. Welcome to the Pizza Cafe. What pizza would you like?* (students respond with a type of pizza). *What extras would you like?* (students choose extras).
- Write on the board:

Waiter:	What	pizza	would you like?
		extras	
Customer:	I'd like	an Italian pizza.	
		cheese	

- Explain the meaning of the phrases, and get students to repeat them.
- Ask another group of students the questions. They respond with *I'd like …* and the type of pizza.
- Students read the dialogue.
- 📼 Play the cassette. Students listen and write the missing words.

Answer key

would   you   like   'd   like   big   Italian   'd like   Italian   cheese

Useful English

- Make sure students understand all the phrases. Help them with the pronunciation of *Would you* /ˈwʊdʒ uː/ and *some* /səm/.
- 📼 Play the cassette. Students listen for the stressed words (see answer key).
- Play the cassette again. Students listen and repeat.

Answer key

Would you like an <u>A</u>mer<u>i</u>can pizza?
<u>Yes</u>, <u>please</u>.
Would you like some lemon<u>a</u>de?
No, thank you. I'd like some <u>wa</u>ter, please.
<u>Me</u> <u>too</u>! … <u>Thank</u> you.

4

- In pairs, students work out a similar dialogue between a waiter and a customer, using expressions from the box. When the dialogues are ready, give students a few minutes to practise, then ask a few pairs to act out their dialogues for the class.

Option

- Ask two students (from different pairs) to come to the front and act the dialogue spontaneously (without practising together first). You may like to add drama by suggesting the 'waiter' greets the customer and politely pulls out a chair for him or her.

Work it out: countable and uncountable nouns

5a

- Teach the verb *count* (remind them of the word *Countdown*). Students look at the two lists of words and guess the meaning of *countable* and *uncountable*.

Answer key

Countable: things we can describe by number – I'd like an egg, two eggs.
Uncountable: things we don't count – I'd like some rice (not some rices).

5b

- To help students, point out that there are three countable and three uncountable nouns.

Answer key

Countable: mushrooms   olives   onions
Uncountable: cheese   chicken   sausage

Option

- Exercise 5b is relatively easy, as the countable nouns are all given in the plural form. As a follow-up task, write more food words on the board. Students decide if they are countable or uncountable, for example: *sugar, carrot, water, meat, apple.*

6

- In groups of four, students play the parts of waiter or customer. They can base their dialogue on the ones they practised in Exercise 4, but include extras in their orders, for example: *What extras would you like? I'd like some mushrooms and some extra onions.*

Pronunciation: numbers 21–100

Background information

- **The Euro** is the new European currency. There are 100 cents to one Euro (€).

7a

- The recording is of someone counting change, first in British currency, then in Euros.
- Teach numbers 30, 40, 50, 60, 70, 80, 90, 100.
- 📼 Play the cassette. Students listen and repeat.

Tapescript

30p … 40p … 50p …60p … 70p … 80p … 90p … a hundred p – that's one pound.
55 cents…95 cents…100 cents – that's one Euro.

Option

- Use number cards (see Materials preparation 4) to teach the numbers, and revise numbers 1–20 at the same time.

7b

- Students look at the numbers and guess how they should be said, and which word will be stressed. Write the number *21* on the board, point to it and ask: *Do we say Twenty-one or Twenty-one?* Do not give the answer yet.
- 📼 Play the cassette. Students listen and confirm their guesses (the second part of the number is stressed).
- Play the cassette again. Students listen and repeat.

7c

- This exercise shows the difference in pronunciation between 13 and 30, 15 and 50 and so on.
- Write two lists on the board, headed A and B. Under list A write numbers 13–19, and under B write numbers 30–90.
- Remind students of word stress (thir*teen*, *thir*ty), and get them to say the numbers.
- Call out numbers from the lists in random order. After each number, the class or individuals call out A or B, according to the number they hear. For example:

Teacher	Students
Six*teen*	A
Good! Thir*teen*.	B
No, listen carefully. Thir*teen.*	A
Seventy	B

- Students practise in pairs, taking turns to test each other.
- In pairs, students practise reading out the numbers in Exercise 7c in preparation for the listening task.
- 📼 Play the cassette. Student listen and circle the right amounts.

Tapescript

1
Steve Oh no! I haven't got any money. Have you got £5.50, Shannon?
Shannon Yeah, here … Five pounds … ten p … and five p - £5.15.
Steve No, Shannon. I want £5.50 – have you got 35p more?
2
A That's six Euros thirteen, please.
B Sorry – 6.13 or 6.30?
A 6.13 … That's right … Thank you.

3
Waitress There you are – one Mexican with extra meat … that's £7.60, please.
Steve … seven … twenty … forty … fifty … fifty-five … sixty. There.
Waitress Thanks.

Answer key

1 *£5.50*   2 *€6.13*   3 *£7.60*

Option

- Give students an addition quiz (see Materials preparation 5). Ask the class a few simple questions first. Students call out the answers as quickly as they can. For example, *What is ten and twelve?* (twenty-two). *What is twenty-three and fourteen?* (thirty-seven). *What is nine and sixteen?* (twenty-five). Divide the class into two teams. For each question, one member of each team should stand up. The student who calls out the answer first (in English, of course!) gets a point for their team.

Suggested Workbook practice

Page 21, Exercises 1 and 3

some and *any*

Aims

In this section, students learn to express preferences when ordering food, and to use *some* and *any* in positive and negative sentences, and in questions. They also learn words for drinks, and practise talking about ingredients. The language is presented through listening and reading exercises, and practised through speaking and writing activities.

1

- Go through the menu with the class to find out which words they recognize. Students match these words to their pictures.
- Put students into pairs, and tell them to look up the remaining words in their dictionaries. To save time, partners look up half the words each and share answers.

Answer key

1 *coffee with milk*   2 *black coffee*   3 *tea*   4 *hot chocolate*
5 *orange juice*   6 *cola*   7 *lemonade*   8 *mineral water*
9 *vanilla milkshake*   10 *coffee milkshake*   11 *chocolate milkshake*
12 *banana milkshake*

2

- Ask students a few questions about their preferences, for example: *Do you like coffee? Do you like black coffee? … coffee with milk? … with sugar? Do you like tea? What milkshake would you like?*
- Tell students they will hear four customers ordering drinks. They must imagine they are the waiter, and write down the customers' orders.
- 📼 Students listen and make notes of the customers' orders. If students find the task difficult, let them compare their answers with a partner, then play the cassette again.

Tapescript

1
Waiter Good morning. Can I help you?
Woman Hello. Coffee, please.
Waiter Do you want any milk? Or do you want it black?
Woman No, I'd like some milk, please, but I don't want any sugar.
2
Waiter Good morning.
Girl Hello, I'd like a milkshake, please … em … chocolate.
Waiter A chocolate milkshake … with ice cream?
Girl No, thanks. I don't want any ice cream.
3
Woman Good morning. Hot chocolate, please.
Waiter Here you are. Do you want any sugar?
Woman Oh, OK. Yes, please.
4
Waiter Here's your coffee. Would you like any sugar?
Man Er…no, thank you.

Answer key

1 *Coffee with milk (no sugar)* 2 *Chocolate milkshake (no ice cream)*
3 *Hot chocolate with sugar* 4 *coffee (no sugar)*

3

- Students use their answers from Exercise 2 to complete the sentences.

Answer key

1 *coffee milk sugar* 2 *chocolate any ice cream*
3 *hot chocolate sugar* 4 *any*

Work it out: *some* and *any*

4a

- Students look again at the sentences in Exercise 3, and formulate rules for the use of *some* and *any*.

Answer key

some *in positive sentences* any *in questions* any *in negative sentences*

4b

- In pairs, students practise ordering food and drinks in a cafe. If you think they need more guidance, let them prepare a written dialogue, then proceed as described in the teacher's notes for Student's Book page 34, Exercise 3.

Options

- For guided practice, students do Workbook page 21, Exercise 2.
- Students work with new partners, and extend the dialogue to include paying the bill. For example:
  Waiter: *Mexican pizza is £7.60 and a large cola is 85p. £7.60 and 85p is … £8.45.*
  Customer: *£8.45? Here you are.*
  Waiter: *Thank you.*

5

- Students read the instructions. In the mother tongue, check that they understand what to do. For example, ask: *What is B going to do?* (go shopping). *Who is A?* (the shop assistant). *What does B want to buy?* (the things on the list). *What language is B going to use?* (*Have you got any …? I'd like some …*). Explain that if the shop assistant hasn't got what they want, Bs should buy something similar to what is on their list.

- Put students into pairs, and tell them to choose their roles.
- Give As time to read the instructions on page 110, then check they understand what to do. For example, ask: *Have you got all of the things on the customer's list?* (no – only some of them). *What will you say when the customer asks for things that you have?* (*Here you are*). *And if you haven't got them?* (*No, sorry. I haven't got any …, but I've got some … / but would you like any …?*).
- Go round the class checking that students are able to use the language correctly, and helping those with any problems.
- When students have finished, ask some 'customers', in the mother tongue: *What did you buy?* Ask some 'shop assistants', from different pairs: *What did you sell?*

'Make a drink' competition

6a

- Students read the description. Ask in English: *What do you think of this drink?* (*It's very good/OK. / It's awful – I don't like bananas*). *What are the ingredients?*

Option

- Students invent a name for the drink, such as *Banana fantastic, Yoghurt and Banana Dream*.

6b

- Students, choose ingredients for their own drinks.

6c

- The word-map acts as a plan from which students can write their description. The word-map should divide into two groups – the liquid ingredients and the solid ones.
- Go round the class, looking at the maps and encouraging students: *That's great / good / very interesting*.
- When most students have finished, put them into groups or pairs to talk about their ingredients: *My drink has got … It hasn't got any …, but it's got some … .*

6d

- Students write a description of their drink, using the description in 6a as a model.

Suggested Workbook practice

Page 21, Exercise 2 (if not done after Exercise 4 above)

The OK Club
Hamburgers

Aims
This section continues the photo-story. It presents informal English in a lively context, and brings together the language students have been practising in the unit. This episode practises the language of likes, dislikes and preferences, and revises *Who …?* and *What …?*

1

Option

- In the mother tongue, get students to remember the story so far. For example, ask: *Why do you think this episode is called 'Hamburgers'?* (the club members have decided to sell hamburgers to make money for the club). *Why does the club need money?* (to buy paint to redecorate the Coffee Corner).

- Tell students to look at the four small pictures and say what they think each is. Do not check the answers yet.
- 🖾 Students listen, look at the pictures and label the four food items.

Answer key

1 *mustard* 2 *ketchup* 3 *chips* 4 *hamburger*

2

- Students should be able to complete the sentences from memory. If not, play the last part of the recording again.

3

- Students discuss their ideas in small groups. Check that they are using the language of opinions: *I think … .* Do not tell students the answer – they will find out in the next episode.

4a

- Ask students which pictures contain the answers (pictures 1 and 2). Students then read the relevant parts of the story again, and answer the questions.

Answer key

1 *The boy wants edtra Ketchup.*
2 *The boy doesn't want any onions.*
3 *The girl doesn't want any mustard.*
4 *Jack likes Harley Davidson bikes.*

4b

- Ask the questions round the class, asking several students the same question. Students respond with short answers (*Yes, I do / No, I don't*).
- Students write their answers.

Suggested Workbook practice

Page 22, Exercises 1 and 2
Page 23, Exercises 1 and 2

Review

Aims

The Review section summarizes and briefly revises the Key language features of Unit 5: the present simple tense, countable and uncountable nouns, and *some* and *any*.

The present simple tense (*like, eat …*)

- See Tip 5, page 30, and revise the forms of the present simple.
- Explain the difference between *like* and *would like*: *Do you like …?* is used to talk generally about likes and dislikes; *Would you like …?* is used for offers and requests.
- Explain that *Would you like …?* is slightly more formal and polite than *Do you want …?*

Countable and uncountable nouns

- Write a list of food items on the board: *tomatoes*, *apple*, *cheese*, *beef*, *olives*, *fruit*, *strawberry*, *carrots*, *milk*. Students put the words into two lists, *Countable* and *Uncountable*. Check answers, then ask which words can have *a/an* before them, and which can have *some*.
- Explain that some nouns can be thought of as countable or uncountable, for example: *Do you like coffee/ice cream? I'd like a coffee/an ice cream.*

some and *any*

- Students read the rules and examples, then write more examples of each point.

1

- Students use the example table for *like* to help them write present simple tables for *want* and *use*.
- Ask students to write example sentences for the forms of *want*. Walk round the class, checking that they understand how to use *do* and *does* and the third person *-s/-es*.

2a

- Students write sentences about their own likes and dislikes.

2b

- In small groups, students ask each other *Do you like …?* questions. They note down the names of any students who have the same opinion about any of the items on their own list.

2c

- Students use the information from 2b to write five sentences about other students' likes and dislikes. Check that they are using *does/doesn't*.

3

- Students look through their lists from 2a, and write *C* (countable) or *U* (uncountable) by each. To check the answers, ask: *Who has got some uncountable nouns?* Students call out their answers. Repeat for countable nouns.

4

- Read out the instructions and example sentences. Say an example of your own, such as *I don't want any chocolates. I want an expensive car.* Ask a few students to suggest some more examples. Students then write their two sentences.

Vocabulary

- *Food and drink.* Students add to the word family tree on Workbook page 76. They add any drinks to the word-map in their vocabulary books.
- *Nationalities.* Students add to the map and chart on Workbook page 75.

Option
- Students could copy these into their vocabulary books instead.

Freewheeling

- To practise numbers, different students read out each sentence about prices.
- Ask a student to read out the questions and the clue, then let students work out the puzzle individually or in pairs.

Answer key

Each letter in a word is worth 5p, so a lemon (5 letters) costs 25p, and a pear (4 letters) costs 20p.

Suggested Workbook practice

Page 22, Exercises 3 and 4
Page 23, Exercise 3

Preparation for Unit 6

Workbook page 23, Exercise 4

Workbook answer key

The best of British

1a 2 *We don't eat a lot of fruit and vegetables.*
3 *I don't like cheese and fruit together.*
4 *We don't eat a lot of meat.*

b 1 *I like tomatoes.*
2 *She uses spicy ingredients.*
3 *They enjoy cooking at home.*

2

1 2 love 3 don't eat 4 love 5 Do eat 6 don't
7 like 8 don't like 9 don't like 10 love

2 1 don't like 2 love 3 love

3 4 *Martin likes chicken and lamb.*
5 *Martin doesn't like beans or carrots.*
6 *Julia likes apples but she doesn't like bananas.*

What would you like?

1 Countable: *people shoes tomatoes*
Uncountable: *orange juice sugar water*

2a 3 *Would you like any sugar in your coffee?*
4 *Would you like any chips or beans with your pie?*
5 *Would you like any ice cream?*

b 1 *any* 2 *any, some* 3 *some* 4 *some, some* 5 *some*

3 2 *b* 3 *a* 4 *f* 5 *c* 6 *e*

4 2 *tomato* 3 *oil* 4 *lamb* 5 *beans* 6 *strawberry*
7 *yoghurt* 8 *tuna* 9 *apple* 10 *egg* 11 *garlic*
12 *cheese*

5b

/s/	/z/	/ɪz/
eats	*enjoys*	*teaches*
likes	*loves*	*uses*
wants	*orders*	

Hamburgers

1 2 *Do you write letters to your friends?*
3 *Mr Smith teaches English at that school.*
4 *Does your sister eat meat?*
5 *My brothers don't like eggs.*

2 1
Customer *Yes, I'd like a Mexican pizza please.*
Waiter *Would you like any extras?*
Customer *Yes, please, I'd like extra cheese.*
Waiter *OK. Would you like a drink with your pizza?*
Customer *Yes, a cola please.*

2
Customer *Yes, we'd like a milkshake and a coffee please.*
Waiter *Would you like any sugar with the coffee?*
Customer *No, thanks, but I'd like some milk.*
Waiter *OK. That's two pounds ninety please.*

3 Food: *cheese onions chips ice cream hamburger*
Drink: *cola lemonade milk coffee orange juice*
Clothes: *T-shirt jeans jumper boots trainers*

4a *Student's own answers*

Skills: a menu

1a 1 *Peggy's Pie Place*

1b 2 *Meat dishes*   4 *Ice cream*
3 *Vegetables*   5 *Drinks*

2 1 *Lamb and apricot pie.*
2 *Cola, lemonade and mineral water.*
3 *£10.40.*

3 Menu
Meat/Fish: chicken beef
Vegetables: beans salad mushroom
Fruit/Sweet dishes: apricot ice cream
Drinks
Hot: coffee hot chocolate
Cold: lemonade mineral water

Prepare for Unit 6

4b *Verbs: dance perform*
People: singer dancer
Other: song studio tour

Consolidation

1

Syllabus

Topic
Revision

Grammar
Revision of grammar points

Function
Revision of functions

Vocabulary
Revision of vocabulary

Reading
Identifying topics in a letter

Listening
Identifying likes and dislikes

Writing
Completing notes
Completing a form
Writing a letter to a friend

Speaking
Meeting people
Offering and accepting food and drink

Vocabulary

Key vocabulary

China	teacher	year
Portugal		

Other vocabulary

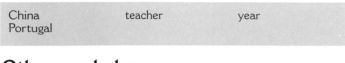

age	herself	pop star
boyfriend	live	sit down
description	music	tell

Grammar

Aims

This section revises the main grammar structures and some of the functions presented in Units 1–5.

1

- These three dialogues revise the verb *be*, *would like* and the present simple of *want*, and pronouns, possessive adjectives and *have got*. The dialogues all have a character called Kevin, a rather silly boy. Ask *Do people like Kevin?* Students read the dialogues and find out. They then complete the dialogues individually.

Answer key
1 *from* 2 *I'm* 3 *Who* 4 *She's* 5 *Would* 6 *like* 7 *like*
8 *do* 9 *got* 10 *'ve* 11 *your* 12 *It* 13 *'s / has*

Option
- Students act out dialogues 1–3 with a partner.

2

- Students read the dialogues again and complete the questions and answers.

Answer key
1 *London* 2 *What   does   like   sausage   ice cream*
3 *has   got   TV* 4 *Has   got   he has*

3a

- This exercise revises countable and uncountable nouns with *a/an* or *some*. Students work individually, putting the words in the right columns.

Answer key
Countable: olive, potato, onion, apple
Uncountable: cheese, bread, ketchup, rice

3b

- Each partner writes a separate list of six food words from the chart, three from each column. Student A asks for a food from their list, using *a/an* for countable nouns and *some* for uncountable nouns. Student B responds according to his or her own list.

Vocabulary

Aims

In this section, students revise some of the vocabulary they have learned in Units 1–5.

1

- Write the categories as headings on the board. Explain that all the words in the box belong to one or other of the headings, but the letters of the words have got mixed up. Students work out the words and write them in their notebooks. If students have difficulty guessing a word, give clues rather than the answer, for example, *It's a colour. It begins with y. The second letter is e.*

Answer key

pizza   brown   coffee   garage   grey   jumper   kitchen   potatoes   shower   sweatshirt   trainers   yellow.

2

- Students copy the chart, and write the words in the columns. Check by asking individual students to write two words each under the headings on the board.

Answer key

Clothes: sweatshirt   trainers
Colours: brown   grey   yellow
Food and Drink: pizza   coffee   potatoes
The home: garage   kitchen   shower

3a

- Students complete the charts individually.

Answer key

Chinese   French   Greece   Indian   Italy   Japan   Polish   Spain   Turkish   American

3b

- Students work in pairs to study the nationality endings and find the patterns.

Answer key

Common endings: 1 -ian/-an   2 -ish   3 -ese
Different forms: French   Greek

Option

- Students write words for nationalities in their vocabulary books, putting them into groups according to their endings. Remind them to begin each with a capital letter.

4

- Students do this individually. Make it a competition to be first to find the extra word.

Answer key

pizza   tomato   lettuce   bread   meat   onion   rice   cheese
Extra word: potatoes

Communication

Aims

This section revises the functions of Units 1–5, including the topics of meeting people and offering and accepting food and drink.

1

- Explain that some gaps can have more than one possible answer. Students read the dialogue, then fill in the gaps.

2

- 📼 Play the cassette. Students listen and compare their answers with the dialogue on the cassette. If students' answers are different but make sense, accept them.

Answer key

How   fine (OK / very well)   This (Here)   fantastic (great / amazing)
living-room (kitchen / dining-room)   Pleased   sister   Hi (Hello)   got
like   please   sugar   any

3

- Students change the names, places and things and, where necessary, the pronouns, in the dialogue. They then practise it in groups of four.

Suggested Workbook practice

Check yourself, pages 24–25, Exercises 1–7. (See Introduction to the course, page 7, 'What does the Workbook contain?' on Consolidation units.)

Project: a letter to a penfriend

Aims

In this section, students practise reading, writing and listening skills by doing a project which leads to writing a letter to a penfriend. It is intended that the project is done partly at home and partly in class.

Reading

1

- This is a prediction exercise. Tell students to look at the pictures, but not the letter, and tick three boxes.

2

- Students read the letter to check their answers.

Answer key

her family   her pets   her home

3

- Students read the letter again for information about Carol's family, then draw a family tree.

Answer key

Top row: father – Roger   mother – Anna
Lower row: brother – Dave, 16   sister – Carol, 14

4

- Students work in pairs to check the statements against the letter, and find the mistakes.

Answer key

1 *Carol's mother Anna isn't a doctor. She's a teacher.*
2 *Carol's got a brother. She hasn't got a sister.*
3 *There are three bedrooms in Carol's house.*
4 *Carol doesn't like TV or computers.*

Listening

5

- 📼 Play the cassette. Students listen to the penfriend's reaction to Carol's letter and decide if she is a good penfriend for Carol.

....

Tapescript
Girl Look, Mum. I've got a letter from my new penfriend, in Britain.
Mum That's good. What's she like?
Girl I think she's nice. Her name's Carol and she's 14. She's got a brother. Her mother's a teacher ...
Mum Oh, interesting. Her mother's a teacher and I'm a teacher.
Girl Yes, she likes pop music, that's great. She likes the same music as me. Gosh, Mum, she likes football.
Mum Really? American football?
Girl No, Mum, their football, you know, soccer. That's OK. I like sports, too, but I love tennis, and I don't like football.
Mum Does she like animals?
Girl Oh, yeah. Listen. She's got two cats and five birds. That's great! I love animals. Oh, but look, she doesn't like TV!
Mum Oh dear ...
Girl Oh no ... I love TV!

....

6a

- 📼 Play the cassette again. Students listen for specific details to complete the chart.

Answer key
Carol: likes pop music, football, animals doesn't like TV, computers
her penfriend: likes pop music, tennis, animals, TV doesn't like football

6b

- Students use the information in the chart to write a sentence about the differences between Carol and her penfriend.

Answer key
Carol likes football but her penfriend likes tennis.

Before you write

7

- This exercise focuses students' attention on the organization of topics into paragraphs.

Answer key
3 4 2 1

8

- These are the kind of notes that Carol might make before writing her letter.

Answer key
14 brother 3 yes animals computers

9

- Students write notes about themselves in preparation for writing their own letters.

Writing: a letter to a penfriend

10a

- Students can follow the organization of paragraphs in Carol's letter, or choose an order of their own.

60

10b

- Tell students to underline any references to photos in Carol's letter. Help them to write comments about their own photos.

10c

- Students write the main part of their letter in their notebooks, using the guide and their notes from Exercise 9.

10d

- Tell students to look at paragraph 5 in Carol's letter. Discuss, in the mother tongue, what to keep and what to change in their final paragraph. Students complete their letters.

Check your vocabulary book

- Write the topics covered in Units 1–5 on the board: *Animals, Buildings/Places, Classroom objects, Clothes, Colours, Countries, Family members, Food and drink, Nationalities, Numbers, Rooms and furniture, Sport.* Students check that they have a page for each topic. In small groups, they compare entries, and add any they have missed to their vocabulary books or on Workbook pages 73–76.

Suggested Workbook practice

Page 26, Exercises 1–3

Workbook answer key

Grammar

1 1 *b* 2 *c* 3 *a* 4 *c* 5 *b* 6 *a* 7 *c* 8 *a* 9 *b* 10 *a*
2 1 *got* 2 *your* 3 *doesn't like* 4 *this* 5 *do* 6 *look*
    7 *that* 8 *next to* 9 *has got* 10 *want*

Vocabulary

3 1 *dog bird* 2 *hair eyes* 3 *mother grandfather*
    4 *bath shower* 5 *books pens*

Communication

4b 1 *d* 2 *g* 3 *b* 4 *j* 5 *i* 6 *a* 7 *h* 8 *f* 9 *c* 10 *e*

Pronunciation

5
/iː/	/e/	/aɪ/	/uː/	/aː/
green	bread	like	blue	last
team	neck	white	fruit	shark

Skills: a recipe
Reading

1 *Student's own answers*
2a 2 *False. It's got fish in it.*
    3 *True.*
    4 *False. You don't cook the tomatoes, lettuce, tuna and olives.*
    5 *False. It's got olives and olive oil in it.*
b *potatoes, beans, salt, eggs, lettuce, tomatoes, tuna, olives, olive oil, pepper*

Writing

3b 1 *Carol* 2 *for* 3 *fifteen* 4 *I live* 5 *haven't* 6 *father's*
    7 *It has got* 8 *kitchen* 9 *I like* 10 *Please*

Unit 6

Syllabus

Topic
Life and times: *the lives of pop stars*
Carnival time: London's carnival
The OK Club

Grammar
Adverbs of frequency
Present simple questions
Object pronouns

Function
Describing routines
Telling the time

Vocabulary
Music and dance

Reading
Skimming a text to identify topic and content

Listening
Identifying context
Finding specific information

Writing
Writing about routines
Writing an advert

Speaking
Interviewing a pop singer
Describing someone's routine
Buying and selling

Pronunciation
Word stress
/æ/ and /ʌ/

Vocabulary
Key vocabulary

advert(isement)	guitar	price
afternoon	half	producer
always	hour	quarter
arrive	huge	sing
breakfast	hungry	special offer
buy	interesting	sport
cameraman	interview	sports centre
carnival	jacket	stall
clock	last	start
colourful	late	(go) swimming
concert	lunch	table tennis
costume	musician	terrible
dancer	never	them
day	night	until
every	noisy	us
exciting	often	usually
exercise (sport)	party	visit
get	past (prep)	weekend
go	pay for	

Other vocabulary

actor	hear	stop
all over	homework	studio
all round	hopeless	swimmer
appetite	lesson	take
baseball	million	take place
beautiful	newspaper	talk
boutique	plane	(on) tour
bring	remember	travel
cards	road	upwards
company	relaxation	wait
competition	(go) shopping	wash (... away)
designer	sound (v)	wear
forget	specialize	win
hat	stay	world

Materials preparation

1   For page 42, Exercise 1 Option 1: bring in a magazine picture of a famous pop star, singer or musician, and a map of the students' country.
2   For page 43, Exercise 1d Option 1: a large model clock with moveable hands.
3   For page 43, Exercise 1d Option 2: a sheet of paper for each student to make a Bingo! card, and a list of times for calling out.
4   For page 43, Exercise 1d Option 3: make one photocopy of Worksheet 2 on Teacher's Book page 147 for each student.
5   Dictionaries for page 45, Writing Exercise 2.

Life and times
Frequency

Aims

In this section, students learn to talk about daily routines, using the present simple tense and adverbs of frequency. The language is presented and practised through listening tasks about a pop group.

1

Background information

Concert tours. Performers of all kinds (singers, musicians, pop groups) often go 'on tour' for several weeks or months, travelling around different countries and cities giving concerts. Although it sounds like a very glamorous lifestyle, it is also very hard work.

Options

- To introduce the topic and vocabulary, pin up a magazine picture and a map (see Materials preparation 1). If a map is not available, write the country's main cities on the board. Say: *(Name of star) is on tour this week. On Monday she/he is in (name of city). On Tuesday …* . Point out a route on the map or board as you speak. Then ask: *Where is (star) on Wednesday? … Thursday?*
- In the mother tongue, discuss with students the good and bad things about life on tour. Ask: *Is this life boring? … interesting? … relaxing? … hard work?*

- Tell students to look at the picture and guess the answers to questions 1 and 2.
- 🔊 Play the cassette. Students listen and check their guesses.

Tapescript

… Now that I don't see you,
Now that I don't hear you,
Now that you don't come round
To my place any more.
DJ … good evening from me, Johnnie Marks! That was the new song from the sensational new British group, Blue Aquarium! And I've got the four members of this great new group in the studio this evening: Denton … Alex … Chris … and Patty.
Group Hi! … Hello! … Hi, Johnnie. … Hello there.
DJ You're on tour now - right? … er … Alex?
Alex That's right, Johnnie. We're here in Liverpool for four days now. Then London for four days … and then Australia for three weeks …

Answer key

1 *b* 2 *b*

2

- Read the questions with the class. Explain any unfamiliar words, particularly the verbs.
- 🔊 Play the cassette. Students tick the questions the interviewer asks.

Tapescript

DJ … on tour in Australia for three weeks? Tell us about your tours, Alex. Do you visit a lot of different places?
Alex Yes, we do. We always visit four or five different cities when we're on tour …
DJ Do you usually travel in the day or at night?
Alex We often travel at night, after our concert. Sometimes we have a tour bus, and sometimes we go by plane …

DJ Do you find time for relaxation or exercise?
Alex Exercise? Oh yes! Exercise is very important when you're on tour. I usually go swimming in our hotel pool in the morning.
DJ And you, Patty? Do you take some exercise every day when you're on tour?
Patty Me?! Exercise?! No way! I never take exercise! I usually stay in bed and listen to the radio or watch a video until about eleven o'clock … Then I sometimes go out to the shops or a park or something …
DJ What about work? Do you start work in the afternoon, er… Denton?
Denton Yes, we usually start work after lunch, at about two o'clock. We often work from then to five or six o'clock.
DJ And do you have a meal before the evening concert … or after?
Denton After, always after. We never eat before a concert. It's often one or two o'clock in the morning before we eat!

Answer key

2   3   5   6   7

3

- Tell students to read the answers then match them with the questions in Exercise 2.
- 🔊 Play the cassette again, twice if necessary. Students listen and complete the group's answers. Tell students they can refer to Exercise 2 for most of the spellings.

Answer key

1 *do   visit*   2 *travel*   3 *exercise   listen   radio   video*
4 *start   work*

4

- Explain the task. Students will probably be able to do the sentences from memory; otherwise play the cassette again.
- Check the answers, and ask students to correct the false sentences.

Answer key

1 *False. The group often travels at night.*   2 *True*   3 *True*   4 *True*
5 *False. The group always eats a meal after the concert.*

Work it out: adverbs of frequency

5a

- Teach *per cent* (%).
- Working in pairs, students use the diagram and the sentences in Exercise 4 to work out the meaning of *always, usually, often, sometimes, never*. They write their translations.
- Ask pairs to read out their translations, then discuss with the class which the best translations are.

5b

- Students look at the percentage at the end of each sentence, check it against the chart, then fill in the right frequency adverb.
- Check the answers, then ask students where the frequency adverbs go in a sentence (before the verb).

Answer key

1 *usually*   2 *never*   3 *always*   4 *sometimes*   5 *often*

6

- Put students into pairs to practise the dialogue in the usual way.

Option

- *Interview with a pop star.* Write question prompts (ideas) on the board. Examples: *places? eat? sleep? work? relaxation? shopping?* The class discusses possible questions, for example for places: *Do you visit a lot of places? Where do you eat? What do you eat?* Keep the prompts on the board. Ask students to tell you the names of their favourite pop singers. List them on the board. Students work in pairs. Student A chooses which pop star to be. Student B asks questions, using the prompts. They then change roles. Ask a few students to the front. Introduce their characters, for example: *Please say hello to Madonna!* The rest of the class asks each 'singer' questions.

Suggested Workbook practice

Page 27, Exercises 1 and 2

Telling the time

Aims

In this section, students learn to tell the time in English, and to describe periods of the day within daily routines.

1a

Option

- Look at your watch, then hold it to your ear and look annoyed. Ask: *What time is it?* When a student tells you the time in the mother tongue, repeat it in English, for example: *It's ten past eleven.* On the board, draw 12 clocks without hands.

Draw hands for 2.00, 2.15, 2.30 and 2.45 on clocks 1, 4, 7 and 10. As you draw, say the time on each clock, for example: *It's quarter past two*, for students to repeat. Tell students that, in English, times are given as either *past* or *to* the hour. Draw 2.05 on clock 2. Point to clock 4, and ask *What time is it?* When a student remembers *quarter past two*, point to clock 2 and ask: *What time is it – five past two or five to two?* Repeat the procedure with *quarter to three* (clock 10) and *twenty to three* (clock 9). Get the class to work out the times on the remaining clocks.

- Students look at the clocks and read the times.

1b

- 📼 Play the cassette. Students listen and repeat. Check that they are saying *quarter* /ˈkwɔːtə/ and *half* /hɑːf/ correctly.

1c

- Students draw six clock faces in their notebooks.
- 📼 Play the cassette. Students listen and draw the times they hear on their clock faces.
- Ask a student to tell you the times on his or her first clock. Play the relevant part of the cassette to confirm the answer. Do the same with other students and clocks.

- Ask students if they noticed another way of asking the time (*What's the time?*).

Tapescript/Answer key

1
Girl What time is it, please?
Boy It's half past ten.
2
Girl What time is it, please?
Boy It's twelve o'clock.
3
Girl What time is it, please?
Boy It's twenty to five.
4
Girl What's the time, please?
Boy It's quarter past eleven.
5
Girl What's the time, please?
Boy It's ten past ten.
6
Girl What time is it, please?
Boy It's quarter to seven.

1d

- Tell students to listen and write the answer. Ask: *What time is it now?* Students write the time.
- Ask the question *What time is it now?* several times in each lesson from now on.

Options

- Use a large model clock (see Materials' preparation 2) or draw a large clock on the board, and use pens or rulers as the clock hands. Move the hands of the clock and ask: *What time is it?* After a few examples, invite individual students to the front to move the clock hands and ask the time.
- *Time Bingo.* Play the game as in Numbers Bingo (Unit 1, Student's Book page 10), using times in place of numbers (see Materials preparation 3).
- In pairs, students do Worksheet 2 (see Materials preparation 4).

Answer key

1a

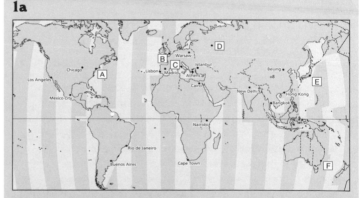

1b 1 *one o'clock* 2 *two o'clock*
- Students start a new page in their vocabulary books with the heading *Time*. They copy the 12 clocks from the board, and write the time under each.

2

- Ask individual students to read out the sentences. Explain any unfamiliar vocabulary.

- Demonstrate the task. Draw the chart on the board and write sentence 1. Add your name and a student's name in the other columns. Read the sentence out loud, then write 80% in the *Your name* column. Point to *80%* and say: *I usually arrive at school before eight o'clock in the morning.*
- Students work individually to complete the *Your name* column with information about themselves. Leave the chart on the board.

Useful English

- Tell students to read the phrases and divide them into two groups. (Students should notice that three phrases begin with *in* and two with *at*.) Point out that the phrase *at night* does not need *the*.
- ▣ Play the cassette. Students listen and repeat each phrase. Check that they are stressing the time word. For further practice, with or without the cassette, see Tip 1, page 9. Encourage students to clap or tap out the rhythm of each phrase.

3a

- Get two students to read the example dialogue. To check that the class understands what to do, turn to the student whose name you wrote on the chart on the board for Exercise 2. Repeat the sentence about yourself, then ask: *(Paula). Do you arrive at school before eight o'clock in the morning?* The student responds, for example: *No, I never arrive at school … .*
- Put students into pairs to ask and answer in the same way, and to complete the chart with information about their partner.

3b

- This exercise provides further practice in using 3rd person singular. Get two students to read the example. Then put students into new pairs (see Tip 8, page 37). Before they start, each tells the other the name of his or her previous partner.
- Walk round as pairs talk, checking that students are using *Does* not *Do* in their questions. Students write down information given by their partner.

4

- Remind students that frequency adverbs go before the verb. Students write a paragraph about their partner from 3b.

Option

- *Group survey.* If you have followed the steps suggested in 3a and 3b, each student will have information about 3 people, including themselves. Students change partners one more time. By sharing information with their final partner, each pair will now have information about 6 people in the class. They share their information, then write statements showing the results of their 'group survey', for example: *In our group, three people never arrive at school before eight. Two people sometimes arrive before eight. One person usually arrives before eight.* For homework, students can produce coloured graphs to illustrate their sentences.

Suggested Workbook practice

Page 27, Exercises 3 and 4

Carnival time

Aims

In this section, students practise reading for gist (general meaning) and detail, and learn to ask open questions (*What …? Where …? When …?*) with the present simple.

1

Background information

1 **Notting Hill** is in West London. The population of this area of London has a mix of races, including quite a large Caribbean community.

2 **Notting Hill Carnival** is a famous three-day event held every August. It is similar to the carnival in Rio de Janeiro, Brazil. Local people work all year on their elaborate costumes. On the days of the carnival, they parade through the streets. Visitors come to watch the parade, and to dance to the music. The party atmosphere continues through the day, and much of the night.

3 **Caribbean music.** The main percussion in Caribbean music is from steel drums, which give the music its strong rhythm and distinctive, tinny sound.

- The music provides a vivid introduction to the reading text. Write on the board:
  1) Is the music …
  interesting   boring   fast   slow   sad   happy   noisy ?
  2) Is the music good for …
  relaxing   dancing   studying   a party ?

- Tell students to listen to the music and choose answers to the questions on the board.

- ▣ Play the cassette. Students listen, then give their opinions, using the ideas on the board.

2

- This is a gist reading task. Students read the possible titles, then read the text quickly for the general idea. They do not need to understand every word. To check that students are reading quickly, tell them to raise a hand as soon as they have chosen the title.

Answer key

3 *London's great street party*

3

- This exercise encourages students to use context (the words that come before or after) to guess the meaning of unknown words and phrases. The task should be done without a dictionary.

- Check that students understand the meaning of the four words and phrases.

- Students work individually, then compare answers with a partner. If necessary, give students clues, such as the paragraph or part of speech, to help them locate each item.

Answer key

1 *street party*   2 *huge*   3 *noisy*   4 *costumes*

4

- Teach the meaning of *take place*, *million* and *a (market) stall*.

- Students read the text in more detail, and answer questions 1–5. Make sure students understand that they do not need to write complete sentences.

Answer key

1 *the last weekend of August* 2 *in Notting Hill in London*
3 *all over the world* 4 *the Caribbean* 5 *colourful costumes*

Work it out: the present simple (3)

5a

- On the board, write: *I like pizza*. Below it, write *Yes, I do*. Ask students: *What's the question?* Students respond: *Do you like pizza?* Write it on the board above the answer. Then point to the statement again, and write *pizza* below it. Ask: *What's the question?* If students have trouble replying, write *What …* on the board as a clue (*What do you like?*).
- Students study the table and complete the questions.

Answer key

wear   do   wear

5b

- Practise this orally first, using simpler questions. Write statements on the board for students to ask two questions about, for example: *She wants a taxi*. (*What does she want? Does she want a taxi?*). *They come from London*. (*Where do they come from? Do they come from London?*).
- Quickly do Exercise 4 again orally to remind students of the answers. Tell them they can give wrong information in the questions so that they get *No* answers. Do the first one with the class, encouraging them to make two questions, for example: *Does the carnival take place in August?* (*Yes, it does*). *Does the carnival take place in May?* (*No, it doesn't*).
- Students work individually, writing one *Yes* and one *No* question for each.

Answer key

1 *Does the carnival take place in August?/(May)?*
2 *Does it take place in London/(New York)?*
3 *Do the musicians and dancers come from all over the world/(London)?*
4 *Does the food come from the Caribbean/(Italy)?*
5 *Do a lot of the dancers wear colourful costumes/(jeans)?*

Suggested Workbook practice

Page 28, Exercise 3

Object pronouns

Aims

In this section, students learn to recognize object pronouns and who they refer to, and practise skimming (reading quickly for gist) a text to identify content. Students also learn to differentiate between the sounds /æ/ (*cap*) and /ʌ/ (*cup*).

1a

- Explain the task and read out questions 1–5. Ask students, in mother tongue: *What do you think of when you hear the word 'disco'?* Students make suggestions, for example *dance*. Ask: *Can* you find the word (dance) in one the adverts? Students look quickly to find the word. They identify advert B, and write B in the box for question 1.

- Students do 2–5 in the same way. Let them compare answers with a partner before you check them with the class.

Answer key

1 *B*   2 *E*   3 *D*   4 *A*   5 *C*

1b

- Quickly revise the object pronouns introduced in previous units (*you, me, them, him, her, it*)
- Get students to tell you the meaning of *us* through an example sentence, such as <u>We</u> don't understand this word. Can you help <u>us</u>?
- Tell students to underline all the people and object pronouns in the texts.
- Students read the texts again and work out who each pronoun refers to.

Answer key

2 *Big John*   3 *Royston and Rosie*   4 *your friends*   5 *your brother*
6 *Rosalind Arasis*   7 *Janet Barton*

Pronunciation: /æ/ and /ʌ/

2a

- Point out that the vowel to listen to is in **bold** in words of more than one syllable.
- 📷 Play the two example words. Students repeat them. Then say the two, similar sounds, /æ/ and /ʌ/. Students should now be able to hear the difference.
- Play the cassette. Students note down their answers.
- Tell students to check their answers in pairs. This allows them to practise saying the words aloud.

Option

- With a more confident class, allow students to try the task before they listen. They then listen to check their answers.

Answer key

/æ/ – *cap   has   hat   jacket   man*
/ʌ/ – *club   come   hundreds   number   some*

2b

- 📷 This is a back-chaining exercise (see Tip 2, page 13). Students listen and repeat in the usual way. Encourage them to clap the rhythm.

Tapescript

…cap
a fantastic cap …
a bag and a fantastic cap …
a jacket and a bag and a fantastic cap …
That man has a jacket and a bag and a fantastic cap

Suggested Workbook practice

Page 28, Exercise 1, 2 and 4

Buying and Selling

Aims

This section of the unit revises and extends language for shopping, including vocabulary for clothes and colours, and revision of *have got*. Students learn to plan, write and edit an advertisement.

1a

- Read the instructions aloud. Students guess from the picture what the girls want to look at.
- 📼 Play the cassette. Students listen to find out if their guess was right.

Answer key

jackets

....

Tapescript

Girl	Hello. We'd like to buy a jacket, please.
Assistant	What colour would you like?
Girl	Have you got any blue jackets?
Assistant	Er … No, we haven't. Sorry.
Girl	Mmm … have you got any green jackets, then?
Assistant	Yes, we have.

....

1b

- Quickly revise colours and clothes. Ask: *What colours do you know? What clothes do you remember?*
- Put students into pairs, and tell them to decide who is A and who is B. The As choose a colour for each garment, but do not tell their partner.
- Pairs act the dialogue in the usual way.

Options

- 📼 To help students prepare for the dialogue, play the cassette again. Students listen and note down phrases that they think will be useful, such as *Hello. We'd (I'd) like to buy …, What colour would you like? Have you got a/any …? No, we haven't. Sorry. Yes, we have.*
- Practise the basic dialogue first by playing the cassette again, pausing for students to repeat.

Writing: an advert

2a

- It is important to follow each stage described in this writing task. Students read the instructions. Check that they understand what to do. Suggest they read the adverts on page 45 again.
- Students carry out the planning stage in pairs or small groups, discussing the details, and making notes.

2b

- The first draft of the adverts can be written for homework. Also for homework, students find suitable magazine pictures.
- In the next class, encourage students to check their draft texts carefully, particularly for spelling mistakes. Alternatively, pairs or groups can swap their work and check each other's texts.

2c

- Students produce a final draft of their text. Encourage them to set out the text and picture(s) in an attractive way. The adverts can then be made into a wall display.

Suggested Workbook practice

Page 29, Exercises 1 and 2

The OK Club
The people from TV 4

Aims

This section continues the photo-story. It presents informal English in a lively context, and brings together the language students have been practising in the unit. In this episode a TV producer visits the club. She wants to make a film about the club and its members.

1

Background information

TV 4 is a fictitious small film company. Such companies typically produce their own documentaries and programmes and then sell them to a TV network.

Option

- In the mother tongue, see if students can remember what has happened so far. Ask: *What did the OK Club members do to get money?* (sell hamburgers). *Why did they need the money?* (to buy paint for redecorating the club). *What extras could people have in the hamburgers?* (onions, ketchup and mustard). *Who didn't sell hamburgers?* (Jack). *What did he do?* (He worked in his brother's garage). *How much money did they earn?* (£78). *Who arrived at the club?* (a man and a woman).

- Students read the words in the box. They then look at the pictures, and guess which words are likely to appear in the story. Do not confirm answers yet.

Answer key

computer   interview   programme   TV company

2a

- 📼 Ask: *Who are the man and woman?* Students listen with their books closed, and answer the question (people from a TV company).
- Play the cassette again. Students listen and read the story.
- Get students to tell you the main events in this episode: that the TV company wants to make a programme about the club, the TV producer promises to buy paint for the coffee bar, and the TV producer interviews the club members. For example, for picture 3, ask: *Why are Dave, Jane and Ricky so happy?*.
- Students listen once more and match actions with people. Check the answers.
- Read the example out loud. Students then write similar sentences for 1–6. Check that they are using the right verb endings.

Answer key

1 *members of the club*   2 *the TV producer and her cameraman*
3 *Jack*   4 *members of the club*   5 *the TV producer and her cameraman*   6 *members of the club*

2b

- Ask students if they do any of the things in 2a, for example: *Do you play table tennis?* When a student says *Yes*, ask more questions, for example: *Where do you play it? When do you play? Do you always play table tennis (in the evening)?* Write the answers as a sentence on the board, for example: *I sometimes play table tennis at my friend's house in the evening.*

- Give students some ideas for sentences, such as verbs from Student's Book page 45. Write them on the board, for example: *I (sometimes/often) do, eat, go, listen, read, stay, travel, visit, watch, write.*
- Students write 5 sentences about their lives. Choose a few students to read out one of their sentences each.

Review

Aims
The Review section summarizes and briefly revises the Key language features of Unit 6: the present simple, adverbs of frequency, telling the time, and object pronouns.

The present simple
- Read the explanation and examples. Remind students of the pronunciation of *watches*, /ˈwɒtʃɪz/. Ask: *Do you know another verb that has -es with* he, she *and* it? (do, teach, use).

Adverbs of frequency
- Say each adverb, in random order. Students tell you the percentage of frequency. Then call out each adverb in turn. Students make up a sentence containing the adverb in the right position.

Telling the time
- Draw clocks on the board. Students say the time.
- Draw circles on the board. Say different times. Individual students draw the times in the circles.

Object pronouns
- Ask students: *Do object pronouns go before or after the verb? What is the object form of 'they' / 'she' / 'I' … ?*

1a
- Explain the task. Read out the examples for 1, and ask students to suggest a third question. Ask them if they can think of any other questions. Tell students to write the three questions they like best, then to do the same with 2 and 3. Tell them to leave space after each question for the answer.

1b
- Put students into pairs. Tell them to swap books. Students suggest answers to the example questions. Make sure they include a frequency adverb in sentences. Students then write answers to their partner's questions.

2
- Students work individually, answering the questions. Make sure they use frequency adverbs.

Vocabulary
- *Music and dance*. Students make word-maps for *Music* and *Dance*. They may also wish to illustrate some words, for example, instruments such as *guitar*.
- *Adverbs of frequency*. Students list and translate these, adding an example sentence and a percentage after each.
- *Time*. If students have already started a page for *Time* (see Student's Book page 43, Exercise 1 Options), they just add in the time expressions *before*, *after*, *late*, and the periods of time, such as *in the morning*. If they have not, they also draw clocks and write the times. Suggest they write a sentence for each time, for example: *I usually get up at quarter to eight. On Sundays, I often get up late, at half past nine.*

Suggested Workbook practice
Page 29, Exercise 3
Page 30, Exercises 1 and 2

Freewheeling

a
- Students work with a partner to complete the song with words from the box. Do not check the answers yet.

b
- 📼 Play the cassette. Students check their answers.

Answer key
music sugar water hear come summer winter street

Option
- 📼 Play the cassette again. Students sing along to the music.

Preparation for Unit 7
Workbook page 30, Exercise 3

Workbook answer key
Life and times
1 2 *visit, Yes, we do.*
3 *travel, No, we don't.*
4 *travel, Yes, we do.*
5 *start, No, we don't.*

2 2 *They usually start work after lunch.*
3 *They sometimes meet friends on tour.*
4 *They never eat before a concert.*
5 *Alex always takes some exercise on tour.*

3 *Student's own answers*

4 1 *It's half past eight.*
2 *It's eleven o'clock.*
3 *It's a quarter past one.*
4 *It's quarter to five.*

Carnival time
1 2 *them* 3 *you* 4 *him* 5 *her* 6 *me* 7 *us* 8 *it*
9 *you*
2 1 *e* 2 *c* 3 *f* 4 *a* 5 *b* 6 *d*
3a 2 *different* 3 *same* 4 *different* 5 *same*

3b 2 *black*   3 *large/huge*   4 *colourful*   5 *boring*
6 *noisy/loud*

4b *black, bag, jacket*

c *Hungry, Come, club, lunch*

The people from TV4

1a 1 *I'd like a green T-shirt, please.*
2 *Have you got any blue T-shirts, then?*
3 *How much is it?*
4 *Are the red T-shirts six pounds, too?*
5 *OK, I'd like one blue and two red T-shirts please.*

b 1 *green*   2 *green*   3 *three*   4 *twenty-three pounds*

2 1 *I'd like to see some baseball caps.*
2 *I'd like a red baseball cap, please.*
3 *Have you got any black caps then?*
4 *How much is it?*
5 *Are the blue caps three pounds fifty, too?*
6 *OK, I'd like a black cap and a blue cap, please.*
£7.50

3 1 *b*   2 *c*   3 *a*   4 *f*   5 *g*   6 *d*   7 *e*

Skills: timetables

1 *8.30 He leaves for school.*
8.50 School starts.
12.20 They stop for lunch.
3.45 He leaves school and goes to the park.
5.15 He goes home.
6.30 He has / They have supper.
10.00 He goes to bed.

2a *Student's own answers*

b *Student's own answers*

Prepare for Unit 7

3a *circle b   rectangle d   square a   triangle c*

b 1 *Earth*   2 *space station*   3 *space*   4 *sun*

Unit 7

Syllabus

Topic
Imagine this…: *space travel*
Clever inventions
The OK Club

Grammar
Demonstratives: *this, that, these* and *those*
Quantifiers: *a little, a few,* and *a lot of*

Function
Describing objects
Expressing quantity

Vocabulary
Space travel
Shapes
Useful things at home or work

Reading
Matching text and pictures

Listening
Identifying key information
Matching descriptions with pictures

Writing
Writing puzzles
Writing a description of an invention

Speaking
Discussing the purpose of objects
Describing the location of objects

Pronunciation
/θ/ and /ð/
Word and sentence stress

Vocabulary
Key vocabulary

behind	little (a …)	ship
between	matches	size
bottle	microphone	solar
circle	move	something
control	ocean	space station
crew	off	square (n & adj)
direction	panel	string
Earth	play	Sun
electricity	produce (v)	teeth
feet	receive	tin (n)
few (a …)	rectangle	tin-opener
in front of	round	triangle
invention	screen	triangular
knives (sing. = knife)	send	wheel
library	shape (n)	wood

Other vocabulary

area	garden	salad
boss	lose	section
cargo	Never mind!	sunny
children	No way!	toy
clever	part	
close (v)	put	

Materials preparation

1   Dictionaries for Student's Book page 48 Exercise 2, and page 51 Exercise 1b.
2   For page 50, Exercise 2b: draw a picture of an unusual cassette player on the board or on a large sheet of paper:

3   A tray of everyday objects that students know for 'Kim's Game', Game 4, page 74.
4   Find one or more mother-tongue nonsense poems or songs that have a strong rhythm for Freewheeling on page 53.

Imagine this ...

Aims

In this section, students work out the use of *this*, *that*, *these* and *those* to describe the location of people and objects. The language is presented through reading and listening activities about a space station of the future. In the pronunciation section, students learn to differentiate between the sounds /θ/ and /ð/.

1

Background information

Space Station 66H, Orbit Q24. This space station is imaginary, but space stations do exist. The Russians sent the first components of a space station called *Salyut* into orbit in the late 1970s, then replaced it with the MIR station in 1986. In 1998, 16 nations joined together to begin building a much larger 'International Space Station' (ISS), which is scheduled for completion in 2004. The ideas of tourism in space, and of a space hotel, are already being discussed by several companies, but there are as yet no plans to start building.

Option

- Do a quick substitution drill with the class to practise the present simple (see Tip 11, page 51). Say: *People travel to work by bus.* Substitute words: *train, I, London, go, she, doesn't, New York, we, space bus, the crew.*

- Use the picture and questions to teach *Earth*, *space bus*, *space station*, *section*, *control centre*, *crew*, *exercise*.

- Give students guidance on what to discuss. Write on the board: *What is on the space station? What part of Earth do you see? How do you think visitors come to the station? How many sections has the station got? Is there really a station in space?*

- Put students into groups of 4–5. Students discuss their ideas in the mother tongue for 2–3 minutes, then prepare answers in English for 3–4 more minutes. The focus of this discussion should be on students' ideas, rather than on using correct sentences. Only comment on mistakes if you have a real problem understanding what they want to say.

- Each group chooses a representative to report their answers to the class.

2

- The texts describe the various sections of the space station in the main picture. Demonstrate the task by reading and matching the first paragraph with them, pointing out the clues *bus, to ... from the space station*.

- To encourage students to read for gist (general meaning), tell them to do the rest of the exercise without looking up words in a dictionary.

- Check answers. Students read the text again, underline any unfamiliar words, and look them up in a dictionary.

Answer key

1 *E* 2 *C* 3 *D* 4 *A* 5 *B*

3a

- Use the cartoon to prepare students for the listening task. Ask: *Who is the visitor, the man or the woman?* (the man). *What part of the station do you think they are in?*

- 🔲 Play the cassette. Students listen to check their guesses.

Answer key

The living-room in section D (see text 3 of Exercise 2)

3b

- Briefly show the meaning of *that* and *those* by pointing to objects in the classroom (pictures, windows, clock, and so on), and asking: *What's that? What are those?* Do not explain the difference between *this/these* and *that/those*.

- Tell students to read the instructions. Make sure they understand that only the words *that* and *those* are missing.

- 🔲 Students listen and fill in the gaps.

Tapescript/Answer key

Tourist What's this room? ... er ... Are all these CDs and videos for the visitors?
Guide Yes, they are. These videos and CDs are all here for you.
Tourist Oh, great! ... and ... er, what's **that**?
Guide **That** round thing's Earth, sir. Do you see **those** blue parts? **Those** are the oceans ... and **those** black parts are the big cities. **That's** New York.
Tourist Really? Isn't it small?

Work it out: *this*, *that*, *these* and *those*

4a

- Students already know *this* and *that* from Unit 2, and have seen *those* as the plural form of *that* in Exercise 3, so they should be able to work out the meaning of *these* easily.

- Students read the examples. In the mother tongue, ask: *Which examples talk about one thing?* (1 and 3). *Which examples talk about more than one thing?* (2 and 4). *Which examples talk about things near us?* (1 and 2). *What about the third and fourth ones?* (things not near).

4b

- Students show they have understood the sentences in 4a by completing the chart.

Answer key

Things near us: this   these
Things not near us: that   those

Option

- For oral practice, students work with a partner, pointing to or touching objects in the room, using *this/that is a ...* or *these/those are ... .*

Pronunciation: /θ/ and /ð/

Option

- These are difficult sounds for many students, so it may help to teach them how to produce the sounds first. Say /θ/, and show students how the tongue is placed between the teeth and air is breathed out with no sound from the voice (or 'voice box'). Students say /θ/. Now say /ð/, and show students how the tongue is behind the upper teeth, and the voice box produces a sound. Students say /ð/. Say both sounds several times for students to repeat.

5a

- 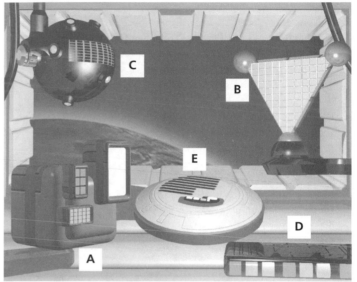 ▣ Play the cassette. Students listen and repeat the words.

5b

- Students put the words into two groups, and check their answers with a partner.

Answer key

/θ/: *thing, think, thanks*
/ð/: *this, these, there*

5c

- This tongue-twister allows students to practise saying the two sounds /θ/ and /ð/ quickly, one after the other. It is said three times on the cassette, a little faster each time.
- ▣ Play the cassette. Students listen only.
- Clap out the rhythm, getting students to clap and say the words with you. Begin slowly, then say the lines and clap the rhythm with a faster and faster beat.
- Play the cassette again. Students repeat.

Suggested Workbook practice

Page 31, Exercise 1

Describing objects

Aims

In this section, students learn to describe objects by shape and use, and talk about the purpose of objects. The language is presented and practised through reading and writing tasks.

1a

- Make sure students understand the meaning of *circle*, *rectangle*, *triangle*, *square*, *circular* and *round*. (See Tip 10, page 50.)
- Remind students where to look for adjectives in a sentence. On the board, write two rows of simple sentences:
    A It's a square.   It's a triangle.   It's a circle.
      It's a rectangle.
    B It's small.   It's large.   It's white.   It's black.
- In the mother tongue, ask: *Which sentences have nouns, row A or row B? How do you know?* (the use of *a* in the sentences, which means singular nouns follow). *What are the words after 'It's' in row B?* (adjectives). Tell students to make new sentences by putting the adjectives in the row A sentences, for example, *It's a large square. It's a small circle.* Ask: *Where do adjectives go?* (either before a noun or after the verb).
- Read the instructions. Check that students have understood what to do. Tell them not to worry about other new vocabulary yet.
- Students look through the texts, and complete the list of adjectives of shape.

Answer key

rectangular   triangular   square

1b

- Tell students to read the instructions, then check that they understand what to do. Do the first item (A) with the whole class. Students do B, C and D individually.
- Check the answers with the class. Ask individual students what words in the descriptions helped them.

Answer key

1c

- Tell students to look at the last piece of equipment in the picture. Then tell them to look at the text, and ask what sort of words are missing from the description of E (adjectives).
- Students look at the picture, then complete the description.

Answer key

round   blue

Useful English

- Tell students to read the list on the left of the box, and ask them: *What does 'shape' mean?* Do the same for *purpose*.
- Explain, or get students to guess the meaning of any vocabulary.
- ▣ Play the cassette. Students listen and mark where the stress falls in each adjective (<u>cir</u>cular, tri<u>an</u>gular, rec<u>tan</u>gular).
- Point out the use of *for* + verb + *-ing* in *It's for sending/receiving.*
- ▣ Play the cassette again. Students listen and repeat.

2

- Make sure students understand the idea of a 'mystery object'. Hide a tennis ball behind your back, and say: *It's small and round. It's for playing.* When students guess the answer, open your hand to show the ball.
- Students work in pairs, taking turns to read the description or guess the object.

Answer key

1 *teeth*   2 *feet*   3 *the sun*

3a

- Students work in groups of 3–4 to prepare descriptions of more mystery objects.
- Tell each group to write down their mystery word. Go round checking the words. If two groups have the same word, make sure that they do not exchange descriptions with each other in 3b. Have some suggestions ready on slips of paper in case any groups cannot think of an object, for example, *door, telephone, pizza, train, sofa.*
- Students write sentences to describe their object. Walk round the room, checking that the descriptions include shape, size, purpose and, if appropriate, colour.

Option

- If some groups finish before others, suggest more details for their description, for example: *Do you use it often? Where do we usually find it?*

3b

- Groups swap descriptions and guess each others' mystery objects.

Option

- Get a representative of each group to stand up and read their group's description to the class. The rest of the class listens and guesses the object.

Game 3 ▼
Mystery objects

- Divide the class into teams. Read out a description of an object, pausing after each clue. Students can call out a guess after any clue. If they guess correctly, their team gets a point. If they call out an incorrect guess, the other teams get a point. The winning team is the one with the most points at the end of the game. Example objects and clues:
  A watch – It's got numbers on it … .it's got a face and two hands … it's small … we wear it on our arms … we sometimes look at it … it's for telling the time.
  Pyramids – They're very big … they're very very old … they're triangular … they're in a country beginning with E … they're in Egypt.
  A television – It's usually rectangular or square … sometimes it's black and white … usually it's colour … it's often in the living-room … we usually watch it in the evening … it receives pictures.

Suggested Workbook practice

Page 31, Exercises 2 and 3
Page 34, Exercises 1 and 2

Clever inventions
Quantity

Aims

The discussion and listening exercises in this section give further practice in describing objects and their purpose. Students learn about expressions of quantity (*a lot of, a little, a few*), and have further practice is using the present simple for general truths.

1

- Get students to think about the dimensions of each machine. For example, get them to use their hands, or objects in the room, to show the actual size.
- Remind students of *It's for (verb) + -ing* to express purpose. Ask: *What's a pen for?* (It's for writing). *What's a watch for?* (It's for telling the time).
- Put students into groups of 3–4 to decide the purpose of the three objects. Allow about 5 minutes for groups to discuss their reasons in the mother tongue, and write sentences using *I think it's for (verb + -ing)*. Go round the class, helping students with vocabulary, or tell them to look up words they want in a dictionary, then check that they have found the appropriate translation.
- A representative reads out each group's ideas. Write these on the board without comment. Students will be able to confirm or adjust their ideas in Exercises 2 and 3.

2a

- Read descriptions 1–5, and explain any unfamiliar words.
- Tell students to read the instructions. Make sure they understand that the exercise refers to pictures A, B and C, and that only three of the names are correct.
- Students work individually, matching the names with the objects. Do not check the answers yet.

2b

- Show your picture of a cassette player (see Materials preparation 2). Say: *What's this?* (a cassette player). *What's it for?* (listening to music). *What are the clues?* (It says 'Music master' and there is a cassette next to it).
- Put students into pairs to compare guesses and clues for Exercise 2a. Then ask the class for their ideas. Write these on the board, without commenting if they are right or wrong. Possible clues are: A – It's got an antenna. It says 'You are here'. B – It's big. There are pictures of food on it. It has the word *MENU* on it. C – There's some paper next to it.

3

- This is a 'gist' listening exercise – students must understand enough to confirm their answers, but they do not need to understand every word.
- 📼 Play the cassette. Students listen and check their answers to Exercise 2.

Tapescript

... Now ... this is a new invention – the Direction-Finder – um ... that's picture A ... it's for crews on space stations. It has these small solar panels for electricity ... and ... er ... there's a small radio for receiving messages from satellites and space stations ... The Direction-Finder puts a lot of different messages together and it tells you where you are in space ...

... and this ... this is a clever invention for space ships ... it's a square box ... er ... The Space Kitchen ... Picture B ... It uses only a little electricity but it produces a lot of good food! ... It shows you a few different dishes on this small screen. ... You choose a dish ... and, um, then it cooks your food. These small solar panels are for the electricity.

... and this is The Message-Writer - Picture C. You speak here, into this microphone, and it ... er ... listens to you. It understands men's and women's voices ... and then it writes your words on this small screen. ... After you read them and check them, the ... er ... Message-Writer writes your message for you.

Answer key

A *a direction-finder*   B *a space kitchen*   C *a message writer*

4

- This is an 'intensive' listening task – students listen for details of the inventions.
- Check that students understand all the sentences, and explain any unfamiliar words, but do not give a grammar explanation for using *a little*, *a few* and *a lot of*.
- Tell students to guess as many of the answers as they can before they listen.
- 📼 Play the cassette again. Students listen and write or check the answers.

Option

- If students find this task difficult, play the cassette again.

Answer key

1 *B*   2 *C*   3 *A*   4 *B*   5 *C*   6 *A*   7 *B*

Work it out: *a little*, *a few* and *a lot of*

5a

- Quickly revise countable and uncountable nouns. Ask: *What words in Exercise 4 are countable?* (men, women, messages, voices, words, screen, dishes). *What words are uncountable?* (electricity, food, space).
- Tell students to underline the phrases *a little*, *a few*, and *a lot of* in Exercise 4, together with the noun they describe. Do the first one with the class as an example (sentence 1: *a little electricity*), then let students do the others individually.
- Students use the examples they have found to complete the chart.
- Check answers, and point out that *only* can go before *a little* and *a few* to indicate a very small quantity.

Answer key

With uncountable nouns: a lot of (food)   a little (electricity)
With countable nouns: a lot of (messages)   a few (dishes)

5b

- Students use the chart in 5a to complete the sentences, working individually, then checking their answers with a partner.

Answer key

1 *a lot of*   2 *a little*   3 *a lot of*   4 *a few*   5 *a lot of*

Suggested Workbook practice

Page 32, Exercise 3
Page 33, Exercises 4 and 5

In the workshop

Aims

Exercises 1 and 2 provide controlled practice of expressions of quantity, together with vocabulary for the following writing task. Exercise 3 guides students through the stages of a project to design and describe their own inventions.

1a

Option

- Teach any new vocabulary. Then ask: *Are there any wheels on the table? Has a bike got four wheels? What about a car? Are there a lot of boxes of matches on the table? Is there any paint on the table? What colour is it? Where does wood come from? Tables have legs. What other furniture has legs? (chairs). What do you use string for? What goes in a bottle?*

- Tell students to read the instructions. Check that they understand what to do. Ask: *What words will you use to complete the sentences?* (*a little*, *a few*, *a lot of*).
- Students work individually, then check their answers with a partner.

Answer key

1 *a few*   2 *a little*   3 *a few*   4 *a little*   5 *a few*   6 *a few*
7 *a lot of*   8 *a few*

1b

- Students find other objects on the table, and look up any unfamiliar words in a dictionary.
- Students describe objects in the picture, using expressions of quantity.

Answer key

banana   book   coffee   cups   envelopes   knife   paper   pencils
pens   scissors

2

- Put students into pairs. Tell them to decide who is A, and who is B.
- Tell students to read the instructions, then ask questions to check that both A and B understand what to do. Partner A studies the picture carefully for about 30 seconds, trying to remember everything in it, then describes the picture to B. Remind students that B can ask questions too, especially questions that get more detail. For example:

  A: There are some cups.
  B: What's in the cups? / Where are they? / Are there a lot of cups?

- Write some useful language for B on the board, such as *Where is/are ...? Are there a lot of ...? What colour is/are...?*

- Tell Bs to think about more questions while you time the 30 seconds for As to study the picture.
- Students play the game for 3–4 minutes, and then change roles.

Game 4 ▼
Kim's game

- This is a traditional memory game. Prepare a tray of everyday objects that students know the English for, such as a small pile of matches, some pencils of different colours, an apple, a watch, two potatoes, a sock and so on. Include at least fifteen small items. Keep the tray covered with a cloth. Students gather around the tray. Remove the cloth for one minute and tell students to take a good look. Then cover the tray again. Students work in pairs, writing a list of the objects on the tray from memory. They should include as many details as they can remember, such as colour, size, number. Allow five minutes, then tell students to stop writing. Each pair in turn names one object on the tray, for example: *There is a red and white sock. It's a man's sock. It's old!* Remove objects from the tray as they are identified, but do not let students see what's still under the cloth.

Writing: an invention

- Tasks a–e guide students through the stages of planning and composing a piece of imaginative writing. As for all project work, the quality of their ideas is as important as the quality of the language they produce. The following is a suggested guide to timing:

Stage	a	b	c	d	e
Time	15–20 minutes	15 minutes	20 minutes	15 minutes	students produce the final text and drawing at home

3a

- This is the 'brainstorming' stage, when students come up with as many ideas for an invention as they can.
- Tell students that their invention can be either practical or 'futuristic', like inventions A, B and C on page 50, but should include things from the picture on page 51.
- Let the initial discussion be in the mother tongue. Students then begin to plan in English, starting by listing the vocabulary they will need to describe their object. They may prefer to organize their words as a list or a word-map.

Option

- Pairs join up to try out their ideas and to compare vocabulary.

3b

- These questions help the students to plan their invention in more detail. They answer the questions with full sentences. Go round the class checking ideas and sentences.

3c

- The listening text provides a model of the sort of description students will write.
- Tell students they are going to listen to the description of object A on page 50 again. Write on the board: *1 What is it called? 2 Who is it for? 3 What parts has it got? 4 What does it do?*

Students look at the picture again and answer as many questions as they can before they listen.

- ▣ Play the cassette from page 50 Exercise 3 again. Students listen and check their answers.

Answer key

1 *The Direction Finder.*   2 *It's for crews on space stations.*
3 *It's got small solar panels. There's a small radio for receiving messages.*   4 *It tells you where you are in space.*

3d

- Students use the notes they have made and the language they have learned to write the first draft of a description of their own invention. Go round the class checking students' work, and helping them organize their notes into a logical sequence.

Option

- After students have written their first draft, they swap work with another pair. The 'readers' check the language, and ask questions about the invention. The 'inventors' use the questions to improve their description.

3e

- Students produce a final draft of their texts, together with a name for their invention and a drawing of it.
- Make a wall display using a title suggested by the class.

Suggested Workbook practice

Page 32, Exercises 1 and 2

The OK Club
Project OK

Aims

This section continues the photo-story. It presents informal English in a lively context. This episode revises the language of expressing preferences and giving opinions, and the use of the present simple. In this episode, the club members buy decorating materials and choose a project leader.

1

Options

- In the mother tongue, get students to remember the story so far. For example, ask: *Who is in the OK Club? What catches fire? What do the club members decide to do? Where do they sell the hamburgers? Who sees them? What does the TV producer want? How does the TV company help the OK Club?*
- Instead of asking questions, write the jumbled sentences below on the board (answers are in brackets). Explain in the mother tongue that the sentences make a summary of the story so far, but are in the wrong order. Students must decide the correct order of the sentences. To help them, get the whole class to decide which is the opening sentence.

  They make some hamburgers and sell them in the street. (5)
  The TV producers gives them money for paint. (7)
  Five teenagers are members of the OK Club. (1)
  They decide to redecorate the club. (4)

The kettle in the club catches fire and burns the coffee area. (3)

One evening, they go to the club and make coffee. (2)

Two people from a TV company see them and decides to make a film about the club. (6)

- Students try to remember what 'Project OK' is. Tell them to look back through the episodes if they are having trouble remembering. (The answer is in Unit 4.)

Answer key

Project OK is the redecoration of the Coffee Corner.

2

- Ask students questions in English about the pictures, for example: *Look at picture 1: Where are they?* (in a paint shop). *Look at picture 2. Where are they?* (they're in a cafe). *Look at picture 3. What do you think is in the box?* (money for 'Project OK'). *Look at picture 4. Who is the girl?* (Emma). *What has she got in her hand?* (the money box). *What is under the coffee cup?* (a message).
- In the mother tongue, ask: *Why do you think Emma's taking the box?*

3

- Play the cassette. Students listen to see if they guessed the story correctly.
- Tell students to cover the story so that they can concentrate on listening. Give them time to read sentences 1–6.
- Play the cassette again. Students listen and correct the sentences.
- They read the story again to check their answers.

Answer key

1 **Jack** wants brown paint for the walls or Jane wants **yellow** paint for the walls.
2 **Jane** doesn't think brown paint is a good idea.
3 **Jane** wants Jack to be to be the boss of Project OK.
4 **Jack** forgets to take the money home.
5 Emma finds the **money box** in the Coffee Corner later.
6 Emma **takes** the money and goes home.

Tip 12 ★
Teaching contrastive stress

- On the board, write two sentences with factual errors in them. Get students to call out corrections. Write these on the board too. For example:
  1 Jane wants brown walls. No. She wants <u>yellow</u> walls.
  2 Emma wants Jack to be the boss. No. <u>Jane</u> wants Jack to be the boss.
  Say both the wrong and the corrected sentences, placing stress on the corrections (*yellow* and *Jane*). Students repeat the sentences, trying to get the stress right. Say more incorrect statements, and get students to correct them, again placing stress on the corrected word. For example:
  Today is Monday. No. Today is <u>Tuesday</u>.
  The month is August. No. It's <u>July</u>.
  There are 23 students in the class. No. There are twenty-<u>five</u>.
  Jack has got straight hair. No. <u>Dave</u> has got straight hair.

Set the pace
4a

- Students use the pictures and dialogue to guess the meaning of each phrase. (Note that *No way* is an informal expression to show strong disagreement. We say someone is *hopeless* at something when they are not good at doing it – Jack is 'hopeless' at remembering things.)

4b

- Students listen and repeat each phrase, trying to copy the intonation.

Options

- Students work in groups of 5 to act out the episode.
- Focus on the plot. Ask: *Why does Jack think 'Thanks Dave' in picture 1?* (Jack is being ironic. He's angry that Dave supports Jane's ideas – especially as both boys like Jane).

Suggested Workbook practice
Page 33, Exercise 2

Review
Aims
The Review section summarizes and briefly revises the Key languages features of Unit 7: the demonstratives *this*, *that*, *these* and *those*, and quantity.

this, *that*, *these* and *those*

- Quickly revise the demonstratives. Students, in groups of 4–6, ask each other questions about things in the classroom or seen through the window.

Quantity

- On the board, write: *oranges*, *milk*, *potatoes*, *meat*, *cola*, *hamburgers*, *ketchup*. The class discusses which words can be described using *a lot of*, *a little* or *a few*.

1

- Students do this exercise orally, in pairs.

2a

- Check that students remember the meaning of each word in the box. Ask: *What do you think is the singular of 'knives'?*
- Students work individually, putting the words into two lists.

Answer key

Countable: children, feet, ideas, knives, legs, men, people, teeth, women
Uncountable: electricity, paint, string, water, wood, work

2b

- Students choose two countable and two uncountable nouns from the box in 2a. They write sentences in their vocabulary books under the heading *Quantity*. Each sentence should use one of the nouns and a quantifier.

2c

- Students look at the words in 2a again. They find the six irregular plurals and write them on a new page in their vocabulary books under the heading *Irregular plural nouns.*

Answer key
children   feet   men   people   teeth   women

Vocabulary

- *Space travel.* Students look back for words to do with space travel. They list and translate them.
- *Shapes.* Students draw and label the shapes on page 49.
- *Useful things.* Students make a list of words from page 50 and 51, together with vocabulary the class used to describe their own inventions. They draw and label objects, and list and translate other words and phrases.

Freewheeling

- Tell students to read the poem quickly. Ask: *What's the poem about?* Get them to say that the poem is nonsense, but funny because the rhyming words are so absurd.
- Remind students of /s/, /z/ and /ɪz/ pronunciation in third person singular (this poem has two examples of /ɪz/ verbs, *washes* and *brushes*).
- 🔊 The poem has a very regular rhythm. Play the cassette. Students listen silently, and mark the stressed syllables (see tapescript).
- Play the cassette again. Students read the words, and clap the rhythm.
- Ask students if they know any similar poems or songs in their own language. Let students who respond perform them. If they cannot think of one, suggest one yourself, and get students to say or sing it.

Tapescript
<u>Desperate</u> <u>Dan</u> is
A <u>dirty</u> old <u>man</u>.
He <u>washes</u> his <u>face</u>
In a <u>frying</u> <u>pan</u>.
He <u>brushes</u> his <u>hair</u>
With the <u>leg</u> of a <u>chair</u> –
<u>Desperate</u> <u>Dan</u> is
A <u>dirty</u> old <u>man</u>.

Suggested Workbook practice

Page 33, Exercise 1
Page 34, Exercise 3

Preparation for Unit 8

Workbook page 34, Exercise 4

Workbook answer key

Imagine this ...

1   2 *These*   3 *those*   4 *these*   5 *this*
      6 *that*   7 *this*

2a 2 *check new words*   4 *write notes and answers in*
      3 *carry things*   5 *brush your hair*

b   2 *It's for checking new words.*
      3 *It's for carrying things.*
      4 *It's for writing notes and answers in.*
      5 *It's for brushing your hair.*

3a 1 *triangle*   2 *rectangle*   3 *circle*   4 *square*

b   *Circular: ball, CD*
      Rectangular: book, envelope
      Square: picture, box
      Triangular: sandwich, cheese

Clever inventions

1a *bottle   bread   coffee   envelope   matches   string   wheel*

b   Countable: *matches, wheel, envelope*
      Uncountable: *paint, string, coffee, bread*

2   1 *are a few*   5 *is a little*
      2 *is a little*   6 *are a lot of*
      3 *are a lot of*   7 *are a few*
      4 *is a little*

3   *Student's own answers*

4   2 *only a few*   6 *a lot of them.*
      3 *a little*   7 *I'd like a little.*
      4 *I'd like some*   8 *How much is that?*
      5 *a few*

5   1 *It's for washing a car.*   4 *Yes, it does. It's got wheels.*
      2 *It's round.*   5 *No, it doesn't.*
      3 *It's quite big.*

Project OK

1   2 *these*   3 *this*   4 *those*   5 *those*   6 *this*   7 *that*

2a 1 *Good! That's a lot!*
      2 *No way! Grey is boring!*
      3 *Yes, please.*
      4 *White? That's a good idea.*
      5 *Never mind. The other shop is open.*

b   a *3*   b *5*   c *1*   d *2,4*

Skills: puzzles

1   1 *d – magazine*
      2 *c – pens*
      3 *b – ball*

2   *a radio*
      b *It's rectangular and it's big. You use it for listening to music.*

3   2 *wood*   3 *meat*   4 *shoes*   5 *toy*   6 *men*

Prepare for Unit 8

4a *Tuesday*
      Wednesday
      Thursday
      Friday
      Saturday
      Sunday

b   *We use a ball*
      basketball, football, volleyball
      One person can do these
      swimming, walking
      We play these with other people
      badminton, basketball, football, judo, volleyball
      We do these in water
      swimming, water aerobics

Unit 8

Syllabus

Topic
That's amazing: *interesting facts*
Do you want to be a champion?
The OK Club

Grammar
can/can't
must
Prepositions of time

Function
Expressing ability
Agreeing and disagreeing
Expressing obligation

Vocabulary
Names of languages
Sports and hobbies
Days of the week

Reading
Matching text with pictures
Finding and checking information
Matching titles with paragraphs

Listening
Identifying context
Checking specific information
Correcting and completing information

Writing
Writing a short article

Speaking
Checking facts
Asking about ability
Making arrangements

Pronunciation
Word and sentence stress
can and *can't*

Learn to learn
Using a dictionary(3)

Vocabulary

Key vocabulary

aerobics	get a move on	study
agree	gym	Sunday
athlete	habit	sure
athletics	Hang on (a minute)!	technique
badminton	horse	... think so
become	judo	Thursday
bicycle	Monday	timetable
can / can't	must	track (running ...)
dangerous	perhaps	train (v)
diameter	piano	Tuesday
east	relax	walk
enough	ride	Wednesday
equipment	run	week
fast	sleep	west
Friday	speak	wide

Other vocabulary

air	dive	open
angry	drum (n)	out
anything	first (thing)	organize
blow (v)	fly (v)	practise
bubble-gum	kilometres per hour	regularly
call (v)	laugh	supper
centimetres	laughter	top
champion	learn	without
dead	minute	

Materials preparation

1 For page 54, Useful English Option: prepare a list of 'facts' about yourself, some true, some not true, for example: *I've got a dog. I drink two coffees in the morning. I like pizza with mustard. I run 5 kilometres before school.*

2 Dictionaries for page 55, Exercise 6b.

3 For page 57, Exercise 1b Option 2: make seven cards with the days of the week on them (see Tip 10, page 50).

That's amazing
can/can't

Aims

In this section, students learn to talk about ability, using *can* and *can't*. They also learn how to express agreement, disagreement and uncertainty. They learn the names of some languages, and the stressed and unstressed ways of saying can. The language is presented through a listening task, and practised through reading, discussion and writing activities.

1a

- Read the titles with the class. Help students to guess the meaning of any new vocabulary such as *bubble*, *dangerous*, *dive* and *fast*.
- Students match the titles with the pictures.

Answer key

1 Dive with your dog 2 Big big bubbles 3 Walking on water 4 The walking dictionary 5 Fast fish and dangerous fish

1b

- Students look at the pictures. Ask: *Which pictures do you think are amazing? Why? What can you see in the other pictures? Look at picture 4. What is 'a walking dictionary'? Look at picture 5. Do you know the names of these fish? Which fish is fast? Which fish is dangerous?*
- Explain the exercise, then check that students understand what to do. Ask students what they think the conversation will be about (one of the pictures).
- 🔊 Play the cassette. Students listen and match the conversation with one of the titles.
- Students give reasons for their choice of title.

Tapescript

DJ …Mr Ruffle, can you speak Chinese, for example?
Mr Ruffle Yes, I can. But I speak only a little Chinese.
DJ Can you write Chinese, too?
Mr Ruffle No, I can't. I can't write it, but I want to learn.
DJ And what about Russian? You can speak it, I know, but… can you write Russian?
Mr Ruffle Yes, I can. I can write it quite well now.
DJ Can you speak any African languages? … Swahili, for example?
Mr Ruffle Swahili? Yes, I can speak Swahili – that's the main language of East Africa.
DJ And can you speak any of the languages of West Africa?
Mr Ruffle No, I can't. But I want to learn Yoruba. That's the main language of West Africa.

Answer key

The walking dictionary

2a

- Read the questions with the class. If students cannot guess the meaning of *Can you …?*, give a simple translation of the first question, but do not give any explanation.
- Explain that students listen for the questions only, and tick only the ones they hear. They do not write in the *Answer* boxes yet.
- 🔊 Play the cassette. Students listen and tick the questions they hear.

Answer key

The interviewer asks questions 1, 3, 4 and 5.

2b

- Get students to work out the short answer forms for *can*. Write on the board:

  Is Mr Ruffle a teacher?   Yes, he is. No, he isn't.
  Can he speak Chinese?   Yes, … … No, … ……

  Students who think they know the answer complete the short forms.
- Read the instructions to the class, and make sure they understand that they remember Mr Ruffle's answers, and put either a tick or a cross in the appropriate boxes.

2c

- 🔊 Play the cassette again. Students listen and check their answers.

Answer key

1 ✓   3 ✓   4 ✓   5 ✗

2d

- 🔊 Play the cassette. Students listen and repeat in the usual way.

Tapescript

DJ Can you speak Chinese?
Mr Ruffle Yes, I can.
DJ Can you write Russian?
Mr Ruffle Yes, I can.
DJ Can you speak any African languages?
Mr Ruffle Yes, I can.
DJ Can you speak any of the languages of West Africa?
Mr Ruffle No, I can't.

3a

- Tell students to read sentences 1–6 and underline any unfamiliar words or phrases, such as *for one hour*, *without air*, *fly*, *kilometres per hour*. Students guess the meaning from context.
- Demonstrate the task, using the first sentence as an example. Make it clear to students that they are guessing – there is no 'right' or 'wrong' answer. Students complete the task individually.

Useful English

- Read the phrases, explaining or helping students to guess the meaning of each.
- 🔊 Play the cassette, pausing after each phrase for students to repeat. Encourage students to copy the intonation of the speakers (from confident, to less certain, to doubtful).

Option

- Practise the phrases before expecting students to use them in a discussion. Using your prepared list of facts (see Materials preparation 1), make statements to the class about yourself. After each statement, students guess which are true and which are false, using the Useful English phrases.

3b

- Put students into groups of 3–4. Group members take turns reading out a sentence from Exercise 3a. Each member of the group then gives an opinion, using phrases from the Useful English box.

4

- Explain that texts 1–5 tell the facts about the photos. Encourage students to complete the task as quickly as they can, looking quickly through the texts for the specific information they need.
- Students check their answers in pairs, underlining the relevant phrases in the text. Discuss answers and clues with the class. Do not give students help with unknown words at this stage.

Answer key

1 *False. 'She can't stay under water for a very long time – only about five minutes'* 2 *False. '... has her own diving equipment',* 3 *True. 'She uses a special sort of bubble-gum'* 4 *False. 'It can walk on water', but there's no mention of flying* 5 *True. 'can speak and write 58 different languages'* 6 *True. '... can move at 109 kilometres per hour'*

5a

- Put students into pairs to discuss probable answers before they read the texts again.
- Students read the texts again, looking for confirmation of their answers. Do not check the answers yet.

5b

- Put students into pairs new pairs (see Tip 8, page 37). Pairs decide who is A and who is B.
- Check that students understand what to do: partner B covers Exercise 5a, and looks at the texts. Partner A asks questions beginning *Who* or *What ...?* based on list A in Exercise 5. Partner B answers from the texts.
- When A has asked all seven questions, partners change roles.
- Check answers with the class. Ask for answers in the form of complete sentences using *can*, for example, *Champion athletes can run at 42 kilometres per hour.*

Answer key

1 *champion athletes* 2 *piranha fish* 3 *Mr Ruffle* 4 *Shadow, the dog* 5 *Susan Williams* 6 *a lizard in Costa Rica* 7 *cosmopolitan sailfish*

Option

- To make the task more challenging the second time, partner A closes his or her book, and answers B's questions entirely from memory.

Learn to learn: using a dictionary (3)

6a

- Students find the words in the text, and underline them.
- To encourage students to make use of context, help them with the first word. Say: *He goes away on holiday.* In the mother tongue, ask: *Why do people often go away? Where are they going? So what does 'on holiday' mean?* Students use context to guess the meaning of the other words.

6b

- Students compare their guesses with a partner. They then share the task of checking the words in a dictionary.

- Discuss with students where in their vocabulary books they are going to put the words, for example, *wide* and *diameter* under *Shapes* and *Measurements*, *athletes* under *Sports*.

Work it out: *can*

7a

- Students read the texts again, and underline examples of *can* and the 'companion' verb, for example, in text 1: *Can dogs swim?*
- Students choose the meaning of *can*.

Answer key

1 *She swims*

7b

- If students are not sure of the negative form, tell them to look for an example in text 1 (*She can't stay under water very long*).

Pronunciation: *can* and *can't*

8a

- These exercises contrast the strong (stressed) forms of *can* /kæn/ and *can't* /kɑːnt/, and the weak (unstressed) form of *can* /kən/.
- Remind students of the changing pronunciation of have (see Unit 3). On the board, write: *Have you got a brother? Yes, I have.* Ask several students to say both question and answer. Choose one who pronounced *have* correctly in each case to come to the board and underline all the strongly stressed words (*got, brother, Yes, have*). Say the sentences. Students repeat them.
- Tell students they are going to listen to some questions with *can*. In the mother tongue, ask: *Do you think 'can' will be strong or weak?* (weak).
- 🔲 Play the cassette. Students listen carefully to the pronunciation of *can* in questions.
- In the mother tongue, ask: *Which did you hear?* Then say *Can you cook?* twice, the first time with the strong form /kæn/, the second time with the weak form /kən/. Write the question on the board.

Tapescript

Can you speak English?
Can you cook?
Can you play football?

8b

- 🔲 Play the cassette again. Students listen and repeat.

8c

- On the board, write: *Yes, I can* under *Can you cook?* Ask students whether they expect to hear the strong form or the weak form of *can* (the strong form /kæn/). Ask the question *Can you cook?* again, and point to the answer. Students answer, using the strong form of *can*. Say: *Let's see if you're right.*
- 🔲 Play the cassette. Students listen carefully, and report back on the pronunciation of positive short answer forms.

Tapescript

A Can you speak English?
B Yes, I can.
A Can you cook?
B Yes, I can.
A Can you play football? …
B Yes, I can.

Answer key
Different

8d

- Add *No, I can't* to the sentences on the board. Ask students to say it. Then ask if it's strong or weak (strong – /kɑ:nt/).
- 📟 Play the cassette. Students listen and repeat questions and short answer forms.

Tapescript

A Can you speak English?
B Yes, I can.
A Can you speak Chinese?
B No, I can't.
A Can you cook?
B Yes, I can.
A Can you play football?
B No, I can't.
A Can you play volleyball?
B No, I can't.

8e

- Explain to students that this time they will hear the questions only, and that they should answer each with information about themselves, using either *Yes, I can* or *No, I can't*.
- Ask students to recall the five questions, but do not let them write them down.
- 📟 Play the cassette. Students listen and answer together.
- Play the cassette again. Gesture to individual students around the class to answer each question.

Tapescript

Can you speak English?
Can you speak Chinese?
Can you cook?
Can you play football?
Can you play volleyball?

9

- Go through the list of activities. Explain any unfamiliar words. Ask individual students round the class to make questions with *Can you …?* Make sure students are using the weak form /kən/, and placing stress on the main verb.
- Students work in pairs, taking turns to ask and answer questions, using phrases in the box.
- Walk round listening to pairs. Stop the activity as the first pairs finish the list. Ask three or four students: *What can your partner do? What can't he/she do?*

10

- Make sure students understand what to do: they ask each other questions with *Can you …?*, or answer questions, until they find six things the whole group can do. Ask the class to suggest other

activities to add to the list in Exercise 9, for example, *dive, make coffee, play tennis*. Write them on the board.

- Put students into groups of 4 – 6. Each group should choose one member to write down the activities they can all do. Members of the group take turns asking questions.
- Write a model sentence on the board, for example: *We can all swim*. A representative from each group reports their findings to the class using sentences like the model sentence.

Game 5 ▼

Party tricks

- This is a game which practises the use of *can* in a fun way. Write a list of 'party tricks' (things that not everybody can do) on the board. For example:

  whistle a song   touch your toes   move your ears
  snap your fingers   touch your nose with your tongue
  walk with a book on your head

  Explain the meaning of each phrase. Students work in pairs, asking each other *Can you …?* and trying out the tricks.

Suggested Workbook practice

Page 35, Exercises 1–4

Do you want to be a champion?

Must

Aims

In this section, students learn vocabulary to do with sport, and to talk about obligation, using *must*. The language is presented through listening and reading tasks.

1

Options

- Find out what sports the students are interested in, and what sports they play. In English, ask: *What is your favourite sport? How often do you play it? Do you do training for your sport? Do you watch sports on TV? What sports do you watch? Do you know the names of any famous athletes?*
- Get students to think about an athlete's lifestyle. In the mother tongue, ask: *Do you think top athletes have got an easy, difficult, interesting or boring life? Why?* The class briefly discusses the last question, using phrases from the Useful English box on page 54.

- In the mother tongue, tell students that they are going to hear some rules for an athlete. Students suggest what some of the rules might be.
- Students read sentences 1–5. Make sure they understand *athlete, competition, organize, technique, train* and *trainer*.
- 📟 Play the cassette. Students listen carefully and complete the sentences.
- Check answers. Then ask: *What do you think 'must' means?*

Tapescript
Right, you want to be a world champion? Listen to me … Here are the rules …
One … You must organize your time carefully. Two … You must train every day. Three … You must eat and drink the right things. Four … You must go to bed early before competitions. Five … You must study the techniques of your sport.

Answer key
1 *your time*   2 *every day*   3 *eat and drink*   4 *go to bed early*
5 *study   your sport*

Option
• If you think students will find the listening task difficult, play the cassette twice, the first time as a gist listening task. Tell them to listen and answer the question: *Who is speaking: an athlete, a journalist, or a trainer?* (a trainer).

2
• Make sure students understand the four titles. Teach *paragraph*. Remind them that in this sort of task, they should just look for words and phrases that help them match paragraphs with titles – they do not need to understand every word.
• Set a time limit of about three minutes. Students read and match.
• Put students into pairs to compare answers, then check answers with the class.

Answer key
a *2*   b *4*   c *1*   d *3*

Option
• 🖭 This text is recorded on the cassette. Get students to listen and read at the same time, matching titles and paragraphs as they do so.

3
• Read the instructions, and ask students to translate the example – this will show you whether or not they understand the meaning of *must*. Do not explain grammar yet.
• Guide students to the relevant parts of the text. Ask: *Which paragraphs talk about these rules?* (paragraphs 3 and 4).
• Students read the text again more carefully, and write a list of rules, as in the example.
• Students check their answers with a partner.

Answer key
1 *You must learn to relax.*   2 *You must also get a lot of sleep.*
3 *You must want/learn to win.*

Work it out: *must*

4a
• Read the exercise with the students, and make sure they understand the meaning of sentences 1–3.
• Students work individually, choosing the sentence which best explains the meaning of *must*.

Answer key
2 *that something is very important to do*

4b
• Help students to think of a topic to write about. In the mother tongue, ask: *Do you play any sports? Do you play a musical instrument? What is your favourite school subject? Do you like cooking? drawing? chess? Do you have other hobbies? Does anyone you know have an interesting hobby?* On the board, make a list of all the interests, sports, school subjects and hobbies that students mention.
• Each student chooses a topic to write about. They can write a title for their list of rules, such as *Do you want to be a good cook? Do you want to play chess? Do you want to study Maths?* They then write four rules like those they wrote in Exercise 3.

Suggested Workbook practice
Page 36, Exercise 1

Days of the week
Aims
In this section, students learn the days of the week, prepositions of time, and more sports words. Tasks provide further practice of *must* and *can*. Students plan and write a short article.

1a

Background information
A Visitors' Book is an information booklet describing facilities and events in a town or area. They are often given away free in tourist information centres, local libraries or at stations.

Options
• Quickly revise clock time. Write on the board:
   3.00   5.30   9.15   10.20   10.45   10.50.
   Students say the time, using *o'clock*, *past*, and *to*, for example: *quarter past nine*.
• Teach the days of the week, using prepared cards (see Materials preparation 3).

• Tell students to read through the Sports Centre programme, and to make a list of all the sports and activities mentioned. Ask: *Which sports do you know?* Explain or translate sports that they don't know. Then, in the mother tongue, ask: *Which sports would you like to try? Look at the programme to see if you can attend the sessions.* Encourage them to make comments, such as *I can't do water aerobics, because I see my friends on Friday night. I can go to badminton on Wednesday.*
• Read the instructions, and make sure students understand what to listen for. Ask: *What sort of information could change?* (times, days, activities).
• 🖭 Play the cassette. Students listen and make a note of programme changes.
• In the mother tongue, ask: *How many changes were there?* (three). Check the answers with the class.

Tapescript

Hello. This is King's Sports Centre. Here are some changes to our evening programme for this week. On Monday there is no water aerobics at half past eight. On Tuesday the badminton starts at nine o'clock, not half past eight. There are no changes for Wednesday. On Thursday children's swimming starts at seven o'clock, not half past seven. There are no changes for Friday or Saturday … Don't forget, the centre is closed on Sunday evening.

Answer key

1   *No water aerobics on Monday*
2   *Badminton starts at 9.00, not 8.30, on Tuesday*
3   *Children's swimming starts at 7.00, not 7.30, on Thursday*

1b

- 📼 Students listen and repeat the days of the week.
- Make sure students stress the first syllable: <u>MON</u>DAY, <u>TUES</u>DAY, <u>WEDNES</u>DAY (/'wenzdeɪ/), <u>THURS</u>DAY, <u>FRI</u>DAY. Ask them which days they think are the most difficult to say or remember. Give extra practice of these words.

Tapescript

Monday… Tuesday …Wednesday …Thursday …Friday …Saturday … Sunday.

2

- Tell students to look through the text and guess what actual words or sort of words are missing (prepositions, days, times).
- 📼 Students listen and complete the text.

Answer key

on Saturday   at six   in   on   on   at

Option

- Get students to close their books so they can concentrate on listening, rather than having to listen and write at the same time. They then complete the gaps from memory. Play the cassette again for them to check the answers.

Work it out: prepositions of time

3

- Students use the examples in the text in Exercise 2 to match prepositions with time expressions.

Answer key

1 *at*   2 *in*   3 *on*

Option

- Practise the prepositions. Students close their books. Call out time expressions at random. Students say the right preposition with the expression. For example:

Teacher		Class
half past five	→	**at** half past five
the winter	→	**in** the winter
the weekend	→	**at** the weekend
Wednesday	→	**on** Wednesday
Friday morning	→	**on** Friday morning
afternoon	→	**in** the afternoon

4a

- Tell students to read through the timetable. Ask questions to check they understand it, for example: *What days of the week can the athletes get up quite late?* (Thursday and Friday). *When do they go running?* (Monday, Wednesday and Friday mornings). *What do you think they do in Video study?* (study techniques). *When are they free?* (Monday at 3.00; Tuesday at 10.00 and 5.00; Wednesday at 10.00 and 3.00; Thursday at 5.00; Friday at 12.00 and all afternoon).
- Tell students to read the instructions. Check that they understand that they must think of other activities, either their own ideas or ideas from the King's Sports Centre programme.
- Students work individually to choose four activities, and to write each on the timetable in a 'free' time.

4b

- Put students into pairs. They decide who is A and who is B. Read the example dialogue. Then demonstrate the task with one student.
- Tell students to hide their timetable from their partner. Point out that partners need to listen carefully to each other's replies. Set a time limit of 3–4 minutes. Any pairs who finish quickly should try to find a time for a second meeting.
- When the time limit is up, stop the role-play and ask round the class: *Can you meet your partner? What day? What time?*

Writing: an article

5a

- Students work independently through the stages of planning a timetable.
- Put students into pairs or small groups. Write a list of instructions on the board:
   1 Choose 5 sports.
   2 Decide what time your club opens and closes (evenings? afternoons? weekends?).
   3 Decide what days it is open, and what days it is closed.
   4 Write the programme. Give two or three times and days for each sport.
   5 Think of a name for the club.
- The pairs or groups work through the list of tasks at their own pace. Go round the class, checking how students are progressing, and helping with ideas and language.

5b

- Read the example article aloud. Make sure that students understand how the article should be organized:
   The [name] club is now open. The sports you can play at the club are [the 5 sports they have chosen]. You can … [students describe the days and times they can play each sport].
- Students individually write their articles.

Option

- Tell students to write final drafts of their timetable and text for homework. If they wish, they can illustrate their article with pictures of sports players or sports equipment.

Suggested Workbook practice

Page 36, Exercises 2–4
Page 37, Exercise 5

The OK Club
Where's the money?

Aims

This section continues the photo-story. It presents informal English in a lively context, and brings together the language students have been practising in the unit, as well as revising language learned previously. In this episode, Jack realizes he has left the money-box at the club. When they get there, they cannot find it – nor do they find Emma's explanatory note.

1a

Option

● Dictate the summary of the last episode. See Tip 13 below.

● Explain the exercise, then get individual students to read sentences 1–4. Check that they understand them. For example, in the mother tongue, ask: *Which situations would make them happy?* (1 and, perhaps, 4). *Which would make them unhappy?* (2 and 3).

● Put students into pairs or small groups to discuss the sentences and pictures, using the phrases from the Useful English section on page 54. Suggest they look at the faces in the story. Ask: *Are they happy?* (they are obviously unhappy).

● Students guess which sentence is most likely.

1b

● 📼 Play the cassette. Students listen and read the story to check their guess.

Answer key

3

2

● Tell students to try and remember the answers without looking back at the text, and then to discuss their ideas with a partner.

● Students read the text again to check their answers.

Answer key

1 *Dave*　2 *Emma, Ricky and Carol*　3 *No, they can't.*

Tip 13 ★

Giving a dictation (1)

● Give a dictation in stages:
 1　Write key words and phrases from the text on the board, for example, *episode, leader, hopeless at remembering, money-box, leave (something behind), coffee cup*. Check that students understand them. If this is the class's first dictation, teach *full stop* and *comma*.
 2　Read the text aloud in a clear voice, and at a natural speed. Students listen only.
 3　Read the text again, including puctuation marks, pausing after every few words to allow students time to write.

Pauses should come at natural points between phrases (see the example text below). Tell students that if they miss anything, they should leave a space.
 4　Read the text once more, without pauses, for students to check what they have written, or to fill in gaps.
 5　When you have finished, students compare their text with a partner.
 6　Ask a student to come to the board and write the first sentence. Then ask another to write the second sentence, and so on. Alternatively, write the correct text on the board yourself. Students swap texts and mark each other's work.
 Example dictation:
 In the last episode, / the club members agree / that Jack can be / the leader of Project OK. / But Jack is hopeless / at remembering things, / and forgets / to take home / the money for the project. / Emma finds the money-box / on the table, / and takes it home with her. / She leaves a message for Jack / under a coffee cup / on the table.

Set the pace

3a

● Students find the three phrases, and use context and pictures to guess the meaning in the usual way.

Option

● If students have difficulty guessing, give more examples: for 1, look at your watch and say: *Oh it's late!* Then gesture for everyone to leave the room quickly, and say: *Let's get a move on!* For 2, pretend to be tired, sit on a chair, and say: *Wait, wait! Hang on a minute!* For 3, pretend to look at a piece of homework, shake your head as if you are not pleased, then say angrily: *This is bad work! It's not good enough!*

3b

● 📼 Students listen and repeat the three phrases. Encourage them to imitate intonation and the speaker's mood, as well as correct pronunciation.

3c

● This story has the three characters expressing their feelings strongly, so it is an interesting episode to act out.

● Discuss the emotions that are expressed in scene 1. Ask in the mother tongue: *How do Jane, Jack and Dave feel and why?* (Jack and Jane are <u>impatient</u> because they want to go shopping for the paint. They are <u>annoyed/irritated</u> because the others are late. Dave arrives out of breath and <u>apologetic</u> because he is late. Then Jack is <u>upset</u> because he realizes he left the money at the club).

● In the mother tongue students describe the characters' emotions in the other scenes.

● Put students into groups of three to practise the dialogue. Go round the groups, encouraging students to read out the dialogue in a dramatic way.

● Call a *Jack* from one group, a *Dave* from another group, and a *Jane* from a third to act out the scenes to the rest of the class.

4

- Read the instructions with the class. Help them to find the answer in the text (it's in scene 2).
- Tell students to think of all the things the club members can't buy, and therefore things they can't do.

Answer key

They can't buy paint, paint brushes or a new kettle. So, they can't paint the Coffee Corner, and they can't make coffee.

5

- Put students into new pairs (see Tip 8, page 37).
- Explain that they should think about their favourite character in the story, and justify their choice to their partner. Remind them of the phrases in the Useful English section.

Suggested Workbook practice

Page 37, Exercise 1

Review

Aims

The Review section summarizes and briefly revises the Key language features of Unit 8: *can/can't* (*cannot*) and *must*, and talking about time.

can/can't (*cannot*) and *must*

- Tell the class to read the explanations and examples, and check that they understand the sentence structure used with modals: no *-s* ending for third person singular; the main verb is an infinitive without *to*. Write this table on the board:

Positive	Negative	Question	Short answers
1 He can cook. 2 She cans swim. 3 They can to play the guitar. 4 We must tell the police.			

Ask: *Which sentences have a grammar mistake?* (2 and 3). *Can you correct them?* Then get them to help you complete the table (see Tip 5, page 30).

Talking about time

- For further practice, do a quick substitution drill (see Tip 11, page 51). Sentence: *You must get up at six o'clock.* Substitutions: *the morning, We, practise, summer, Tuesday, can, the weekend, relax, Sunday, night*.

1

- Get the class to give one or two suggestions for situations 1–4.
- Students write sentences individually, using *can*, then share their sentences with a partner.

2

- Put students into pairs to think of rules for the English class. After 2–3 minutes, tell pairs to join up to form groups of four and

share their ideas. Allow groups another 4–5 minutes to prepare a written list of rules, using *must*. Walk round, helping with language and ideas.

3

- This exercise revises the language of routines, and practises prepositions of time.
- Do the exercise orally with the class. Students write their answers in class or at home.

Vocabulary

- *Languages.* Students add the languages from Exercise 1b, page 54 to the map on Workbook page 75. Where necessary, they also write the countries and nationalities.
- *Sports and hobbies.* Students add new sports to the word family on Workbook page 76. They start a new page in their vocabulary books for Hobbies and Interests.
- *Time.* Students write sentences combining days of the week and prepositions of time on the *Time* page of their vocabulary books. The sentences should say how they feel about each day, for example: *I like Monday. On Monday I sometimes go to the cinema in the evening. Saturday is a good day. I often see my friends on Saturday evening.* Students could also write acrostic poems (see Tip 14 below) about days of the week.

Tip 14 ★

Creative writing: acrostic poems

- One way of practising both specific vocabulary and the written language is to get students to write 'acrostic' poems. These are poems based around one word or phrase, which is highlighted. Poems should look attractive. For example:

Tuesday

It's no**T** a bad day.

I **U**sually have a good time.

In the **E**vening I can play my favourite sport.

Sport, **S**port, sport

My frien**D**s and I play.

Wh**A**t is our favourite sport?

Volle**Y**ball, of course.

Write the example on the board. In pairs or groups of three, students choose another word from the vocabulary set and write a similar poem.

Freewheeling

- Say: *I feel happy. I feel sad. I feel angry.* Get students to guess the meaning of *feel*. On the board, write: *Feelings: happy, sad, angry*.
- 📼 Play the cassette. Students listen to the music, and read the lyrics.
- 📼 Play the cassette again. Students sing along to the music.

Suggested Workbook practice

Page 38, Exercises 1 and 2

Preparation for Unit 9

Workbook page 38, Exercise 3

Workbook answer key

That's amazing

1 3 *No, she can't.*
   4 *Yes, he can.*
   5 *Yes, she can.*
   6 *No, he can't.*
   7 *Yes, they can.*

2 4 *Carlos can walk for 20 kilometres but he can't run fast.*
   5 *Eleni can't play the drums or swim.*
   6 *Levent can swim and he can run fast.*

3a *riding a bike* 2
   playing football 1
   cooking 4
   playing volleyball 3

b 1 *He can't play football.*
   2 *She can ride a bike.*
   3 *He can play volleyball.*
   4 *She can't cook.*

4 *Student's own answers*

Do you want to be a champion?

1 2 *We must wear trainers in the gym.*
   3 *We must pay for aerobics classes before they start.*
   4 *We must use the correct equipment.*
   5 *We must put the equipment away after games classes.*

2a 1 *in* 2 *on* 3 *on* 4 *at* 5 *in* 6 *at* 7 *in*
   8 *at* 9 *on* 10 *at*

b 2 *The English class starts at four o'clock on Tuesday.*
   3 *The club closes at eleven o'clock.*
   4 *The swimming pool closes at a quarter past six in the summer.*

3 3 *Monday* 4 *Wednesday* 5 *Saturday* 6 *Thursday*
   7 *Friday* 8 *Sunday*

4a 2 *judo* 3 *running* 4 *swimming* 5 *badminton*
   6 *aerobics* 7 *volleyball* 8 *basketball*

b 2 *volleyball*
   3 *judo*
   4 *Student's own answers*

5 *My friend's gym is open every day of the week. It's open from seven o'clock in the morning until eleven o'clock at night from Monday to Friday. On Saturday it's open from eight in the morning to eleven at night and on Sunday it's open from nine o'clock in the morning to ten o'clock at night.*

Where's the money?

1 1 *How are you?*
   2 *Monday evening*
   3 *That's not good enough!*
   4 *Hang on a minute.*
   5 *What time?*
   6 *in the morning*

Skills: sports routines

1 2 *He plays basketball for his city.*
   3 *He trains for a few hours every day.*
   4 *He starts his day at the swimming pool.*
   5 *He works in the mornings.*
   6 *He goes running on Wednesdays and Thursdays.*
   7 *He's usually free on Sundays.*

2

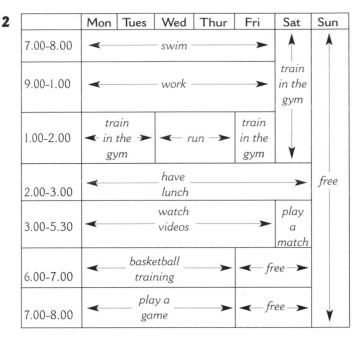

	Mon	Tues	Wed	Thur	Fri	Sat	Sun
7.00-8.00	←		swim		→	↑	↑
9.00-1.00	←		work		→	train in the gym	
1.00-2.00	train in the gym →	←	run	→	← train in the gym	↓	free
2.00-3.00	←		have lunch		→		
3.00-5.30	←		watch videos		→	play a match	
6.00-7.00	←	basketball training		→		← free →	
7.00-8.00	←		play a game		→	← free →	↓

Prepare for Unit 9

3a 1 *h* 2 *g* 3 *a* 4 *d* 5 *e* 6 *c* 7 *f* 8 *b*
b 1 *c* 2 *b* 3 *h* 4 *d*

Unit 9

Syllabus

Topic
Travelling: *coral reefs*
Having a wonderful time ...?; *holidays*
The OK Club

Grammar
The present continuous
Adverbs of manner

Function
Describing what is happening
Talking about the weather

Vocabulary
The weather
Directions
Holidays

Reading
Finding information
Guessing meaning from context
Understanding mood

Listening
Identifying key information
Identifying main message
Identifying a speaker from manner and main message

Writing
Writing a postcard
Creating an extended dialogue

Speaking
Discussing holidays
Checking information
Asking about spending habits

Pronunciation
/ŋ/

Vocabulary

Key vocabulary

beach	miserable, -bly	tent
boat	north	thousand
camp	package holiday	tour guide
climb	pollution	tourist
cloudy	raining	traveller
coast	sea	warm
comfortable	shine	weather
coral reef	skiing	wet
cruise	slow, -ly	What's going on?
environment	snow	windy
grow	south	wonderful
island	steady, -ily	

Other vocabulary

break(v)	floor	metres
business	happen	mountain
danger (in ...)	hard (adv)	piece
die	high	slope
everything	immediate, -ly	soon
explain	independent	stand
fishermen	kill	through

Materials preparation

1 Dictionaries for page 60 Exercise 1a, page 61 Exercise 6b, and page 63 Exercise 4c.

2 For Game 6 page 90: make cards suggesting actions.

3 For page 63, Exercise 5 Option: make cards suggesting actions and adverbs (see Game 6 page 90).

4 For page 63, Exercise 1a Option 1: make cards with simple drawings depicting types of weather, for example, the sun (*It's sunny*), a snowflake (*It's snowing*), a scarf and hat (*It's cold*). See Workbook page 40, Exercise 3 for ideas.

5 For page 63, Exercise 3 Option: make one photocopy of Worksheet 3 on Teacher's Book page 148 for each pair of students. Cut each worksheet in half.

Travelling
The present continuous

Aims

In this section, students learn to talk about activities and processes that are taking place at the present moment, using positive, negative, question and short answer forms of the present continuous. They also learn to describe causes and consequences, and to talk about travel and tourism.

1a

Background information

Package holidays are offered by travel companies as an 'all-inclusive' holiday. The company has responsibility for organizing all holiday arrangements, such as flights, accommodation, excursions, and meals. They are often able to offer very good prices because they arrange cheap group bookings with large hotels. It is usual for a package holiday group to be accompanied by a tour guide, who will deal with any problems during the holiday.

Options

- Quickly revise *must* and *can*. Ask students to tell you three rules: one for home, one for school, and one for a public place like a restaurant or cinema, for example, *You mustn't talk loudly in a cinema.* Then do a question-and-answer chain round the class (see Tip 9, page 39) for *can*, for example: *Can you speak Swahili, Bob? No, I can't. Can you spell 'photograph', Joan?*

- Brainstorm vocabulary and associations linked to the word *holiday(s)*. Note that singular and plural can be used interchangeably: *Where are you going for your holiday(s)?* Draw a circle or an eye-catching shape on the board, and write *Holidays* in the centre. Ask questions to get ideas from students of words and activities they associate with holidays, for example: *Do you like holidays? Why? Where do you go? What do you do? Who do you see?* Gradually build up a word-map. For example:

- Students look at the picture. In the mother tongue, ask: *Where are these people? What does 'Customs' mean? What happens at Customs?* (officials check your baggage). *Can you see an exchange bureau? Are there a lot of people in front of it? What do they want to do there?* (change money).

- Students look up *package holiday* in a dictionary. If their dictionaries do not have the whole phrase, let them look the words up separately, then ask them to guess what the two words together might mean (clue: in a package you put everything together).

- Each student looks at the picture again, and tries to identify which passengers are on a package holiday. Do not give the answer yet.

1b

- Explain the meaning of *local, stay together* and *tour guide*.

- To show they have correctly understood the concept, students read the four descriptions and tick those which describe what happens on a package holiday.

Answer key
1   3   4

1c

- Students look at the picture again and find people who are not on a package holiday. Ask: *Why do you think he/she isn't on a package holiday?* Help students with vocabulary to explain their reasons, for example, *They haven't got holiday clothes. They've got briefcases. They aren't in a big group.*

- Read the instructions and descriptions 1 and 2. Ask: *Which people are business travellers/independent travellers?*

2

- Ask: *Where is the tour guide?* (at the front of the picture. He's the man with the phone). *What is the name of his company?* (*Sunset*).

- Explain that students are going to listen to the tour guide describing the groups of passengers. They need only understand the gist of the conversation to find out who is being described, then write the order numbers in the boxes.

- 📼 Play the cassette. Students listen and write the order of the descriptions.

....

Tapescript

Elizabeth Ramli?
Ramli Yes … oh, hi, Elizabeth.
Elizabeth Are you at the airport?
Ramli Yes, I am. I'm waiting for my new group of tourists … but I can't see them here.
Elizabeth Is their plane there?
Ramli Yes, it is. A lot of the passengers are standing in the baggage hall now – they're waiting for their bags to come through …
Elizabeth Your new group is all young people, I think …
Ramli I know, but there are a lot of young people here … two young men are standing near the door … but they're carrying small computers and things – I think they're business travellers. Yes, a man's taking their bags out to a taxi now.
Elizabeth Can you see any other young people?
Ramli There are two young people in jeans and T-shirts near the Exchange desk, but they're independent travellers, I think. They're changing some money. … Ah, it's OK. A group of young tourists is coming into the baggage hall now, Elizabeth. … Yes, I think it's my group … They're looking round for me. I must go and say hello.
Elizabeth OK Ramli, bye!

....

Answer key

the package holiday makers 3   the business travellers 1
the independent travellers 2

3

- Tell students that they are going to match parts of sentences that explain what people are doing in the picture.

- All the verbs in this exercise are in the present continuous form. If students are unsure of its meaning, give a simple example. Say:

I am standing. You are sitting. Sit down, and say: *Now I am sitting*. Keep the explanation short.

● Do the first one with the students, by giving a wrong answer, and letting them correct it. Say: *The tour guide is … um … changing some money.* Choose a student to give the right answer. Students continue in pairs.

Answer key
1 *talking on the telephone*   2 *answering a question*   3 *smiling at the two young visitors*   4 *changing some money*   5 *looking for the tour guide*

Work it out: the present continuous (1)

4a
● Students underline *is/are* at the end of the first half of each sentence in Exercise 3, and the verb + *-ing* at the beginning of the second half of each sentence.
● Students work individually, then compare answers with a partner.

4b
● Students read the rules, check back to the sentences, then complete the rules.

Answer key
1 *be*   2 *be   not*

4c
● Check that students fully understand the sentence, but allow them time to decide individually if the description is true or false.

Answer key
True

4d
● Students look at the picture again, and tell you whose actions have not been described in Exercise 3 (the old woman, the porters, the business travellers). Write them on the board.
● Do this exercise orally. Ask students about each person or group. Individual students respond. Help them with vocabulary and the verb.

Answer key
Possible sentences: A man is helping an old woman.   The business travellers are talking to a man.   One business traveller is holding a newspaper.   A man is taking their bags.

5

Background information
Coral and coral reefs. Students probably know of coral as a dark or bright red rock-like material that can be made into jewellery. It is, in fact, an organic substance made from the bodies of tiny sea animals. It grows very slowly in great underwater formations known

as *reefs*, which are home to many types of underwater animals. They are therefore very important for the oceanic ecosystem, but unfortunately easily damaged. The text on Student's Book page 61 describes the environmental causes and results of this damage.

● This is a gist reading exercise – students do not need to read every word, only enough to find out the general topic of each paragraph.
● Make sure students understand the questions, especially the key words *coral* and *reef*.
● Give students no more than two minutes to find the answers. Check them orally, and for each ask: *What words helped you to decide?*

Answer key
3 *(clue: Australian, Africa, Central America, the Pacific Islands)*
4 *(clue: tourists are visiting/walking/breaking)*
2 *(clue: grow from the dead bodies …).* Note that the first is a general, introductory paragraph.

6a
● Students look at the words, find them in the text, and underline them.
● 🔊 Play the cassette. Students listen with their books closed.
● Students read the text again, and use context (the words and phrases on either side) to guess the meaning of the unfamiliar words.

6b
● Students look up the words in their dictionaries to check them.
● Discuss the best heading for a word-map of the main text vocabulary, such as *Nature* or *The Environment*. Words to include: *reef, coral, island, environment, sea animals/plants, floor (of the sea), coast, diver, fishermen, pollution*.
● Discuss where to write other words from the text, such as *dead, die/dying, body/ies, visit, kill*.

6c
● This exercise practises the use of pronouns as reference words to avoid repetition in a text.
● Do the first one with the class. Say: *Find the word 'they' in paragraph 1. Underline it. Read the sentence.* Then ask in the mother tongue: *Is 'they' singular or plural? How many plural words are there in the first sentence? What are they? Which one can 'bring good business to these places'?*

- Students work individually to answer questions 2–4.

Answer key

1 *tourists*   2 *coral reefs*   3 *reefs*   4 *divers and fishermen*

7a

- Make sure students understand the question, including the verb *cause*.
- Students guess the answer before they listen.
- 📼 Play the cassette. Students listen and confirm their guesses.

Tapescript

Guide … and we're starting to have problems with the environment in this country, in the towns, on the islands, and in the sea, too … on the reefs around the islands …
Interviewer Are the tourists causing these problems, too?
Guide Yes, they are. More and more tourists are visiting the reefs these days … more people are walking on the reefs …
Interviewer Is the coral dying?
Guide Yes, it is. People are killing it when they walk on it … and people are taking pieces of coral away with them …
Interviewer And more divers are diving near the reefs here too, aren't they? Are all these divers breaking the coral?
Guide No, they aren't. Divers usually know that you can easily break it and they're usually very careful.
Interviewer What about the local fishermen? Is the pollution from their boats killing the coral?
Guide No, it isn't. Not now. Before, yes. But the local fishermen now understand about pollution, so they don't go near the reefs.

Answer key

tourists

7b

- In this exercise, students listen more carefully to hear specific answers to specific questions.
- 📼 Play the cassette again. Students listen and match questions with responses.

Answer key

1 *Yes, they are.*   2 *Yes, it is.*   3 *No, they aren't.*   4 *No, it isn't.*

Work it out: the present continuous (2)

8a

- Students use the sentences in 7b to help them complete a grammar chart for the present continuous.

Answer key

be: *am   am   is   are*
Statement: *is*
Question: *Is*
Short answer: *is*

8b

- Remind students how questions are formed in English. Write statements on the board: *He has got a big car. They like coffee. I want some eggs. The children have got a problem*. Ask individual students to write the questions below them. Then erase the statements, leaving the questions, and ask other students to write the statements again.

- Students look at the questions in Exercise 7 again, and write the statements. Check answers orally.

Option

- Students work in pairs, asking and answering questions about coral reefs, using prompts on the board. For example:
  1 tourists / cause / problems ?   2 coral / die ?
  3 divers / break / coral ?   4 pollution / boats / kill / coral ?

Suggested Workbook practice

Page 39, Exercises 1 and 2

Having a wonderful time
Adverbs and adjectives

Aims

In this section, students learn vocabulary for describing conditions, experience and feelings encountered by people on holiday, including adverbs of manner, and types of holiday.

1

Option

- Write the following on the board:

	skiing holiday.
	camping holiday
I'd like a	cruise.
	city holiday.
	beach holiday.
	walking holiday.

Check that students understand all the vocabulary. Ask several students: *Which holiday would you like to have?* Then, for each holiday ask: *Where can you have a (skiing) holiday?*

- Students match pictures with types of holiday.
- Check answers. Ask students, in the mother tongue, what the clues are in the pictures.

Answer key

Top: E   Middle: B   Bottom: A

2a

- Tell students they have 30 seconds to look quickly through the postcards to see which is the only writer who is having a good time. This will make students scan the texts (read bits of, not every word).

Answer key

2

2b

- Students read the texts more carefully and match each text with a picture.
- When checking answers, have students tell you the words in the postcards which helped (1 *pool*, 2 *mountains, skiing, slopes*, 3 *Camp, tent*).

Answer key

1 *E*   2 *A*   3 *B*

Option

- Play *Mimes* (see Game 6 below, and Materials preparation 2).

3

- Students discuss their dream holidays in groups of 3–4. They decide which is their group's 'dream holiday', and discuss the reasons for their choice.

Game 6 ▼
Mimes

- This is an excellent way of practising continuous tenses. The version described here is for the present continuous. Prepare cards with actions on them. For example:

  Play basketball. Buy a car. Eat a pizza. Run for a bus.
  Read a book. Watch television. Dive into a pool.
  Play the guitar.

  Student A takes a card and thinks how to mime the action. He or she asks: *What am I doing?* and then performs the mime. The class tries to guess the activity. The student who guesses correctly, using a present continuous verb (example: *You're running for a bus*), does the next mime. Shyer students do not always enjoy performing in front of all the class, so do not insist if a student seems reluctant to do a mime.

Work it out: adverbs of manner

4a

- Tell students to look at the postcards again, and to find and underline any adverbs of manner. Give them an example to help. Say: *Look at postcard 1. How are the people sitting round the pool?* (miserably).
- Students complete the lists of adjectives and adverbs of manner.

Answer key

warmly   badly   miserable   immediately

Options

- To check that students understand the difference between adverbs and adjectives, write example sentences on the board: *1 Jack has got a loud voice. 2 Jack talks loudly.* Explain that in sentence 1 *loud* (an adjective) describes *voice* (a noun). Write *Adjectives describe nouns*. Ask: *What does 'loudly' describe?* (*talks*). *So what part of speech do adverbs describe?* (verbs).
- To check that students understand the concept of manner, explain that 'manner' is a way of doing things. Ask: *What ways are there of driving?* (slowly, fast, well, badly, dangerously).

4b

- Remind students of the same change from *-y* to *-i* in plural nouns and third person verb forms, for example, *family – families, study – studies*.
- Ask students to think of any other adjectives that end in *-y*. Get students to say the adverb form, for example, *happy – happily*.
- Students write the adverb form of *steady*.

Answer key

steadily

4c

- Tell students to look at the adverbs in the postcards again. Ask: *Are there any that do not end in -ly?* (hard).
- Ask: *What other irregular adverbs are there?* Look at 4c. Students read and find the irregular adverbs *hard*, *well* and *fast*, and look them up in their dictionaries.

4d

- Students use the verbs and adverbs of manner to write six sentences about their own abilities. Walk round as they work, checking that they are using the adverbs correctly.

5

- Students work with a partner to ask and talk about their abilities, using the sentences they made in Exercise 4d.

Option

- Play *Mimes* (see Game 6, above), but with adverbs as well as verbs. On each card, write an action and a way of doing that action. The student must mime the action in the given manner. The rest of the class guesses the activity. Possible cards:

play tennis slowly	shop quietly	cook angrily
read a book fast	play the piano sadly	walk happily

Suggested Workbook practice

Page 40, Exercises 1 and 2
Page 41, Exercises 1 and 2

The weather

Aims

In this section, students learn weather expressions, and continue to practise adverbs of manner through listening tasks. They also learn about the sound /ŋ/.

1a

Options

- Use picture cards (see Materials preparation 4) to teach weather words and phrases.
- Remind students of the question *What's he/she like?* from Unit 3, and the sort of response: *He's tall. He's got brown hair.* Now ask: *What's the weather like? Is it sunny?* Students answer. Tell students to look at the postcards on page 62 again. Ask: *What's the weather like in postcard 1/2/3?* Students look for weather words and phrases in the texts of the three postcards.

- This is a gist listening exercise. Tell students they are going to hear the writer of one of the postcards making a phone call. The information about the holiday and the writer's mood should tell them which writer it is.
- ▣ Play the cassette. Students decide who is telephoning.
- Check answers. Then ask what information on cassette gave them the answer (raining, wet clothes, terrible food, immediately).

Tapescript

… the weather's terrible. It's raining all the time and it's really cold. In fact, maybe it's snowing now … all my clothes are wet, … and I can't eat these meals here – you know, they just give us potatoes the whole time … I want to come home immediately, please.

Answer key

Postcard writer 3

1b

- Students complete the sentence describing the speaker's mood and manner.
- 🔲 Play the cassette again to check answers.

Answer key

miserably   quietly

Vocabulary: the weather

- Tell students to look at the phrases in the box. In the mother tongue, ask: *Which words are stressed in each sentence?* (the weather words).
- Say the sentences for students to repeat (see Tip 1, page 9).

2

- 🔲 Play the cassette. Students listen and tick the phrases they hear.
- Ask: *Which phrases are not on cassette?*

Tapescript

A What's the weather like?
B It's terrible … It's beautiful … It's warm … The sun's shining … It's raining … It's snowing … It's sunny … It's cloudy … It's windy.

Answer key

All of them except *It's hot* and *It's cold*.

Options

- Students repeat the expressions, placing the stress on the correct syllable.
- Students look back at the pictures on page 62. Ask: *What's the weather like in picture E? … picture B? … picture A?* Students describe the weather, using the language they have learned.

Pronunciation: /ŋ/

3a

- This exercise makes students aware of the pronunciation of the *-ing* ending /ɪŋ/. The letter *g* is not pronounced separately but, with the letter *n* it forms the sound /ŋ/.
- 🔲 Play the cassette. Students listen and repeat.
- Practise with individual students. Say, for example: *snow*. The student responds: *snowing … It's snowing*. Do this quickly so that more students can participate.

Tapescript

rain…raining…It's raining.
snow…snowing…It's snowing.
shining…The sun's shining.

3b

- Explain to students that they are going to hear a weather forecast for Britain. After the forecast, there are some questions for them to answer about what they heard.
- Teach points of the compass: *north, south, east* and *west*.
- 🔲 Play the cassette up to the end of the weather forecast. Students listen and identify the places on the map.
- Say: *Listen again, then answer the questions*.
- Play the cassette again, this time with the questions, too. Students listen carefully and answer each question. Pause between questions. Students answer the questions orally or in writing.

Tapescript

A And finally, here are today's weather reports from around the country … In London and the south it's a warm, sunny day. In the east it's cold and cloudy. In the west it's raining at the moment and there's a lot of water on the roads, so drive carefully. In the north of Britain we have some snow on the mountains today.
B What's the weather like in London and the south?
What's the weather like in the east?
What's the weather like in the west?
What's the weather like in the north?

3c

- Discuss today's weather with the class.
- Students individually write two or three sentences about the weather today.

Option

- Give out one copy of Worksheet 3 to each pair of students (see Materials preparation 5). Pairs ask and answer questions in turn to find the missing weather information. Check that they understand that they must fill in the empty thermometers, and direct their attention to the key of symbols.

Writing: a postcard

4

- Help students to think of ideas and to plan their writing by following these stages:
  1 Brainstorming – students in pairs choose the type of holiday, the place, the month or time of year, activities and weather.
  2 Planning – students write notes in the form of answers to the questions.
  3 Writing a first draft – this can be done in class or for homework. Remind students to keep it short, as it is a postcard, not a letter.
  4 Editing – students comment on and check each other's first draft.
  5 Students write a final draft.

Option

- Students write their text on one half of a piece of paper shaped like a very large postcard, and draw a picture of their holiday location next to it. Display the postcards.

Suggested Workbook practice

Page 40, Exercises 3 and 4

The OK Club
Detective work

Aims
This section continues the photo-story. It presents informal English in a lively context, and brings together the language students have been practising in the unit, as well as revising language learned previously. In this episode, Jack, Jane and Dave are still worrying about the missing money-box, but find out what has happened to it. Emma, Ricky and Carol are plotting something which they find very amusing.

1a

Option
- Get students to summarize what happened in the last episode. Write some word prompts on the board, and ask students to connect the words to tell the story:

      Jane   Jack   Dave   meet   paint
      Carol   late   shops
      Jack   not got   money   in club
      look for   money-box   not find   or note
      Jack   police   Dave   Emma   ideas

- Students look at the pictures and work out their answer to each statement.

1b
- 📼 Play the cassette. Students listen and check their answers.

Answer key
*Jack is talking to Ricky: False   Ricky is sitting with Carol: True
Ricky and Carol are laughing: True   Jack is laughing too: False*

2
- Explain what students have to do, and read out the example. Remind students that if they think their partner has answered incorrectly, they can say *No, that's wrong*, and ask the question again.
- Put students into pairs to take turns asking and answering questions from the prompts. Walk round, checking that they are using present continuous correctly.

Set the pace

3a
- 📼 Do this exercise in the usual way, playing the cassette and pausing it for students to work out the meaning of the phrases from the context and tone of voice.

Answer key
1 *Yes, of course.*   2 *What's happening?*   3 *Ricky's home.*

3b
- 📼 Play the cassette. Student listen and repeat the three phrases, paying special attention to intonation.

4
- Students close their books. Read out Ricky's first sentence in picture 2: *Hi, Jack …* in the mother tongue, ask: *What do you*

think that Jack said before this? (*Hello, Ricky. It's Jack here.*). *What do you think Jack will say next?* Students make guesses.
- Tell them to open their books and look at the speech, then ask again: *What do you think Jack will say next?* Students revise their ideas. Write the dialogue so far on the board.
- Put students into pairs to work out Jack's side of the rest of the dialogue. They then write the whole dialogue.

5
- Students take the parts of Jack and Ricky and practise the dialogue in their pairs.
- Choose pairs to read their dialogues to the class. The class discusses the details.

Option
- Students change partners between Exercises 4 and 5.

6
- Put students into groups of four. Tell them to look at pictures 3 and 4 again.
- Ask: *What are Emma, Carol and Ricky laughing about?* The groups discuss possibilities for 2–3 minutes. If any groups appear to be having difficulty thinking of ideas, ask: *Who likes who in the story?*
- A representative of each group shares the group's ideas with the rest of the class. The class briefly discusses which idea they think is most likely.

Suggested Workbook practice
Page 42, Exercises 1 and 2

Review
Aims
The Review section summarizes and briefly revises they Key language features of Unit 9: the present continuous, and adverbs of manner.

The present continuous
- Students read the explanation, then close their books. Ask: *When do we use the present continuous?*
- Do a quick substitution drill (see Tip 11, page 51) to see how fluent students are in forming the present continuous. Starting sentence: *I'm washing some clothes.* Substitutions: *She, Is she?, they, not, the car, he, we, drive.*
- Write as a list on the board: *I stand   2 change   3 sit.* Ask individual students to come and write the *-ing* form of each verb. If a student is wrong, ask another student to try. When all three *-ing* forms are right, ask: *How do we form type 1 verbs?* (just add *-ing*). *How do we form type 2 verbs?* (take off the *-e* and add *-ing*). *How do we form type 3 verbs?* (double the final consonant and add *-ing*). Tell students to look back through pages 60–62, find more verbs, and add them to the lists.

Adverbs of manner
- See Tip 5, page 30, and revise the adverbs of manner.

1a
- Students look at the pictures and write sentences. Writing correct sentences is more important than having right answers.

1b

- Students compare their ideas with a partner. Check that students are using the language correctly, for example, A: *I think number 1 is an elephant. It's eating an apple. What do you think?* B: *Yes, I agree it's an elephant. But I think it's playing football.*

Answer key

1 It's an elephant. It's playing football.   2 It's an elephant. It's standing in a box. 3 It's a Mexican. He's riding a bicycle.   4 Its a koala. It's climbing a tree.

2a

- Students individually find the six adjectives, and write their adverb form.

Answer key

Horizontal: loud – loudly   good – well
Vertical: slow – slowly   noisy – noisily   bad – badly   hungry – hungrily

2b

- Students write sentences using the adverbs. Students can write about themselves or about someone or something else. Check that they are using the right adverb form in the right position in their sentences.

Vocabulary

- *Weather*. Students can draw or copy a weather map with different symbols, and add labels.
- *Directions*. Students draw a compass and label the four main directions, *north*, *south*, *east* and *west*.
- *Holidays*. Students make small word-maps for each type of holiday.

Suggested Workbook practice

Page 39, Exercises 3 and 4
Page 41, Exercise 3

Freewheeling

a

- Students use the symbols and rhymes as clues to the missing words.

Option

- 📻 Students listen to the cassette with books closed.

b

- 📻 Play the cassette. Students listen and check their answers.

Answer key

raining   grey   hot   snowing   blue   sun   shining   sunny

c

- 📻 This chant has a very strong rhythm, so it is excellent for practising word and sentence stress. Play the cassette again. Students listen and repeat the chant.

Option

- Students learn the chant for homework, and look up on a map to find out where the places mentioned are located.

Preparation for Unit 10

Workbook page 42, Exercise 3

Workbook answer key

Travelling

1 2 *He's changing some money. He's carrying a big bag.*
3 *He's running for a bus. The bus is leaving.*
4 *He's riding a bike. He's smiling.*
5 *He's swimming and scuba diving in the sea.*
6 *He's relaxing on a beach. He's sleeping.*

2 2 *Is he changing his money?*
3 *Is he running for a taxi?*
4 *Is he riding a horse?*
5 *Is he swimming in a lake?*
6 *Is he sleeping on the beach.*

3 + ing: *looking, relaxing, sleeping*
-e + ing: *changing, diving, leaving, riding, smiling*
+ consonant + ing: *swimming*

4a 2 *sea* 3 *beach* 4 *mountain* 5 *island* 6 *coast*

b 7 *lake* 8 *forest*

c 1 *island* 2 *coral reef* 3 *coast* 4 *mountains*
5 *beaches* 6 *sea*

Having a wonderful time … ?

1 1 *badly* 2 *carefully* 3 *hungrily* 4 *loud* 5 *miserably*
6 *quietly* 7 *steady* 8 *good* 9 *hard* 10 *fast*

2 2 *She's running fast.*   3 *They're dancing badly.*
4 *He's walking carefully.*

3 2 *It's cloudy* 3 *It's sunny* 4 *It's cold* 5 *It's snowing*
6 *It's warm* 7 *It's raining* 8 *It's windy*

4a *North of England and Scotland* ❄️☀️🌂   *London* ☁️
West of England and Wales 🌂   *South* ☀️🌂
East 🌫️

b *Student's own answers*

Detective work

1 2 *… is playing badly.*   3 *… are talking loudly.*
4 *… is running quickly.*   5 *… is carrying (things) carefully.*
6 *… are sitting miserably.*

2 1 *I'm fine, thanks* 2 *Are you enjoying the camp?*   3 *What's the weather like?*   4 *The sun's shining and it's warm.*   5 *I'm watching football on TV.*   6 *I'm going now, Mum.*

3 2 *nationality* 3 *sing* 4 *airport* 5 *police officer* 6 *local*
7 *pollution* 8 *package holiday*

Skills: postcards

1a 2 *awful* 3 *wet* 4 *uncomfortable* 5 *noisy* 6 *don't like*
7 *miserable* 8 *terrible* 9 *sitting in our room*
10 *watching the rain*

b 1 *Maria* 2 *the weather* 3 *the hotel* 4 *the people*
5 *the food* 6 *Alan and Susan*

2 Suggested answers
(Maria), a great time here, fantastic, comfortable, friendly, delicious, sitting in the sun, reading (Alex and Susan)

Prepare for Unit 10

2 *February, April, May, July, August, October, November, December*

Unit 10

Syllabus

Topic
Diet and lifestyle
Pocket money
The OK Club

Grammar
The present simple and present continuous
How much/many?
Ordinal numbers

Function
Discussing lifestyles and spending choices

Vocabulary
Everyday actions
Food
Numbers over 100
Per cent and fractions
Months and dates

Reading
Responding to a questionnaire
Finding and checking information

Listening
Completing a questionnaire
Understanding meaning from context
Checking specific information
Discriminating between numbers
Identifying context

Writing
Describing spending habits

Speaking
Buying a present

Pronunciation
Word and sentence stress
Ordinal numbers

Vocabulary

Key vocabulary

April	height	October
August	How many?	per cent
birthday	How much?	pocket money
biscuit	January	second
(a) bit	July	September
cake	June	shy
couch potato	leave	spend (on)
date (day)	magazine	sweets
December	March	third
diet	May	ticket
fat	month	weight
February	November	
go out	occasion	

Other vocabulary

at the moment	increase (n)	reason
(on) average	just	(tell the) truth
brilliant!	length	way
give	Lucky you!	

Materials preparation

1   For page 66, Exercise 1 Option: bring in a mixture of healthy and 'junk' food, such as an apple, a packet of crisps, a chocolate bar, some nuts, sweets, a fizzy drink, milk.

2   Dictionaries for page 66 Exercise 1, page 67 Exercise 3, and page 70 Exercise 1b.

3   For Game 7 (see page 96): prepare some cards on which are written a time and two actions: the first a routine one, the other an alternative, for example: *7 o'clock 1. have a shower 2. sleeping.* Make all times o'clock.

4   For page 69, Exercise 1 Option: make 12 cards with the months of the year written in English on one side, and in the mother tongue on the other.

Diet and lifestyle
The present simple and continuous

Aims

In this section, students learn to talk about diet and lifestyle, using the present simple and continuous, depending on whether they are discussing regular habits or temporary actions happening at the moment of speaking. The language is presented through amusing reading and listening tasks, and practised through an oral task.

1a

Background information

1 **Junk food** is the collective name for food such as crisps, fizzy drinks and sweets, all of which are tasty but not very nutritious.

2 **A couch potato** is a humorous name for someone who is very inactive. A typical couch potato is someone who sits on the sofa watching hours of television. The name suggests that such people develop a potato shape as they sag into their seats.

Option

- Offer mixed healthy and junk food (see Materials preparation 1) round the class. Ask: *What would you like? An apple? Some chocolate? Some crisps?* In a joking way, show disapproval of those who ask for 'junk' items, and approval of those who ask for the 'healthy' ones. Use the food items to teach the words *junk food* and *healthy food*.

- Get students to tell you the items in the picture they already know. They then look up the remaining words in their dictionaries.

1b

- In pairs, students discuss which category each food item belongs to.

- Discuss ideas with the class. Note that some foods do not fall clearly into one category or the other. For example, it is a matter of opinion whether chocolate is junk food or not.

2

- Use the little cartoon at the top of the questionnaire to elicit the meaning of 'couch potato'.

- Read the instructions aloud. Draw a table on the board for students to copy:

Me	My partner
1	
2	
3	
4	
5	
6	

- Explain the task by getting individual students to answer questions orally. They should not mark their answers yet.

- Students answer the questionnaire individually, writing their answers in the *Me* column of the table.

- Put students in pairs to take turns asking and answering the questions. They write their partner's answers in the second column. They then turn to page 110 and work out their scores, and compare them.

3

- Tell students they are going to hear an interview with a girl called Sally. She is asked similar questions, but in a different order. Students should write her answers in the third column of the table.

- 🔊 Play the cassette. Students complete the questionnaire with Sally's answers. They then work out her score.

- Ask: *Can you remember – does Sally eat chips or other fried food?* (No).

Tapescript

Interviewer Sally, you're an average fifteen year old. Do you think you're fit and healthy?
Sally Oh, yes. I know I am!
Interviewer Well, tell me about your diet.
Sally My diet, erm, well, I eat fruit and vegetables every day. I don't eat sweets or chocolate, er, and I don't take sugar in tea or coffee.
Interviewer Yes, that's very healthy! Do you eat chips or other fried food?
Sally Um, no, I don't.
Interviewer And what about exercise? Do you take any exercise?
Sally Oh, yes. I love tennis and I play badminton too, and I walk to school every day!
Interviewer Excellent, and do you watch TV in the evening at home?
Sally No, I never watch TV.
Interviewer Well, Sally, that's all very good. You must be extremely fit and well.

Answer key

1 *c* 2 *b* 3 *a* 4 *a* 5 *a* 6 *c*
Score: 24

Option

- 🔊 If you think students will find this task difficult, put them into pairs. Tell partner A to listen for answers to questions 1, 3 and 5, and partner B to listen for answers to questions 2, 4 and 6. Play the cassette, and then tell A and B to share their answers. Play the cassette again. Students check their answers to all six questions.

4

- Students describe Sally's actions, using the present continuous tense. Do the exercise orally with the class first. Students then write a sentence for each picture.

- Students decide if Sally is telling the truth in the interview (No).

Answer key

2 *Sally's eating chocolate.*   3 *Sally's not eating fruit and vegetables. She's eating chips.*   4 *Sally's watching TV.*

Work it out: the present simple and continuous

5a

- Write on the board: *she eats* and *she's eating*. In the mother tongue, ask: *Which form is called the present simple and which is called the present continuous?*

- Put students into pairs to discuss the meaning of each tense, using the definitions given. Go round the class listening to students' ideas.

- Have students tell you the correct answer. Students then write their answers.

Answer key

1 *present simple* 2 *present continuous*

5b

- Students use the questionnaire, Sally's answers, and the sentences they wrote in Exercise 4 to contrast Sally's words and actions.
- Put students into new pairs (see Tip 8, page 37). They take turns saying what Sally claims and what she is doing in the pictures. Walk round the class, checking that students are using the tenses correctly.

Answer key

1 *Sally says she walks to school. But in the pictures she's going to school by car.* 3 *Sally says she eats fresh fruit and vegetables every day. But in the pictures she's eating chips.* 4 *Sally says she never watches TV. But in the pictures she's watching TV.*

Game 7 ▼
Changes

- This game practises the contrast between the present simple and continuous. Explain the game to the class. Pairs of students are given cards (see Materials Preparation 3), and come to the front, a pair at a time, to act out the actions on the cards. Student A in the pair holds up fingers to tell the time, for example, three fingers for 3 o'clock. The rest of the class calls out the time to check they've understood. Student A then mimes the first action on the card, for example, practising the piano. Student B then mimes the second action, for example, playing tennis. Students who think they have understood the mime raise a hand. The pair at the front names one of them. This student explains the mimes, for example: *At three o'clock, she usually practises the piano. But today she's playing tennis.*

  Other possible cards:

  8 o'clock. Do homework / Watch TV
  1 o'clock. Have lunch / Swim.
  11 o'clock. Have English lesson / Go doctor
  7 o'clock. Eat breakfast / sleep

Suggested Workbook practice

Page 43, Exercises 1 and 2

Numbers over 100

Aims

In this section, students learn written and spoken forms of numbers over 100 through an article on why British children are getting fatter. Vocabulary for measurement is also introduced. The language is practised through listening exercises and a general knowledge quiz.

1a

Option

- To introduce ways of talking about measurement, draw two stick figures on the board:

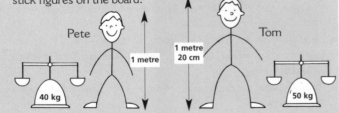

Say: *This is Pete and his friend Tom. What is Pete's weight?* (40 kg). *What is his height?* (1 metre). *What is Tom's height?* (1 metre 20 cm). *What is his weight?* (50 kg). *What does 'weight' mean? What does 'height' mean? Their average weight is 45 kg.* (Do the calculation on the board.) *What does 'average' mean? What is their average height?* (1 metre 10 cm). Then do a question-and-answer chain (see Tip 9, page 39) about weight and height. For example: *What is your weight, Ali? Fifty-five kilos. What is your height, Freda? One metre forty-nine centimetres. What's your …?*

- Check that students understand the headline and the instructions.
- Put students into groups of 4–5. Groups discuss their ideas in the mother tongue for 2–3 minutes. A representative of each group then reports to the class on their group's ideas.

Option

- If some groups are having difficulty thinking of ideas, tell them to look again at the questionnaire on page 66 of their Student's Books.

1b

- Students read the article quickly to check their guesses. Ask: *Which paragraph has the answers?* (paragraph 2).
- Tell students to read the second paragraph again, and to underline those parts of the text which answer the question.

2

- This exercise checks students' understanding of key vocabulary. Students match the words with their examples, then check the answers with a partner.

Answer key

1 *75 kilos* 2 *160 cm* 3 *meat, bread, fruit*
4 *swimming, walking, aerobics*

3

- Put students into pairs to read the sentences, and underline any unfamiliar words. They look these up in a dictionary.
- Pairs do the exercise from memory, then check their answers in the text.
- Check the answers, and ask students to correct the false answers.

Answer key

1 *False. Their height is different from their parents' height at ten.*
2 *False. They are 141 cm tall.* 3 *True* 4 *True*

Work it out: numbers over 100

4a

- Point out the use of commas in numbers over a thousand. Read the examples aloud. Students listen but do not repeat.
- Write the numbers on the board in random order. Point to them one at a time. Students say the number. Repeat the procedure, but with different first numbers, for example, *5,000, 12,000, 4,000,000.*

4b

- Read the examples aloud. Point out that a single hundred, thousand or million is said as either _a hundred/thousand/million_, or _one hundred/thousand/million_. Point out, too, the use of _and_ to connect numbers up to 99 to hundreds, thousands and millions.
- Do number 1 with the class. Students then work individually, writing the rest of the numbers in their notebooks. They check answers with a partner.

Answer key
1 _2,736_   2 _30,205_   3 _328,514_   4 _5,200,410_

Option
- Tell students to cover the exercise, convert the numbers in their notebooks back to the written form, then look at the exercise again to check their answers.

4c

- These are the numbers from Exercise 4b.
- 🔊 Play the cassette. Students listen and read the numbers.
- Play the cassette again. Students listen and repeat the numbers.

4d

- Students write the numbers as words.

Option
- To make this task more challenging, turn it into a pairwork reading task. Student A says the number, then Student B writes the number in figures.

5a

Background information
1 **The CN Tower** in Toronto, Canada was built between 1973 and 1975 to improve TV and radio reception. It is one of the tallest towers in the world.
2 **The Statue of Liberty** is in New York. This gigantic figure of a woman holding a torch in her raised right arm is one of the most famous sights in America.

- Make sure students understand how to work out a group average. Ask five students to come and write their heights on the board. In the mother tongue, ask: _How can you find the average height?_ (add the numbers together and divide by five).
- Put students into groups. Students ask each other their height, write down the numbers, and work out the average. Each group then reports their findings to the class, using the phrase _Our average height is … ._

5b

- Make sure students understand place names 1–5 (see Background information). Tell them to first match the pictures with places 1–5.
- Get students to decide the correct question to ask about place (_What is the height of …?_ for 1, 2 and 4. _What is the length of …?_ for 3 and 5). Do not teach _How long/tall …?_ yet.
- Read the measurements in the box. Ask students to decide which measurements they think describe height, and which describe length (kilometres are probably for length, and metres for height in this exercise).

- Students match places with measurements.
- In pairs, students use the model sentence to compare their answers: _I think the height of Everest is … I think the length of the Nile is … ._

5c
- 🔊 Play the cassette. Students listen and check their answers.

Tapescript/Answer key
1 The height of Mount Everest is eight thousand, eight hundred and forty-eight metres.
2 The height of the Statue of Liberty is forty-six metres.
3 The length of the Great Barrier Reef is two thousand and ten kilometres.
4 The height of the CN Tower is five hundred and fifty-three metres.
5 The length of the Nile is six thousand, six hundred and ninety-five kilometres.

Suggested Workbook practice
Page 44, Exercise 3 (first column)

Pocket money
How much/many?

Aims
In this section, students learn to talk about spending habits, using _How much?_ or _How many?_ to ask about uncountable or countable objects. Students also learn to say percentages and fractions in English. The language is presented through listening tasks, and practised through discussion leading to a writing activity.

Vocabulary: buying and spending

1

Background information
1 **Pocket money** is a regular (usually weekly) sum of money that parents give their children to save or spend as they wish. Most parents feel that this practice helps children to 'learn the value of money'. Children may also 'earn' small amounts of money from parents or other family members by doing jobs such as washing the car or baby-sitting.
2 **Going out** covers leisure time activities outside the home, such as going to a coffee shop with friends, to the cinema, to a disco, or to a party.

- This exercise introduces vocabulary relating to teenagers' hobbies and interests.
- Make sure that students understand all the words in the box. Students then do the matching task.
- Check answers. Then ask the class a few questions about each item, for example: _What magazines do you like? What are they about? Have you got any favourite clothes? Do you play computer games? What games? Where do you play? Do you buy people presents for special occasions? What occasions? birthdays? What presents do you buy? Do you go out with your friends at the weekend? Where do you go? What do you do? What sort of music do you like? Have you got any CDs or cassettes? Which are your favourites?_

Unit 10, Student's Book page 68

Answer key

1 *music*   2 *books and magazines*   3 *food and drink*   4 *special occasions*
5 *going out*   6 *clothes*   7 *sports*   8 *computers*

2

- Tell students to read the instructions. Explain the meaning of *pocket*. Students have to work out the meaning of 'pocket money' by listening to the dialogue between three teenagers.

- 🔊 Play the cassette. Students listen and decide the topic of conversation, and therefore the meaning of *pocket money*.

- Put students into pairs to discuss their ideas. Then ask for the answer (see Background information).

Tapescript

Laura I never have enough money, you know. How much pocket money do you get a month, Gemma?
Gemma Me? Oh, Mum and Dad give me ten pounds a week, so about forty a month.
Martin Mmm, what do you spend it on?
Gemma I suppose I spend about half of it on new clothes, yeah about twenty pounds. Then I spend about eight pounds on magazines ...
Martin That's a lot! How many magazines do you buy a month?

Option

- Ask what clues helped students to guess the meaning of *pocket money*.

3

- Draw two circles on the board, divide the first in half vertically, shade in a half and say: *half*. Then divide it in half again, this time horizontally. Point to one section, shade it in, and say: *a quarter*. Divide the other circle into three, point to one section, and say: *a third*.

- Make sure students understand the purpose of the pie chart. Ask: *What does person 1 spend their money on?* (food and drink, clothes, magazines, sports). *What about person 2?* (presents, music, food and drink, books). *Who spends half their money on clothes?* (person A). *How much does person 2 spend on presents?* (a quarter of their pocket money).

- Tell students to read the instructions. In the mother tongue, ask: *Who will you hear on the cassette?* (the people from Exercise 2). *What are you going to write under the two charts?* (names).

- 🔊 Play the cassette. Students listen and decide whose spending habits are described by the two pie charts.

- Play the cassette again. Students listen and check their answers by ticking off the sections of the pie charts as they are mentioned.

Tapescript

Laura I never have enough money, you know. How much pocket money do you get a month, Gemma?
Gemma Me? Oh, Mum and Dad give me ten pounds a week, so about forty a month.
Martin Mmm, what do you spend it on?
Gemma I suppose I spend about half of it on new clothes, yeah about twenty pounds. Then I spend about eight pounds on magazines ...
Martin That's a lot! How many magazines do you buy a month?
Gemma One a week, usually. They're about two pounds each.
Laura Mmm, I see.
Gemma Then I spend about about five or six pounds a week on sport – I play tennis every week, and the rest on, erm, yeah, on sweets, drinks

and chocolate I'm afraid! How much money do your parents give you then, Martin?
Martin Well, I get about sixty pounds a month because I do little jobs in the house, but I spend about thirty on going out, you know, to the cinema or to a coffee bar with friends.
Laura That's half of your money. That's a lot!
Martin Yeah, so that leaves me about thirty pounds for football and computer games.
Gemma How many computer games do you buy then, Martin?
Martin About three or four a year. I save up for them – at about five pounds a month.
Gemma What about you, Laura?
Laura Well, I get about thirty pounds a month ...
Gemma Yeah.
Laura ... and I spend about a third, about ten pounds a month on music – I love music.
Martin Cassettes or CDs?
Laura Cassettes. And I spend about six pounds on sweets and drinks.
Gemma That's not much.
Laura And about six or seven pounds on books. Then I keep about seven pounds for special occasions, you know, birthdays and so on.

Answer key

1 *Gemma*   2 *Laura*

Work it out: *How much ...? How many ...?*

4a

- Tell students that they have already heard sentences 1–4 in the dialogue in Exercise 3. Ask them to read the sentences and try to guess which word, *much* or *many*, completes each sentence. They should not write yet.

- Check that students understand the question *How much/many ...?* but do not explain the grammatical difference between the two. In the mother tongue, ask: *When you ask 'How much ...?' or 'How many ...?', what do you want to find out?* (the quantity of something).

- 🔊 Play the cassette for Exercise 3 again. Students listen for the questions, and complete the sentences.

Answer key

1 *much*   2 *many*   3 *many*   4 *much*

4b

- 🔊 Play the cassette. Students listen and check their answers.

- Play the cassette again. Students listen and repeat.

4c

- Put students in pairs. Using the examples in 4a, they discuss when to use *much*, and when to use *many*. Walk around, listening to discussions, and checking if they have worked out the difference (*How much ...?* is used with uncountable nouns, *How many ...?* is used with countable nouns).

- Students write their answers.

Answer key

1 *How many ...? (apples, books, pencils, tickets)*
2 *How much ...? (sugar, bread, money)*

98

Useful English

- 🔲 Teach and practise the phrases in the usual way.

5a

- Ask the class some questions about their spending habits. Make clear that you are asking about money given to them for their own use (not things that parents buy for them). For example, ask: *Who buys magazines? Who spends money on food and drink?*
- Students work individually to write a list of five things they spend money on. They can invent these things if they want.

5b

- Take the part of B, and read the dialogue with a student, adding information as appropriate.
- On the board, write: *How many (cassettes) do you buy a month? How much money do you spend on (cassettes) a month?* Students practise the questions, using other items from Exercise 1.
- Put students into pairs. Students take turns asking and answering questions about their spending habits.

Writing: describing your spending

6a

- Students draw a pie chart to represent the five items they discussed in Exercise 5. They can either draw small pictures or write words to label the sections.

6b

- Students choose how they want to describe the amounts they spend: by the actual sums of money, by percentages, or by fractions. They then make notes of the amounts they spend, using their chosen method of description, for example, *clothes: 2/5, food and drink: 1/10, magazines: 1/5, music: 1/5, sport 1/10*, and write them on the chart.

6c

- Ask: *Do you write in present simple or present continuous?* (present simple). *Why?* (because they are regular actions). Students use the information on their charts to write a paragraph about their spending habits.
- Students check their first draft with a partner. The final writing can be done as homework.

Suggested Workbook practice

Page 44, Exercise 1

Month and dates

Aims

In this section, students learn the months of the year, ordinal numbers and their pronunciation, and how to write and say calendar dates. The language is presented through a listening task about birthdays, and practised through listening and speaking tasks.

1

- Say: *Look at the calendar. Is it for a month or a year?* (a year). Ask students to read the days of the week along the top of the calendar (M = *Monday*, T = *Tuesday*, and so on). Then, in the mother tongue, ask: *What do you think the words down the side are?* (months).
- Tell students they are going to hear how to say the months. Ask them to listen carefully for which syllable is stressed in each month (see Tapescript).
- 🔲 Play the cassette. Students listen and note pronunciation.
- Play the cassette again. Students listen and repeat.

Tapescript
<u>Ja</u>nuary, <u>Fe</u>bruary, March, <u>A</u>pril, May, June, Ju<u>ly</u>, <u>Au</u>gust, Sep<u>tem</u>ber, Oc<u>to</u>ber, No<u>vem</u>ber, De<u>cem</u>ber

2a

- Discuss with the class other dates that they might circle, such as birthdays of other members of the family, national days, anniversaries, exam dates. Students work individually and circle three dates on the calendar.

2b

- Tell students to read the instructions, then check that they understand what to do. Suggest they use a pen of a different colour this time, and make it clear that students record the dates, not the names.
- 🔲 Play the cassette, pausing it after each date. Students listen and circle the dates they hear.
- Students check their answers with a partner. If students are unsure of their answers, play the cassette again.
- On the board, write the six months mentioned on the cassette. For each month, ask: *Which day in (November)?* Students say the number, for example, *Six*. Do not expect ordinal numbers yet, but write them on the board as students say the numbers, for example, *6th November*. Leave the answers on the board.

Tapescript
A One. Jack.
Jack My birthday's on the sixth of November.
A Two. Carol.
Carol My birthday's in June; it's the eleventh of June.
A Three. Emma.

99

Emma My birthday's on the first of April.
A Four. Dave.
Dave I'm afraid my birthday's on the twenty-ninth of February so I only have a birthday every four years!
A Five. Jane.
Jane My birthday's on the twenty-eighth of August.
Presenter Six. Ricky.
Ricky My birthday's on the twelfth of December.

Answer key

*6th November   11th June   1st April   29th February   28th August
12th December*

Pronunciation: ordinal numbers

Option

- Using the birth dates on the board, point out the pronunciation of the first three numbers, and the use of *the* in dates (*the sixth, the eleventh, the first*). Students guess how to say the other numbers (*the twenty-ninth, the twenty-eighth, the twelfth*). Say the first three dates in full, emphasizing the word *of* (*the sixth **of** November, the eleventh of June, the first of April*). Students guess how to say the other dates.

3a

- ▣ Play the cassette again. Students listen and mark the stress pattern in the dates, for example, *the sixth of November*.
- Play the cassette again, pausing after each date. Students listen and repeat.

3b

- Students guess how to say each number.
- ▣ Play the cassette. Students listen and repeat.

Work it out: ordinal numbers

4a

- Students read the numbers and words. Then ask them to explain why we write *4th, 5th, 6th, 7th* and so on for all numbers except *1st, 2nd, 3rd* (because all ordinal numbers are followed by the last two letters of the word).

Option

- Point out the spelling changes in *fifth, fifteenth* and *twelfth* (*v* changes to *f*), *eighth* (add *h* only), *ninth* (no *e*), and *twentieth* (*y* changes to *i*).

4b

- Using the examples in 4a, students work out the written form of more ordinal numbers. Walk round, checking students are spelling the words correctly.

Answer key

second   thirteenth   eighteenth   twenty-first   twenty-fourth   thirtieth

5

- This exercise focuses on both the written and spoken forms of dates.
- Students cover the phrases on the left, and say the dates on the right.

- ▣ Play the cassette. Students listen and repeat with books closed.

6

- Point out the use of the preposition in *It's on* … Ask a few students: *When's your birthday?* They respond with *It's on the (date) of (month)*.
- Put students into groups of four to find out each other's birthdays. They write the dates in their notebooks.

7

- This is best done as a question-and-answer chain (see Tip 9, page 39) with the question *When's your birthday?* Students listen carefully to each other to find someone with the same birthday as themselves.

Suggested Workbook practice

Page 44, Exercises 2 and 3

Buying a present

Aims

This section revises and extends language for shopping.

1a

- This is a gist listening exercise. Students only need to work out what shop the speaker is in, and who she is buying a present for.
- Ask students to suggest possible answers before they listen.
- ▣ Play the cassette. Students listen and note down the answers.

Tapescript
Assistant Good morning. Can I help you?
Laura Er, yes. I'm looking for a birthday present.
Assistant Right. Who is it for?
Laura My mother.
Assistant OK. And what sort of present are you looking for?
Laura I'm not sure, maybe a jumper.
Assistant A jumper. OK. What colour would you like?
Laura Blue. Yes, blue's her favourite colour.
Assistant How about this? It's very nice.
Laura Yes, it is. How much is it?
Assistant It's quite expensive. It's twenty-two fifty.
Laura Oh dear, I've only got twenty pounds.
Assistant Ah, well, maybe this jumper. It's blue and it's eighteen ninety-nine.
Laura Oh, OK. Yes, I'd like that, please.

Answer key
She's in a clothes shop and the present is for her mother.

Option

- Ask students to note down the present that she wants, too (a jumper).

1b

- Ask: *Can you remember any questions the shop assistant asked?* Write suggestions on the board.
- ▣ Play the cassette again. Students listen and write the rest of the questions.

Answer key

Can I help you? Who is it for? What sort of present are you looking for? What colour would you like? How about this?

1c

- Put students into pairs to guess how to say the prices.
- 📼 Play the cassette again. Students listen and check their ideas.

Answer key

1 b 2 a 3 b

2

- Students use their notes from Exercise 1 to make a similar dialogue.
- Practise the dialogue with the whole class first. Ask a different student to suggest each line of the dialogue.
- Put students into pairs to practise the new dialogue. Walk round, listening to pairs.
- Ask a 'shop assistant' from one pair, and a 'customer' from another to act out the dialogue in front of the class.

Suggested Workbook practice

Page 45, Exercises 3

The OK Club
The trick

Aims

This section continues the photo-story. It presents informal English in a lively context, and brings together the language students have been practising in the unit, as well as revising language learned previously. In this episode, Emma, Carol and Ricky plot to get Jane and Dave to the cinema together.

1a

Option

- In the mother tongue, ask: *What were Emma, Carol and Ricky doing in the last episode?* (laughing). Explain the meaning of *trick*, then ask: *Who do you think is going to play a trick?* (Emma, Carol and Ricky).

- Students read the questions, then look at the pictures to find the answers.

Answer key

1 at the cinema 2 the money-box 3 (cinema) tickets

Option

- Ask further questions, using the present continuous, for example: *What are the people doing in picture 1?* (They're talking and laughing). *What are they doing in picture 2?* (They're leaving the house. Ricky is shutting the door. He's talking to Jane). *What are they doing in picture 3?* (They're buying cinema tickets).

1b

- Students work in pairs to look up any unfamiliar words in a dictionary, and guess which words will appear in the story.

2

- 📼 Play the cassette. Students listen, read, and check their answers.

Answer key

cinema shy tickets

Set the pace

3a

- Students use the context of the dialogue to decide the meaning of the phrases in the usual way.

3b

- 📼 Play the cassette. Students listen and repeat the phrases.

4

- Students read the five parts of the plan, and underline any words or phrases that they do not understand. Explain these.
- Students work individually to order the texts. They then check their answers with a partner.

Answer key

a 4 b 3 c 1 d 5 e 2

Option

- Use the correctly ordered text as a dictation exercise (see Tip 13, page 83).

5

- Students discuss their opinions of Emma's plan in the mother tongue. To start them off, ask: *Would you play a trick like this on your friends? How would you feel if you were Jane/Dave?*

Suggested Workbook practice

Page 45, Exercises 1 and 4

Review

Aims

The Review section summarizes and briefly revises the Key language features of Unit 10: the present simple and the present continuous, *How much …?* and *How many …?*, and ordinal numbers.

The present simple and the present continuous

- Write the four example sentences on the board. Ask students to explain why the first two sentences use the present simple tense, while the second two use the present continuous. Students then read the explanation.

How much …? and *How many…?*

- Again, have students explain the difference before they read the explanation.

Ordinal numbers

- Write the following numbers on the board: *1, 2, 3, 5, 9, 13, 21, 30, 45*. Get students to call out the ordinal forms of the numbers (*the first, the second …*).

1

- Put students into pairs. Each student looks through past episodes, and chooses one picture to discuss.
- Partners take turns asking and answering questions about their chosen pictures.

2a

- Have students suggest possible questions. Write the key words, for example, *books, money*, on the board as prompts. They then each write five questions with *How much …?* and *How many …?*

2b

- Students take turns asking and answering their questions.

3

- Students can use the dates they circled for Exercise 2a, page 69. They write the date in numbers and words, then explain its significance.

Suggested Workbook practice

Page 45, Exercise 2
Page 46, Exercises 1 and 2

Vocabulary

- *Everyday actions*. These can be organized into different groups, such as *Eating habits, Keeping fit*. Encourage students to write example sentences or phrases rather than a list of verbs.
- *Food*. Students add any new words to their *Food and drink* page and to the Word family tree on Workbook page 76..
- *Per cent and fractions*. These can be added to the *Numbers* page. Students should write both figures and words.
- *Months and dates*. Students write the months of the year and dates on the Time page of the vocabulary books. They can use the dates from Review Exercise 3.

Freewheeling

- This game has already appeared as a suggestion for Unit 9 (see Game 6, page 90). This time students must think up their own actions and manner of doing it.

Suggested Workbook practice

Page 45, Exercise 2
Page 46, Exercises 1 and 2

Preparation for Unit 11

Workbook page 46, Exercise 3

Workbook answer key

Diet and lifestyle

1   2 *goes, is going*   3 *studies, is speaking*   4 *wears, 's wearing*
  5 *watches, 's dancing*   6 *goes, 's going*

2   Lucy *No, I usually have breakfast at eight o'clock.*
  Steve *What are you eating?*
  Lucy *I'm eating fruit and yoghurt.*
  Steve *Do you usually have fruit and yoghurt for breakfast?*
  Lucy *No, I usually have an egg.*
  Steve *What are you drinking with breakfast today?*
  Lucy *I'm drinking fresh orange juice.*

3   1 *110*   2 *237*   3 *4,792*   4 *16,131*   5 *96,502*   6 *728,487*

Pocket money

1   2 *How much water is there?*   3 *How much sugar is there?*
  4 *How many passports are there?*   5 *How many sweets are there?*   6 *How much ice cream is there?*   7 *How much money is there?*   8 *How many cakes are there?*

2   1 *f*   2 *e*   3 *a*   4 *h*   5 *c*   6 *d*   7 *b*   8 *g*

3   2 *30th March*   3 *18th May*   4 *1st June*   5 *23rd August*
  6 *2nd October*   7 *10th December*

b   *Student's own answers*

The trick

1   2 *play*   3 *listen*   4 *'re watching*   5 *Are, staying*   6 *stay*
  7 *come*   8 *is, doing*   9 *'s training*   10 *plays*

2   *Student's own answers*

3   1 *birthday*   2 *brilliant*   3 *find out*   4 *how much*
  5 *fifteen pounds*   6 *expensive*   7 *silly*   8 *What about*
  9 *We'd like*   10 *See you*

4   1 *Six is fine.*   2 *That's brilliant!*   3 *That's silly.*   4 *See you in a minute.*   5 *What about Jack?*

Skills: diagrams

1a   2 *£4.00*   3 *£3.00*   4 *£1.50*   5 *£2.00*   6 *£0.50p*

b   *(clockwise)*
  £4.00 presents and clothes
  £3.00 magazines and cassettes
  £2.00 going out with friends
  £1.50 swimming
  £1.00 coffee and biscuits

2   *Suggested answers:*
  '… *about half of it on clothes. I spend about two pounds on magazines and another two pounds on going out with my friends. I spend the other pound on sweets and chocolate.*'

Prepare for Unit 11

3   *Positive meaning: safe, survival, alive*
  Negative meaning: terrifying, violent, frightening

Consolidation

Syllabus

Topic
Revision

Grammar
Revision of grammar points

Function

Revision of functions

Vocabulary
Revision of vocabulary

Reading
Finding information to complete graphs

Listening
Checking information
Identifying key information

Writing
Writing a survey report

Speaking
Revision of shop dialogues
Discussing sports activities

Vocabulary

Key vocabulary

billiards	horse-riding	survey
chess	once	unusual
cricket		

Other vocabulary

double
(musical) instrument

Grammar

Aims
This section revises the main grammar structures and some of the functions presented in Units 6–10.

1

- This task revises the present continuous and the days of the week through the character of Kevin. It should be done orally. Read the example sentence, which explains that they should only describe Kevin's action in each picture, not how often he does the activity.

Answer key

In picture B Kevin's playing the piano/having a piano lesson.
In picture C Kevin's playing chess.
In picture D Kevin's studying history/listening to his history teacher.
In picture E Kevin's doing his homework/studying French.
In picture F Kevin's reading a sports magazine/reading in bed.
In picture G Kevin's playing football.
In picture H Kevin's playing a computer game.
In picture I Kevin's swimming.
In picture J Kevin's dancing.

2

- This time, students note whether the actions are done usually or just that day, so they must decide whether to use present simple or present continuous. They must also choose a suitable verb. Go through the example with the class, getting students to explain the choice of verb and tense. They then complete the text individually.

Answer key

2 *isn't going to school*   3 *is reading*   4 *doesn't read*   5 *goes*
6 *plays*   7 *isn't playing*   8 *is playing*

3

- Students continue the description of Kevin's usual routine and what he is doing during his holidays.

Answer key

1   *It's Thursday. On Thursday Kevin sometimes studies history after school, but this Thursday he isn't studying history. He's swimming. It's Friday. On Friday Kevin usually does his homework after supper, but this Friday he isn't doing his homework. He's dancing.*

4a

- This exercise revises and extends the topic and language of ability. For questions 4–6, make sure students know how to form follow-up questions: *What musical instrument …? What sport …? What meals …?*
- Read the questions aloud. Check students understand them. Ask for a few example ideas, and write these on the board.

- Put students into groups of 4–6. Each group adds two more questions.
- Students ask and answer the questions, and note all the group's answers.

Option
- Students first make a chart on which to record their answers.

4b
- Get a student to read out the example. Ask a representative of each group to report on their group. Students then write about their group's abilities.

Coffeepotting

5

Background information
Coffeepotting is a game that families play to pass the time on rainy days, holidays, or long car journeys. The mystery verb is traditionally called *to coffeepot*, but any word would do as well.

Option
- Ask students what games their families play on long journeys or on rainy weekends.

- This game practises *Yes/No* questions and short answers with present tenses and *can*. Students look at the picture, read the dialogue, and discuss briefly what order they think the children speak in. Explain that this is a real, traditional game.
- 🎧 Play the cassette. Students listen and confirm their guesses. Play the cassette again. Students listen, and work out how to play the game (one person thinks of an action and, by asking up to ten *Yes/No* questions, the others work out what the action is).
- Play the game once with the whole class. Then put students into groups of 4–5 to play the game a few times.

Tapescript
Boy 1 OK, I've got an idea.
Girl 1 Are you coffeepotting now?
Boy 1 No, I'm not.
Boy 2 Do you coffeepot every day?
Boy 1 Yes, I do.
Girl 1 Can you coffeepot in the house?
Boy 1 Yes, you can.
Girl 2 Do you coffeepot with food?
Boy 1 No, I don't.
Boy 2 Do you coffeepot in the morning?
Boy 1 Yes, usually.
Girl 2 Is it brush your hair?
Boy 1 Yes, it is!

Option
- Do not play the final section of the recording, where a player guesses the answer. Once students have understood the rules of the game, play the cassette again. Students try to guess what the mystery activity is.

Vocabulary

Aims
In this section, students revise some of the vocabulary they have learned in Units 6–10.

1
- Do the first one with the class, getting them to give reasons for their choice. Students then do 2–8 individually, and check them with a partner.

Answer key
1 *rain* 2 *shopping* 3 *gym* 4 *tall* 5 *city* 6 *March* 7 *old*
8 *chips*

2
- Students work individually to find the opposites.

Answer key
1 *never* 2 *true* 3 *evening* 4 *different* 5 *receive* 6 *well*
7 *hot* 8 *loud* 9 *impossible* 10 *slowly* 11 *unhealthy*

3a
- This is a two-part exercise. Students first identify and complete the list of words individually. They then work with a partner to categorize them.

Answer key
Words: aerobics, airport, beach, cake, chess, chips, coral reef, diver, inventor, library, mountain, shop assistant, sports centre, sweets, volleyball
Jobs: shop assistant   diver
Places in a town: airport   library   sports centre
Sports and games: aerobics   chess   volleyball
Places outside a town: beach   coral reef   mountain
Food and drink: cake   chips   sweets

3b
- Students each think of ten more words, two for each category.

Option
- Students write their words but remove the vowels. They show the words to a partner, who tries to guess what they are.

Communication

Aims
This section revises the functions of Units 6–10.

1a
- Remind students how to work out the sort of word that fits a gap (see Tip 6, page 34). Students work individually to complete the dialogue. Then put them into pairs to compare answers and act out their dialogue. This will help them see if it makes sense.

Option
- 🎧 If you think this task is difficult for your students, play the cassette before students attempt the task. Students listen with books closed. They then try to fill in the gaps from memory. Play the cassette again for students to check their answers.

1b

- 📼 Play the cassette. Students listen and check their answers.

Answer key

help you   is it for   looking for   music   likes   songs   How much   another CD   (£12)

2

- Put students in pairs. They prepare a similar dialogue and act it out to another pair. Speaking in front of another pair should make students take more care with pronunciation and intonation.

Suggested Workbook practice

Check yourself, pages 47–48 Exercises 1–7

Project: a sports survey

Aims

In this section, students practise listening, reading, speaking and writing skills by doing a project which leads to writing the results of a survey. It is intended that the project is done partly at home and partly in class.

1a

- 📼 These exercises introduce useful ideas and vocabulary. Students listen to a number of sports being played, identify them, and match them with eight of the pictures.

Answer key

2 A   3 L   4 H   5 E   6 N   7 G   8 K

1b

- Students identify all the sports in the pictures and write the letters next to the names of the sports.

Answer key

*badminton I   basketball D   billiards L   cricket M   diving B
football E   horse-riding H   judo A   riding a bike G   running K
swimming N   tennis J   volleyball C*

1c

- Students add any new sports to their vocabulary books. They could also add them to the word family on Workbook page 76.

Reading

2

- This is a scanning exercise. Students quickly read the text to find specific information.

Answer key

1 swimming   2 football, basketball, volleyball   3 tennis, aerobics

3

- Students read the text again, and write the information on the bar charts according to the percentages.

Answer key

*Boys: running   football   cricket   basketball   tennis   volleyball
Girls: swimming   volleyball   tennis   running   aerobics   basketball
football*

Option

- 📼 This text is recorded on the cassette. You may wish to play it to the students after they have read the text again, and while they are checking their answers.

Listening

4

- 📼 Play the cassette. Students listen and write the sports each teenager plays.

Tapescript

Interviewer Michael, which sports do you play outside school?
Michael Outside school? Well, football, of course. We all play football, and I play billiards a lot – with my friends at a club.
Interviewer What about you, Kelly? Do you do any sports outside school?
Kelly Oh, yes, I go swimming a lot, and in the summer I play tennis.
Interviewer Do you play tennis at school?
Kelly Yes, but not a lot – I probably only have one game a week. I go to the park with my friends after school and we play tennis there. I also do a lot of aerobics.
Interviewer Aerobics?
Kelly Yes, all my friends like it. We go to a class two evenings a week – it's great fun.
Interviewer Mmm. James, do you play sports outside school?
James Not really sports. I don't like football or cricket, but I ride my bike a lot. I go on long rides with my friends at the weekend. And I'm just starting a new sport now. I do judo on Tuesday evenings.
Interviewer Do you like it?
James Yes, I do.
Interviewer Finally, Fiona, what about you?
Fiona Well, I like sport at school. I play volleyball and tennis at school, but I don't play them outside school.
Interviewer Do you do any sports outside school?
Fiona Well, I love horse riding. It's my favourite sport, but it's quite expensive.
Interviewer Have you got a horse?
Fiona No, I haven't. I go to a riding school on Saturday mornings.

Answer key

Kelly: swimming, tennis, aerobics   James: riding a bike, judo   Fiona: volleyball, tennis, horse riding

5

- 📼 Students decide which verb is used with each activity. Play the cassette for students to check their answers.

Answer key

Do: judo   Go: swimming, horse riding, (cycling)   Play: billiards, football, tennis, volleyball   Ride: a bike

Speaking

6

- Make sure students understand how to use the prompts. Follow through an example question with the whole class. Students work with a partner asking each other about sports A–N in Exercise 1.

7a

- Students now collect data for a group survey on the topic *Sports*. Put students into groups of 5–6. Each student copies the chart, leaving space for more questions. Groups discuss further questions to ask, such as *Who/Which team do you play with?* then add them to the chart.

7b

- Students take turns to ask one other person in the group the questions. Everyone in the group notes the answers on their chart.

Before you write

8a–d

- Read the instructions for Exercises 8a–8d with the class. Each group transfers their data to a bar chart.

Writing

9a

- Students, working individually, use the information from their chart to write a descriptive paragraph about their group. They can use the text in Exercise 2 as a model.

9b

- Students glue their description and bar chart on to a piece of paper. Display the results on the wall, or in a booklet.

Check your vocabulary book

- Write the topics covered in Units 6–10 on the board. Students check that they have a page for each topic. In small groups, they compare entries, and add any they have missed to their vocabulary books or on Workbook pages 73–76.

Suggested Workbook practice

Page 48, Exercises 6 and 7
Page 49, Exercises 1 and 2

Workbook answer key

Grammar

1 1 *b* 2 *c* 3 *a* 4 *c* 5 *b* 6 *a* 7 *c* 8 *b* 9 *c* 10 *a*

2 1 *can* 2 *well* 3 *come* 4 *on* 5 *at* 6 *past* 7 *me*
     8 *o'clock* 9 *much* 10 *standing*

Vocabulary

3a 2 *hot* 3 *volleyball* 4 *Friday* 5 *rectangle* 6 *lake*

b 1 *Friday* 2 *hot* 3 *rectangle* 4 *lake* 5 *volleyball*

Communication

4 1 *d* 2 *i* 3 *g* 4 *c* 5 *h* 6 *j* 7 *a* 8 *e* 9 *b* 10 *f*

Pronunciation

5a 1 '*that* 2 *amazing* 3 *start* 4 *seventh* 5 *the*

b *man* /ae/: *fat, stand*
     must /ʌ/: *drum, junk, sun*

Skills: surveys
Reading

1a 2 *languages*

b 1 *French* 2 *Spanish* 3 *Russian* 4 *Hindi* 5 *German*

c 1 ✗ 2 ✗ 3 ✗ 4 ✓ 5 ✗ 6 ✓

Writing

2 1 *do/play football* 2 *girls* 3 *half of us* 4 *Film* 5 *films*
     6 *Music* 7 *popular* 8 *of us/students* 9 *Chess club*
     10 *History* 11 *five per cent*

Unit 11

Syllabus

Topic
Typhoon Opal
Survival
The OK Club

Grammar
The past simple: *be, have, go*
The past simple: questions
Why?/Because ...
Adverbs of past time

Function
Asking about and explaining past events
Giving reasons

Vocabulary
Extreme weather
Adjectives to describe feelings
Adverbs of past time
Adverbs of manner

Reading
Organizing and sequencing information
Identifying topic
Finding and checking information

Listening
Understanding meaning from context
Ordering information
Checking specific information

Writing
Writing about a personal experience

Speaking
Asking about past events
Giving and explaining opinions
Re-telling a story from memory

Pronunciation
was and *were*
Sentence stress

Vocabulary
Key vocabulary

alive	hospital	strong
both	lovely	terrifying
clear (adj)	race (competition)	thirsty
completely	rescue	tired
enormous	safe	typhoon
extremely	spy	violent
freezing	still (adj)	wave
frightened	storm	yesterday
hope		

Other vocabulary

across	meeting	signal
building	middle	stand up
damage	mystery	strange, -ly
emergency	navy	suddenly
experience	over	upside-down
heavy	passport	zoo
inside	ready	

Materials preparation

1   For page 76, Exercise 1 Option 1: the weather cards prepared for Unit 9.
2   Dictionaries for page 76 Exercise 4b.

Typhoon Opal
The past simple: *be*

Aims

In this section, students learn how to ask about and explain past events, using the positive, negative and short forms of the past simple of the verb *be*. The language is presented through reading and listening tasks. They also learn the strong and weak ways of saying *was* and *were*, and how to give and explain opinions.

1

Background information

Typhoons are violent winds which occur in the western Pacific Ocean. The same phenomena in the Atlantic Ocean are known as *hurricanes*. There is a long tradition of giving names to both typhoons and hurricanes. These names may be male, for example, *Hurricane Bob*, or female, for example, *Typhoon Opal*.

Options

- Explain that the topic of this unit is the weather. Revise weather words, using the cards from Unit 9 (see Materials preparation 1). Then point to picture 2 and say: *In picture 2 you can see a typhoon. It's a very strong wind.* Make a sound like the wind blowing through the trees, and ask: *What does 'typhoon' mean?* Students translate.
- If students have studied this topic in their geography syllabus, ask: *Where can typhoons happen?* (accept places which experience typhoons or hurricanes, such as the Florida coast in the USA, the Pacific China coast.

- Students look at the pictures then read the text quickly to find another word for *typhoon*.

Answer key

(violent) storm

2

- This is a prediction exercise. Teach *during* with an example sentence: *You have breakfast before school, you study during school, and you watch TV after school.*
- Put students into pairs to read the sentences, and underline any unfamiliar words. They then discuss possible answers. Remind them of the Useful English phrases on page 54, Unit 9. Do not check answers or explain vocabulary yet.

3

- 📻 Play the cassette. Students listen for some of the sentences in Exercise 2 to confirm their guesses.

Tapescript

Before the typhoon.
Typhoon 'Opal' was a really awful experience. It was all so quick and so powerful! We were at the beach one morning. It was a beautiful sunny day. The sky was clear. There wasn't any wind that morning. It was very quiet and still. It was about eleven o'clock, I remember … then suddenly the sky over the sea in the east wasn't clear and blue. It was a strange grey or white colour …
During the typhoon …
About fifteen minutes later we were back at our house. The wind was extremely strong. It wasn't possible to stand up in it. The noise of the rain was terrible. Then an hour later, we were in the 'eye' (the middle) of the

typhoon. There were about twenty minutes with no wind or rain. It was strangely quiet. Then the wind and rain and terrible noise were suddenly back. That was the second part of the typhoon.
After the typhoon …
It was all over in about three hours – no more wind, no more rain. The whole village was a complete mess. There weren't any undamaged buildings in the whole place. Our house wasn't badly damaged but some of the houses were in pieces. We weren't ready for a terrifying experience like that at all!

Answer key

1 *during*   2 *before*   3 *during*   4 *after*   5 *after*   6 *before*

4a

- Students look for the words in Exercise 2, and try to guess their meaning from the context.
- 📻 Play the cassette again. Students listen and look at the photos to see if they guessed correctly.

4b

- Students look up the words in their dictionaries.

Option

- Students guess and then look up the meaning of the other vocabulary they underlined.

5a

- Explain to students that they are going to hear the mother of the man who experienced the typhoon. She is phoning him to ask about the typhoon. Tell students to look at his answers, which are in a different order to the questions.
- Students read the answers, and suggest what the questions were.
- 📻 Play the cassette. Students listen and decide which answer is most appropriate to each question. They write the order numbers in the boxes.

Tapescript

Hello, Joe. Can you hear me? That typhoon – Typhoon 'Opal' – it was on TV here. Are you all OK? Were you in the middle of it? Where were you? Were you inside a building?
Was there a lot of damage to the house? How much damage was there? Were other people's houses OK? Was it an interesting experience?

Option

- 📻 If you think students will find this listening task difficult, have them listen with books closed first. Then play the cassette again for them to note their answers.

Answer key

4   2   1   3   6   5

5b

- 📻 Play the cassette again. Pause after each question to allow students to read out the correct response.

Work it out: the past simple (1)

6a

- Students use the sentences in Exercises 1 and 2 to complete the chart in the usual way.

Answer key

Positive: I was   he/she/it was   we/they were
Negative: he/she/it wasn't   we/they weren't

6b

- Make sure students understand that they must pretend it is now July. They tick the boxes of months which are past.

Answer key

April   June

> **Option**
> - Revise months before starting this exercise. Write numbers 1–12 in random order on the board. Students 'translate' the numbers into months, for example: 9, 5, 11 = September, May, November.

6c

- Assuming it is now July, students write the tense name under the correct month.

Answer key

June

> **Option**
> - Help students to label the other two lines: July = *present*, August = *future*.

7a

- Students complete the sentences with the right form (past simple) of the verb *be*.

Answer key

1 *weren't*   2 *was*   3 *wasn't*   4 *were*

7b

- Students work out the short forms first (see Tip 7, page 36).
- Ask: *Which question doesn't have a short answer?* Students identify the first question as an 'open' question (the other two are yes/no questions). They then match the questions with the answers.

Answer key

What sort of experience was it? It was terrifying.
Was it a really awful experience? Yes, it was.
Were any of the houses undamaged? No, they weren't.

Pronunciation: *was* and *were*

8a

- Tell students to look at the two groups of sentences. In the mother tongue, say: *Write 'S' next to the sentences you think will have the strong form of 'was' or 'were'*. Then ask them to write W by the sentences with the weak form.
- ▣ Play the cassette. Students listen carefully to check their guesses.

Answer key

1 *It was a lovely day.*   2 *We were very frightened.*

In the positive statements, the verb be *is weak (was /wəz/, were /wə(r)/). In questions and short answer forms, it is strong (was /wɒz/, were /wɜː(r)/).*

8b

- ▣ Play the cassette. Students listen and repeat, using strong and weak forms of *was/were* as appropriate.

9

- Demonstrate the activity with a good student, using the example. Make sure the student understands he or she should concentrate on how to say *was/were*.
- Put students into pairs to take turns asking and answering about various times yesterday.

> **Option**
> - Do a quick question-and-answer chain (see Tip 9, page 39) round the class first. For example, Student A: *Where were you at three o'clock last Sunday, Emil?* Student B: *I was at home. Where were you at two o'clock in the morning yesterday, Janet?*

10

- Ask students to tell you briefly, in the mother tongue, what happened to the man and his family who experienced Typhoon Opal.
- Explain the task, then do the first sentence with the students. Read the sentence aloud, and ask: *Do you think they were all very tired after the typhoon?* Tell them to tick the box if they think the answer is *Yes*.
- Students do sentences 2–7 individually. Tell them that there are no right or wrong answers to these questions; their answers are a matter of opinion.

Useful English

- These phrases are useful for expressing opinions and giving reasons. Remind students of the phrases they learned in Unit 4 to express opinions.
- ▣ Play the cassette. Students listen and repeat in the usual way (see Tip 1, page 9 and Tip 2, page 13).

> **Option**
> - Practise *Why?/Why not?* with a few statements, for example, *I like the colour red.* (*Why? Because it's a happy colour*). *I can't go to the cinema tonight.* (*Why not? Because I haven't got any money*). *I want to stay at home this evening.* (*Why? Because I'm tired*).

11

- Put students into pairs. Taking A's part, demonstrate the example with a student, and complete the reason, for example: *Because it was a terrifying experience.* Pairs take turns explaining their responses to the statements in Exercise 10.

12

- Do the first one with students, writing sentences on the board as they make them, for example, *It was August. I was extremely hot because I was at the beach. I was with my family.* Students write short accounts of their own experiences. Students need to keep these descriptions, as they will be referring to them again in the next unit.

Suggested Workbook practice

Page 50, Exercises 1–5

Survival
The past simple: *have*, *go*

Aims

In this section, students learn the positive and negative forms of the past simple of *have* and *go*. The language is presented and practised through reading activities about a survival story.

1

> **Option**
>
> - Put students into small groups, with their books closed. Tell them that they are going to hear a true story. Write key words on the board: *yacht, crew, Indian Ocean, race, enormous, waves, freezing, rescue, plane, crew, race*. Groups look up any unfamiliar words in a dictionary. They then discuss ideas of what the story will be about, based on the vocabulary.

- Students look at the map and the photograph. They then read the three story descriptions, and choose one. Do not provide the answer at this stage.

2

- Tell students to read the story and underline any words that help them check their guess.

Answer key

c

3

- Students read the story again to find specific information. They tick or cross statements 1–6.
- Check the answers, and ask students to read out the relevant sentences in the text that give the answers.

Answer key

1 *True. '…there was an awful storm. There were strong winds …'*
2 *True. 'Suddenly … there was one enormous wave …'*
3 *True. '…the yacht went over, upside-down. … the yacht didn't go down.'*
4 *False. 'He had … some chocolate …'*
5 *True. '… an Australian Navy ship went to rescue him …'*
6 *False. '… the ship was next to the yacht. Some men went over to the yacht …'*

> **Option**
>
> 🔊 This text is recorded on the cassette. You may wish to play it to the students after they have read the text again, and while they are checking their answers.

Work it out: the past simple (2)

4a

- Read the examples aloud. Ask: *What does 'went' mean? What does 'had' mean?* Students translate the past simple verbs. Tell them to find examples of *went* and *had* in the text and underline them.
- Students complete the sentences. Check answers with the class.
- Ask: *What's the past simple of have/go with 'I'? …with 'he'? …with 'they'?*
- Tell students to read the third paragraph again, and find examples of the negative forms of *went* and *had* (*didn't go, didn't have*).

Answer key

1 *had, went*   2 *went, had*

4b

- Tell students to complete the sentences with positive or negative forms of the two verbs.

Answer key

1 *didn't go*   2 *went*   3 *went*   4 *didn't have*

Past simple questions

Aims

In this section, students learn the question and short answer forms of the past simple of *have* and *go*. The language is presented and practised through listening and speaking activities, leading to students re-telling the survival story, in writing, from memory.

1a

- Tell students they are going to hear a journalist interviewing one of Tony Bullimore's rescuers. Students read the questions. Check that they understand them. Explain that the questions are listed in the correct order.
- 🔊 Play the cassette. Students listen to hear which questions the journalist asks.

Tapescript

Interviewer Did you have any real hope that he was alive in there? Inside the yacht?
Rescuer Well yes, we did … but it was only a small hope really.
Interviewer Did you have a doctor with you in the rescue boat?
Rescuer No, we didn't. The doctor was on the main ship, of course, and he was ready to help. We were on top of the upside-down boat and then suddenly Bullimore was there, in the sea, next to the yacht. It was fantastic!
Interviewer Did you go into the water to help him?
Rescuer Yes, I did. I went in immediately.
Interviewer How many men went with you in the rescue boat?
Rescuer I was with four other men.
Interviewer What were Bullimore's first words to you?
Rescuer His first words were 'It's great to see you'. And it was great to see him, too!

Answer key

2 4 5 6 7

1b

- Students read the instructions.

- Tell them to read the five questions heard in 1a again. Say: *There are two questions that don't have a short 'Yes' or 'No' answer. Which two are they?* Students use their knowledge of question forms to work out which two are 'open' questions (6 and 7).

- 🔲 Play the cassette again. Students listen and write the answers.

Answer key

2 *Yes, we did.*   4 *No, we didn't.*   5 *Yes, I did.*   6 *four men*
7 *'It's great to see you.'*

1c

- Put students into pairs. Demonstrate the first question with a student. Pairs then take turns to ask and answer the questions.

Work it out: the past simple (3)

2a

- Students look at the examples in Exercise 1 again, and then complete the sentences.

- Students compare answers with a partner.

Answer key

1 *Did, did*   2 *Did, didn't*   3 *did, go, went*

2b

- Students complete the chart for *have*.

Answer key

Questions: have   they
Short answers: did   didn't

Option

- For further practice, students close their books, and act out the dialogue from 1c again, using questions prompts on the board :

    have / real hope/ Bullimore / alive? have / doctor / rescue boat? go / water / help him? How many men / with you / rescue boat? What / Bullimore / first words?

3

- Students find the sentences they wrote for Exercise 12 on page 77. They take turns asking and answering questions about them.

- Ask a few students to report back to the class on one of their partner's experiences.

Writing: a short story

4a

- Students plan a short story of a past experience, basing it on the questions in Exercise 3. Explain that they need not answer the questions in the same order.

4b

- Students write the story in class or at home.

4c

- Students check the verbs, then swap stories with a partner and check the whole text.

Suggested Workbook practice

Page 51, Exercises 1–3

The OK Club
Ricky the spy

Aims

This section continues the photo-story. It presents informal English in a lively context, and brings together the language students have been practising in the unit, as well as revising language learned previously. In this episode, Ricky reveals that he watched Jane and Dave's meeting, and tells Emma, Carol and Jane what he saw.

1

Option

- Dictate a gapped summary of the last episode. See Tip 15, page 112.

- Students try to remember the last episode, and answer the questions. Tell them to write full answers. This will give them further practice in past simple.

Answer key

1 *Emma had a plan.*   2 *Yes, she did.*
3 *Jane and Dave went to the cinema.*

2a

- Students look at the pictures, but cover the text. By answering the questions, they guess what happens in this episode.

Answer key

1 *At the OK Club*   2 *Ricky is telling them about Jane and Dave at the cinema.*   3 *They are laughing about what happened.*

2b

- 🔲 Play the cassette. Students listen, read, and check their guesses.

Option

- Ask further questions about the pictures, for example: *Who can you see in picture 2? Where are they? What are they doing? What about in picture 3? Look at picture 4. Does Jane look happy or angry? Did she and Dave have a good time or a bad time?*

3

- Students complete the sentences with the right verbs. Check them with the class.

- Students work with a partner, asking and answering the questions.

Answer key

1 *had – Jane and Dave.*   4 *went – Jane and Dave.*
2 *was – Jane.*   5 *had – Jane and Dave.*
3 *was – Ricky.*

4

- Put students into new pairs (see Tip 8, page 37). Students close their books, and take turns to tell the story again. Suggest that each partner tells the story of two of the pictures.

Tip 15 ★

Giving a dictation (2)

- Giving a 'gapped dictation' is a useful way of summarizing a story or story episode. Write the summary on the board, but replace parts with a line for each missing word. Students copy the text, including the gaps.

  Example gapped text:

  The other members ___ ___ ___ ___ can see that Jane ___ ___ ___ each other. But Dave is ___ ___ ___ ___ person , so Emma persuades the others ___ ___ ___ in a plan to bring ___ ___ ___ ____. She buys two ____ ____ ____ ____ Jane and Dave that ____ ____ ____ are going. The truth is that the others ____ ____ _____. They don't even know ___ ___ ___ ___ ___!

  Read the text once at normal reading speed. Students listen without writing. Read the text a second time, also at normal reading speed. Students listen and fill in the missing words. Let them check their answers with a partner. If students request it, read the text a third time.

  Example dictation:

  The other members / of the OK Club / can see that Jane / and Dave / like each other. / But Dave is / a very quiet, / shy person, / so Emma persuades the others / to help her / in a plan / to bring Jane and Dave together. / She buys two cinema tickets / and tells Jane and Dave / that all the friends / are going. / The truth is / that the others / haven't got tickets. / They don't even know / the name of the film!

Suggested Workbook practice

Page 52, Exercises 1 and 2

Review

Aims

The Review section summarizes and briefly revises the Key language features of Unit 11: the past simple tense of *be*, *have* and *go*, and adverbs of past time.

The past simple tense of *be*, *have* and *go*

- Students read the notes, then close their books. Ask quick questions, for example: *What's the past of 'go'? What about with 'he', 'she' or 'it'? What's the negative form of 'We were'? What about 'It was'? Make a 'Yes/No' question from these sentences. Ricky was across the street. The ship went to his rescue. Jane and Dave had a good time.* Then say: *Now answer these questions. Did you go to the cinema yesterday? Did (student's name) have a bad experience last year? Were Jack and Carol at the cinema? Was Jane angry?*

Adverbs of past time

- Although the unit did not focus on these, students have been using them throughout. Ask students to look through the unit and find examples of *yesterday*, *last* and *in* + month. Then have

individual students make sentences using the adverbs, for example, *(Elise) was extremely frightened last Tuesday.*

1a

- Students make short (one or two word) notes to complete the chart.

1b

- They extend the notes into full sentences, using verbs in the past simple.

2

- Students, in turn, check each other's report from 1b. Student A asks questions from the chart, for example: *Where were you on Sunday at 10 o'clock in the morning?* Student B gives a full answer.

Option

- For further practice of past simple questions and answers, play *Guilty or not guilty?* (See Game 8 below.)

Game 8 ▼

Guilty or not guilty?

- This game of 'alibis' /'ælɪbaɪz/ is useful for practising past tenses. Explain the situation to the students in the mother tongue:

  There was a murder in your town at the weekend. There are several suspects, but they say that they were together all day. The police want to test the suspects' alibi. They prepare some questions, and then interview the suspects one by one. If the suspects' stories are the same, they are innocent. If their stories are different, they are guilty.

  Put students into groups of five. Each group chooses one member to be a suspect. The suspects leave the room, or go into a corner, and work out the details of their weekend together. Meanwhile, the other students in each group think of questions to ask, for example: *Where were you on Saturday morning? What was the weather like? Who was there first? What clothes did your friends have on? What did you have for lunch on Sunday? What did your friends have for lunch?*

  The suspects return to their groups, and try to answer questions. The suspects cannot say *I don't remember* or *I don't know*. When the questioning is finished, each suspect goes to another group to answer that group's questions. They must not talk with other suspects at any point.

  When the questioning is over, ask the groups: *Are the suspects guilty or not guilty?* If the group says *Guilty!* ask: *Why?*

Vocabulary

- *Weather* and *Adjectives to describe feelings*. Students look back through the unit and add new words to the appropriate pages in their vocabulary books.
- *Past time adverbs*. Students add these to the *Time* page in their vocabulary books.

Suggested Workbook practice

Page 52, Exercise 3

Freewheeling

a

- By writing questions, students will remember the obects on the table better. Go through the objects first, helping with vocabulary, such as *passport*, *zoo*, *key/keyring*.
- Read the example questions, and then ask students to suggest one more.
- Students study the objects and each write six questions.

b

- Students give their list of questions to another student, and take someone else's questions. They close their books, then read and answer the questions from memory. Set a time limit of about 5 minutes.
- Students return the questions, and then check the answers to their own questions.
- Point out the question under the picture. Ask: *Where was the spy on 6th May?* Students look at the picture again, and try to answer the question. (They need to look at the air ticket.)

Answer key
The spy was in London on 6th May.

Suggested Workbook practice

Workbook page 53, Exercises 1 and 2

Preparation for Unit 12

Workbook page 53, Exercise 3

Workbook answer key

Typhoon Opal

1 2 *was, were, wasn't*   3 *was, was, were*   4 *was, weren't, wasn't*   5 *was, weren't*

2 2 *In his garden.*   3 *At seven o'clock on Saturday.*
4 *His brother.*   5 *Because there wasn't any work.*
6 *At the swimming pool.*

3 *Student's own answers*

4 2 *My little sister was frightened because the room was very dark.*
3 *We were all happy because the party was very good.*
4 *We were very thirsty because it was a hot day.*
5 *The dog was under the bed because it was frightened of the storm.*

5 1 *sky*   2 *rain*   3 *storm*   4 *sun*

Survival

1 2 *go under the water*   3 *did it go upside-down*
4 *did you go*   5 *you have any food*   6 *you go home*
7 *have any visitors in hospital*   8 *did you go home*

2a 1 *yacht*   2 *wave*   3 *boat*   4 *navy*   5 *ship*

b 1 *frightened*   2 *tired*   3 *hungry*

3 2 *wasn't*   3 *wasn't*   4 *went*   5 *didn't go*   6 *went*
7 *were*   8 *went*   9 *didn't have*   10 *had*   11 *went*
12 *wasn't*   13 *went*   14 *didn't have*   15 *went*   16 *was*
17 *didn't have*   18 *was*

Ricky the spy

1 2 *went*   3 *wasn't*   4 *were*   5 *were*   6 *was*   7 *were*
8 *went*   9 *was*   10 *had*   11 *had*   12 *didn't have*
13 *went*   14 *were*   15 *wasn't*   16 *went*   17 *didn't go*
18 *went*

2 1 **Carol** *We went to the beach.*
2 **Carol** *Yes, we went swimming in the sea.*
3 **Jane** *What did you have for lunch?*
   Carol *We had fish and chips and a fruit pie.*
4 **Jane** *Did you go home after lunch?*
   Carol *No, we went on a boat trip.*
5 **Jane** *Was the boat trip good?*
   Carol *No, it wasn't. There were some huge waves in the sea.*
6 **Jane** *Where did you go in the evening?*
   Carol *We went to the cinema.*
7 **Jane** *Did your mum and dad go with you?*
   Carol *No, they went to visit some friends.*

3 1 *lovely*   2 *frightened*   3 *strong*   4 *lost*   5 *terrifying*
6 *enormous*   7 *tired*
hidden word: violent

Skills: story-telling

1a 1 ✗   2 ✓   3 ✗

b *Sunday: the boat   Monday and Tuesday: was lovely*
Wednesday: Malta   Thursday: was awful   Friday: Italy

2 *Monday: went out on, lovely, was beautiful*
Tuesday: were, was lovely
Wednesday: an idea, to Malta, storm, frightened
Thursday: awful, other boats
Friday: went away, back to Italy, went to the airport.

Prepare for Unit 12

3 a *accident*   b *bus stop*   c *passengers*   d *crash*   e *circus*
f *seats*   g *acrobat*

Unit 12

Syllabus

Topic
Lost and found: *an evening that went wrong*
In the news: *newspaper reports*
The OK Club

Grammar
The past simple: regular verbs
Sequencing words

Function
Telling and completing stories
Expressing likes and dislikes in the past
Preparing newspaper reports

Vocabulary
Verbs for telling stories and writing reports
Sequencing words

Reading
Making predictions from pictures and written clues

Listening
Discriminating between and comparing accounts of events
Listening for main and specific information
Dictation: completing a text

Writing
Preparing and writing short stories

Speaking
Summarizing a story
Telling a story from picture clues
Roleplay: asking and answering questions
Agreeing accounts from clues
Giving opinions

Pronunciation
-ed endings
Word stress and intonation

Vocabulary

Key vocabulary

accident	bus-stop	job
after	circus	jump
ago	clean (v)	news
airport	decide	next
argument	diary	report
arrest (v)	end	return
back	finally	search
because	headache	Switzerland
brush	horrible	

Other vocabulary

(on) board	hero	show
bomb	hijack	squid
break (n = rest)	lift	theme park
disaster	passenger	undersea
flat (n)	president	van
hangman	seat (n)	

Materials preparation

1   Dictionaries for page 84 Exercise 1b.
2   For page 82, Exercise 5 Option 2: make one photocopy for each student of Worksheet 4 on page 149.
3   For page 85, Options after Exercises 7 and 8d: make one photocopy of Worksheets 5 and 6 on page 150 for each student. Cut the page in half.

Lost and found
The past simple: regular verbs

Aims

In this section, students learn to use the positive and negative forms of regular past simple verbs for telling a story. The language is presented through reading and listening tasks.

1a

> **Options**
>
> - Revise the past tense of *be*, *have* and *go* by doing a quick substitution drill (see Tip 11, page 51). Sentence: *The wind was extremely strong*. Substitutions: *Tony, tired, the girls, not, at the cafe, go to, Dan, We, meeting, have, dinner, Sally, Did?, a shower*.
>
> - In the mother tongue, ask students about their experiences of circuses: *What can you see in a circus show?* (acrobats, animals, clowns, trapeze/high wire artistes). *Did your parents take you to a circus when you were young? How old were you? Did you enjoy it? What did you see?* Ask students about their feelings, for example: *Some people like circuses and some people don't like them. What about you? Are circus animals happy? What do you think? Would you like to work in a circus? Why/Why not?*

- Tell students to look at the picture. Say: *This is Gemma. She has a story to tell. What do you think it's about?* (the circus). *Why?* (because there's a circus poster behind her). Read what Gemma says.

- Students read Gemma's speech bubble. Then ask: *Were you right?* Ask: *When was it?* (last summer). *Who wanted to go to the circus?* (her sister, Alex). *How old is Alex?* (12). *Who said 'Yes'?* (Gemma).

- Tell students to read the three summaries of Gemma's story, and to decide which one seems the most likely story. In the mother tongue, ask a few students which summary they chose and why.

Options

- To check students' understanding of the three summaries, ask: *Which summaries have a happy ending?* (none of them).

- Write titles for the summaries on the board:
  - A Gemma loses Alex B A boring day
  - C The day everything went wrong

  Students match the titles with the summaries. (Answers: 1c, 2a, 3b)

1b

- Tell students they are going to listen to the story as it happened, and check their guesses.

- 📟 Play the cassette. Students choose the true summary.

Tapescript

Gemma Come on, Alex. … Two tickets, please.
Woman Near the front?
Gemma Yes, please …
Woman That's ten pounds, please.
Gemma Thank you. We've got seats right near the front.
Alex Great! Let's go in.

Ringmaster Good evening ladies and gentlemen, girls and boys … Welcome to this evening's show! First, we have our amazing acrobats from China – the Lee Sisters! … And now the big moment of the evening, please welcome our beautiful horses from Arabia!
Gemma I really enjoyed that! Especially the horses.
Alex Oh yeah! Me too! Gemma? I'm hungry now. Can I have a hamburger?
Gemma No Alex, not now. We must get to the bus-stop before all these other people.
Alex But we can wait for another bus. I want a hamburger.
Gemma No, Alex.
Alex Oh, please. I won't be a minute.
Gemma Alex? ALEX! … Oh, where is she? That's twenty minutes now! Maybe she went on another bus. … Oh, what can I do?
Bus driver Well? Are you coming or not?
Gemma Er … yes…

Answer key

Summary 2

Work it out: the past simple (4)

2a

- Read the instructions. Students find the past simple of the verb *want* in the sentences in the speech bubble. They use these to work out the past simple positive and negative forms for regular verbs.

- In the mother tongue, ask: *What are the last two letters of a regular past simple verb?* (-ed). *Does the verb change for 'he', 'she' or 'it'?* (No). *How do you make the negative form?* (use *didn't* and the verb without an ending).

Answer key

wanted   didn't want

2b

- Students work individually, putting the verbs into past simple. They check answers with a partner. Then ask individual students to read out a sentence each. Do not worry about pronunciation at this point.

Answer key

1 *wanted* 2 *didn't want* 3 *enjoyed* 4 *was   wanted* 5 *jumped*

Pronunciation: *-ed* endings

3a

- Write the three verbs on the board. Tell the class that the ending of each is pronounced slightly differently: one is pronounced like a *d*, one like a *t*, and one as an extra syllable, pronounced *id*.

- 📟 Play the cassette. Students listen only.

- Play the cassette again. Students listen and repeat.

- Point in random order to the verbs on the board. Students try to pronounce their endings correctly.

3b

- Tell students to look at the list of verbs. Explain the task.

- Students guess which ending they will hear for each.

- 📟 Play the cassette. Students listen and write *1*, *2* or *3* in the boxes, according to how each verb is pronounced. You may need to play the cassette twice.

Answer key

1 /ɪd/ *started   waited*   2 /t/ *asked   hoped   watched*
3 /d/ *arrived   moved   opened*

3c

- 📼 Play the cassette again. Students listen and repeat the verbs.

> **Option**
>
> - 📼 If students find this task difficult, play the cassette again. Students listen with their eyes closed to concentrate better on hearing the sounds.

4

- Put students into pairs. Students tell Gemma's story again. Suggest that they take it in turns to add to the story. For example, Partner A: *Gemma's sister, Alex, wanted to go to the circus.* Partner B: *Their parents asked Gemma to take her, but Gemma didn't want to go.* Partner A: *They arrived at the circus, and … .*

> **Option**
>
> - To help students tell the story, write word prompts on the board:
>
>   Alex – go circus – parents – ask – Gemma – take Alex – not want – said yes – arrive – circus on time – very good – after – Gemma – hamburger – Gemma wait – bus stop – wait – wait – not come – jumped – last bus

5

- 📼 Play the cassette again. Students listen to Gemma's own account of the story, and compare it with their own.

Tapescript

Last summer there was a circus in our town. My sister, Alex, wanted to go – she's twelve – and my parents asked me to go with her. I didn't want to go, really, but I said yes, and my sister and I went one Thursday evening. We went by bus. I really enjoyed the circus in the end, actually, especially the horses and the acrobats. They were brilliant!
After the show, Alex really wanted a hamburger but I wanted to go to the bus-stop. We had an argument. Alex went to buy a hamburger and I waited at the bus-stop. It was quite late by that time, nearly dark. I waited for nearly twenty minutes but Alex didn't come. Then a bus arrived. The bus driver waited for me. I didn't know what to do. I didn't want to miss the bus, and maybe Alex was already on another bus. I jumped on the bus, but I was really frightened. Alex was lost!

> **Options**
>
> - 📼 Students listen again and take notes of further details, then tell Gemma's story again, adding in the extra details.
> - Put students into pairs. Give each student a copy of Worksheet 4 (see Materials preparation 2). Students complete a page of a diary, then ask each other questions about it, using the past simple.

Suggested Workbook practice

Page 54, Exercise 2

What happened next?

Aims

In this section, students learn to consider, discuss and relate events in a story, using regular past simple verbs and sequencing words. They also learn how to show interest when listening to a story, and practise asking and answering questions in the past simple.

1

> **Option**
>
> - To introduce sequencing words, write *first*, *then*, *next*, *after that* on the board. Do not explain them. Say: *Yesterday, I went shopping. First I went to the market to buy some vegetables. Then …* Stop talking, and look at the class, waiting for a student to continue. The student makes a suggestion. Say: *Next, …* Wait for a student to continue the story, then say: *And after that …*, and have another student give one more idea.

- Read and explain the instructions. This is an 'information-gap' activity. Partner A looks at the pictures on page 83. Partner B looks at page 111. Students should not look at each other's books.
- Partner A tells Gemma's story according to the pictures. Partner B corrects A's statements if they are different from the account in Gemma's diary, for example: *That's not right. Gemma didn't go home immediately. She waited for a long time before she went home.*
- Walk round, listening to pairs and helping when necessary.

2

- In pairs, students discuss the details of each ending. They should question details and how they fit with the story so far, for example: *Why was Alex in hospital? Why did Alex come home without her parents?*
- They choose the ending they think is most probable. There is no right or wrong answer at this stage, but ending 3 is the most probable one.

Useful English

- Teach the words and phrases in the usual way.
- 📼 Play the cassette. Students listen and repeat. Encourage students to copy the speakers' intonation so that they sound genuinely interested.

3

- Pairs read their chosen story ending again, and work out the details. Encourage them to make notes to remind them of the story, but do not let them write out the story ending in full.
- Each pair joins another pair. Pairs take turns telling their story ending from their notes. The pair listening should show interest, using the Useful English phrases.

> **Option**
>
> - Write some questions on the board to help students brainstorm ideas for their endings, for example: *Why was Alex a long time at the hamburger shop? How did she go to the airport? Why did she go to the airport? Who helped her? How long did she wait at the airport?*

4

- In the mother tongue, ask students to remind you of what Gemma was doing while her parents were finding Alex.

- Explain that Gemma's parents want to question her about what happened.

- Put students into new pairs (see Tip 8, page 37), and tell them to choose their role. Partner A takes the part of the parents, and asks the questions. Partner B takes the part of Gemma, and answers them.

5

- Students work individually to write questions. They then compare their answers with a partner.

Answer key

2 *Did they like the horses?* 3 *Did they have an argument?*
4 *Did she arrive home at about 11 o'clock?* 5 *Did she call the police?*

6

- Students read the final part of Gemma's diary on that day. They discuss with their partner for Exercise 3 how their ending compared with the real ending.

Options

- Use the text in Exercise 6 as a dictation (see Tip 13, page 83, and Tip 15, page 112). Students check their own texts, or exchange books and check each other's work.

- Discuss the story in the mother tongue with the class. If they were Gemma, what would they have done differently? What did they think of Alex's behaviour? And Gemma's. How would their own parents have reacted in the situation?

Suggested Workbook practice

Page 54, Exercises 1, 3 and 4

In the news
Preparing newspaper reports

Aims

In this section, students practise reading and writing past simple narratives in the form of newspaper stories and story summaries.

1a

Background information

Wimbledon is a famous international tennis tournament which takes place every summer at Wimbledon, in London.

Option

- Explain that the lesson is about newspaper stories. On the board, write:

      TYPHOON DAMAGES MOST HOUSES ON ISLAND
      A typhoon damaged most of the houses on the island yesterday …

  Students discuss the difference between the newspaper headline and the story (Answer: in the headline, there are no articles and the verb is in the present simple).

Write another sentence on the board: *A team of men rescued a yachtsman from the sea*. Students make a headline from it, for example:
TEAM OF MEN RESCUES YACHTSMAN FROM SEA.

1a

- Tell students to read the headlines quickly. Do not explain new vocabulary yet.

- Ask: *Which are the most important words in each headline?* Students suggest the key words in each headline. Explain that these are the words to listen for.

- 📻 Play the cassette. Students listen and match the newspaper stories with their headlines.

Tapescript

1 **Newscaster 1** A telephone caller warned of a large bomb at Disneyworld near Los Angeles in California early yesterday morning. Police immediately closed the park but decided to open it again four hours later after a careful search.

2 **Newscaster 2** In Washington the American President named his new dog yesterday. The brown dog, only three months old, arrived a week ago, but it had no name. Hundreds of American suggested names for it. The people's favourite name was 'Brownie', but the President and his family liked the name 'Buddy' and so the new …

3 **Newscaster 1** Bad weather again continued to cause problems at Wimbledon, when rain delayed the start of the fourth day's tennis. The London Weather Centre predicted more bad weather to come.

4 **Newscaster 2** A hijacked Russian plane landed safely at Moscow airport at 2pm yesterday. Three hijackers took over the plane, with more than 140 people on board, two hours after they left the city of Magadan, in eastern Russia, on a flight to Moscow. There is a suggestion that the three hijackers are students.

5 **Newscaster 1** The great French undersea explorer and film-maker, Jacques Cousteau, died at his home in Paris yesterday at the age of 87.

Answer key

Stories match headlines in the order: 3 1 4 2 5

1b

- Students look up any new words in their dictionaries.

2a

- For each headline, ask: *What country did this happen in? What town do you think it happened in?*

- 📻 Play the cassette again. Students listen and match the places with the newspaper reports.

Answer key

a *5* b *1* c *3* d *4* e *2*

2b

- Students choose a headline, and expand it, adding any further details they can remember from the cassette.

- Ask a few students to read their summaries to the class.

Option

- If you think students may find this difficult, let them work in pairs.

3

- Find a student who chose the Russian hijacker report in Exercise 2. Ask him or her to read out their summary to remind the class of the story. Explain in the mother tongue that the hijacking is still front page news the next day, and that there are three possible continued stories, only one of which is correct.

- Students read the reports, and choose the one that they think is most probable.

4

- In groups of 4–5, students discuss their ideas in the mother tongue. They should think about the information from the first report, then look at the new reports to see which one is the most logical follow-on.

Answer key

The cassette clues are: The plane landed safely in Moscow. There is a suggestion that the three hijackers are students.

Option

- 📼 If necessary, play the Russian hijack report on the cassette again. Students make brief notes of information they think is important, and then discuss the other reports.

5

- 📼 Play the cassette. Students listen and check their guesses.

Tapescript

Reports from Moscow say that Russian police stormed the hijacked plane at Moscow airport last night and arrested the three hijackers of the plane. The three men are students from the university of Magadan – police cannot understand the reasons for the hijacking. All the passengers and crew are safe.

Answer key

Report 1

Dictation

6a

- Tell students to read the text, and to try and guess what words to write (see Tip 6, page 34).

- 📼 Play the cassette. It is the same as for Exercise 5, but with pauses. Students listen and complete the report.

6b

- Students compare their texts with a partner.

- 📼 Play the cassette again. Students check their answers.

7

- Tell students to look at the first two pictures. Have them suggest what is happening in each. Give vocabulary as necessary.

- Students read the first text. Ask questions about the pictures and text: *What animal is in the box in the first picture?* (a squid). *Where is the man putting the box?* (in his van). *Who is behind the van?* (Jean Grillette /ʒɒ(n) griː'jet/). *How old is he?* (20). *What sort of car is he driving?* (an open-top sports car). *Is this a good car to drive in winter?* (no). *Why not?* (It's too cold!). *What happened next?*

- Repeat the procedure with the second text and pictures. Ask: *Where did the brothers live before?* (Newcastle). *When did one*

brother move to Australia? (1969). *When did he come back?* (1999). *Why?* (to see his brother). *Who is the man in the first picture?* (the brother who went to Australia). *Look at the woman's face. Has she got good news?* (no). *What can you see in the second picture?* (the two brothers, the Sydney opera house). *What do you think happened?*

- Put students into pairs to discuss how they think each story ended.

Option

- Students do Worksheet 6 (see Materials preparation 3) before they attempt Exercise 7. Students look at the pictures and describe what happened before and after.

Writing a story

8a

- Working with a partner, students expand one of the stories from Exercise 7. Tell them to choose which story they want to write.

8b

- Explain the task. Partner A makes notes about the background to the story, while partner B makes notes about the ending.

Option

- To help students make notes, remind them of the note-taking activities in Exercise 8 on page 41 of the Student's Book.

8c

- Students close their text books and tell their part of the story to their partner, using only their notes.

8d

- Put students into groups of four to take turns telling or listening to each other's stories. The pair listening should show interest, using the Useful English phrases on page 83. If the story is unclear, they should ask questions.

Option

- Students do Worksheet 7 (see Materials preparation 3) to practise reducing a text to the required number of words. Tell students to read the first four sentences of the text. Then read the first sentence of the gapped text, and ask: *What's the man like?* (tall) *And the woman?* (young). *Where did they meet?* (a park). *What sort of park?* (a city park). Students complete the text individually.

Answer key

A tall man and a young woman met in a city park. First, they went to sit on a bench. Then, they looked carefully around. Next, the man opened his briefcase and took out some paper. The man gave the paper to the woman and she put it in her big winter coat. Finally, the man shut his briefcase and they both left.

9a

- Students write their story without considering length, then reduce their text to 120 words. The aim here is to help them write more concisely with fewer repetitions. Remind them to use sequencing words.

9b

- Pairs exchange stories, and check each other's texts for errors of fact, spelling and language, as well as past simple verbs and the number of words.

9c

- Students write their stories out again, correcting anything their partner has pointed out to them.

Option

- Students illustrate their stories, and then stick text and pictures on a larger piece of paper. Make a wall display, or a booklet of the stories.

Suggested Workbook practice

Page 55, Exercises 1–3.
Page 57, Exercises 1–3

The OK Club
Come on, Carol!

Aims

This section continues the photo-story. It presents informal English in a lively context, and brings together the language students have been practising in the unit, as well as revising language learned previously. In this episode, Jack finds out that Jane and Dave went to the cinema together. Because he is angry, he gives Dave a lot of work to do. Carol doesn't want to work, but when the film crew come in, she suddenly discovers that she really wants to help!

1a

Option

- Ask questions about the pictures, for example: *Look at picture 1. Who can you see?* (Jack and Dave). *What do you think Jack's feeling?* (angry/annoyed/hurt). *Look at picture 2. What's happening?* (They're painting the Coffee Corner). *Who's in the middle of the picture?* (Jack and Emma). *What's Jack's job in Project OK?* (he's project leader). *What new people can you see in picture 3?* (the TV producer and cameraman). *Why are they there?* (to film the OK Club members). *Who can you see in picture 5?* (Carol and Jane). *How do you think they're feeling?* (tired).

- Students read the verbs, look at the pictures, and guess which verbs will be used in the story. They underline the verbs they think will be used.

1b

- 📼 Play the cassette. Students listen, read and check their guesses.

Answer key

arrived   helped   started to   worked

Option

- Revise the pronunciation of the *-ed* verb ending. Ask students to say all the verbs in the box.

2

- Tell students to read the episode again.
- Explain the task, and go through the example with the class.
- Students write five questions about the story, using a choice of the verbs in the box in Exercise 1.

Option

- Write question prompts on the board to help students make questions: *Did …? When did …? Why did …? Where did …? How did …?*

3

- Put students into pairs to take turns asking and answering their questions. If their partner does not understand the question, or answers it incorrectly, they should look at the question again, and re-phrase it.

4

- The class give their opinion of Carol. Focus particularly on her behaviour <u>before</u>, <u>during</u> and <u>after</u> the TV people film the group.

Review

Aims

The Review section summarizes and briefly revises the Key language features of Unit 12: the past simple (regular verbs), and sequencing words.

The past simple simple: regular verbs

- Tell students to close their books. in the mother tongue, ask: *How do we form a regular past simple? How do we form the negative?* Ask students for example positive and negative sentences about any of the stories in the unit, for example, *Alex wanted to go to the circus. Gemma didn't wait for Alex.*

- On the board, write: *arrive   damage   decide*. Ask students to remind you how to form the regular past tense. Add *-ed* to each verb, and ask: *Is that right?* Students should realize that the verbs are not right. Ask: *What's the rule for verbs that end in -e?* Students work out that verbs ending in *-e* add only *-d* for past simple.

Sequencing words

- On the board, write four sentences in the wrong order: *A He decided to eat the bread and cheese that was on the table. B He finished the food and went to watch TV. C He walked to the table. D John went into the kitchen.* Ask individual students to help you put the sentences in the right order, using sequencing words.

Answer key

1 D   2 C   3 A   4 B

1

- Students say each verb to themselves and decide which category it belongs to.

Answer key

*listened 3   looked 2   opened 3   searched 2   stopped 2   wanted 1
walked 2*

Unit 12, Student's Book page 87

2a

- Students read the sentences, and complete them with the verbs from Exercise I. Make sure they understand that they use one of the verbs twice.

Answer key

2 *looked* 3 *searched wanted* 4 *closed*
5 *walked stopped listened closed*

2b

- In pairs, students brainstorm answers to the questions about the story in 2a.
- They make notes of their ideas.

2c

- They write the complete story with sequencing adverbs.
- Check that students are using verbs in the correct tense, and help them with vocabulary.

Vocabulary

- *Stories*. Students start a new page in their vocabulary books for verbs used for telling stories and making reports.
- *Sequencing adverbs*. Students write a very short story sequence, and underline the sequencing adverbs.

Suggested Workbook practice

Page 56, Exercises 1–3

Freewheeling

- Students may already have played the game of *Hangman* in Unit 4. If so, they will need no explanation.
- Tell the class to read the instructions. Make sure they understand the game.
- Tell one student to look through the unit and find a word they could use for the game, but not to say what it is.
- Divide the rest of the class into two teams.
- Students play the game. The person who guesses the word can choose the next word. The first person takes his or her place in that team.

Preparation for Unit 13

Workbook page 57, Exercise 4

Workbook answer key

Lost and found

1 2 *didn't* 3 *happened* 4 *did you wait* 5 *opened*
6 *didn't ask* 7 *miss* 8 *wanted*

2 2 *No, Alex didn't like the acrobats best. She liked the horses best.*
3 *No, the lesson didn't start at ten o'clock. It started at half past ten.*
4 *No, Martin didn't call a friend in London last week. He called a friend in Paris.*
5 *No, Julie didn't wait for the bus for twenty minutes. She waited (for the bus) for ten minutes.*

3 2 *Who did you telephone last night?*
3 *What did you watch on TV last night?*
4 *What did you like best on TV last night?*
5 *What did you enjoy at school yesterday?*

4a a *5* b *I* c *3* d *6* e *2* f *4*

b 1 *waited* 2 *arrived* 3 *closed* 4 *opened* 5 *went*
6 *started* 7 *awful* 8 *watched* 9 *went* 10 *arrived*

In the news

1 1 *arrived* 2 *arrest* 3 *climb* 4 *lift* 5 *looked* 6 *move* 7 *telephoned* 8 *try* 9 *waited* 10 *want*

2 2 *waited* 3 *looked* 4 *climbed* 5 *tried* 6 *moved*
7 *arrived* 8 *telephoned* 9 *lifted* 10 *arrested*

3 2 *Bob Smith wanted her TV.*
3 *One day he waited outside Mrs Jones' house.*
4 *Mrs Jones went to work by car.*
5 *Bob went into her house by a window.*
6 *He moved the TV a few centimetres.*
7 *Mrs Jones telephoned the police.*
8 *The police arrested Bob Smith.*

Come on, Carol!

1 2 *arrived* 3 *asked* 4 *rescued* 5 *stopped* 6 *called*

2a 1 *crashed* 2 *stopped* 3 *called* 4 *rescued* 5 *arrived*
6 *asked*

b 1 *crashed*
2 *stopped*
3 *called*
4 *rescued*
5 *arrived*
6 *asked*

c (a) *... did you do?*
(b) *What happened next?*
(c) *Really?*
(d) *What did the police do?*

3b *arrived* /d/: *cleaned, died, enjoyed, returned*
asked /t/: *crashed, liked, missed, stopped*
started /ɪd/: *decided, reported, waited, wanted*

Skills: news reports

1 1 *c* 2 *a* 3 *b*

2 A *3* B *I*

3 moved to another town
wasn't with them
searched the country
did not find her
walked into a police station
tired and hungry
to the hospital

Prepare for Unit 13

4a *critic, environmentalist, farmer, explorer, lawyer, painter, poet, politician*

b *direct, filmscript*
silence

c 1 *farmer* 2 *critic* 3 *painter* 4 *lawyer* 5 *explorer*
6 *politician*

Unit 13

13

Syllabus

Topic
Behind the camera: *A Hollywood Director*
The world of silence: Jacques Cousteau
The OK Club

Grammar
The past simple: irregular verbs
Object pronouns (revision)

Function
Talking about films
Talking about someone's life

Vocabulary
Films
Jobs

Reading
Finding and organizing information
Finding key points
Matching headings with paragraphs
Editing: adding new information

Listening
Listening for specific information
Completing a text

Writing
Preparing and writing a life history

Speaking
Sharing information about films
Asking and answering questions using a picture clue
Giving opinions and reasons

Learn to learn
Taking notes

Vocabulary

Key vocabulary

adventure	explore, -er	lawyer
architect	farmer	lazy
attack (v)	fight (fought)	movie (... camera)
believe	filmscript	office
born (was ...)	greedy	poet, -ry
critic	helpful	politician
director	hit (n = success)	sink (sank)
edit	hunt, -er	writer
escape		

Other vocabulary

omelette	hate	pain
against	hostel	period
amount	ill	prize
aqualung	instead	promise
chief	interest (n)	silence
cookie	nowhere	still (adv)
court (law ...)	nuclear test	survive
death	oxygen	underwater
fluent, -ly	packet	watch (n)
free time		

Materials preparation

1 For Tip 16 on page 123: prepare test papers of the irregular verbs found on pages 88–90 with both questions and answers.
2 Dictionaries for page 91 Exercise 2, and page 93 Exercise 2.

Behind the camera
The past simple: irregular verbs

Aims

In this section, students learn some irregular past simple verbs through simple narrative accounts from a book, films, and a biography. They also learn to read a text in detail in order to take notes.

1a

Background information

1   **Steven Spielberg** is one of Hollywood's most successful directors, and has made some of the most popular films of all time. In chronological order these include:
Jaws: Spielberg's first big hit, starring Richard Dreyfuss, Robert Shaw and Roy Scheider, is about an enormous man-eating shark.
Duel: The story of a car driver (Dennis Weaver) who finds himself doing battle against a mad truck driver.
E.T.: A children's story about an Extra Terrestrial (a creature from another planet) who is stranded on Earth. A small boy (Henry Thomas) protects him and helps him to get home again.
Raiders of the Lost Ark: This is an adventure story in which the hero, Indiana Jones (Harrison Ford), sets out to rescue a holy and magical treasure from the Nazis.
Jurassic Park: A science fiction adventure in which a group of scientists visits a new animal park inhabited by dinosaurs that have been created from the DNA of long-extinct monsters. Everything goes terribly wrong and the group becomes trapped in the park. It stars Richard Attenborough and Sam Neill.
Schindler's List: A true-life story of a German businessman (Liam Neeson) who saves his Jewish workers from the Nazis during World War 2.
Saving Private Ryan: This film, also set in World War 2, is about a group of American soldiers who go to the fighting in France to try and rescue Private Ryan, who is now his mother's only surviving son. Tom Hanks is the star.
2   **The Oscar awards** are very important film awards given each year for categories such as Best director, Best actor, Best actress, Best film music.

Option

- Ask questions about the cinema and films: *How often do you go to the cinema? Once a month? Every week? Who do you go with? Your family? Friends? Did you go to the cinema this month? What films are on at the cinema at the moment? What would you like to see next? What are your favourite films?* In the mother tongue, make a list of the films on the board. In small groups, students talk for a few minutes about their opinions of each film: *What do you think of …? It was fantastic/awful/boring/interesting. I liked it. I'd like to see it.*

- Students look at the 'map', try to recognize some of the films, and name the director.

Option

- If students can't guess, write some names connected with cinema on the board: *George Lucas, Walt Disney, Steven Spielberg, Brad Pitt, Stanley Kubrick, Harrison Ford, Indiana Jones.*

1b

- Students discuss their ideas in small groups, for example: *Indiana Jones isn't a director, he's the hero in Raiders of the Lost Ark.*
- Give students 2–3 minutes to agree, then a representative from each group gives their group's answer. Do not tell them whether they are right yet.

Answer key

Steven Spielberg

2

- Students work in the same groups, and talk about each film using the questions provided as a guide.

3

- 📼 Play the cassette. Students check their answer to Exercise 1.
- Students read the dates and facts in the text.
- Play the cassette again. Students listen and match facts with dates.
- Ask: *What happened in (1949)?*

Tapescript

Stephen Spielberg was born in Cincinnati in 1947. Today he is one of the great film directors of Hollywood.
Some of his famous films are *Jaws* in 1975, *E.T.* in 1982, *Jurassic Park* in 1993, and *Saving Private Ryan* in 1998.
His film-making started when he was only about 12 years old. That was in 1959. His father gave him his first small movie camera and he made his first, very short film about his toy trains. He called it *The Great Train Crash*. Two years later, in 1961 when Spielberg was only 14, he wrote a short film called *Escape to Nowhere* – his first film with actors. His friends and family were the actors.
From 1968 to 1970, Spielberg studied film-making in California. He made five short films during this time at college. Then, in 1969 he went to work for Universal Studios in Hollywood, and from 1974 to 1975 he made his first really famous film, *Jaws*. It was immediately an enormous hit.
Over the next 20 years he made several other famous and very successful films, but he only won his first Oscar, for *Schindler's List*, in 1994.

Answer key

1947 – He was born in Cincinnati.
1959 – His father gave him his first small movie camera …
1961 – He wrote and then made his first film with actors: Escape to Nowhere.
1968–70 – He studied film-making at Long Beach College …
1974–5 – He made Jaws …
1994 – He won a Hollywood 'Oscar' for his film Schindler's List.

Option

- 📼 If you feel your students can manage a slightly more difficult task, play the cassette again. Students make more detailed notes.

Work it out: the past simple (5)

4a

- Students read the text in Exercise 3 again, and underline all the verbs.
- Students match the irregular past simple forms with the infinitive forms in Exercise 4.

Answer key

1 *became*　2 *gave*　3 *made*　4 *win*　5 *wrote*

4b

- Write some verbs on the board: *arrive, have, ask, wait, say, go.* Ask students to tell you the negative form of each, for example, *didn't arrive.*
- Students write the past simple negative form of the irregular verbs in Exercise 4a.

Answer key

1 *didn't become*　2 *didn't give*　3 *didn't make*　4 *didn't win*
5 *didn't write*

4c

- Tell students to start a new page in their vocabulary books, and to write the heading *Irregular verbs.* They write the infinitive and past simple versions of the verbs in Exercise 4a, and those of *be, have* and *go.* Tell them to add other irregular verbs as they learn them.

Option

- Tell students to learn the irregular verbs for the following lesson, when they can work in pairs and test each other (see Tip 16 below):
  - A: What is the past tense of 'give'?
  - B: Gave.
  - A: That's right, well done.

Tip 16 ★
Student-to-student tests

- This approach to classroom tests makes students more responsible for their own learning. It also replaces the usual pen and paper exercise with oral practice. The example here is a test of past simple forms.

  Prepare a test paper with both question and answer on the sheet. For example:
  - What is the past tense of …?
  - 1 give (gave)　2 have (had)　3 leave (left)
  - 4 become (became)

  Put students into pairs. Give a copy of the questions and answers sheet to partner A in each pair. Partner A then tests partner B. For example:
  - A: What is the past tense of 'give'?
  - B: Gave?
  - A: Yes, that's right. One point! What's the past tense of 'leave'?
  - B: Leaved?
  - A: No, 'left'.

  At the end of the test, partner A tells partner B (or you, the teacher) partner B's total score. A and B then change roles. If you want to make the test fair to both partners, prepare different question sheets for A and B.

5

- Say: *Look at the picture. Who wrote the book 'Jaws'? Did he write the book before or after the film? Do you know this film? What happens in the film?*
- Allow students 2–3 minutes to read the text and underline any information that is new to them.

6a

- Read the instructions. Ask the class if they can guess what *fictional* means (they should be able to work it out because of the contrast with *real people*).
- Students find the names in the texts, then read around each name to find out if they are real or fictional people.

Answer key

Quint *F*　Verna Shields *R*　Hooper *F*　Martin Brody *F*
Peter Benchley *R*　Steven Spielberg *R*

Option

- 📼 These two texts are recorded on the cassette. You may wish to play them to the students after they have read the text again, and while they are checking their answers.

6b

- Students check the texts, and answer the question.

Answer key

1 *fictional*　2 *real*

7

- Ask students to guess what the words in the text will be.
- Students search quickly through the texts for the synonyms.

Answer key

1 *terrifying (text 1, paragraph 1)*　2 *killer fish (text 1, paragraph 2)*
3 *began (text 2, paragraph 1)*

Learn to learn: taking notes

8a

- Write the first date, place name, and facts on the board as an example:

Dates	1974	Universal Studios asked Spielberg to make the film
	April 1974	....
Places	North-east coast of USA	filming began
	Los Angeles	....
Cinema		*Jaws* opened in 464 cinemas
Money		....

- Students make a similar chart of notes on the film text.

Answer key

Dates	1974	Universal Studios asked Spielberg to make the film
	April 1974	Filming began
	October 1974	Verna Shields and Spielberg started to edit
	20th June –1975	Jaws opened
	by December 1977	made $250 million
Places	NE coast of USA	filming began
	Los Angeles	edited film
Cinema		Jaws opened in 464 cinemas
		954 cinemas showing the film
Money		$14 million in first week
		$250 million by December 1977

8b

- Discuss what facts students need to make notes of (people, their jobs, actions).
- Students make a chart for the book text.
- They compare their notes with a partner, making changes if necessary.

Answer key

People	Jobs	Actions
Peter Benchley	–	wrote the book
A young woman	–	went for a swim – a shark killed her
A little boy	–	the shark took him from the beach
His mother	–	never saw the boy again
Martin Brody	police chief	asked for help – went out to hunt the shark – survived
Quint	shark hunter	knew what to do – went out to hunt the shark – shark killed him
Hooper	scientist	went out to hunt the shark – shark killed him

9

- Students match the negative verbs with the positive ones in the texts. They then complete the crossword with the positive verbs.

Answer key

1 *found* 2 *saw* 3 *wrote* 4 *took* 5 *came* 6 *attacked*
7 *knew* 8 *began*

Options

- Students cover the texts and use their notes to talk about the book and the film.
- Students add new irregular verbs from the texts to their vocabulary books.

Suggested Workbook practice

Page 58, Exercise 2

The world of silence

Aims

In this section, students read a detailed biography, and learn some more irregular past simple verbs. They also learn the new editing skill of adding new information to a text.

1

- This task helps student to think about the topic and to make predictions before they read. Tell students to read the questions and underline any words they do not know. Explain these briefly. They are all jobs to record later.
- Put students into new pairs (see Tip 8, page 37). They look at the picture and make guesses about the man in it by answering the questions.
- Ask individual students to tell you their answers, and to give reasons for them. Do not confirm the answers yet.

2a

- Give students 4–5 minutes to read the text, check their guesses, and underline answers.

- Check answers with the class. Students should quote the parts of the text that answer the questions in Exercise 1.

Answer key

1 *Paris (in the background you can see the famous* Arc de Triomphe*).*
2 *He was all of these things.*
3 *The sea (clues are the whale in the main picture, the aqualung, the fact that under water you cannot hear very much).*
4 *Jacques Cousteau* /ʒæk kuˈstəʊ/.

2b

- Students read the text again, and underline all the verbs.
- They match infinitive forms 1–6 with their past simple forms in the text.
- Point out the pronunciation of *read* in the simple past, /red/.

Answer key

1 *read* 2 *spoke* 3 *said* 4 *thought* 5 *understood* 6 *fought*

2c

- Students write the new irregular verbs in their vocabulary books.

3

- To improve students' skimming skills (reading quickly for gist), make this a competition to see who can get the order first.
- Students match the headings with the text paragraphs.

Answer key

a *2* b *5* c *4* d *1* e *3*

4

- Students scan the text for specific information in the text, to learn more about Jacques Cousteau.
- Put students in pairs to check their answers. They take turns asking and answering the questions. To practise past simple verbs, they should answer with full sentences.

Answer key

1 *He was 87 when he died.* 2 *His environmental organization was The Cousteau Society.* 3 *He invented the aqualung in 1943.*
4 *He spoke French, English and German fluently.* 5 *He only understood Spanish, and only read Russian.*

Option

- 📼 This text is recorded on the cassette. You may wish to play it to the students after they have read the text again to help them answer the questions.

5a

- Demonstrate the task first. Read additional sentence 1. Then ask: *What is this sentence about?* (a ship). *Which paragraph in the text is about a ship?* (paragraph 2). Tell students to write 1 in the box at the end of paragraph 2. Have a student read the complete paragraph, including the new sentence.
- Students work individually adding sentences 2–4 into the text.

5b

- Students check their answers with a partner by reading whole paragraphs out loud.

Answer key
2 *paragraph 1*   3 *paragraph 5*   4 *paragraph 4*

Suggested Workbook practice
Page 61, Exercises 1 and 2

Jobs and hobbies

Aims
In this section, students revise object pronouns, learn the names of more jobs, and plan and write a description of a famous person.

Vocabulary: jobs

1
- Students circle Jacques Cousteau's areas of work and interest in the text. Students circle all references to any area.

Answer key
1 *explorer: 'underwater explorer' (paragraph 1), 'exploring' (paragraph 3)*
2 *environmentalist: 'His environmental organization' (paragraph 1), 'fought … for the environment' (paragraph 3)*
3 *film-maker: 'The French film-maker' (paragraph 2), 'film-maker' (paragraph 5)*
4 *writer: 'writing books' (paragraph 4), 'a writer' (paragraph 5)*
5 *'inventor' (paragraph 4)*
6 *'adventurer' (paragraph 5)*
7 *'businessman' (paragraph 5)*
8 *languages: 'He spoke French, English … read Russian' (paragraph 5)*

2

Background information
Ms is a woman's title which does not indicate whether she is married or single. It is particularly used by professional women.

- Read out the jobs in the box. Ask: *Which jobs do you know?*
- Students look up the other jobs in a dictionary.
- Students read the clues and match them with the jobs. They compare answers with a partner.
- Ask individual students for the answers. Get them to tell you which words helped them.

Answer key
1 *doctor*   2 *politician*   3 *secretary*   4 *film-star*   5 *lawyer*
6 *architect*

Option
- Ask students to write a clue for *farmer*.

3
- Quickly revise object pronouns. Say a subject pronoun, for example, *she*. Students respond with the object pronoun, for example, *her*.
- Students read the clues again and work out who or what the object pronouns refer to.

Answer key
1 *the politician*   2 *His boss, Ms Take*   3 *critics*   4 *my father and I*
5 *the plan for the new office*

Writing: a famous person

4a
- In groups of 4–5, students briefly discuss their own interests. They should start by discussing which, if any, of Cousteau's jobs they would like to do. They then talk about their ideas for jobs in the future. Help with vocabulary if asked.
- Students individually think of a famous person who has a job that interests them, and write as many facts as they know about their chosen person. They should organize their information in the form of notes as in Exercise 8 on page 89.

4b
- Students read the example, and look back at the texts on pages 88–90 for ideas on how to write their information. They then use their notes to write full sentences.

4c
- Students go back to their groups and read out their sentences. The new partners can suggest more information, or ask questions.

Option
- Students insert new information into their texts, as they practised in Exercise 5.

Suggested Workbook practice
Page 59, Exercise 1 and 2

The OK Club
Chocolate chip cookies

Aims
This section continues the photo-story. It presents informal English in a lively context, and brings together the language students have been practising in the unit, as well as revising language learned previously. Students practise describing people and reasons for their actions, using *because*. In this episode, Carol and Jane agree to clear up after the decorating. Carol arrives late, but doesn't start work. Instead, she eats a whole packet of chocolate chip cookies. The other members of the club are very annoyed to find no biscuits when they arrive. Dave thinks he knows what has happened.

1a

Background information
Cookies is more often used by Americans. The British call them 'biscuits'. However, some varieties of biscuit that originated in the USA are called 'cookies' by the British.

Options

- Dictate a summary of the last episode (see Tip 13 page 83 and Tip 15 page 112).

  Dave tells Jack / that he and Jane / went to the cinema together. / Jack is not happy / when he hears this. / Later, / at the club, / Jack gives Dave / all the horrible jobs. / Emma tells Jack / that it's not fair. / Jack says he is sorry, / and tells Dave / to have a break. / Carol says / she has a headache, / but when the film crew arrives, / she is suddenly / the first to help / with the work.

- To practise the present continuous, ask what is happening in each picture: *Who can you see in picture 1?* (Jane and Carol). *What are they doing?* (They're talking). *What are they wearing?* (jackets and trousers). *Look at picture 2. Where is Jane?* (at the club). *What's she holding?* (some biscuits). *What's Carol doing in picture 3?* (She's sitting/reading/eating). *Who can you see in picture 4?* (Jane, Dave, Ricky, Emma and Jack). *Who's missing?* (Carol). *Where do you think she is?* Students make suggestions.

- Read out the verbs in the box. Ask students to guess the meaning of the new past simple forms *ate, came, left* and *sat*.

- Students look briefly at the pictures, then cover them and underline the verbs in the box they think will be in the story. Do not give the answers yet.

1b

- Explain the task. Ask: *What's the infinitive of ate/came/left/read/sat?*

- Students write any new irregular past simple verbs in their vocabulary books.

1c

- 📟 Play the cassette. Students listen, read and check their ideas.

Answer key

ate   came   left   read   sat

2a

- Put students into pairs. They read the adjectives and check which ones they know. If one partner knows an adjective that the other doesn't, he or she should explain it. They then share the task of looking up any adjectives that neither of them knows.

- Pairs discuss Carol's behaviour and choose appropriate adjectives to describe her.

Answer key

greedy   hungry   late   lazy

2b

- Read the example out loud.

- Ask students to suggest first sentences for each adjective, for example, for *greedy*: *She ate all the biscuits*.

- Students write pairs of sentences. They then join them and write a third sentence with *because*.

Answer key

Carol ate all the biscuits because she was greedy.
She didn't see Jane because she was late.
She took the biscuits because she was hungry.

3

- Put students into groups of 3–4 to discuss their opinions of Carol's behaviour, and give reasons for their views.

Suggested Workbook practice

Page 60, Exercises 1–3

Review

Aims

The Review section summarizes and briefly revises the Key language features of Unit 13: the past simple (irregular verbs), and object pronouns.

The past simple: irregular verbs

- Tell students to close their books and tell you all the irregular verbs they can remember.

Object pronouns

- Students read the explanation.

- On the board, write: *Carol ate the biscuits*. Ask students to write the sentence again, using pronouns instead of nouns (*She ate them*). Ask: *Which is the subject pronoun? Which is the object pronoun?*

1

- Students write the positive past simple forms of as many verbs as possible. They then check back through the unit to find the others. They check their list in their vocabulary books and add any that are missing.

Answer key

was/were   became   began   came   did   ate   fought   found   gave went   had   knew   left   made   read   said   saw   sent   sank sat   spoke   took   told   thought   understood   wrote   won

2

- Students write sentences 1–5, changing the underlined words into subject or object pronouns.

- Students check their answers with a partner.

Answer key

1 *He*   2 *She   them*   3 *He   it*   4 *They   her*   5 *She   us*

Vocabulary

- *Films*. Students look back through the unit for any film words. They list and translate them.

- *Jobs*. Students add new items to their *Jobs* page. They could draw a small symbol to represent the job, for example, a stethoscope for a doctor, a pitchfork for a farmer.

Suggested Workbook practice

Page 58, Exercise 1
Page 59, Exercise 3

Freewheeling

a

- Go through the vocabulary in the box to check students know all the words.
- 📼 Play the cassette. Students listen and complete the words of the song.

b

- 📼 Play the cassette again. Students check their answers.
- Play the cassette again. Students sing the song.
- The class looks carefully at the song and discusses what the title probably is.

Answer key

fingers   life   life   heard   sang   heard   had   came   was   crowd found   read
The title is 'Killing me softly'.

c

- Students search for three more irregular verbs. Ask them what they think the infinitive form of each one is. They then add them to their vocabulary books.

Answer key

heard   felt   kept

Preparation for Unit 14

Workbook page 61, Exercise 3

Workbook answer key

Behind the camera

1a 2 *made*   3 *won*   4 *wrote*   5 *came*   6 *took*   7 *found*
8 *knew*   9 *gave*   10 *saw*

b 2 *make, made*   3 *win, won*   4 *write, wrote*
5 *come, same*   6 *take, took*   7 *find, found*   8 *know, knew*
9 *give, gave*   10 *see, saw*

2b 2 *They didn't watch a film on the radio. They watched it on TV.*
3 *She didn't go home in the evening. She went home in the afternoon.*
4 *They didn't go swimming in the cafe. They went swimming in the lake.*
5 *They didn't find a shark in the water. They found a frog.*
6 *She didn't write a book to her penfriend. She wrote a letter.*

The world of silence

1 1 *was born*   2 *became*   3 *made*   4 *won*   5 *invented*
6 *fought*   7 *spoke*   8 *played*   9 *wrote*   10 *died*

2a 2 *films*   3 *the aqualung*   4 *undersea divers*
5 *the natural environment*   6 *Jacques Cousteau*

b 1 *Please give it to me.*
2 *Let's invite them to the party.*
3 *Did you see her there?*
4 *Please tell us.*

3a 1 *director*   2 *painter*   3 *farmer*   4 *doctor*   5 *politician*
6 *architect*

b 2 *A painter paints pictures.*
3 *A farmer works on a farm.*
4 *A doctor checks people's health.*
5 *A politician works for his/her country.*
6 *An architect designs houses.*

Chocolate chip cookies

1 2 *She went to her bedroom. She put her bag on the floor and her jacket on the bed.*
3 *She went to the kitchen and ate her father's supper.*
4 *She went to the living-room and watched TV.*
5 *She went back to her bedroom and read a magazine. She didn't tidy her room and she didn't do her homework.*
6 *Her mother came home and she was (very) angry.*

2 *Student's own answers*

3 2 *because*   3 *so*   4 *so*   5 *because*   6 *so*

Skills: inserting new text

1 1 *C*   2 *B*   3 *D*   4 *A*

2 1 *Because she wanted to be like Marilyn Monroe.*
2 *She went to an acting college.*
3 *No, it didn't.*
4 *No, she didn't.*
5 *She found a job as a waitress.*

Prepare for Unit 14

3b *You can eat and drink here: cafe, restaurant*
You can buy things here: market, shop
You can look at things here: cinema, gallery, library, museum, theatre, zoo
You can stay here: hostel, hotel

c *bank*
You can get/change/save money here.

Unit 14

14

Syllabus

Topic
Great journeys: *explorers*
On the town: *a visit to London*
The OK Club

Grammar
The present continuous with future meaning
Shall we/Why don't we …?
How about …?
Let's …

Function
Talking about the future: plans
Suggestions and arrangements

Vocabulary
Jobs
Places in a town
Travel and exhibitions
Time phrases

Reading
Ordering events
Identifying locations on a map

Listening
Selecting relevant information
Recording main information
Transferring specific information to a chart

Writing
Writing a letter explaining future arrangements

Speaking
Sharing information
Making future arrangements
Discussing possible plans and suggestions

Pronunciation
/w/ and /v/
Sentence stress

Vocabulary

Key vocabulary

book (v = reserve)	market	theatre
blouse	North Pole	travel agent
expedition	palace	trip (n)
gallery	preparation	waistcoat
How about …?	relative	wax (… museum)
Jamaica	Shall I/we …?	Why don't we …?
let's		

Other vocabulary

complete	invitation	rock (music)
Cool!	model	silk
history	pull	

Materials preparation

1 For page 95, Exercise 1 Option 2: bring in something made of silk.
2 For page 95, Exercise 4 Option: make one copy of Worksheet 7 on page 150 for each student.
3 For page 96, Exercise 1: if possible, bring in books, pictures and postcards of London.

Great journeys
Sequences of events

Aims

In this section, students learn to order events to produce a simple narrative summary. They revise past simple verbs, sequencing words, and dates, and learn the names of more jobs. The language is presented through a reading text, and practised in reading and writing tasks.

1

Background information

Women explorers. On 24 January 2000, some of the team who took part in the walk to the North Pole described in the text completed a similar walk to the South Pole, becoming the first all-women team to do both Poles.

Options

- Revise past simple in telling stories. On the board, write sentences in the wrong order, and with verbs in the infinitve form:

    A   'I (think) you (know). I must go to Paris tomorrow,' she (tell) him.
    B   Thomas (come) into the living-room.
    C   'No, I (not know),' Thomas (reply). 'When (you decide) to go?'
    D   'What's wrong?' he (ask).
    E   He (give) her a smile, but she (not smile) back.
    F   'I (not decide),' she (answer). 'My parents want me to go away from you!'
    G   He (see) Maria by the open window.

    Give students a minute or two to read the sentences and think of the order. Then ask a student to say the first sentence, with the verb in the past simple. The rest of the class corrects the sentence if necessary. Ask another student for the next sentence, and so on.

Answer key

1B *came*   2G *saw*   3E *gave, didn't smile*   4D *asked*
5A *thought, knew, told*   6C *didn't know, replied, did you decide*
7F *didn't decide, answered*

- Quickly revise dates. On the board, write dates that are important to you, for example, *3/11/ 63, 6/76, summer 1991*. Students read them out, for example, *the third of November nineteen sixty-three, June nineteen seventy-six*. Explain the dates, for example: *My sister was born on 3/11/63. My family moved house in June 1976. In the summer of 1991, I had a holiday in Germany*. Students each think of one or two dates that are important to them. Send a piece of paper round the class on which students write their dates. Call out the dates in random order, for example: *What happened in April 2000?* The student who wrote that date explains its importance, for example: *That's me! In April 2,000 I went to Paris*.

- Tell students to look at the photo. Ask: *Where are they? What is different about them?* Students offer suggestions. Do not confirm answers yet.

- Draw students' attention to the headline 'At the top of the world'. Ask: *Where do you think the top of the world is?*

2

- Students quickly read the text to check their answers. Remind them that they do not need to understand every word.

Answer key

They are at the North Pole.   They are all women.

Option

- 📼 Play the cassette. Students listen with their books closed. Ask: *How many explorers arrived at the North Pole this morning?* (4). *How did they get there?* (they walked). *How long was the walk?* (700 km). *How many teams were there?* (5). *So how many women took part?* (20). *Did all the teams complete the walk?* (Yes). *Who organized the expedition?* (Caroline Hamilton). *What did the women do for six months?* (they trained and planned the trip).

3

- Students read the exercise before they read the text again.
- Explain any unfamiliar words, such as *relatives, organizer, expedition*.
- Put students into pairs. They number the order of events, then write the date of each.
- Pairs compare their answers with another pair. Then check answers with the class.

Answer key

A *5, 28/5/97*   B *6, 28/5/97*   C *7, 3/6/97*   D *3, 14/3/97*
E *4, 18/5/97*   F *1, 9/96*   G *2, 9/96–3/97*

4

- Remind students of the sequencing words *first, then, next* and *after that*. Use the small story in Exercise 1 Option 1 to do this, for example, *First, Thomas came into the room. Then he saw Maria by the open window …*
- Students put the sentences from Exercise 3 in sequence to produce a simple summary.

Option

- For homework, students could write the summary again, using pronouns where possible, and adding other information into the text, as they practised in Unit 13.

Vocabulary

5

- Tell students to look at the example. In the mother tongue, ask: *How do you make the verb into a noun?* (add -r). *What do you think you add if the verb doesn't end in -e?* (add -er). *So, what is the noun from 'teach'?* (teacher). *Do all nouns describing a person's job end in -er? Look back at Unit 13* (No, some end in -or, -ist or -man).
- Students individually remember and write the noun forms.
- Students compare answers with a partner. Then check them with the class.

Answer key

2 *teacher*   3 *TV producer*   4 *writer*   5 *inventor*   6 *scientist*
7 *businessman*   8 *cameraman*

Talking about the future

Aims

In this section, students learn to talk about the future, using the present continuous to discuss plans and arrangements. They also learn to differentiate between the sounds /w/ and /v/. The language is presented in a listening task, and practised through written and oral activities.

1

Background information

The Silk Road was a famous trading route as far back as the fourteenth century. Starting from the city-state of Venice, traders travelled through Turkey, Persia and India on a journey that could take years. The *Silk Road* was so named because traders brought back silk, as well as other goods from China. The most famous explorer to travel this route was the Italian, Marco Polo.

Options

- Write the following lists on the board. Ask students to try to match the people with the places.

1	Roald Amundsen	The Nile
2	Marco Polo	America
3	Christopher Columbus	The Antarctic
4	David Livingstone	China

  Students discuss their ideas in pairs, for example, A: *I think Roald Amundsen explored the Nile.* B: *Really? I'm not sure. I think it was …*

Answer key

1 *The Antarctic* 2 *China* 3 *America* 4 *The Nile*

- Show students something made of silk (see Materials preparation 1). Allow students to look at and feel it. Teach the word silk. Ask: *Where did silk come from?* (originally from China). *What animal makes it?* (the silkmoth). *Is it cheap or expensive? What clothes can be made of silk?*

- Give students time to read the introduction. Explain any unfamiliar words.
- Tell students to look at the map. Familiarize them with all the place names. Say a place name, for example, *Moscow/Antioch*. Students find it.
- 🔲 Play the cassette. Students listen and make notes on the map, ticking towns and writing dates.

Tapescript

Interviewer Roger, you're planning an exciting trip for this autumn. Can you tell me something about it?
Roger Yes. Some friends and I are travelling part of the old Silk Road in October and November. You know, the road people used hundreds of years ago to bring silk from China to the Mediterranean.
Interviewer Oh, yes. Are you going to China, then?
Roger No. Our route starts in Tashkent, in Uzbekistan. We're flying to Tashkent and then walking to Bukhara.
Interviewer How far is that?
Roger About 500 kilometres, and it's quite difficult because there are mountains and desert areas.
Interviewer When are you leaving?
Roger We're leaving in October – 10th October.
Interviewer Are you starting the walk immediately?
Roger No, we're spending two or three days in Tashkent first.

Interviewer Mmm, and where are you staying on the way?
Roger Well, when we can – when we're in towns – we're staying in hotels, or rather hostels, but we're taking tents with us too.
Interviewer And are you flying back from Bukhara?
Roger No, we're taking the train from Bukhara to Moscow. We're hoping to get to Bukhara on about the third of November and we're leaving there on the seventh. Then we're arriving in Moscow on the 18th November. We're stopping in a couple of places on the way.
Interviewer It all sounds wonderful – but hard work! Are you doing a lot of preparation for it at the moment?
Roger Oh, yes, we're doing a lot of long walks, and we're planning the route carefully.
Interviewer Are you reading about the area?
Roger No, we haven't got time!

Answer key

Tashkent 10th October   Bukhara 3rd to 7th November
Moscow 18th November

2a

- 🔲 Play the cassette again. Students listen carefully, and complete the interviewer's questions.
- Ask: *What sort of words did you need?* (verbs). Then check answers.

Answer key

1 *leaving* 2 *starting* 3 *staying* 4 *flying* 5 *doing* 6 *reading*

2b

- These questions follow on from each other very quickly. Sharing the questions will allow students time to both listen and write notes.
- Put students into pairs. They decide who listens to which questions.
- 🔲 Play the cassette again. Students make notes of the answers to their three questions.
- Walk round the class, checking notes, but do not give answers.

Option

- If necessary, play the cassette again for students to complete or check their notes.

2c

- Pairs share their information by asking and answering the questions. This should be oral only. Students do not write notes to the other three questions. Walk round, checking that students are using the right tense in their answers.

Work it out: the present continuous with future meaning

3a

- Students work individually. They read the sentences and answer the questions.

Answer key

the future: 2 (next week)   the present: 1 (at the moment)

Option

- Students think of other words that can follow *next*, for example, *month, year, summer, Tuesday, July, weekend.*

3b

- Students study the sentences carefully to decide if the events are present or future. They complete the sentences with the time expressions.

Answer key

1 *next week*   2 *at the moment*   3 *at the moment*   4 *next week*

3c

- Students read the questions in Exercise 2 again. They decide if they refer to the present or the future, and write *P* (= *present*) or *F* (= *future*) next to each.
- Students compare their answers with a partner. Then check the answers with the class.

Answer key

1 *F*   2 *F*   3 *F*   4 *F*   5 *P*   6 *P*

4

- Put students into new pairs (see Tip 8, page 37). They take it in turns to ask and answer questions to find a time they can meet. Walk round listening to pairs, and checking that they are using the present continuous.

Option

- Give out copies of Worksheet 5 (see Materials preparation 2). Students complete the diary, then ask and answer questions with a partner, using the present continuous with future meaning.

Pronunciation: /w/ and /v/

5a

- 📼 Play the cassette. Students listen and repeat the two sounds, /w/ and /v/, and then the phrase..

5b

- 📼 Play the cassette. Students listen and write the words they hear.
- Play the cassette again. Students listen, and tick the right column for each word.

Tapescript

1 leaving   2 wet   3 weather   4 volleyball   5 television   6 shower
7 travel

Answer key

2 /w/   3 /w/   4 /v/   5 /v/   6 /w/   7 /v/

Option

- Teach students this tongue twister:
    Whether the weather is cold
    Or whether the weather is hot
    We'll travel together
    Whatever the weather
    Whether you like it or not!

Suggested Workbook practice

Page 62, Exercises 1–4

On the town
Suggestions and arrangements

Aims

In this section, students learn language for making and responding to suggestions. The language is presented through listening tasks, and practised through guided role-play activities and writing.

1

Background information

London tourist attractions. All of these are found on the map in Exercise 3.

London Zoo is situated in 36 acres of Regent's Park. It has more than 650 species of animals, including 112 on the World Conservation endangered list. The zoo aims to house all the animals in conditions as close to their natural habitat as possible.

Madame Tussaud's is a waxworks museum. Madame Tussaud brought her original collection from France to London in 1835. The museum now contains thousands of extremely life-like models of famous people, past and present, including pop stars, politicians, and sports men and women.

At *The Rock Circus*, animated models of rock stars (made at Madame Tussaud's) tell the history of rock music.

Buckingham Palace has been the official London home of British Kings and Queens since 1837. It houses many great art treasures and is magnificently furnished.

The London Dungeon is London's 'Museum of Horror', recreating scenes from the darker side of European history. Exhibitions include the executions of two of Henry VIII's wives, the legend of Dracula, and the murderous exploits of Jack the Ripper and other serial murderers.

The Tower of London was built in the eleventh century. Used first as a king's castle, the fortress then became a prison for important prisoners. Since the fourteenth century, the tower has also been the place where the crown jewels are kept safe.

Covent Garden is a district of London, but the name is particularly associated with the fruit and vegetable market that was at its centre for centuries. The market has been replaced recently by a fashionable shopping centre with boutiques, craft stalls and cafes.

- In the mother tongue, find out what students know about London and what they think it is like. Ask: *What famous buildings are there? Is it cheap or expensive? What are the people like? Do you know what colour the buses are? What colour are the traditional London taxis? How else can people travel?* (by the underground). *Do you think it's the same as other big cities? How is it the same? How is it different? If you went to London, what would you go to see?* If possible, show students pictures, books and postcards about London (see Materials' preparation 3).

2

- Teach any new vocabulary from column A, for example, *palace, gallery, wax*.
- Students match the places with the words and phrases in column B.

Answer key

1 *pictures*   2 *food, clothes to buy*   3 *an important family*
4 *actors and musicians*   5 *models of famous people*   6 *animals*

3

- This exercise familiarizes students with the map of the area and some of its attractions. Students look at the picture and map, and try to find examples of any of the places in Exercise 2. Ask, for example: *Can you find a gallery?* (Yes). *What's the name of the gallery?* (National Gallery). *Where is it?* (in the south of the map). *Can you find a market?* (No). Continue with the other places in the same way.

Answer key

On the map – a gallery: the National Gallery
In the pictures – picture 1 a zoo: London Zoo   picture 4 a palace: Buckingham Palace

4a

- Students read the instructions. Say: *Alison and Luke are making plans. What tense do they use?* (the present continuous). *Read the example and check*. Students confirm their answer.

- 🔊 Play the cassette. Students listen and make notes on the plans Luke and Rachel have already made. Write the names on the board.

Tapescript

Luke   Hello.
Alison   Hi, Luke. It's Alison here.
Luke   Ali! How are you?
Alison   Fine. Luke, would you like to go to London on Saturday? With Rachel if she's around?
Luke   Yeah, that'd be great, but I've got a bit of a problem.
Alison   Oh, what's that?
Luke   I'm playing football with some friends from school in the morning.
Alison   Oh, that's OK. I'm doing the shopping for Mum in the morning anyway. What time does your football finish?
Luke   At half past twelve, I think.
Alison   So can we meet at about half past one?
Luke   Yes. Oh, I know that Rachel wants to be at home in the evening – she's watching a concert on TV with a friend of hers at half past nine.
Alison   Well, we can be back by then, can't we?
Luke   Yes. Why don't you come here this afternoon and we can decide where to go in London?
Alison   Good idea. See you later then. Bye.
Luke   Bye.

Answer key

Luke's playing football in the morning.
Rachel's watching a concert on TV in the evening.

4b

- 🔊 Play the cassette again. Students listen for the time they can meet.

Answer key

Saturday at about 1.30 p.m.

5a

- 🔊 Play the cassette. Students listen and write down the opening and closing times only of the places on the chart.

Tapescript

Hello. Thank you for phoning London Call – London's information service…
Buckingham Palace, the home of Britain's royal family, is open to the public from half past nine in the morning to quarter past four in the afternoon. Allow about two hours for your visit.

The London Dungeon, London's museum of horror, is open from ten in the morning to half past six in the evening. Allow about an hour and a half for your visit.
London Zoo, in Regent's Park, has an amazing collection of animals from all over the world. It is open daily from ten to half past five. You need five to six hours to see the zoo.
Madame Tussaud's, the famous wax museum, opens every day at ten o'clock and closes at half past five. Allow about three hours for your visit.
Rock Circus is part of the Trocadero Centre in Piccadilly Circus. Here, all your favourite rock musicians come to life! It is open from eleven in the morning to nine in the evening every day and you need about an hour here.
The Tower of London is one of the main historical sights in London and parts of it are nine hundred years old. You can visit it from nine o'clock to five o'clock every day. Allow three to four hours for your visit.
If you would like any other information …

5b

- 🔊 Play the cassette again. Students listen and note down the length of time suggested for each visit.

Answer key

	Opens	Closes	Time for visit
Buckingham Palace	9.30	4.15	*2 hrs*
The London Dungeon	10.00	6.30	*1 1/2 hours*
London Zoo	10.00	5.30	*5–6 hours*
Madame Tussaud's	10.00	5.30	*3 hours*
Rock Circus	11.00	9.00	*1 hour*
The Tower of London	9.00	5.00	*3–4 hours*

6a

- Ask: *What time can Alison and her friends meet on Saturday?* (1.30).

- Put students into groups of 4–5. Tell them look at the chart and the map, and discuss which places Alison, Luke and Rachel could visit in an afternoon.

- Students plan a day out in London for Alison and her friends. They should take into account the time needed for a visit, and where the attraction is located.

- Allow about 5 minutes for discussion, then ask some groups to tell the class their ideas. Encourage students from other groups to comment.

Option

- Use this exercise as a role-play. Students, in groups of three, imagine they are Alison, Rachel and Luke. Have them work out a) the approximate time that they can stay in London, and b) the time they would like to stay in each place. Tell them to allow time to travel to and from home, and from one place to another. These times need not be accurate, but will add to the realism of the role-play.

6b

- 🔊 Play the cassette. Students listen carefully and find out what the final arrangements are.

Tapescript

Alison   OK, then. Shall we meet at the station?
Rachel   Yes, good idea. At half past one – OK?
Alison   Where shall we go, then?
Rachel   How about going to the zoo?
Luke   No, a visit to the zoo takes hours, and it closes at half past five.
Rachel   Mmm, you're right. I know, let's go to Covent Garden Market.

Alison No, I hate markets! Perhaps we can visit some different places. I know, why don't we go to the Rock Circus? That's open in the evening too.

Luke Yeah! I love that! Let's go there in the evening.

Rachel But what shall we do in the afternoon?

Alison How about visiting the National Gallery? That's quite near.

Luke Oh, no. I hate art galleries!

Alison Yeah I agree. Look, why don't we go to Madame Tussauds? That's fun.

Rachel Yes, great idea! There are lots of new wax models there.

Alison OK, so we're meeting at half past one and we're going straight to Madame Tussaud's.

Luke Yes, then we're going to the Rock Circus.

Rachel We can have something to eat at Planet Hollywood first, and then go to the Rock Circus at about six. Then I can still be home by about nine!

....

Answer key

First they're going to Madame Tussaud's, then they're going to Planet Hollywood (to eat), and after that they're going to the Rock Circus (at about 6.00).

Work it out: making suggestions

7a

- Students close their books. Read out the text in the speech bubbles. Then, in the mother tongue, ask: *What do all the phrases have in common?* (they are all ways of making suggestions).

- Students read the phrases. Still in the mother tongue, ask: *Are they all questions?* (no). *Which phrase do you think is the strongest way of making a suggestion? Why?* (*Let's*, because it's a statement, not a question. *Perhaps* is a rather tentative word).

7b

- Explain the task. Suggest students look carefully at the verb endings and punctuation before they decide.

- Students complete the chart.

Answer key

Shall we/Why don't we go out for the day?
Let's/Perhaps we can go out for the day.
How about going out for the day?

Useful English

- 📼 These phrases are possible responses to suggestions given in Exercise 7. Teach them in the usual way.

Pronunciation: sentence stress

8a

- Tell students to close their books, and to listen carefully.

- 📼 Play the cassette. Students listen only.

- Play the cassette again. Students listen and mark the stressed words in each sentence.

Answer key

2 *How about going to the zoo?*
3 *Let's go to Covent Garden Market.*
4 *Perhaps we can visit some different places.*
5 *Why don't we go to the Rock Circus?*

8b

- 📼 Play the cassette again. Students listen and repeat, taking care to stress the words they underlined in Exercise 8a.

8c

- Put students into pairs. They take turns making suggestions 1–5 and responding to them, using expressions from the Useful English box.

9

- Join pairs to make groups of 4. Students use the information from the exercises on pages 96–7 to plan a day in London. Walk round the groups, checking that they are making and responding to suggestions correctly.

Writing: plans

10a

- Students plan a weekend itinerary for their 'visitor'. These activities take students through the stages of brainstorming for ideas, planning events, and drafting and editing a reply to the penfriend.

- On the board, write some notes:
    Arriving: this weekend – Monday 26th – 12.30
    Leaving: Friday 23rd – 2.30 – train at 2.00

- Tell students to read the letter, then copy the notes. Wait for a student to notice a mistake. Apologize, and correct it. Ask: *Are there any more mistakes?* Students look and help you correct the notes. This should fix the facts in their minds.

- Students make a list of places in or near their own town. They plan the visit. Tell them to make notes, for example, *Friday – 1) lunch Tosca's, 2) Tate Gallery 3.00–4.30, 3) 7.25 theatre: Shakespeare.*

10b

- Students make their notes into sentences, for example, *On Friday we're eating lunch at Tosca's. In the afternoon we're visiting the Tate Gallery.*

10c

- Students check their sentences, and make any corrections. They should particularly check that they are using the present continuous for future meaning.

10d

- Students invent a name for their penfriend. They copy the beginning of the letter, then add their plan. Remind them to link their sentences, using sequencing words (*first*, *then*, *next*, *after that*).

Suggested Workbook practice

Page 63, Exercises 1 and 2

The OK Club
Plans for a party

Aims

This section continues the photo-story. It presents informal English in a lively context, and brings together the language students have been practising in the unit, as well as revising language learned previously. In this episode, the club members discover they have some money left over from Project OK. They decide to spend it on a party, and plan the party.

1a

Option

- To revise the story so far, ask students about pictures 1 and 2, for example: *Why is everyone looking at Carol in picture 1? What did she do in the last episode? Look at picture 2. Why are all the club members happy? What did they do for their club?*

- This exercise gets students thinking about the new topic in the story: a club party.
- Copy the word-map from the book onto the board. Students call out their ideas for a party. Accept all their suggestions, as there are no right or wrong answers, and write them on the board.

Option

- Add *Clothes* as another heading in the word-map.

1b

- ▣ Play the cassette. Students listen and compare their ideas for a party with those in the story.
- Ask: *Which categories on the word-map are talked about in the story? Which ones aren't discussed?*

Option

- Students briefly discuss what drinks and music the OK Club members would probably choose.

2

- Go through the example with students. Students work individually to match the people with the food, then write sentences joining the two parts.

Answer key

2 *The TV people are making a film of the party.*
3 *Dave and Carol's mother is making some cakes.*
4 *Ricky's parents are making some Caribbean food.*

3

- In pairs, students use the list of ideas to practise the language of making and responding to suggestions.

Tip 17 ★
Simulations

- In some ways a simulation activity is similar to a role-play, requiring students to think about an imaginary situation. The difference is that role-plays require students to act out a scene and to be a character in that scene, for example, a shopkeeper or customer in a shop. In a simulation activity, on the other hand, students are free to express their own ideas and do not have to act a part. The example given here is 'Planning a party'. Explain that you want to organize a class party. Write some question prompts on the board. For example:

  LET'S HAVE A PARTY!
  people to invite?   place?   date?   time?
  music?   food?   drink?   party games?   clothes?

  Get the class to make suggestions for three or four of the questions, for example: *Let's invite our friends. We can have pizzas. Let's have the party on Friday afternoon*. Put students into groups of 4–5. Each group plans their own party, using the question prompts on the board. They appoint a 'secretary' to make a note of their group's ideas. Go round checking how students are progressing with their plans.

  When groups have almost completed their plans, teach some useful phrases of giving a general invitation, for example, *Listen everybody! We're having a party, and we'd like you to come! We're having our party on (place/day/time). We're making (type of food). Please bring …* Give groups a few more minutes to practise their announcements. Each group chooses a representative to tell the class about their plans, and to invite the others.

  Groups can then write a poster to advertise their party.

Review

Aims

The Review section summarizes and briefly revises the Key language features of Unit 14: present continuous with future meaning, and making suggestions.

Present continuous with future meaning

- Ask students to read the explanation and examples. They then each write two sentences using the present continuous, one with present meaning, and the other with future meaning. Their examples should make the difference clear.

Making suggestions

- Students close their books. Ask five students to each make a suggestion. Every suggestion should begin a different way.

1

- Students read the diary, then write sentences about Emma's plans for next week.

Answer key
(possible answers)
Emma's playing tennis with Ricky at half past four on Tuesday.
Emma's playing chess with Jack at the club at quarter past seven on Wednesday.
Emma's meeting Carol at the burger bar at twenty-five past twelve on Thursday.
Emma's going to a disco at the club at quarter to eight on Friday.
Emma's going swimming at quarter past three on Saturday.
Emma's going on holiday to France on Sunday.

Option
- If you think students have mastered the language quite well, do this exercise as a quick oral activity.

2
- Check that students understand each advert. Ask: *Who are the Spice Girls? What is the Odeon? What is Hollywood Pizza? When is the circus coming to Battersea Park?*
- Students work with a partner to decide where they would like to go.
- Ask pairs: *Where are you going? Why are you going there?* Find out which is the most popular choice and why.

Vocabulary
- *Travel.* Students add any new language to the appropriate page in their vocabulary books, for example, *Countries, Transport.*
- *Places in a town.* Students add any new words to their *Places* page. They may like to do this as a word-map.
- *Time phrases.* Students add these to their *Time* page.

Suggested Workbook practice
Page 63, Exercises 3 and 4
Page 64, Exercises 1–3
Page 65, Exercises 1–3

Freewheeling
- Demonstrate the game with a student. The student thinks of a place. Ask questions like the examples. Encourage the rest of the class to join in. If a student asks an open question, such as *What street is it in?*, tell him or her that they must try again.
- Put students into groups of 4–5 to play the game.

Preparation for Unit 15
Workbook page 65, Exercise 4

Workbook answer key

Great journeys
1 Present: *now, at the moment*
Future: *tomorrow, next month, next week, the day after tomorrow*

2a 2 *F*   3 *F*   4 *F*   5 *P*   6 *P*   7 *P*   8 *F*   9 *F*   10 *P*

b 1   ... *is sitting in her bedroom. She is writing a letter to her penfriend.*
2   ... *she's playing volleyball with some friends.*
3   ... *she's going to France for a day (with her Mum and Dad).*
4   ... *she's visiting her grandparents.*

3a *writer, businessman, explorer, inventor, producer, teacher*

b 1 *businessman*   2 *teacher*   3 *inventor*   4 *producer*
5 *writer*   6 *explorer*

4b *was /w/: window, worried, swap, why*
have /v/: adventure, clever, move, relative

On the town
1 2   ... *have a pizza.*
3   ... *watching a film?*
4   ... *visit the wax museum?*
5   ... *go to the disco?*

2 1   ... *don't we go to the zoo?*
2   ... *we can have a milkshake.*
3   ... *about going swimming?*
4   *Shall we play basketball? / Let's play basketball.*
5   *Shall we visit a gallery? / Let's visit a gallery.*

3a *hostel, library, cinema, restaurant, theatre, bank, cafe, zoo, gallery*

b 1 *station*   2 *hostel*   3 *zoo*   4 *theatre*   5 *restaurant*
6 *gallery*

4 *Luke   I don't know. How about going swimming?*
Ellen   No, I don't think so. I'm playing badminton in the morning.
Luke   Perhaps we can go shopping.
Ellen   I haven't go any money. Let's watch a video.
Luke   Yes, good idea.

Plans for a party
1 A *Great idea! I love barbecues.*
B *Oh yes, I love hamburgers.*
2 ... *don't we have milkshakes?*
C *Oh no! I hate milkshakes.*
3 *have cola*
D *Yes, a lot of people like cola.*
4 *Shall we/Why don't we, her guitar*
E *I'm not sure.*
5 *Let's/Perhaps we can, a radio*
6 *How about inviting/Why don't we/Shall we invite*
F *Yes, why not?*

2 1 *having*   2 *birthday*   3 *having*   4 *cola*   5 *taking*
6 *radio*   7 *inviting*

3 *Student's own answers*

Skills: writing about plans
1 *Student's own answers*
2 *Student's own answers*
3 *Student's own answers*

Prepare for Unit 15
4a 1 *bag*   2 *bracelet*   3 *briefcase*   4 *(baseball) cap*
5 *glasses*   6 *wallet*   7 *pocket*   8 *purse*   9 *umbrella*

b 1 *purse*   2 *glasses*   3 *umbrella*

Unit 15

Syllabus

Topic
Losing things
More mix-ups: *finding your property*
The OK Club

Grammar
I'll, Shall I, let me used for offers
Possessive pronouns
one and *ones*
-'s or *-s'* (revision)

Function
Making offers
Talking about possessions

Vocabulary
Personal property
Offers

Reading
Skimming a text for key information
Finding and transferring information to a chart

Listening
Identifying key information
Checking information
Transferring specific information to a chart

Writing
Completing a story from a picture clue

Speaking
Making a phone call about lost property
Giving an account of past events
Talking about possessions
Summarizing the OK Club story

Pronunciation
Word and sentence stress
/s/, /ʃ/ and /z/

Vocabulary

Key vocabulary

belong to	hers	push-chair
bracelet	one	schoolbag
briefcase	ours	theirs
cap	owner	umbrella
coat	plate	wallet
credit card	(lost) property	Whose?
give someone a	purse	yours
hand		
glasses		

Other vocabulary

absolutely	disappear	mine
babies	dozen	pocket
bone	fall out of	skeleton
cage	false	underground
carry	human	

Materials preparation

Dictionaries for page 100, Exercise 1b.

Losing things

Aims

In this section, students are introduced to the language of making and responding to offers, and vocabulary concerned with personal property. The language is presented through reading and listening tasks.

1a

- Students close their books. Ask a few students: *Do you lose things at school or in town?* Students respond. Then ask: *What sort of things do people often lose?* Accept one or two suggestions, then say: *Make a list.*
- Give students about three minutes to make their lists of items that are frequently lost, for example, *keys*, *purse*, *sunglasses*. Let them write a word in their mother tongue if they do not know it in English.

1b

- Put students into pairs to compare lists, and to look up words in their dictionaries.

1c

- Students read the instructions, and briefly discuss the lost property system in the school. If you do not already know, find out before class where lost property is kept in your school.

1d

- Students translate *lost property*.

Option

- Before the lesson, talk to the person in charge of lost property in your school and find out what the most common lost property items are, and some of the more unusual items that have been handed in. Ask students to guess what these are.

2a

- Give students 30 seconds to read the text and find the two places where people often lose things in London. Tell them that they do not need to understand every word.

Answer key

buses   underground trains

2b

- Students read the text again to find an address.

Answer key

Baker Street

3a

- Students read the text carefully to find more detailed information. Set a longer time limit of 1–2 minutes. Then check answers.

Answer key

1 *wallets   purses   a pair of glasses*
2 *umbrella   book   camera*
3 *human skeleton   false teeth   musical instruments
  babies' push-chairs   stuffed animal or bird*

Option

- This text is recorded on the cassette. You may wish to play it to the students after they have read the text.

3b

- Tell students to look at the picture on page 100 and, with a partner, to find as many of the things from Exercise 3a as they can.
- Ask: *Did you find the (wallet)?* Tell students the letter of objects they do not know, for example, *Did you find the skeleton?* (No). *Look at B.*
- Teach the other objects in the picture. For each item, ask: *Does anyone know what (E) is?* If no student knows, tell them the English word.
- Students check the list against their own ideas from Exercise 1a. Ask a few students what is on their list that isn't in the photo or text.

4

- Tell students they are going to hear three people phoning the Lost Property Office about things they have lost. Students have to identify the lost items in the picture, and write the letter of each item.
- Play the cassette. Students look at the picture on page 100 and decide which three items the speakers have lost.

Tapescript

1 **Man** Hello, is that the Lost Property office?
  Officer Yes, it is. Can I help you?
  Man Yes, please. … er … I lost a keyboard … you know, an electronic piano, on a bus the other day …
  Officer Oh yes. I think we've got a keyboard here. It came in last week … mmm … last Friday. Shall I take your name and address?
  Man Oh, thanks! Yes, please. It's Tom Allen – that's A L L E N. Can I come in and get it later today?
  Officer Yes, of course you can. I'll have it ready for you.
  Man Thank you very much.
2 **Woman** … I left my sister's birthday present on an underground train the other day … er … it's a gold bracelet and it's in a red box with a name on the front.
  Officer Let me look at the computer here for you … mmm … yes, we have got a gold bracelet. In a red box, you say? That's right. Let me take your name, then perhaps you can come and collect it?
  Woman Oh, that's wonderful! …
3 **Old lady** … this is a bit difficult … you see, I left my false teeth on a bus the other day …
  Officer Don't worry, madam – we have a whole box of false teeth here.
  Old lady Oh, I see. Shall I give you my name, then?
  Officer Er, no thank you, madam. Come in and see me tomorrow and I'll show you all the teeth here.
  Old lady Oh, all right. Thank you.

Answer key

1 *E – keyboard*   2 *G – gold bracelet*   3 *F – false teeth*

Offers

Aims

In this section, students learn how to make and respond to offers and suggestions through listening and speaking activities.

Useful English

- 📼 Teach the phrases for making and responding to offers in the usual way.

1a

- Tell students that they should complete the text with Useful English phrases and other missing information. Point out that brackets round a phrase means that the information within them can be changed, for example, *Shall I (help you find them)? Shall I (phone you back)?*
- Students work individually, then compare their answers with a partner.

1b

- 📼 Play the cassette. Students listen, and check their answers.

Answer key

Can I help you   Yes, please   Let me take   I'll phone you   your wallet
Thank you very much

1c

- Put students into pairs to practise the dialogue, taking turns to be the man or the woman.
- Students suggest changes to parts of the dialogue, for example, Man: *I lost my guitar on the London to Manchester train yesterday*. Woman: *I'll have a look for you and phone you back.* Man: *Shall I give you my number?*
- Students make new dialogues. Check that they are using phrases from the Useful English box.

2a

- These activities prepare students for the role-play in Exercise 3. Students decide first who they are, for example, two old men, and what they have lost, for example, a pair of false teeth. They then read the possible situations and choose one, for example, brothers buying a birthday present in the city.

2b

- In pairs, students prepare a story by discussing answers to the questions.

2c

- Students rehearse their stories together. Student A asks the questions, and B answers. If you feel they need further practice, A and B can change roles.

Finding your lost property

3a

- This is a whole class activity. Each pair in turn tells their story and has to prove that the item really belongs to them. The rest of the class asks them the questions in Exercise 2b to establish the facts.

3b

- The class votes whether they believe each pair's story or not.

Suggested Workbook practice

Page 66, Exercises 1 and 2
Page 68, Exercise 4

More mix-ups
Possessive pronouns

Aims

In this section, students learn to talk about possession, using *Whose …?* and possessive pronouns. The language is introduced through a picture story and listening tasks.

1a

Background information

A **bowling alley** is where you can play an indoor game called ten-pin bowling. Players take turns to roll a heavy ball down an 'alley' (or 'lane') to knock down objects called 'pins'. The alleys are long stretches of smooth wood, so special soft shoes are worn to protect them. Players leave their own shoes at the front desk, as in the picture on page 102.

Option

- 📼 Students close their books. Play enough of the first two speeches for students to hear the sounds of a bowling alley. Ask: *Where are these people?* Students make guesses. After a few answers, explain that they are in a bowling alley. Ask: *Is there a bowling alley in our town? Do you go? What special clothes do you need?*

- Explain the situation: there's a mix-up over the shoes. Students look at the pictures and text carefully, and work out who is being referred to in each speech.
- Students read the list of pronouns, and complete the speech bubbles with them. They should be able to guess the meaning of each possessive pronoun because of their similarity to the possessive adjectives. Do not explain the grammar.

1b

- 📼 Play the cassette. Students listen and check their answers.

Answer key

yours   mine   mine   hers   Mine   yours   ours   theirs   ours

2

- Explain the task. Point out that the players have T-shirts with their names on.
- 📼 Play the cassette. Students listen, look at the pictures, and match the shoes with the people.

Answer key

1 *hers*   2 *theirs*   3 *his*   4 *theirs*

Option

- If you think the students will find this task difficult, let them read the text at their own pace, rather than play the cassette again.

Work it out: possessive pronouns

3

- Students use the completed example sentences in Exercise 1 to help them fill in the gaps. Then, in the mother tongue, ask: *What question word do you use to ask about belongings? (Whose?)*.

How do you say that something belongs to you/them/her? (It's mine/theirs/hers).

Answer key

Questions: Whose, Whose
Answers: mine, your, hers, his, ours, theirs

4

- Put students into groups of 4–6. Each member of the group should place several items on a desk, such as pens, a pencil case, a watch, a jumper.
- Students take it in turns to pick up an item and ask questions. When someone answers *Yes, it's mine*, their item is returned to them. Walk round, checking students are varying the questions, and not just asking *Is this yours?* to each person in turn.

Suggested Workbook practice

Page 67, Exercises 1 and 2

one and *ones*

Aims

In this section, students practise talking about possession, and learn to use *one/ones* to avoid repeating words. They also revise *'s*, and learn the plural possessive form, *-s'*. The language is presented and practised in reading, listening and speaking tasks.

1

- Go through the chart with the class, checking that they understand it. Explain any vocabulary. Then ask: *What information is missing?* (two names, two addresses, two descriptions of food, and the letters of the three cages).
- Explain that they are going to complete the chart, but some information is in the reading text, and some is on cassette. Tell them that they can find the first two pieces of information in the text, and work out a third piece of information.
- Students read the text slowly and carefully, and then fill in two boxes of the chart.

Answer key

*Cage **C** is the dog who likes dog food from a tin and biscuits (middle column). **Bella** lives in Station Street (first column). Consequently, **Carol** must be the woman at the top of the middle column.*

2

- Tell students they are now going to work out the rest of the information for the chart. They will need to take quite detailed notes as they listen. Explain that it is the food each dog eats that will help them to work out everything else.
- 🔊 Play the cassette. Pause after each conversation to allow students time to complete their notes, and to think about the clues.
- Students complete as much of the chart as they can.
- Remind them that information in the reading text may help, so they should check the new information against the text.
- Play the cassette again. Students listen for any information they missed, or check their answers. Do not confirm answers yet.

Tapescript

1 **Bella** 138 Hello. Is that the Dogs' Home?
   Officer Yes, it is. How can I help you?

Bella Well, I lost my dog, Buster, in the park today. He's small and brown.
Officer Ah yes. We have three dogs here – they're all small and brown.
Bella Oh dear!
Officer Can you tell me what your dog ... er ... Buster, likes to eat?
Bella Eat? Well, he doesn't really like tinned dog-food, but he loves dog-biscuits. He always has biscuits in the evening – did he eat biscuits?
Officer Yes, one dog only ate biscuits. Now can you give me your name and address, please? You can come and get him immediately.
Bella Oh, thank you so much! My name's Bella Brown – that's B-E-L-L-A and I live in ...

2 **Woman** Hello. Is that the Dogs' Home?
   Officer Yes, it is. Can I help you?
   Woman Yes, please! I lost my dear little Buster in the park today ...
   Officer Ah, yes. Your dog, you mean? Well, we have three dogs here. What colour is your dog?
   Woman He's small and brown.
   Officer Oh dear. I've got three small, brown dogs here. Can you tell me what your ... er ... 'Buster' likes to eat?
   Woman Food, you mean? ... er ... Well, actually, he's a bit difficult. He only eats bones, you see ...
   Officer Bones? Oh, good.
   Woman You've got him?! I'm coming round to get him now!
   Officer Hello! Hello? Are you there? Aargh! I wanted her name!

3 **Woman** Hello. Is that the Dogs' Home?
   Officer Yes, it is. Did you call me a moment ago?
   Woman Me? No, I didn't.
   Officer Oh. I'm sorry. ... Can I help you?
   Woman I'm sure you can. I lost my dog, Buster, in the park this afternoon ...
   Officer I see. Well, we have three dogs here ... and ... er ... they're all small and brown ...
   Woman Oh really? How funny. Buster is small and brown, too.
   Officer Can you tell me what your dog likes to eat?
   Woman Of course. He eats anything – always hungry. Loves his food.
   Officer You mean tinned dog-food, dog-biscuits, that sort of thing?
   Woman Yes, anything.
   Officer Oh good! I think your dog is here and you can have him immediately.
   Woman That's very kind. I'm at number 88 Atlanta Avenue. My name's ...

Answer key

*Dialogue 1: This dog loves **dog biscuits**, so it must be in cage **A** (see text), and belongs to Bella. This completes the first column.*
*Dialogue 2: This dog only eats **bones**, so must be in cage **B** (see text).*
*Dialogue 3: This dog eats anything – tinned dog food and biscuits – so must be Carol's dog (see chart), and the caller lives in **Atlanta Avenue**. This completes the middle column.*
*Consequently, Amy must be the caller in dialogue 2, whose dog eats bones, and she must live in **New Drive** (see text).*

3

- On the board, write: *There are three dogs.* Below it write: *Which one eats bones?* Then, pointing to the question, ask: *What does 'one' mean here?* Students work out that it means 'dog'. Draw an arrow from dog in the sentence to *one* in the question. Then write: *The one in Station Street is called Bella.* Ask: *What does 'one' mean here?* (woman).
- Read the instructions and example out loud. Ask students to suggest other questions (in past simple) they could ask, for example, *Which one ate (dog biscuits)? Which one lived in (New Drive)?*

- Students compare answers with a partner by asking each other questions about the chart, using *one/ones* to describe the dogs and women.

Work it out: -'s or -s' (review)

4

- Students read the rules.
- Ask students to suggest an example of each type of noun, for example, *1 dog, 2 women, 3 cages*. Write them on the board, and tell students to close their books. Point to each noun in turn, and ask: *Apostrophe -s or -s apostrophe?* Students try to remember the rules.
- Students work individually to complete the sentences.

Answer key

1 *s'* 2 *'s* 3 *'s* 4 *'s* 5 *s'*

Pronunciation: /s/, /ʃ/ and /z/

5a

- 📼 Students listen and repeat the tongue-twister.

5b

- The class practises saying the tongue-twister (see Tip 1 page 9, and Tip 2 page 13).

Suggested Workbook practice

Page 67, Exercises 3 and 4

The OK Club
The OK Club on TV!

Aims

This section concludes the photo-story. It presents informal English in a lively context, and brings together the language students have been practising in the unit, as well as revising language learned previously. In this episode, the OK Club members discuss the party, enjoy the video of it, and resolve relationships within the group. There is even the hint of a new romance.

1a

- Put students into groups of 4–5. Students use the pictures to help them answer the questions and make guesses about the episode.

1b

- 📼 Play the cassette. Students listen, read, and check their guesses.

Answer key

The OK Club members are on TV.
They're at the club.
They're dancing.

2

- Tell students to look at the picture. Ask: *Who's in the picture? What's happening? Where are they going? What are they saying? Are they going to meet again? What are the OK Club members doing afterwards?*

- Put students into groups of 3–4 to discuss ideas and take notes.
- Students use their notes to write the end of the story. This can be done in class or at home.
- Students swap notebooks with a partner, and check each other's work.
- Choose one or two students to read out their story endings to the class.

Option

- Give students a gapped dictation (see Tip 15, page 112).
  Gapped text:

    The OK Club members worked hard and _____ _____ _____ _____. They were very pleased ___ ____ ____. They had some extra money, so they ___ ____ ___ ___ party. They planned to have food and music. The television company promised ___ ____ ___ ____ for the last time. The next day, they ____ ____ ____ video of their party. Then the teenagers said 'goodbye' to the TV producer and her _____, ____ ____ ____, 'When are _____ ____ the film? We want to be ___ ___!'

- Dictation:

    The OK Club members / worked hard / and finished the club kitchen. / They were very pleased / with their work. / They had some extra money, / so they decided / to have a party. / They planned to have food and music. / The television company / promised to film them again / for the last time. / The next day, / they all watched / the video of their party. / Then the teenagers said 'goodbye' / to the TV producer / and her cameraman, / and asked them, / 'When are you showing / the film? / We want to be TV stars!'

3a

- In groups of 4–5, students use the episode titles to remember the whole story.

3b

- Still in their groups, students discuss the parts of the story they liked most, giving reasons for their choice. They may look back at previous episodes to do this.

Suggested Workbook practice

Page 68, Exercise 3

Review

Aims

The Review section summarizes and briefly revises the key language features of Unit 15: possessive pronouns, and *one* or *ones*.

Possessive pronouns

- Students read the explanation. Tell them to look at the example and make it plural (*Whose are these cassettes? They're ours*).

one or ones

- Read the explanation aloud. Do a question-and-answer chain round the class, for example, *Which apples do you like, Rosa? The green ones. What colour car have you got, Selim? A red one.*

1

● Students work individually, underlining the right possessive adjective or pronoun.

Answer key

2 *your   yours*   3 *my   mine*   4 *her   hers*   5 *their   theirs*

2

● Students complete the dialogue individually, and then check their answers in pairs by acting it out.

Answer key

1 *one*   2 *one*   3 *ones*   4 *ones*   5 *ones*   6 *ones*   7 *one*

Vocabulary

● *Possessive pronouns*. These could go on the same page as possessive adjectives and object pronouns.
● *Personal property*. Students add new vocabulary from page 100 to the relevant pages of their vocabulary notebooks.
● *Offers*. These could be done as a dialogue.

Suggested Workbook practice

Page 66, Exercise 3
Page 68, Exercises 1 and 2

Freewheeling

Can you remember?

a

● This is a form of Kim's Game (see Game 4, page 74). Students look at the picture on page 100 for one minute.

b

● Students close their books. They try to remember all the objects and where they are located. They write sentences.

c

● Students in groups of 3–4 compare sentences. They then look at the picture again, and check their ideas.

Suggested Workbook practice

Page 69, Exercises 1 and 2

Workbook answer key

Losing things

1   *Possible answers:*
  A *I'll pay for your coffee.*
  B *No, thank you. It's OK.*
  A *Let me carry your briefcase.*
  B *Oh, thank you very much.*
  A *Shall I help you with your homework?*
  B *Yes, please, Mum.*
  A *Can I take your dog for a walk?*
  B *Yes, that's a good idea.*

2   2 *Can I help you?*   3 *I'll do that for you.*   4 *Let me carry your bag.*   5 *Shall I open the door?*   6 *I'll answer the phone.*

3a *umbrella, apple, egg, glasses, show, wallet, trip, purse, sell, lamb, bracelet, taxi*

More mix-ups

1   Possessive adjective: *your, his, her, it, our, their*
  Possessive pronoun: *mine, yours, his, hers, ours, yours, theirs*

2   1 *whose, mine*   2 *yours, ours*   3 *mine, my friend's*
  4 *his*   5 *theirs, theirs*

3   1 *ones*   2 *one*   3 *ones*   4 *one*   5 *one*

4b *see* /s/: *bracelet, disappear, glass, steak*
  as /z/: *lose, size, whose, zoo*
  show /ʃ/: *politician, push, situation*

The OK Club on TV

1   2 *our*   3 *his*   4 *ours*   5 *theirs*   6 *yours*   7 *hers*
  8 *mine*

2   1 *It's Ricky's waistcoat.*
  2 *It's the film crew's camera.*
  3 *They're the club members' biscuits.*
  4 *It's the club's back entrance.*
  5 *He's Carol's brother.*
  6 *She's Carol's mother.*

3   *Thank you.*
  Yes, I'd like that.
  Thanks. I'd love to meet them.
  Yes, please. Can I have one with milk and sugar?
  No, thank you. I'm not hungry.
  I'm sorry. There isn't a film in it.
  Yes, I'd like to become a member.
  OK. I live at …

4   1 *… open the door for you.*
  2 *… open the window*
  3 *… buy/get some crisps for you.*
  4 *… I help you*
  5 *I'll cook supper for you.*
  6 *Let me pay for you/buy your ticket.*

Skills: vocabulary round-up

1a *Food: hamburger, potato*
  Furniture: armchair, bed, table
  Places in towns: bank, cinema, museum
  Sports: basketball, judo, swimming
  Weather: cold, sunny, windy
  Animals: elephant, fox, giraffe
  Jobs: farmer, lawyer, shop assistant
  Clothes: jeans, shirt, trainers

b   *Student's own answers*

2   *Student's own answers*

Consolidation

3

Syllabus

Topic
Revision

Grammar
Revision of grammar points

Function
Revision of functions

Vocabulary
Revision of vocabulary

Reading
Completing a text from cues
Finding information in a leaflet

Listening
Comparing accounts of events and dialogues
Completing texts
Identifying location from clues

Writing
Preparing and writing a mini tourist guide

Speaking
Phone-calls: catching up on news and arranging to meet
Describing a tourist location

Vocabulary

Key vocabulary

award (n)	Egypt	system
bravery	river	transport
cliff	station	Zimbabwe
daughter	supermarket	

Other vocabulary

ballet	flower	opera
cave	guide	path
cheap	health	upset (adj)
fitness		

Materials preparation

For page 109, Exercise 7 Option: bring in books, brochures, town plans and or/maps which provide tourist information on towns in your country. Alternatively, ask students to bring in any tourist brochures that their families may have at home.

Grammar

Aims
This section revises the main grammar structures and some of the functions presented in Units 11–15.

1
- This task revises the past simple, the present simple, and the present continuous for both present and future meaning.
- Students fill in the gaps with the correct form of verbs from the box.
- Students check their answers with a partner first.
- To check answers with the class, first get students to tell you the correct verb, and then the correct tense, for example: *What verb goes in number 5?* (want). *And what tense?* (past simple). *So, what's the answer?* (wanted).

Answer key
3 *was* 4 *left* 5 *wanted* 6 *weren't* 7 *heard* 8 *looked*
9 *saw* 10 *put* 11 *met* 12 *said* 13 *didn't know* 14 *think*
15 *ran* 16 *are doing* 17 *am/'m staying* 18 *is learning*

2a
- This task revises telling a story in the past tense, and sequencing words.
- Students work with a partner to decide the most probable order of the events in the pictures.

2b
- Students write the story of Kevin's rescue of the little girl. They write a sentence for each picture (in order), using the verbs in the box, and sequencing them with *first*, *then*, *next* and *after that*.

3
- 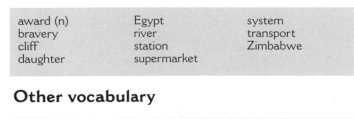 Play the cassette. Students listen to Kevin's account of the rescue, and check their answers.

Tapescript
... and when I went back to the path, my friends weren't there. They didn't wait for me. Anyway, I walked for about two hours and tried to find them, but I didn't. Then I heard a sound from the beach. I looked down and saw that it was a little girl, so I climbed down the cliff to the beach. She was very upset and frightened. First, I sat with her and talked to her for about half an hour; I wanted to find out where her parents were, but she didn't know. Then we began to walk back along the beach to the path, but we saw that the path was now under water!

I didn't know what to do, but then I saw a cave in the cliff and I carried Amy through the water and climbed up to the cave. It was tiny and freezing, and very dark! Next I found some pieces of wood and made a small fire. We were very hungry but I only had some chocolate and some biscuits. We ate those, and after that we tried to sleep. I gave Amy my jacket. In the morning, the sea went out and we left the cave. We went back on to the path and a policeman found us. He took us …

Option
- 📼 Play the cassette again. Students take notes of further details in Kevin's story. In pairs students re-tell his adventure using the pictures and their notes.

4a
- In this task, students practise using the present continuous with future meaning.
- Put students into pairs to decide their roles. Students taking the part of Kevin think about other people who want to meet him, for example, Amy and her family, TV news companies, advertising companies. They then write six more appointments in their diary. Students taking the part of B think of four more everyday plans, for example, going to a party, playing a sport, going shopping, and to write them in their diary.

4b
- Explain the task, and read out the example.
- Remind students of the language of making suggestions. Do a quick question-and-answer chain (see Tip 9, page 39) to revise them.
- Tell B students to try hard to meet Kevin, for example, *Let's meet late/early. What time does your meeting finish? Why don't we meet after/before …?*
- Pairs try to find a time to meet. Walk round, listening to and assessing them.

Vocabulary

Aims
In this section, students revise some of the vocabulary they have learned in Units 11–15.

1
- Tell students to look at the words in the box and the example. Then ask: *What do you think an anagram is?* (a word with the letters mixed up).
- Students work individually to work out the anagrams of weather words. They then categorize the words on a word-map. After each stage, let them compare their answers with a partner.

Answer key
Anagrams: clear windy wet rain storm sunny (typhoon) snow warm
Good weather: clear sunny warm
Bad weather: windy wet rain storm snow

2
- In this task, students work individually to match the situations with the adjectives describing emotion and senses. They compare their answers with a partner.

Answer key
1 *excited* 2 *miserable* 3 *embarrassed* 4 *tired* 5 *thirsty* 6 *hungry*

3
- Set a time limit of 1–2 minutes for students to find the places in the wordsquare.

Answer key
Horizontal: museum theatre zoo university palace market bank
Vertical: cinema restaurant hotel hostel

4
- Do this in the usual way.

Communication

1a
- Remind students how to work out the sort of word that fits a gap (see Tip 6, page 34). Students work individually to complete the dialogue. Let them compare answers with a partner, and then act out their dialogue.

1b
- 📼 Play the cassette. Students listen and check their answers.

Answer key
1 *fine* 2 *And you?* 3 *me* 4 *musician* 5 *week* 6 *great* 7 *staying* 8 *shall we* 9 *Why don't we*

2
- Students work with a partner, thinking of alternative ideas to those in bold. They then act out the new dialogue. Walk round, listening and assessing.

Option
- Students do this as an impromptu pair-work activity. They think of alternative words as they act out the dialogue.

Suggested Workbook practice
Check yourself, pages 70–71, Exercises 1–7

Project: a tourist guide

Aims
In this section, students practise listening, reading, speaking and writing skills by doing a project. The end product is a tourist guide. The earlier tasks provide language and ideas that students will find useful for the project writing task that follows.

1
- Students think back to Unit 14 and try to remember something about Covent Garden (see Background information to Student's Book page 96).

Listening

2
- Students look at the map, and read the labels round it. Point out that some names of places are missing from the labels.

Consolidation 3, Student's Book pages 108–109

- With a partner, students look at the places names in the box, and make guesses about which place goes with which label.
- 📼 Play the cassette. Students listen, and match places with names.

Answer key
5 *Sofra*   6 *The London Transport Museum*   7 *Covent Garden Market*   9 *Costa Coffee*   10 *Tesco Metro*   12 *The Sanctuary*

Reading

3

- This is a scanning exercise. Students look quickly through the map labels to find out what each place has to offer. If necessary, tell them that Zimbabwe /zɪmˈbɑːbwe/ is in Africa.

Answer key
1 *3*   2 *11*   3 *4*   4 *8*

4a

- This is a gist reading exercise. Students read to understand the general topic of the text, in this case, what place is being described. They do not need to understand every word.

Answer key
The London Transport Museum (label 6)

4b

- Students read the text in more detail, using a dictionary if necessary, and answer the questions.

Answer key
1 *an old flower market*   2 *yes*   3 *drive a London bus, explore trains from the past*   4 *Yes. You can buy postcards, posters, models (students should be able to think of these and other ideas)*

Speaking

5a

- 📼 Play the cassette. Students listen and decide where the speakers are.
- Ask students what words they heard that helped them find the answer (*pool*, *swim*, *members only*).

Answer key
The Sanctuary Health and Fitness Club

5b

- Do an example with the class first. For example, for the Banana Bookshop, get students to tell you a) who the speakers could be, b) what sort of dialogue they might have, and c) what words they could try to include as clues.
- Students prepare their own dialogue with a partner, and then practise it.
- Pairs join to form groups of four. Pairs take turns acting out their dialogues, or listening and guessing.
- Congratulate all pairs whose places were guessed straightaway.

6

- In this exercise students brainstorm ideas for their writing project.
- Put students into groups of 4–6. They discuss the questions, and make notes of their decisions.

Writing

7a

> **Option**
> - Distribute any tourist brochures, and so on (see Materials preparation). Let groups look through them, then alter or expand their notes from Exercise 6.

- Each group decides which places they made notes on that they wish to describe in their guide.

7b

- Groups draw a map, with places of interest numbered, using the map of Covent Garden as a model.

8a

- The aim of this exercise is to get students thinking about what information they would like to include, and where to put the different sorts of information. Students tick the first column of boxes for information that might be found on the map labels.

Answer key
1   3   4   5   6

8b

- Students tick the second column of boxes, for information found in the text in Exercise 4.

Answer key
1 2 3 4 5

9a

- Groups discuss the content of labels, decide who writes which, and then write the labels for their map. Check that they understand that these should be only a summary.

9b

- Each student in the group writes a text about one of the places they wrote a map label for. They should refer to their answers to Exercise 8b when deciding what to write. It is important that students do not translate sentences from original brochures, nor copy phrases from English versions of tourist guides – the language should be their own.

Options

- Students write the map labels in class, and prepare the longer texts for homework.
- In the next class, they can check each other's work and write the final text.

10

- This is the final outcome of the project. Groups arrange their work in a suitable order, make a cover, and stick in or draw any illustrations of places mentioned, so producing an interesting and clearly set out guide book.

Option

- Make a classroom display of the finished guides.

Suggested Workbook practice

Page 72, Exercises 1–3

Workbook answer key

Grammar

1 1 *a* 2 *b* 3 *c* 4 *a* 5 *c* 6 *c* 7 *a* 8 *b* 9 *b* 10 *c*

2 1 *gave* 2 *did she buy* 3 *wanted* 4 *didn't have* 5 *one*
6 *Shall I get* 7 *ours* 8 *didn't look* 9 *Let me* 10 *first*

Vocabulary

3 1 *plate* 2 *scarf* 3 *purse* 4 *video camera* 5 *waistcoat*
6 *watch* 7 *glasses* 8 *passport* 9 *credit card* 10 *diary*

Communication

4 1 *f* 2 *i* 3 *a* 4 *g* 5 *c* 6 *e* 7 *b* 8 *d* 9 *j* 10 *h*

Pronunciation

5a 1 *weather* 2 *wave* 3 *sight* 4 *Spanish* 5 *ours*

b *asked /t/: booked, hoped*
joined /d/: returned
wanted /ɪd/: hated painted

Skills: a news story
Reading

1 1 *cat boys climb tree*
2 *girl beach boat sea*

b *2*

2 2 *(She did it) last week.*
3 *She was on Brighton beach.*
4 *She was with her family.*
5 *She saw a small child in the sea.*
6 *She found a small boat and went out to the little girl.*
7 *She took the girl back to the beach.*
8 *She returned the child to her family.*
9 *They were really happy.*

Writing

3 1 *a cat* 2 *tree* 3 *his garden* 4 *a friend*
5 *an unusual sound* 6 *box* 7 *climb into the tree*
8 *carried it down* 9 *phoned the number* 10 *very pleased*

Worksheet 1

Student A

Talk to your partner. Find 10 differences in the pictures.
Use *Is there...?/Are there...?*

Student B

Talk to your partner. Find 10 differences in the pictures.
Use *Is there...?/Are there...?*

Worksheet 2

1 a 🗩 **Work with a partner. Write the letters of the cities in the boxes on the map.**

A New York 7.00 a.m.	B London 12.00 a.m.	C Rome 1.00 p.m.
D Moscow 3.00 p.m.	E Tokyo 9.00 p.m.	F Sydney 10.00 p.m.

b 1 It's 7 o'clock in the morning in New York. What time is it in Rome?
2 It's 9 o'clock in the evening in Tokyo. What time is it in Moscow?

2 **Ask and answer questions. Student A, look at part A. Student B, look at the bottom of the page.**

Example

12.15 a.m. Rome → London (11.15 a.m.)

A It's quarter past twelve in the morning in Rome. What time is it in London?

B Quarter past one in the afternoon? / Is it quarter past eleven in the morning?

A No, that's wrong. / Yes, that's right.

> **A**
> 1 5.10 p.m. Tokyo → Rome (9.10 a.m.)
> 2 6.25 p.m. London → Rome (7.25 p.m.)
> 3 2.00 p.m. Rome → Sydney (11.00 p.m.)
> 4 3.50 a.m. Moscow → New York (8.50 p.m.)

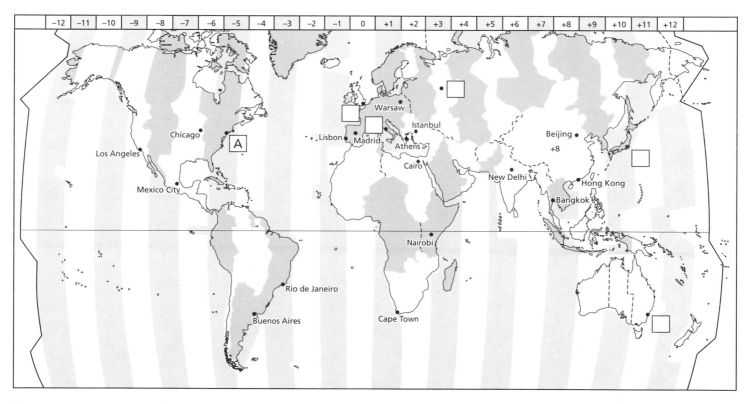

3 Write three questions to ask other students.

It's .... in .... What time is it in ....?

4 Make a group of four. Ask the other pair your questions. Answer their questions.

> **B**
> 1 9.20 a.m. New York → Moscow (4.20 p.m.)
> 2 4.45 p.m. Rome → Moscow (5.45 p.m.)
> 3 2.30 p.m. London → New York (9.30 a.m.)
> 4 1.05 a.m. Rome → Tokyo (9.05 a.m.)

Worksheet 3

Student A

Ask your partner questions. Draw
or fill in the symbols.

Example

<u>What is the weather like in France?</u>
<u>Is it hot? Is it sunny?</u>

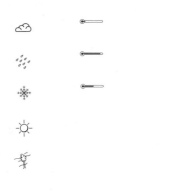

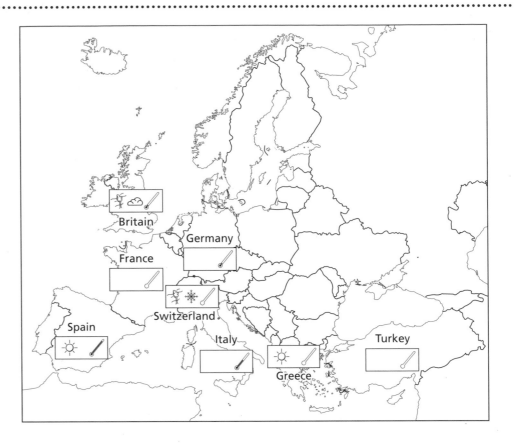

%--

Student B

Ask your partner questions. Draw
or fill in the symbols.

Example

What is the weather like in Britain?
Is it cold? Is it raining?

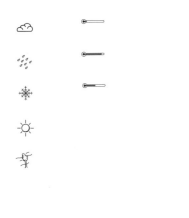

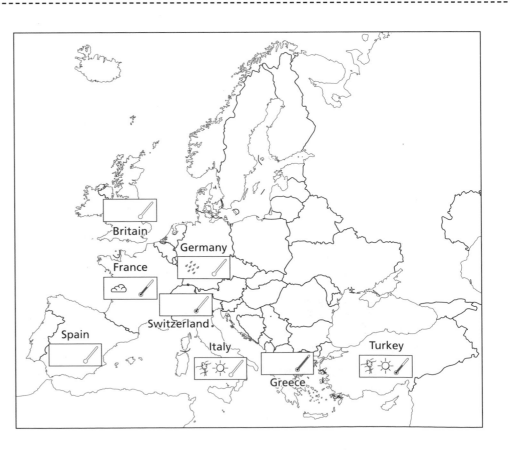

Worksheet 4

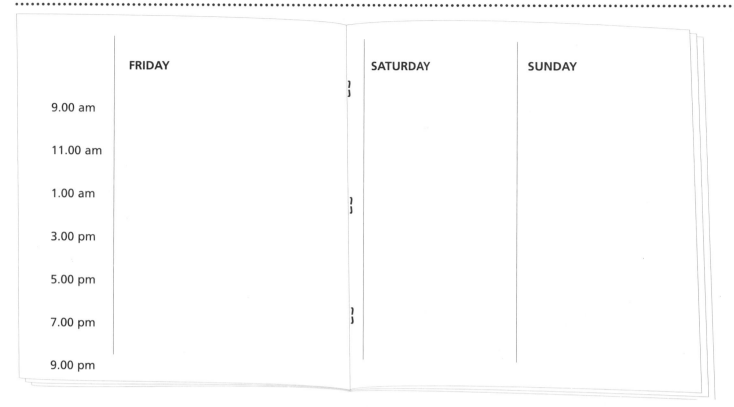

	FRIDAY		SATURDAY	SUNDAY
9.00 am				
11.00 am				
1.00 am				
3.00 pm				
5.00 pm				
7.00 pm				
9.00 pm				

What did you do last weekend?

1 Look at the pictures. In the diary, write six things that you did last week.

Example

	Friday	Saturday	Sun
11.00 a.m.		11.30 I visited my grandmother.	
1.00 p.m.	1.15 I went shopping.		

2 Work with a partner. Take turns to be A and B.

A Look at your page for a minute. Then give it to your partner, and answer B's questions.

B Ask questions about A's diary.

Example

B *What did you do on Friday afternoon?*
A *I went shopping.*
B *What time did you go shopping?*
A *Was it half-past one?*
B *No, quarter-past one.*

go / cinema

go / shopping

phone / friend

do / homework

have / coffee in town

visit / grandmother

watch TV

be / circus

listen / music

read / book

Worksheet 5

Student A

Look at the pictures below. Think of a story. Make notes about what heppened. Use the ideas on page 85 to help you. Tell your story to your partner

Student B

Look at the pictures below. Think of a story. Make notes about what heppened. Use the ideas on page 85 to help you. Tell your story to your partner

Worksheet 6

Read the text. It has 98 words and it is too long. Use the infomation from the text to complete the second text. Do not lose any information.

> A man and a woman had a meeting in a park. The park was in a city. The man was tall. The woman was short. The man and woman went to sit down. The man opened his briefcase. The man looked around first. The woman looked around too. There was some paper in the briefcase. The man took the paper out of the briefcase. He gave the paper to the woman. The woman put the paper in her coat. She had a big winter coat. The man closed the briefcase. The man went away. The woman went, too'.
>
> [98 words]

A _tall_ man and a _____ woman had a meeting in a
city park. First _____ went to sit on a bench Then,
_____ _____ carefully around. Next, the man
_____ his briefcase and _____ some paper
_____. The man _____ the paper to the woman
and _____ put _____ in her big _____ coat.
Finally, the man closed his briefcase and _____ both
went away. [66 words]

Worksheet 7

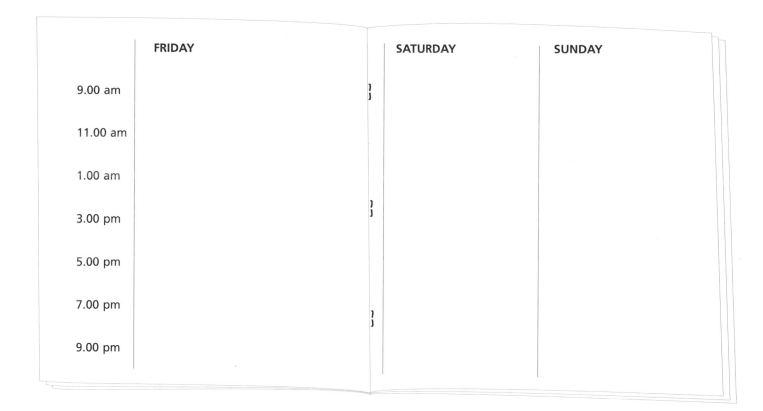

	Friday	Saturday	SUNDAY
9.00 am			
11.00 am			
1.00 am			
3.00 pm			
5.00 pm			
7.00 pm			
9.00 pm			

Talking about the future

1 Look at the pictures. In the diary, write six things that you are doing next weekend.

Example

	Friday	**Saturday**	**Sun**
11.00 a.m.		*11.30 visit my grandmother*	
1.00 p.m.	*1.15 meet friends in town*		

2 Work with a partner. Ask and answer about your plans for the weekend and find a time to meet. Try to find a time when you can both meet.

Example
A   What are you doing on Friday afternoon?
B   I'm meeting some friends in town. What are you doing on Friday morning?

go / theatre   go / pop concert

go / party   do / homework

meet / friends in town   visit / grandmother

watch TV   play / tennis

listen / Top Twenty   play / computer games

Unit test
Grammar

1 Write the long forms.

Example

David	*You're from Australia.*	*You are*
David	**Here's** the new student!	_____
	Hello. **What's** your name?	_____
Anna	**I'm** Anna.	_____
Ricky	Hi Anna! Are you from Brazil?	
Anna	Yes, **that's** right.	_____
Ricky	My **name's** Ricky and this is David.	_____
Anna	Pleased to meet you.	
David	**We're** from Britain.	_____

[6]

2 Look at text A. Read and complete text B.

Text A

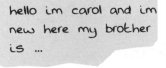
hello im carol and im new here my brother is …

Hello. I'm Carol and I'm new here. My brother is …

Text B

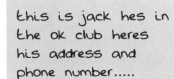
this is jack hes in the ok club heres his address and phone number…..

This _____
_____
_____
_____

[4]

Vocabulary

3 Complete the word-maps.

A

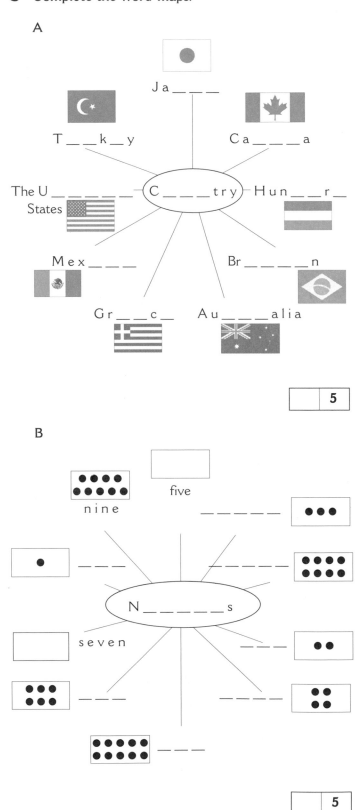

Ja_____

T__k__y   Ca____a

The U_____   C____try   Hun___r_
States

Mex____   Br_____n

Gr___c_   Au____alia

[5]

B

nine   five   _____ •••

•   ____ ____   ••••••

N_____s

seven   ____ ••

•••   ____ ••
••

••••••   ____

[5]

152   **Photocopiable** © Oxford University Press

Skills

Speaking

4 Match the phrases in A with the answers in B.

A	B
1 Hi, Dave.	That's wrong!
2 Hey, be careful!	Listen.
3 Hi, Emma. How are you?	Hello.
4 Are you Jane?	Sorry!
5 What does  mean?	Brazil. And you?
6 28 + 23 = 52	I'm fine, thanks.
7 Where are you from?	That's right.

6

5 Complete the telephone message.

H_ello_ Peter. Th__s is Magda – Magda fr_ _ _ Poland! How are you? Listen! I'm here, i__ London wi _ h my family . Please phone m__ at m__ hotel. The telephone number i__ : 672 88 45. Good b _ _!

8

6 Read the fax message. Complete the address.

England   University Road   12   Peter   SE13 9LB
London   ~~Denton~~

FAX MESSAGE   Page 1 of 1

To: M. Bila
From: P. Denton

Hi Magda
Here is my address in Britain:

_____ Denton,

___ _____,

_____ _____,

_____

3

7 Complete the 'thank you' message.

please	thanks	dear	pizza	Kerry	coffee

_____ Steve,
_____ for the _____ and _____.
_____ ring me at 8.00 p.m.

_____

3

Listening

8  Peter is on the telephone. Listen and complete the dialogue.

Peter

Woman	Good _____ . Grand *Hotel* . Can I help you?
Peter	Oh, hello. Room number _____ please …
Woman	Just a moment …

Magda	Hello?
Peter	_____ , Magda!
	_____ _____ Peter!
Magda	Peter! _____!
	_____ _____ in Oxford?
Peter	No. _____ _____ in London. Listen, …

Magda

	10
Total	50

Unit test
Grammar

1 Choose the right word.

Example
Who's / (What's) your name?

1 **A** **Who's/What's** this film about?
  B **It's/He's** about **a/an** elephant.
  A Is his **name/name's** Jumbo?
  B Yes, **it's/that's** right!

2 **A** **Who's/What's** Jane Pond?
  B She's **spy/a spy**.
  A Is she **British/a British**?
  B Yes, **she's/she is**.

| | 9 |

2 Complete the dialogue.

Where's this hotel? *It's* in France.

A _____' that boy?
B _____' my brother.
A And _____ _____ they?
B _____' my friends.
A _____ _____ from France?
B Yes, _____ _____.

| | 6 |

3 Correct these sentences.

1 **A** ~~Are~~ I right?   *Am I right?*
2 **B** Yes, you're.   _____
3 **A** Im fifteen.   _____
4 **B** Oh! I not fifteen.   _____
5 **A** How old you are ?   _____
  B I'm fourteen.
6 **A** Where you're from?   _____
  B I'm from Canada.

| | 5 |

Vocabulary

4 Write the words in the correct list.

agent bird ~~boy~~ chair desk ~~elephant~~ fish
friend girl pencil shark table

Animals   *elephant* _____ _____ _____
Classroom _____ _____ _____
People   *boy*   _____ _____ _____

| | 5 |

5 Write the numbers.

1 ten + four   = *fourteen*
2 fifteen + four   = _____
3 eleven + seven   = _____
4 five + seven   = _____
5 nine + eleven   = _____
6 one + five + seven   = _____

| | 5 |

Skills

Speaking

6 Put the sentences in the correct order. Write the dialogue.

☐ Are Ricky and Jack members, too?

☐ Are you a member of the club?

☐ *1* What's the OK Club?

☐ Yes, they are. Come with me this evening!

☐ It's a club for young people.

☐ Yes, I am.

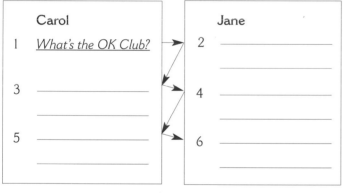

Carol		Jane
1 *What's the OK Club?*	→	2 _____
3 _____		4 _____
		_____
5 _____		6 _____
		_____

☐ **5**

Pronunciation

7 Write the letters in the correct list.
B, D, E, F, G, L, M, P, S, T, V, X

/iː/ *B* _____

/e/ *F* _____

☐ **5**

Listening

8 📼 Listen and complete the dialogue.

Steve! …Here's _____ _____. Come on!

Where is it? Ah, here _____ _____ – *Two brothers*.

How _____ are _____?

I'm _____, and my _____'s seventeen.

No, _____. You're not _____.

	10
Total	**50**

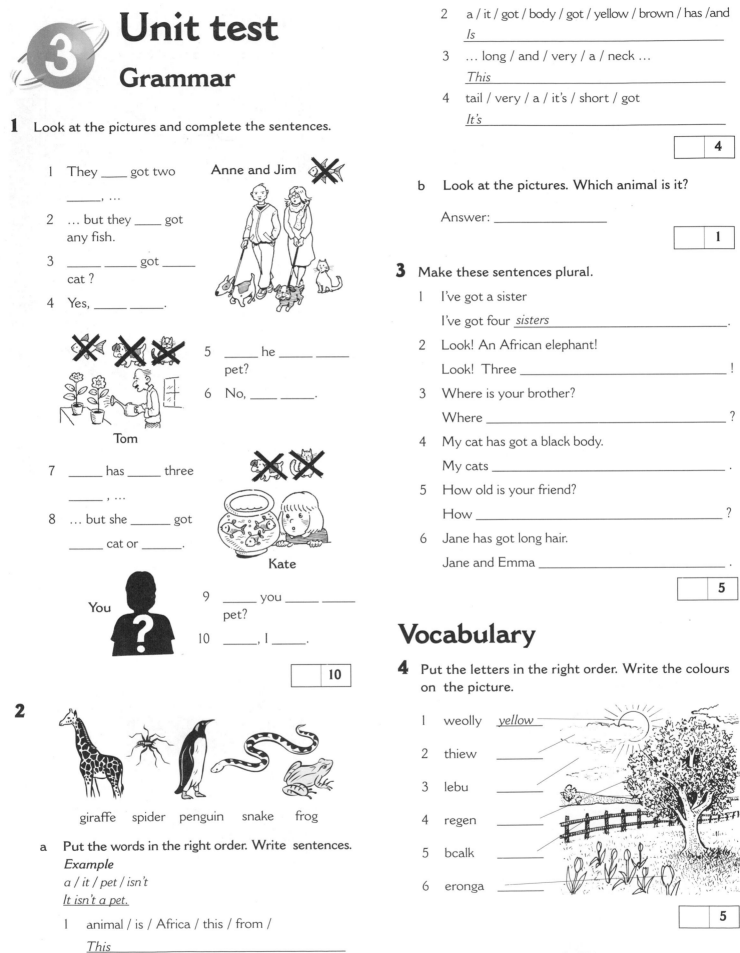

Unit test 3

Grammar

1 Look at the pictures and complete the sentences.

Anne and Jim

1 They ____ got two ______, …

2 … but they ____ got any fish.

3 _____ _____ got _____ cat ?

4 Yes, _____ _____.

Tom

5 _____ he _____ _____ pet?

6 No, _____ _____.

Kate

7 _____ has _____ three _____ , …

8 … but she ______ got _____ cat or ______.

You

9 _____ you _____ _____ pet?

10 _____, I _____.

	10

2

giraffe spider penguin snake frog

a Put the words in the right order. Write sentences.

Example

a / it / pet / isn't

It isn't a pet.

1 animal / is / Africa / this / from /

This ______________________

2 a / it / got / body / got / yellow / brown / has /and

Is ______________________

3 … long / and / very / a / neck …

This ______________________

4 tail / very / a / it's / short / got

It's ______________________

	4

b Look at the pictures. Which animal is it?

Answer: ______________

	1

3 Make these sentences plural.

1 I've got a sister

I've got four *sisters* ______________.

2 Look! An African elephant!

Look! Three ______________________ !

3 Where is your brother?

Where ______________________ ?

4 My cat has got a black body.

My cats ______________________ .

5 How old is your friend?

How ______________________ ?

6 Jane has got long hair.

Jane and Emma ______________________ .

	5

Vocabulary

4 Put the letters in the right order. Write the colours on the picture.

1 weolly *yellow*

2 thiew _______

3 lebu _______

4 regen _______

5 bcalk _______

6 eronga _______

	5

Photocopiable © Oxford University Press

5 Look at the picture and complete the text.

Here is a photo of me and my _____. My name is
Alex. I'm fifteen. Fay and David are my mother and
_____. Louise is my _____. John and Luke
are my _____, and Hannah is my _____.

| | 5 |

Skills
Reading

6 a Look at the pictures in Exercise 2 again. Match
the texts.

1 This small animal
has got four legs and

2 This animal is a big
bird. It has got

3 This animal has got a
very long tail, but

4 This animal hasn't got
a neck but it has got

5 This animal has got a
long neck and a short
tail.

eight legs. It's got a
grey body.

it hasn't got any
legs.

a black and white
body.

It has got a small
head.

very big eyes. It's
got a green body.

| | 4 |

b Write the name of the animal in the box.

Number one is a   _frog_____

Number two is a   _____

Number three is a   _____

Number four is a   _____

Number five is a   _____

| | 4 |

7 Look at the picture, then read the descriptions.

Who are they? Write the correct letters.

1 My sister Pat is 13. She's got short, curly hair,
Her eyes are dark and she has got a long nose.
Pat is not short. ☐

2 Pat's friend Bill is 16. He's got straight dark hair
and blue eyes. He's tall. ☐

| | 2 |

Writing

8 Describe another boy or girl in the picture.

_____

_____

_____

_____

Listening

| | 5 |

9 📼 Listen to the questions. Write answers about
yourself.

1 I am a _student._

2 I am _____ _____.

3 I am _____.

4 I've got _____ _____.

5 They are _____.

6 _____, I _____.

	5
Total	50

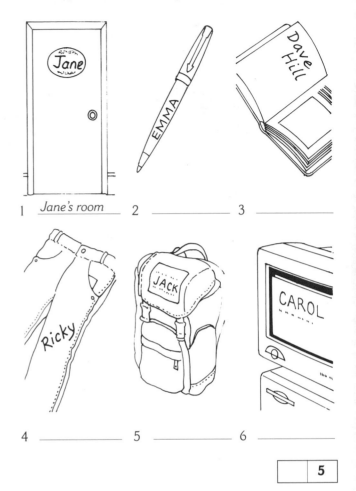

Unit test
Grammar
4

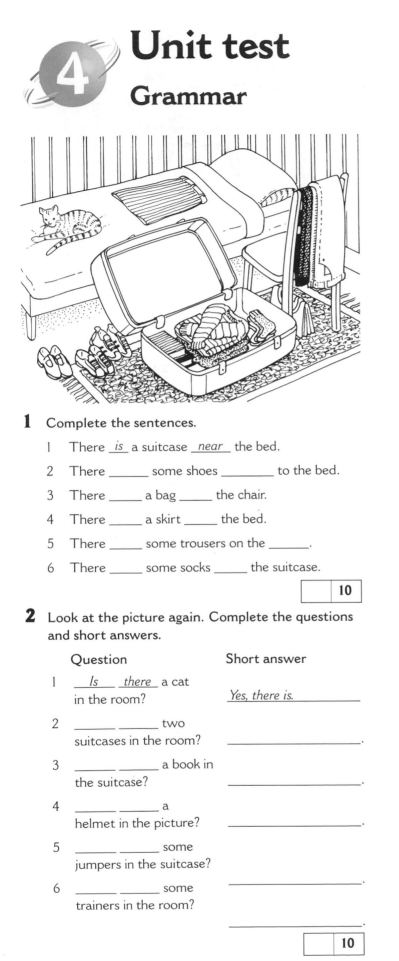

1 Complete the sentences.

1 There _is_ a suitcase _near_ the bed.

2 There _____ some shoes _____ to the bed.

3 There _____ a bag _____ the chair.

4 There _____ a skirt _____ the bed.

5 There _____ some trousers on the _____.

6 There _____ some socks _____ the suitcase.

[10]

2 Look at the picture again. Complete the questions and short answers.

Question	Short answer
1 _Is_ _there_ a cat in the room?	_Yes, there is._
2 _____ _____ two suitcases in the room?	_____.
3 _____ _____ a book in the suitcase?	_____.
4 _____ _____ a helmet in the picture?	_____.
5 _____ _____ some jumpers in the suitcase?	_____.
6 _____ _____ some trainers in the room?	_____.

[10]

Vocabulary

3 Write a phrase under the pictures.

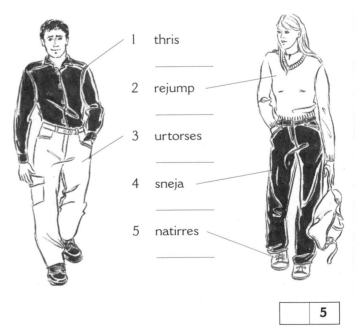

1 _Jane's room_ 2 _____ 3 _____

4 _____ 5 _____ 6 _____

[5]

4 Put the letters in the right order. Label the clothes in the picture.

1 thris

_____

2 rejump

_____

3 urtorses

_____

4 sneja

_____

5 natirres

_____

[5]

158

Photocopiable © Oxford University Press

Skills

Speaking

5 Complete the dialogue. Use words from the box.

| my | our | isn't | your | her | his | haven't | their | 's | 's |

Carlos	Is this _____ Mum?
Tina	Yes, it is, but _____ hair _____ curly now. It's straight. And this is _____ Dad. He's got black hair and blue eyes – like me.
Carlos	Who is the tall man?
Tina	That's Dad___ brother, and that's _____ house. He's got a swimming pool in the garden.
Carlos	Where is your family _____ house?
Tina	This is _____ house. We've got a big garden but we _____ got a swimming pool.
Carlos	Who are these people?
Tina	They're friends. _____ house is next to my school.

	10

Writing

6 Look at the picture. Write five sentences about Tina's house. Write about the rooms, what is in each room, and where each thing is in the room.

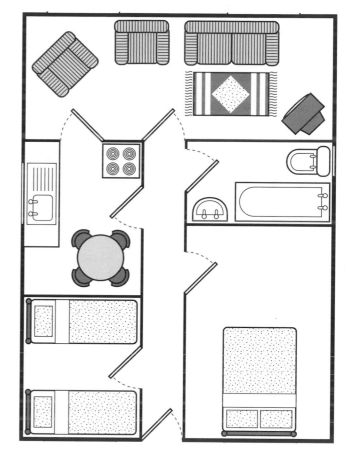

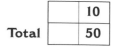
Tina's house has got five rooms.

_____

_____

_____

_____

_____

_____

_____

	10
Total	50

Unit test
Grammar

1 Complete the dialogues.

   A Dave   Do ¹ _you_ _like_ olives?

       Ricky   Yes I ² _____ . And my sister

                  ³ _____ olives too.

   B Customer Waiter! We' ⁴ ____ _____ two

                 American pizzas please, and ⁵ _____

                 large salad and some bread.

       Waiter   ⁶ _____ you ⁷ _____ Italian pizzas or

                 American pizzas?

       Customer American pizzas please, with

                 ⁸ _____ extra cheese, but we don't

                 want ⁹ _____ onions.

   C Customer Waiter! We've got a problem!

       Waiter   What's wrong? Don't ¹⁰ _____ _____

                 your pies?

       Customer No, we ¹¹ _____ . They're cold!

   D Jane   My mother and I like Indian food, but

                 we ¹² _____ eat it at home.

       Emma   Why not?

       Jane   My Dad ¹³ _____ _____ spicy food.

                                   | 12 |

2 a Write C (countable) or U (uncountable) for each word in the list.

    1 pie ☐

    2 money | C |

    3 food ☐

    4 chilli ☐

    5 meat ☐

    6 banana ☐

    7 cheese ☐

                      | 3 |

3 Correct these sentences.

  1 Our family **eats lot** of fruit.   *a lot of*

  2 There is **a** food in the fridge.   _____

  3 I haven't got any **moneys**.   _____

  4 Would you like **sugars** in your

     coffee?   _____

  5 British people **loves** Indian food.   _____

  6 My favourite pudding is **apples pie**.   _____

                      | 5 |

Vocabulary

4 Underline the odd one out in each group. Then add these words to the right list.

   chicken ~~pepper~~ potatoes strawberry

  1 banana lemon <u>carrot</u> cherry   _____

  2 pear tomato mushroom onions   _____

  3 beef cheese lamb sausage   _____

  4 chillies salt milk coriander   *pepper*

                      | 6 |

5 Complete the menu with words from the box.

   Coffee Drinks Fish Hot juice menu Milk
   Vegetables

                     Today's ¹ _____

   Pies   ⁴ _____

   Lamb pie

   Beef pie   *Cold drinks*

   ² _____ *pie*   ⁵ _____

   Cheese and potato pie   *Cola*

                       Lemonade

   ³ _____   *Orange* ⁶ ____

   Potatoes   ⁷ _____ *drinks*

   Carrots

   Tomatoes   *Tea*

                    ⁸ _____

                    Hot chocolate

                              | 4 |

Skills

Reading

6 Read texts A, B and C. Answer the questions.

A

There is a very good Italian restaurant near my house. My favourite dish is Neapolitan pizza. It's got olives, cheese and tomatoes. Mushrooms or spicy sausage are extras. I eat it with lettuce and tomato salad and some Italian coffee.

True or false?

1 Neapolitan pizza has got mushrooms. T/F
2 The restaurant has got Italian coffee. T/F

B

Food in Japan is very different from British food. For example, Japanese people don't eat a lot of bread or potatoes. They use a lot of rice in their dishes. They also eat a lot of fish. Meat and vegetables are also ingredients in Japanese cooking, but not milk or cheese.

Complete these sentences.

3 Japanese people eat a lot of _____, _____, _____ and _____.

4 They don't eat a lot of _____, _____, _____ or _____.

C

In Spain, a favourite dish is tortilla. The main ingredients are eggs and potatoes. Other ingredients are salt, pepper, tomatoes and other vegetables. They are delicious hot or cold!

True or false?

5 Tortillas are from Spain. T/F
6 Tortillas have got a lot of meat. T/F

	6

Writing

7 a Answer the questions.

What is the favourite dish in your country?

_____

What are the main ingredients?

_____

What are some other ingredients?

_____

Do you like it? _____

	2

b Use your answers from Exercise 7a to write a paragraph about the dish.

The favourite dish in my country is _____

_____

_____

_____ .

	2

Listening

8 a 🔊 Listen and underline the right prices: a, b, c, or d.

1 a £13.50   b £13.15   c £30.50   d £30.15
2 a £20.60   b £12.16   c £20.16   d £12. 60
3 a 60p   b 50p   c 16p   d 15 p

	3

b 🔊 Listen and write the correct prices.

1 6 oranges   _____

2 2 kilos potatoes   _____

	2

c 🔊 Listen and complete the dialogue.

Waiter   Hello. _____ I help you?

Customer Yes … _____ _____ an _____ cream, please.

Waiter   OK. _____ _____ like chocolate _____ vanilla?

Customer Have _____ _____ a strawberry ice cream?

Waiter   No, sorry.

Customer OK. _____, please.

	5
Total	50

1 Consolidation test
Grammar

1 **a** Kevin is a new student in an American school. Read the dialogue. Put Tony's words in the right order.

Tony   Hi, / Tony / I'm. / name / your / what's?
      Hi, I'm Tony. What's your name?

Kevin   I'm Kevin.

Tony   to / Kevin / meet / pleased / you
      _____ , Kevin.

Kevin   Thank you!

Tony   from / are / where / you?
      _____

Kevin   I'm from Britain.

                          2

b Read Tony's answers. Put Kevin's words in the right order.

Kevin   there / other / students / British / are / here?
      Are _____ ?

Tony   No, but there's a French boy, Marcel, in my class.

Kevin   that / who / is / woman?
      _____ ?

Tony   That's Mrs Green. She's a teacher.

Kevin   any / have /brothers / got / you ?
      Have _____ ?

Tony   Yes, Jack and Dan. They're students here too.

                          3

c Complete Kevin's questions.

Kevin   What _____ Mrs Green _____?
Tony   She's OK. She's very nice, really.

Kevin   _____ _____ _____ your brothers?
Tony   Jack is 12 and Dan is 14.

Kevin   _____ you eat in _____ school dining-room, Tony?
Tony   No, I go home to eat.

Kevin   _____ the teacher eat at home, too?
Tony   I don't know, Kevin! Ask her!

Kevin   Which _____ _____ classroom?
Tony   We are in room 203. Come on! Let's go there now!

                          5

2 Correct these sentences. There are two mistakes in every sentence.

1   My friend's Sally got a short, curly hair.
   My friend Sally's got short curly hair.

2   She eyes is blue.
   _____

3   She's got French mother and a English father.
   She _____

4   He got's a moustache black.
   He _____

5   There are a lot of French books on your house.
   There are a lot of French _____

6   Hers grandmother and grandfather lives in London.
   _____

                          5

3 Make these sentences negative.

1   Sally's got long hair.
   No, Sally hasn't got long hair.

2   Sally has got two sisters.
   No, Sally _____ any sisters.

3   Her parents are teachers.
   No, her parents _____ teachers.

4   Her mother teaches French.
   No, her mother _____ French.

5   They've got a big garden.
   No, _____ a big garden.

6   There's a tree in it.
   No, _____ a tree in it.

                          5

Vocabulary

4 Complete these word trees.

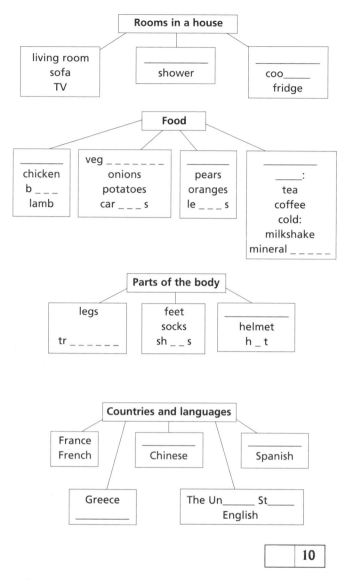

Rooms in a house

| living room sofa TV | shower | coo_____ fridge |

Food

| chicken b _ _ _ lamb | veg _ _ _ _ _ _ onions potatoes car _ _ _ s | pears oranges le _ _ _ s | _____: tea coffee cold: milkshake mineral _ _ _ _ _ |

Parts of the body

| legs tr _ _ _ _ _ _ | feet socks sh _ _ s | helmet h _ t |

Countries and languages

| France French | Chinese | Spanish |
| Greece _____ | The Un_____ St_____ English | |

[ ] 10

Skills
Reading

5 Look at the picture. Find six mistakes in the text.

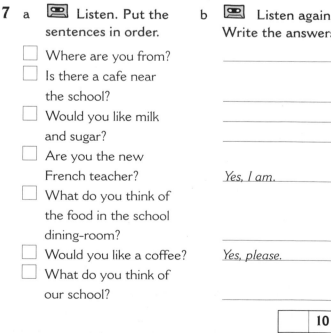

This is my bedroom. *It's* (very) *small*. It's got two beds – a bed for me, and a bed for my sister. We are very tidy. There is a sofa, a desk and two chairs in the corner. There's a computer under the window. It's our computer, but Dad uses it all the time! We've got lots of books in our room too. We like pop music, and we've got three posters of our favourite groups on the door. Our cat loves the chair. He sits on it. His name is Blacky. He …

1 *The bedroom isn't very small. It's big.*
2 *They aren't very* _____
3 _____
4 _____
5 _____
6 _____

[ ] 5

Writing

6 Write five sentences about your bedroom.

1 _____
2 _____
3 _____
4 _____
5 _____

[ ] 5

Listening

7 a 📼 Listen. Put the sentences in order.   **b** 📼 Listen again. Write the answers.

[ ] Where are you from?   _____

[ ] Is there a cafe near the school?   _____

[ ] Would you like milk and sugar?   _____

[ ] Are you the new French teacher?   *Yes, I am.*

[ ] What do you think of the food in the school dining-room?   _____

[ ] Would you like a coffee?   *Yes, please.*

[ ] What do you think of our school?   _____

| | 10 |
| Total | 50 |

6 Unit test
Grammar

1 Complete the text with these prepositions: *after, at, before, by, for, in, to, with*.

My name's Anna and I work in a studio. I start my day at 5 o'clock in the morning. I go swimming _____ two hours _____ work every day. At 8.30, I go to work _____ bike. I start work at 9.00 a.m. I go home again _____ 7 o'clock _____ the evening. I don't cook. My mother always cooks a meal _____ me. I eat, then _____ the meal, I go swimming again. My sister sometimes comes swimmimg _____ me.

What do I do for relaxation? Well, I visit my friends _____ the weekend. I don't watch TV, but I sometimes listen _____ music.

| 10 |

2 Put the words in the right order.

1 don't / I / drink / coffee
   I don't drink coffee. _____

2 go / do / time / to work / you / What?
   What _____

3 day / go swimming / doesn't / Anna 's sister / every
   _____

4 your family / What / usually / do / does / for relaxation ?
   What _____

5 you / Do / often / your friends / visit?
   _____ *you?*

6 TV / Why / you / don't / watch?
   _____

| 5 |

3 Choose the right word.

Example

Tina   Anna's sister (sometimes)/never goes running, but not very often.

1 Carol   What do you **always/usually** have for breakfast, Jane?

2 Jane   I have the same thing every day. I **always /usually** have bread, cheese and milk.

3 Emma   We **sometimes/never** eat dinner in the kitchen – we always eat in the dining-room.

4 Dave   We usually eat in the dining-room, but we **often/sometimes** eat in the kitchen.

5 Ricky   I **often/always** have my lunch in the OK Club, but I sometimes eat it in the classroom.

| 5 |

Vocabulary

4 **a** Write the words in the correct list.

~~colourful~~ ~~do~~ hopeless huge interesting meet noisy paint play read work

Verbs: *do* _____

_____

Adjectives: *colourful,* _____

_____

| 5 |

b Use words from Exercise 4a to complete the sentences.

Producer   What do you do in your club?

Emma   We _____ books.

Ricky	And we _____ cards.
Carol	Dave sometimes _____ his homework here.
Dave	Yes, and Carol and Jane sometimes play _____ music!
Jack	But we've got a problem. We want to _____ the walls.
Producer	OK, I've got an idea …

5

Skills
Reading

A   Would you like to join our student club?
We'd like to start a new club in our school. Would you like to join us? Come to a meeting about it next Saturday in Room 201 at 11.00 a.m.
Tim and Jane

B   Where is Fox?
This is my grandmother's cat. His name is 'Fox'. Fox has got a black body and a white tail. Please help us to find him. My grandmother's name is Mrs Black.
Please telephone her before 9 o'clock in the evening (Tel: 981 3541).
Thank you!
Jane

C   Help the Carnival
Have you got any colourful old clothes? We'd like to use them to make costumes for the August carnival. Please look at home. We pay 20p for a jumper, 50p for trousers!
Contact: Anne and Robin, 625 5532

5 Read messages A, B and C. Are these sentences true (✓) or false (✗)?

1 Jane's family have got a fox.   [✗]
2 Mrs Black is Jane's grandmother.   [ ]
3 Mrs Black would like a new pet.   [ ]
4 The club meeting is at the weekend.   [ ]
5 The club meeting is in Tim and Jane's house.   [ ]
6 Anne and Robin sell colourful old clothes.   [ ]

5

6 Read the messages again. Find the object pronouns. Who or what are they?

Message A	1	us	_____
	2	it	_____
Message B	3	him	_____
	4	her	_____
Message C	5	them	_____

5

Listening

7 a 🔲 Listen and draw the time of each radio programme.

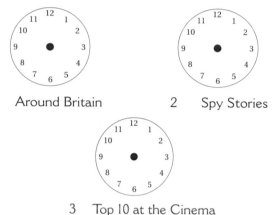

1   Around Britain   2   Spy Stories

3   Top 10 at the Cinema

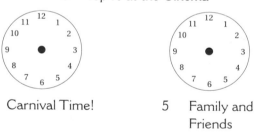

4   Carnival Time!   5   Family and Friends

5

b 🔲 Listen again. Complete the sentences.

1 'Around Britain' is on Radio __. It's about _travel_.
2 'Spy Stories' is on Radio _4_. It's about _____.
3 'Top 10 at the Cinema' is on Radio __. It's about films.
4 'Carnival Time!' is on Radio 2. It's about _____ in _____.
5 'Family and Friends' is on Radio 5. It's about children in _____.

	5
Total	50

Unit test
Grammar

1 Look at the people in the picture. Write *this*, *that*, *these* or *those*.

A What are _____ plants in the corner?

B Where is _____ cheese from?

C Mmm! _____ pies are very good.

D I'd like _____ apple, please.

4

2 Look at the picture. Complete the sentences with the words in the box.

| are are are few four is is lot some some |

1 There _____ a _____ of food on the table.

2 There _____ _____ sandwiches.

3 There _____ only a _____ apples.

4 There _____ _____ water.

5 There _____ _____ visitors next to the table.

10

3 Write the words in the chart.

| water apple table people knives food plants orange juice bread women fruit cheese |

	Countable	Uncountable
singular	plural	

6

Vocabulary

4 a Put the letters in the right order and write the shapes.

1 ircelc _____

2 ragtniel _____

3 aqresu _____

4 tertnagelc _____

2

b Use the words from Exercise 4a to label the parts of the body.

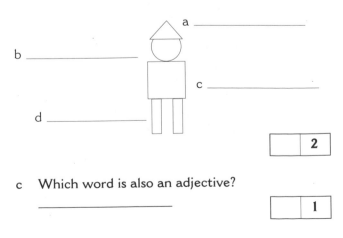

a _____

b _____

c _____

d _____

2

c Which word is also an adjective?

_____

1

Space

5 Match the sentences with the inventions. Write A, B or C in the boxes.

A computer   B wheel   C frying pan

1   It has got a rectangular screen   <u>A</u>

2   It is round and there are four on cars.   ☐

3   It uses electricity.   ☐

4   It is circular. There is usually one in a kitchen.   ☐

5   You can write messages and receive information with it.   ☐

6   It's for cooking your favourite dishes.   ☐

	5

Skills
Reading

6   a   Match the descriptions with the inventions.

1 This is a very useful invention. It's small. It's for opening tins of food, and there is one in every kitchen. It doesn't use electricity. You often use it when you cook.

camera

2 This invention has got a circular 'head' and a rectangular 'body'. Singers and musicians use them for producing very loud music. It's usually black or grey and it uses electricity.

matches

3 This invention is usually black or grey, too. It's used for making TV programmes or videos. It uses electricity and it has got a film in it and a microphone with it.

tin opener

4 This invention comes in a box and there are a lot of them in every box. They are very small. You use them for making fires and for cooking, but they don't use electricity. They are very useful.

microphone

	4

b   True or false? Read the sentences and write ✓ or ✗ in the boxes.

1   Three of the inventions use electricity.   ☐

2   One of the inventions is useful in the kitchen.   ☐

3   Two of the inventions are the same colour.   ☐

	3

Writing

7   a   Look at the picture. Answer the questions.

What is it for?   _____

What shape is it?   _____

What has it got?   *4 wheels, a driver* _____

Do you use it?   _____

	3

b   Use your notes from Exercise 7a to write a description of the bus.

_____

_____

_____

_____

	10
Total	50

Unit test

Grammar

1 Are these sentences right (✓) or wrong (✗)? Correct the mistakes.

1 ✓ Do you speak English?

_____

2 ✗ Do your brother speak English?
      Does your brother speak English?

3 ☐ Can your brother to speak English?

_____

4 ☐ I don't can swim.

_____

5 ☐ Athletes must want to win.

_____

6 ☐ My brother can play the guitar.

_____

7 ☐ I'm must go.

_____

8 ☐ You always must do your homework.

_____

              [6]

2 a Match the phrases.

I'm sure that the Earth is round!

1 I think that's …   … possible.
2 No, it …   … agree.
3 I'm not sure …   … wrong.
4 I don't think …   … about that.
5 Yes, I …   … so.
6 Yes, it's …   … isn't.

              [5]

b What do you think about this idea? Use one phrase from Exercise 2a.

Only a few people can be good athletes.

_____

              [1]

3 Write _in_, _at_ or _on_.

Goodbye. See you!

1 Yes, see you _____ the weekend.
2 Yes, see you _____ Friday night.
3 Yes, see you _____ the summer.
4 Yes, see you _____ the morning.
5 Yes, see you _____ 5.30.
6 Yes, see you _____ Monday.

              [3]

4 Add the extra word in the right place.

1 I can speak five languages. (different)
   I can speak five different languages.

2 He can write Russian. He can't speak it. (only)

_____

3 The basilicus basilicus lizard is amazing. (really)

_____

4 She can swim for twenty minutes. (about)

_____

5 Athletes must eat the right food. (always)

_____

6 Champion athletes must train. They must study the techniques of their sport. (also)

_____

              [5]

Vocabulary

5 Complete the chart with sports and other activities.

Sports	Other activities
play volleyball	_dance_
play football	

              [5]

6 What is the missing word? Look at the picture and complete the sentences.

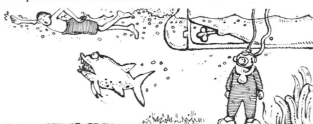

1 This _diver_ can't move fast.
2 He is un__r the water.
3 He's got heavy diving eq_____ .
4 Walking under water is difficult; divers must do a lot of tr____g .
5 There is a swimmer on the s___ace of the water.
6 He must be careful: the fish with teeth is d__ger____!

	5

Skills
Speaking

7 Put the sentences of the dialogues in the right order.

a

☐ Oh, never mind – I can ask Susan.
☐ Bye, see you.
☐ Would you like to come to a concert this weekend?
☐ Hang on a minute! Look, can I tell you tomorrow ?
☑ [2] Maybe. I must ask my Mum and Dad.
☐ OK, tell me tomorrow! Bye.

	5

b

☐ I'm sorry, he's not here today.
☐ Here's our telephone number. Please telephone if you can't come.
☐ Well, Doctor Cope is quite busy on Wednesday – can you come at half past seven?
☐ I'd like to see Doctor Cope, this afternoon please.
☑ [3] Oh. What about Wednesday morning?
☐ Yes, I think that's OK. It's before school.

	5

Reading

8 a Read the text. Write the paragraph numbers next to the right headings.

A Emma's weekends ☐
B Emma's school ☐
C What Emma does at the Sports Centre ☐
D Emma's timetable on Mondays to Fridays ☐

	4

Emma Green is a 16-year-old student from Manchester in England. On Mondays to Fridays she goes to school by car. Her favourite school subjects are French and Science.

Emma is also a top athlete. She can run at 35 kilometres an hour. She wants to be a champion but it takes a lot of her time. She is very busy and she must organize her time carefully. She trains for one hour before school every day and for two hours after school. She sometimes trains at the weekend, too. Her mother and father want her to become a champion, but they say she must do her school homework, too. She does her homework in the evenings after she finishes her training.

She trains at the Sports Centre near her house. Her trainer, Janet Haywood, does a lot of work with her. She says, 'Emma is a great athlete, but she must learn all the techniques of her sport and get a lot of sleep.' Emma runs about 10 kilometres every day on the running track. After she runs, she goes swimming and she does some aerobics in the gym.

Emma gets some relaxation at the weekends. She has got a lot of friends. She meets them when she isn't training. She goes to a club with them and plays table tennis and computer games there. Sometimes she watches TV but usually she is too busy!

b Read the text. True or false? Write ✓ or ✗.

1 Emma is a champion athlete. ☐
2 Emma trains for three hours a day on Mondays to Fridays. ☐
3 Emma knows all of the techniques of her sport. ☐
4 Emma plays table tennis and computer games with her friends. ☐

	2

Writing

9 Write four things that Emma must do.

1 _____
2 _____
3 _____
4 _____

	4
Total	50

Unit test
Grammar

1 **a** Complete the chart with the present continuous verbs.

Present simple	Present continuous
make	*making*
have	
sit	
die	
cause	
kill	

b Complete the dialogue with verbs from the chart. Use the present continuous tense.

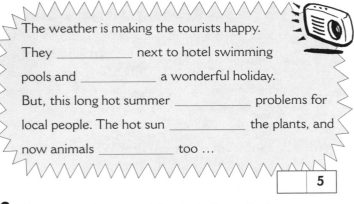

The weather is making the tourists happy. They _____ next to hotel swimming pools and _____ a wonderful holiday. But, this long hot summer _____ problems for local people. The hot sun _____ the plants, and now animals _____ too ...

| 5 |

2 Complete the text with words from the box.

| are | aren't | doesn't | Don't | I'm | is | isn't |

Lisa and her husband _____ enjoying their holiday. Lisa's mother, Hanna, _____ on holiday with them – but Hanna _____ like the hotel, the food, or the town! Only James and Tony _____ having a good time. 'Why _____ Grandma happy?' Tony asks.

'_____ having a great time!'

'_____ ask me,' says his father. 'Ask your grandmother!'

| 7 |

3 Complete the dialogue between Lisa and her mother.

Hanna   Where *are* you _____?

Lisa   To the bank in town.

Hanna   _____ _____ going in the car?

Lisa   No, I'm _____. Mum, please stay with the children.

Hanna   _____n't Dan staying here?

Lisa   Yes, he _____, but he's sleeping.

Hanna   Why _____ _____ sleeping?

Lisa   Because he can't sleep at night.

| 4 |

4 Complete the chart.

Adjectives	Adverbs
bad	*badly*
comfortable	
happy	
hard	
immediate	
miserable	
steady	
terrible	
warm	

| 4 |

Vocabulary

5 Complete the postcard from Hanna to Jack, her husband. Use adjectives and adverbs from Exercise 4.

Dear Jack,
You probably think that I'm having a wonderful time. You probably think I'm sitting _____ in the _____ sun. Well I'm not!!
In fact, I'm really _____! The weather is _____ – it rains _____ every day from morning to evening.
I don't want to stay another day, so I'm coming home _____!
Hanna

| 6 |

6 Who is speaking? Choose people from the box.

| business traveller | holiday-maker | ~~local people~~ |
| tour company advertisement | | tour guide |

1 Thank you for coming to our country!

Local people

2 Can you come over here, please? Thank you.

_____

3 Wait for me! I don't speak the language!

_____

4 Taxi-driver, I'm late! Please take me to the International Centre.

_____

5 Your holiday is our business!

_____

| | 4 |

Skills
Reading

7 Read the notice and answer the questions.

> ### INFORMATION ON THE CORAL REEFS
> We want you and your children to enjoy these beautiful reefs. When you dive from your boat, please be careful. The reefs take thousands of years to grow but some tourists think it's OK to walk on ¹them. Sometimes ²they break pieces of coral and take ³them home at the end of their holidays. PLEASE DON'T DO ⁴THIS! The reefs are in danger. Help us to save the reefs.

1 Who or what is *them*? _____
2 Who or what is *they*? _____
3 Who or what is *them*? _____
4 Who or what is *this*? _____

| | 4 |

Listening

8 Listen and draw the weather on the map.

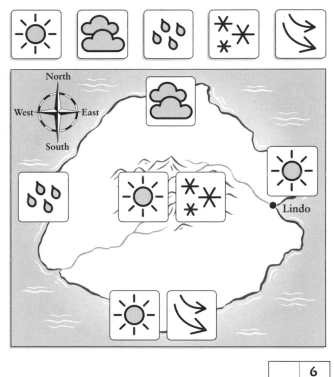

| | 6 |

Writing

9 a You are on holiday in Lindo. Make notes.

Who is on holiday with you? _____

What is the weather like? _____

Are you having a wonderful time, or a terrible time? _____

What are you doing at the moment? _____

What are the others doing? _____

| | 5 |

b Use your notes from Exercise 9a to write a postcard to friends or family at home.

_____
_____
_____
_____

| | 5 |
| **Total** | 50 |

Unit test
Grammar

1 Martin is from Britain, but at the moment he is on holiday with his American friend, John. Read Martin's letter to his mother. Then <u>underline</u> the right verb forms.

Dear Mum

How are you? I write/<u>I'm writing</u> this letter in Jake's bedroom. To me, this room and the rest of the house are huge, but John **says/is saying** it's only an average house. He says lots of families in America **live/are living** in big houses.

I have/I'm having a great time here, and the family **gives/is giving** me a really good time. John's father is a doctor. He **works/is working** a long way from home, so he **goes/is going** to work before 7.00 a.m. The family **eats/is eating** the main meal when he gets home. Mum, **I eat/I'm eating** a lot at the moment. I'm sure I **get/I'm getting** fat!

How are you all? **Do you have/Are you having** a good summer too?

Please write soon.

Martin

| | 10 |

2 John's family are very interested in Martin's life in Britain. Complete their questions.

1 How *many brothers* and *sisters have you* got, Tim?
   I've got one brother and one sister.

2 How _____ _____ _____ do you get?
   I get £10 pocket money a week.

3 How _____ _____ homework do your teachers give you?
   They give me about ten hours homework a week.

4 How _____ _____ are there in your class?
   There are 25 students in my class.

5 How _____ _____ do you spend in school?
   I spend six to eight hours a day in school.

6 How _____ _____ TV do you watch in the evenings?
   I watch TV for about two hours a day – that's a lot, I know!

| | 5 |

3 Complete the chart.

We say	We write
the twenty-first of May	*21st May*
the thirteenth of August	
the twelfth of June	
	8th December
	20th November
the thirtieth of March	

| | 5 |

Vocabulary

4 Write these numbers.

1 6,000,000   *six million*

2 50%   *half*

3 £3.20   _____

4 25%   _____

5 33%   _____

6 21, 869   _____

7 66%   _____

| | 5 |

5 Complete these sentences.

1 The first month of the year is *January* .

2 The fourth month of the year is _____ .

3 The fifth month of the year is _____ .

4 The _____ month of the year is July.

5 The _____ month of the year is August.

6 The _____ month of the year is December.

| | 5 |

Skills

Speaking

6 Complete the dialogue between Martin and a shop assistant.

Shop assistant	Good morning. _____ you?
Martin	Yes, I'm _____ for a birthday _____ .
Shop assistant	OK. Who's it _____ ?
Martin	It's for my sister. She wants a new tennis racket.
Shop assistant	This racket is a very good one.
Martin	Yes, it looks great. How _____ is it?
Shop assistant	It's £75.99.
Martin	Mmm. It's very nice, but _____ only _____ £45.
Shop assistant	Well, _____ _____ this blue racket? It's only £42.50. She _____ use this racket for training – it's fine.
Martin	Well, OK then. I'd like that, please.

[ ] 5

Reading

7 Look at the picture and complete the text.

Mary   Sonia

1m 48

55kg   65kg

Mary and Sonia are in the same class. They are 15 years old. Mary's weight is _____, and Sonia's weight is _____, so their average _____ is _____. The average height of Mary and Sonia is 1m 50 cm, so Sonia's height is _____.

[ ] 5

8 a Read the conversation between Bill and Gemma. Put these topics in order. Write 1 to 5.

[ ] sports [ ] healthy food [ ] snack food

[ ] television [ ] sleep

Bill	Gemma, I'm doing a project for school – a survey about teenagers. Can you help me?
Gemma	Yes, sure.
Bill	OK, the first question is about TV. Do you watch a lot of TV or not?
Gemma	Well, I have a TV in my room, so yes, I watch it a lot! But not at the weekend. On Saturday and Sunday I do other things – go shopping, meet friends, things like that.
Bill	OK, thanks. Second question. What about sleeping? How many hours do you sleep a night?
Gemma	Well, I go to sleep late, about 11 o'clock, and I wake up at about 6 o'clock.
Bill	Wow, that's not much!
Gemma	I know.
Bill	OK … Next is food. Do you think you eat in a healthy way, or do you eat a lot of snack food?
Gemma	Well, I love apples and oranges, all fruit really. I eat carrots too because I think they're good for me.
Bill	Apples, oranges, carrots … What about snack food – chocolate and cake, for example?
Gemma	No, I don't eat chocolate or cake. I sometimes eat sweets, but not often.
Bill	OK. Thanks. And the next question … What sports do you like?
Gemma	Ugh, sport! I'm not really interested.

[ ] 5

b Are these statements true or false? Write ✓ or ✗.

1 Gemma eats a lot of fruit and vegetables. [ ]
2 She does a lot of sport. [ ]
3 She likes cakes and other sweet things. [ ]
4 She watches TV during the week, but not at the weekend. [ ]
5 She sleeps six hours a night. [ ]

	5
Total	50

Consolidation test
Grammar

1 Read the dialogues. Choose the right answers.

1   A   Look at _____ bird over there in the tree.
        a this   b those   c that

    B   Do you mean _____ tall tree at the end of the garden?
        a the   b a   c an

2   A   Excuse me, _____ time is it?
        a what's   b what   c which

    B   It's _____ seven.
        a half past   b half to   c thirty

3   A   How _____ have you got with you?
        a money   b much money
        c many money

    B   _____ got any money, sorry!
        a I don't   b I'm not   c I haven't

4   A   There's only _____ food in the fridge.
        a a little   b a lot of   c a few

    B   Yes, we must _____ shopping this afternoon.
        a going   b to go   c go

5   A   What sports does your brother _____?
        a play   b plays   c playing

    B   He loves football, and he _____ play tennis, too.
        a must   b can   c is

6   A   Where's Jack _____ evening?
        a those   b these   c this

    B   He _____ his grandmother
        a visits   b visit   c 's visiting

7   A   Do you often _____ horse-riding?
        a go   b do   c play

    B   Only _____ the summer holidays.
        a at   b on   c in

| 14 |

2 a   Make negative sentences.

1   I've got a birthday present for you.
    I haven't got a birthday present for you.

2   I go to the cinema on Friday nights.

_____

3   She can speak English very well.

_____

4   The visitors are getting on the bus.

_____

| 3 |

b   Make questions.

1   The visitors are getting on the bus.
    Are the visitors getting on the bus?

2   Dad has got a birthday present for me.

_____

3   The OK Club members usually meet on Friday evening.

_____

4   The Dictionary Man can speak and write Chinese.

_____

| 3 |

Vocabulary

3 Underline the odd one out in each group.

1   sister brother <u>friend</u> mother father
2   doctor tour guide visitor diver shop assistant
3   library beach sports centre hotel school
4   half a quarter two thirds five thousand a third
5   sunny slowly rainy cloudy snowy
6   great fantastic good awful brilliant

| 5 |

4 a   Match the words.

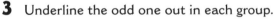

1   healthy   shape
2   birthday   music
3   noisy   holiday
4   space   present
5   round   food
6   beach   station

b Use phrases from Exercise 4a to complete the sentences.

1 Don't eat a lot of chocolate. Eat fruit and other _healthy food_ .

2 Many families have a _____ in Spain every year.

3 I'm looking for a _____ for my little brother. He's 10 next Sunday.

4 What is that _____? It's my drawing of Earth!

5 The _____ has a crew of 55 men and women.

6 Why do you like that awful _____? It sounds terrible!

5

Skills
Reading

5 Complete the text using the words in the box.

grow   danger   late   run   height   tall
average   noise   a lot   them

Giraffes are very _____ animals. They live in Africa. They are brown and yellow and they can _____ up to 5 metres tall and their _____ helps _____ to find food. Giraffes mainly eat in the morning or _____ in the evening.

Giraffes can _____ very fast – 56 kilometres per hour. A champion athlete can only run at 42 kilometres per hour. Their _____ weight is about 800 kilograms.

Giraffes can live for 36 years, but _____ of them die before they are 25 years old. They don't like _____ and they run from _____ (for example other animals).

10

Speaking

6 Complete the dialogue.

Ann like/you/do/sport

_____?

Bill Yes, I love sport.

Ann sports/which/play/you/do

_____?

Bill I play football and tennis.

Ann times/how/a/week/play/do/tennis/many/you

_____?

Bill I play on Mondays and Thursdays.

Ann you/play/do/where

_____?

Bill At the Sports Centre.

Writing

4

7 Look at the chart about pocket money. Write sentences using the words below.

1 a lot   2 a little   3 half   4 a third   5 a quarter
6 two-thirds   7 75%

What do you spend your pocket money on?

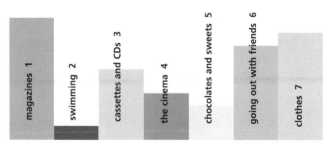

1 _I spend a lot of my pocket money on magazines._
2 _____
3 _____
4 _____
5 _____
6 _____
7 _____

	6
Total	50

Unit test
Grammar

1 Look at the picture, then complete the dialogue between a police officer and Mr Black.

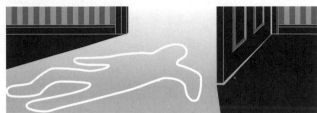

Police officer	Mr Black, ___*did*___ you ___*go*___ to Mr Grady's house yesterday evening?
Mr Black	No, I _____!
Police officer	No? So, where _____ you yesterday, Mr Black?
Mr Black	I _____ at my brother's house all day. It _____ his 50th birthday. We _____ lunch together at his house.
Police officer	What _____ you have for lunch?
Mr Black	We _____ lamb with potatoes and carrots.
Police officer	What did you do after lunch?
Mr Black	We _____ for a walk and then we _____ to the cinema.
Police officer	What time _____ you _____ to the cinema?
Mr Black	Erm … about seven o'clock I think.
Police officer	And _____ you _____ a good time?
Mr Black	Yes we _____.
Police officer	Well, that's interesting Mr Black, because the cinema _____ open yesterday.

[10]

2 Correct the underlined words.

1 It was a very <u>wind</u> day today.   *windy*

2 The typhoon was awful, but we are all safe and <u>good</u>.

   _____

3 In the centre of a typhoon, the air is <u>complete</u> still.

   _____

4 In 1987, the south of Britain had a <u>violently</u> storm.

   _____

5 Many old trees <u>was</u> badly damaged.

   _____

6 I was lucky because my home wasn't <u>undamaged</u>.

   _____

[5]

Vocabulary

3 a Write the words in the correct list.

after before clear during ~~in~~ safe ~~terrible~~ violent

Adjectives	Time prepositions
terrible	*in*

[3]

b Use the words in Exercise 4a to complete these sentences.

1 In 1999, there was a ___*terrible*___ storm.

2 _____ the storm, the sky was _____ and blue.

3 _____ the storm, the winds were extremely _____.

4 _____ the storm, I was happy that all my family were all _____.

[3]

4 Complete the sentences with words from the box.

amazing ~~dangerous~~ freezing enormous terrifying

Danger at sea

The situation was very *dangerous*. The water was _____, and the waves were _____. The experience was _____, but all the people escaped. The rescue was _____.

[4]

Skills

Reading

5 Read the paragraphs. Decide the correct order. Write 1–5.

> **The London Marathon**
> A ☐ During the first half of the Marathon, I had a good time. I was with some friends, and the weather was really good – not very hot, and not cold.
> B ☐ I was very happy to finish. My time was three and a half hours. The first athlete's time was two hours eight minutes, but my time was good enough! It was a great day, and I want to run again next year.
> C ☐ The London Marathon takes place each year in Spring. It is 42 kilometres long. Last year, I was one of the athletes. I was number 3001, and there were a lot of athletes running.
> D ☐2 At 10 o'clock, all the top athletes went to the starting place. I was in the next group, of course. On all the roads, there were hundreds of people. There were also lots of places to get water, because it's important to drink a lot.
> E ☐ The second half was quite hard for me. After two hours, I had some problems with my feet but other athletes were very kind and helpful to me.

	4

6 Read the texts again. Are these sentences true (✓) or false (✗)?

1 A marathon is 42 kilometres. ☐
2 There were 3,001 people in the race. ☐
3 The writer was in the first group of athletes. ☐
4 The weather was good. ☐
5 During the race, it is important to drink a lot. ☐
6 The writer didn't finish the race. ☐

	6

Listening

7 a 📼 Listen to an interview with an athlete. Make notes of her answers.

1 Are you tired? _Yes I am_
2 Was this your first marathon? _____
3 Did any friends run with you? _____
4 Was your husband there at the end? _____

	3

b 📼 Listen again, and answer the questions.
1 What was your running time? _____
2 What was the weather like? _____

	2

Writing

8 Look at the pictures and complete Peter's diary.

...... **August 19th**

We had quite a a good day today. At nine o'clock

we _____.

Then, at 11 o'clock, we _____

In the afternoon, _____,

so we _____. But in

the evening, the weather was cold, so

_____

......

	10
Total	**50**

Unit test
Grammar

1 Read the sentences and <u>underline</u> the right answers.

A Martin ¹___ at school last week.

B I know, he ²___ an accident at the weekend.

A That's terrible! What ³___ to him?

B He ⁴___ his brother's bike.

A Really? That's awful. ⁵___ he go to hospital?

B Yes, he ⁶___ in hospital for five days.

A Which hospital ⁷___ to?

B The City Hospital. His mother ⁸___ me to tell me.

A Did you ⁹___ him in hospital?

B No, I ¹⁰___ time, but I'd like to visit him at home next weekend.

1	a	didn't	b	wasn't	c	weren't
2	a	had	b	has	c	have
3	a	happens	b	happened	c	did happen
4	a	crashes	b	did crash	c	crashed
5	a	Was	b	Did	c	Is
6	a	did	b	is	c	was
7	a	he went	b	did he go	c	he did go
8	a	call	b	did call	c	called
9	a	visit	b	visiting	c	visited
10	a	don't had	b	didn't have	c	didn't had

	10

2 Write the verbs in the correct list.

arrived asked closed crashed helped jumped
moved opened started stopped waited
walked wanted

/d/   _arrived,_____

/t/   _asked,_____

/ɪd/ _started,_____

	10

Vocabulary

3 Read the two texts.

A News report

Last night, the plane ____crew____ of a Boeing 707
helped police   to _____ three
_____ at Madrid _____. The police
say,'We are happy to say that the 96 _____ on
board were all _____. The plane was on its way to
Rome when

B The Circus is in town!

TODAY ONLY!

We are giving free _____ to children under
seven years old.
The _____ starts at 6.30 p.m.
We have famous _____ from Russia,
elephants from Asia, and horse-riders from
Hungary.
Don't _____ this wonderful experience! If
you want a _____ near the front, then
please arrive early!

a Which texts do these words come from? Put the words in the correct groups.

acrobats ~~airport~~ arrest ~~crew~~ hijackers
~~miss~~ passengers ~~safe~~ ~~seat~~ show ~~tickets~~

A **News report**   _airport_   _crew_

safe   _____   _____

_____

B **The Circus is in town!**   _miss_

seat   _tickets_   _____

_____

	5

b Use words from the lists in Exercise 3a to complete the texts.

	5

178

Skills
Reading

4 Paragraphs A–E come from two different newspaper stories. Look at the pictures, and read the texts.

BEARS

A But that is not Terry's story. 'I didn't want to give the bears my food. I wanted to take photographs with my new camera!' So what do Terry's parents say? 'We're not sure how the accident happened. We only want to say a big "thank you" to Terry's rescuer!'

B Terry Adams, a 10-year-old tourist at London zoo had a very lucky escape yesterday. He was at the zoo with his family for his birthday. He wanted to take a photograph of the bears with his new camera. But a bear pulled young Terry into its swimming pool.

C 'It was very frightening,' says one of the scientists. 'There were three bears very near us. People think these animals are friendly, but that's not true. They are also very strong, so it was very dangerous. Luckily, they weren't interested in us. They were interested in our food. They opened three bags of food and went away. We didn't have much sleep after that!'

D A team of scientists had an interesting experience last week, says our science reporter. They were in their tent when there was a terrible noise near them. 'We all jumped up and looked outside …'

E A zoo keeper immediately jumped into the water and helped him to get away. The man was quite angry. 'He had a sandwich in his hand – we tell all our visitors that they mustn't give food to animals,' he said.

a   Complete the chart.

	Part 1	Part 2	Part 3
Story 1	B		
Story 2			–

4

b   Are these sentences true (✓) or false (✗)?

1   Bears are friendly animals. ☐
2   Terry Adams was at the zoo. ☐
3   Terry said he wanted to give the bears his sandwich. ☐
4   The scientists wanted to give the bears some food. ☐
5   The scientists were terrified of the bears. ☐
6   The bears arrived at their tent during the night. ☐

6

Listening

5 a   🔲   Listen and tick (✓) the right headline.

A **HIJACKER LEAVES BOMB AT AIRPORT** ☐

B **TRAVELLER LOSES HIS SUITCASE** ☐

C **POLICE ARREST THE WRONG MAN** ☐

b   🔲   Listen again, and complete the text.

Newsreader   Here is a news report from
_France_____ . Police closed the _____ in
Paris for nearly _____ _____
yesterday. A French police officer said, 'We had a
report about a _____ . In these situations,
we must always think about the safety of the
public first.' Later, an _____ _____
talked about the experience. Over to our reporter
in Paris. Hello, Anne.

Anne   Hello. I'm here in Paris with Mr Smith.
Mr Smith, you were in the airport this afternoon.
Tell us what happened.

Mr Smith   Yes, my wife reported that there was a
_____ near Customs. The police _____
to ask all staff and visitors to leave the _____
. But when they opened the bag, it was full of
clothes. It _____ a bomb at all!'

10

Total   50

Unit test
Grammar

1 a Write the past tense of these verbs.

1 become   _became_
2 know   _____
3 say   _____
4 sit   _____
5 tell   _____
6 understand   _____

     5

b Use the verbs in Exercise 1a to complete the text.

Why I love languages

My grandfather was a very intelligent man, and I think he _knew_ a lot about children, too. When I was a little girl, he _____ me that languages are not difficult to learn.

'For example, let's try Italian. Listen to me and do what I say.' Then, he _____, 'Siediti!' (Sit down!) I didn't know any Italian, but I _____ him easily because he looked at a chair. I _____ on the chair, and my grandfather laughed. 'Good! You see – you speak Italian.'

After that, I _____ interested in languages, and now I can speak five of them – English, Spanish, Greek, Turkish and, of course, Italian.

     5

2 a Complete the first half of the sentences. Use verbs from the box.

eat	give	kill	~~tidy~~	win	write

1 My mother didn't _tidy_ my room, …
2 An American didn't _____ the competition, …
3 I didn't _____ all the biscuits, …
4 Our penfriends didn't _____ to my brother and me, …
5 The police didn't _____ the man, …
6 Ricky didn't _____ the tickets to Jane, …

     5

b Complete the second half of the sentences. Use past tense verbs and object pronouns.

1 … I _tidied_ _it_ .
2 … a Frenchman _____ _____.
3 … my greedy brother _____ _____.
4 … their family _____ to _____.
5 … the hijackers _____ _____.
6 … Emma _____ _them_ to _____.

     5

Vocabulary

3 Complete the dialogues. Use adjectives from the box.

annoyed	greedy	hungry	lazy	terrible	tidy	tired

1 **Father** Carol, don't be _____! Leave some biscuits for other people.

     Carol Sorry, Dad. I didn't eat anything last night, so I'm really _____.

2 **Mother** Carol, please tell Dave to clean his room. It's a _____ mess. Why can't he be _____ like you?

     Carol I don't want to have an argument with him. He's already _____ with me because I left his new CD at a friend's house.

3 **Father** Ricky, go and take the dog for a walk. You watch TV all day, and you never get any exercise – you're getting very _____.

     Ricky That's not true. I'm _____ because I studied all night for my exams!

     7

4 Read about the people. What are their jobs? Use these clues to help you.

a _t e_ ach _e_ r   d do _ _ _ _   g explo _ _ _
b f _ rm _ _   e a _ ch _ _ ect
c a _ t _ r   f l _ _ y _ _

1 I hope you enjoy my lessons. _teacher_
2 Have you got a health problem? See me. _____
3 I can help you design your new home. _____
4 Are you going to court? I can help you. _____

5 I work outside in the fresh air. I get up very early in the morning. I don't want to live in a city.

_____

6 I want to travel to lots of interesting places.

_____

7 I work in the theatre. I like to entertain people.

_____

	3

Skills
Reading

5 Read the text. Match the paragraphs of the text with these headings. Write 1–5.

a   His first film ☐
b   His time at school ☐
c   When he was a child ☐
d   His family life ☐
e   His other films ☐

1 Mel Gibson is a famous Australian film star, but he was born in 1956 in New York and he lived in America until he was 12-years-old. He came from a very large family.  He had ten brothers and sisters. When he was 12, his father won a competition on a television show and the family moved to Sydney in Australia.

2 Mel had a hard time at school. The other students laughed at him because he spoke like an American. He found it difficult to make friends at first. ☐

3 When he left school he decided to become a reporter but then he changed to study drama. ☐ He was very lucky. His sister helped him and sent him to interviews. The night before his interview for the film *Mad Max* he had a fight, so he looked terrible at the interview. But the directors wanted to choose someone who enjoyed fights, so they chose him! ☐ The film made a lot of money and Mel Gibson became famous.

4 Mel Gibson acted in a few other Australian films, but he also began to act in American films. In 1987 Mel went to Hollywood and starred in *Lethal Weapon* with Danny Glover. It was about two police officers. People loved it and he starred in other *Lethal Weapon* films. He also started to direct films. His 1995 film *Braveheart* won lots of Oscar awards. ☐

5 Mel's films are often violent, but outside the movies his family is very important to him. He loves his wife, Robyn, very much and they have seven children. ☐

	5

6 Read the text again. Are these sentences true (✓) or false (✗)?

1   He was born in Australia. ☐
2   His first years in Australia were difficult for him. ☐
3   His sister helped him to get into his first film. ☐
4   He directed Lethal Weapon with Danny Glover. ☐
5   He doesn't like acting in violent films. ☐

	5

7 Answer the questions about Mel Gibson.

1   When did Mel's family move to Australia?

_____

2   How did Mel's sister help him?

_____

3   Why did the directors of *Mad Max* choose him to star in their film?

_____

4   Why was *Braveheart* an important film for Mel?

_____

5   What does Mel feel about his family?

_____

	5

8 Find the best place to add these new pieces of information to the text. Write the number of the sentence next to the right place in the text.

1   Mel's father is American. His mother is Australian.
2   The film was about an Australian police officer.
3   He is very careful to choose very good schools for his children.
4   Some of his other films are *Conspiracy Theory*, *Ransom*, and *Payback*.
5   Later he made more friends.
6   He was very frightened when he first started acting.

	5
Total	**50**

Unit test
Grammar

1 Which sentences have got present meanings (P), which have got future meanings (F)? Circle the right answer.

1 My brother's working very hard for his exams. (P) F
2 What do you do at the weekends?   P   F
3 My sister's going to Spain in the summer.   P   F
4 Please be quiet, I'm trying to study.   P   F
5 We're going to the cinema tonight.   P   F
6 Paul goes to school on Saturday mornings.   P   F
7 Hey! Stop! Where are you going?   P   F

     6

2 a Put the verbs in the past tense.

The Great Wall of China

A   ... my dream (come) _came_ true. We _____ (go) to China and I (walk) _____ along the famous Wall. It (be) _____ fantastic.

B   ... we (telephone) _____ lots of tourist companies and (find) _____ a cheap flight.

C   ... we (book) _____ a hotel near the Great Wall, and (wait) _____ excitedly for the summer holidays.

D   ... I (decide) _____ that I (want) _____ to see the Great Wall of China.

E   ... I (ask) _____ a friend to come with me, and she (agree) _____ .

     5

b Write the correct order of the sentences in Exercise 2a.

1 [D]   2 [ ]   3 [ ]   4 [ ]   5 [ ]   **4**

c Write about the holiday. Use the sentences from Exercise 2a, in the right order, and the words from the box. Think carefully about punctuation.

ago   finally   first   next   so

Three years _____
_____
_____
_____
_____
_____
_____

     5

Vocabulary

3 Complete the letter with prepositions from the box.

about   at   for   for   in   on   to   to

Dear Mary
Thanks _____ your letter. I am very busy _____ the moment, but next week, I am coming _____ London, and I'd love to see you. What are your plans _____ the weekend? Are you free _____ Saturday _____ the afternoon? How _____ having lunch together? Please write _____ me, or telephone. Then we can organize a time and place to meet.
Bye for now.
Linda

     4

4 a Add verbs in the past tense.

book   ~~organize~~   plan   pull   read   stay   train

1 Our friends *organized* visits to interesting places.
2 We _____ the expedition carefully.
3 A tour guide _____ the plane tickets for us.
4 We _____ a guidebook about the country.

5   We _____ our equipment across the ice.

6   We _____ hard for two months.

7   We _____ with friends.

b   Write the sentences under A or B.

     A   A trip to Italy   [1] [ ] [ ] [ ]

     B   A journey to the North Pole   [ ] [ ] [ ]

[6]

Skills
Writing

5   a   A group of students from another school is visiting your town for one day. Complete the plans.

> **Plans for the visit**
>
> 9.30:   Meet all the students at the bus station.
>
> Morning: ¹ Go to _____
>
> Lunch: ² Eat _____
>
> Afternoon: ³ Go to _____
>
> 5.30:   ⁴ Take the students to the bus station.

[3]

b   Write a letter to the group organizer.

> Dear
>
> I am very happy that you are coming to visit my town. These are my plans.
>
> At 9.30, _I am meeting you at the bus station_ . In the morning ¹ _____
>
> _____
>
> At lunch time ² _____
>
> _____ .
>
> In the afternoon,
>
> ³ _____
>
> _____ .
>
> At 5.30
>
> ⁴ _____
>
> _____ .
>
> I hope that's OK.
>
> Best wishes,
>
> _____

[4]

Speaking

6   Steve and Gemma are talking about their mother's birthday. Complete the sentences.

Gemma   How about ¹ _____ a birthday tea for her?

Steve   OK. Good idea. Shall I ² _____ a cake?

Gemma   No! Let's ³ _____ a cake from this book.

Steve   What sort of cake ⁴ _____ we make?

Gemma   Why ⁵ _____ look at pictures in the book …

1	a to prepare	b preparing	c prepare
2	a buying	b to buy	c buy
3	a make	b to make	c making
4	a do	b let's	c shall
5	a we do	b we don't	c don't we

[5]

Listening

7   Steve and Gemma are still talking about their mother's birthday. Look at the shopping list. Listen to the dialogue, and tick (✓) the things that Steve must buy.

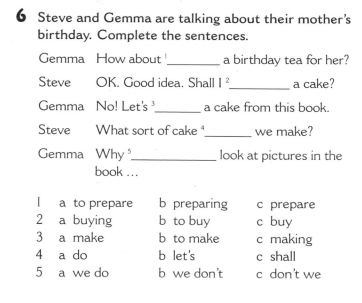

> Steve's shopping list
>
> [ ] eggs
> [ ] lemons
> [ ] chocolate
> [ ] sugar
> [ ] book about plants
> [ ] flowers
> [ ] birthday card from me
> [ ] birthday card from Gemma

[8]

Total   [50]

Unit test
Grammar

1 **Put apostrophes (') in these sentences.**

1 Jack's got two sisters.
2 Jacks sisters are called Alison and Anna.
3 Theyre both ten years old.
4 There are two beds in the girls room
5 One is Alisons bed and the other one is Annas.
6 Annas best friend is called Anna too.
7 Alison and the two Annas all go to Jacks school.

| | 6 |

2 **Complete the dialogues with** *cap, caps, one,* **or** *ones.*

1 Child   Oh look, Dad, _____! Can I
            have _____, please?

   Father   OK, let's ask the _____ seller
            for a black _____.

2 Father   Excuse me. How much are your
            black _____?

   Cap seller The small _____ are £4. The
            large _____ are £5.

3 Cap seller Which size would you like?

   Child   I'd like a large black _____, please.

   Cap seller I'm sorry, I haven't got any large
            black _____.

   Child   OK. I'll have a large white _____.

| | 10 |

3 **Correct these sentences.**

1 Is this your coat?   No, it's **he**.
                          his

2 **Who's** are these shoes?   They're mine.
   _____

3 Are these your books?   No, they're **her's**.
                          _____

4 Who do these bags belong to? They're **us**.
                          _____

5 Excuse me. This is my coat. No, it isn't. It's **my**!
                          _____

| | 4 |

Vocabulary

4 **What are the objects in the bag? Complete the words.**

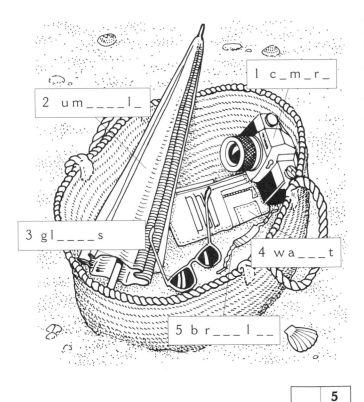

1 c _ m _ r _

2 u m _ _ _ _ l _

3 g l _ _ _ _ s

4 w a _ _ _ t

5 b r _ _ _ l _ _

| | 5 |

5 Complete the sentences. Use words from the box.

absolutely   easily   missing   unusual   usually

My dog can do amazing and _____ things. For
example, when I lose something, he always knows
where to find it. I tell him what is _____ (I never repeat
the words because he understands English _____),
then he runs to get it, and brings it back to me. People
don't _____ believe this story, but it's _____ true!

	5

Skills
Writing

6 Imagine that you lost something yesterday. Today,
you go to a Lost Property Office.

a   Answer the questions. Make notes.

What did you lose? _____

Where/What time did you lose it? _____

_____

What colour/shape/size is it? _____

_____

b   Use your notes to write a dialogue.

	6

Officer   Good morning. Can _____ ?

You   Yes, please. _____

_____

Officer   Where did you lose it?

You   _____

Officer   _____ ?

You   _____

Officer   What is it like?

You   _____

_____

Officer   I'm sorry _____ .
          Please come back again tomorrow.

	7

Speaking

7 Complete these sentences. Use the words and
phrases in the box.

about   don't   'll   please   shall   thank you   would

	Children	Mother
A	_____ worry. I _____ cook dinner!	Ok, but what _____ Dad helping you!
B	_____ you like a hot drink?	Yes, _____. I'm very thirsty.
C	_____ I read to you?	No, _____. I'm very tired.

	7
Total	**50**

Consolidation test

3

Grammar

1 **Choose the right answers.**

1 Good morning. _____ I _____ you?
   (a) can/help b would/ help c can/to help
   d would/help

2 I'd like _____ Italian pizza and _____ extra cheese, please.
   a some/a b an/some c the/a d a/some

3 What _____ like to drink?
   a you b you do c would you d you'd

4 _____ you got _____ money with you?
   a do/a b have/any c are/some d does/the

5 What time _____ your school day _____ ?
   a do/finishes b does/finishes c do/finish
   d does/finish

6 My friends _____ me at the weekend.
   a visits often b visit often c often visits
   d often visit

7 See you _____ Sunday _____ 12.30.
   a at/on b in/at c on/at d to/on

8 She is busy at the moment. She _____ her homework
   a does b is doing c did d 's do

9 We haven't got _____!
   a many time b much times c much time
   d many times

10 Where _____ you _____ last night?
   a were/go b were/went c did/went d did/go

11 Were you at the party last night? No, I _____
   a didn't b weren't c wasn't d don't

12 My sister sings _____ and she's _____ dancer too.
   a well/a good b good/a well c good/well
   d well/good

13 He _____ Titanic and it _____ am enormous hit.
   a is making/becomes b makes/is becoming
   c made/became d made/becomes

14 _____ carry your bag?
   a Shall I b Shall you c Let's d Let me

15 I'd like to see you again. How about _____ at the weekend?
   a don't we meet b meeting c to meet
   d let's meet

16 I'm sorry, I _____ to Paris next weekend.
   a can go b 'm going c go d went

17 _____ is this bag?
   a Where's b What's c Who's d Whose

18 The black _____ is _____
   a one/my b ones/mine c one/mine
   d ones/my

19 Look at the time! I _____ go. Bye!
   a must b can c can't d am

20 Magda is Jack's penfriend. He wrote _____ a long letter yesterday..
   a she b her c hers d her's

21 They _____ French at college from 1997 to 2000.
   a studied b studyed c are studying d study

20

Vocabulary

2 **Complete the sentences with words from the box.**

> dark embarrassed excited expedition
> frightened miserable noisy sock tired wet

1 I saw that I had one green _____ and one red one on my feet. I felt very _____.

2 When the lights went out, it was completely _____. I felt quite _____.

3 It rained all day. The travellers were cold, hungry and _____. They felt extremely _____.

4 The night before the _____, the explorers were very _____.

5 There was a very _____ party last night and I didn't sleep, so now I feel _____.

5

3 Complete the sentences with the past simple of these verbs and the time phrases.

| after | become | before | during | find | in | last |
| see | sink | write | | | | |

1 The ship _____ to the bottom of the sea _____ 1797.

2 Divers _____ the old ship and filmed it under water _____ week.

3 _____ the 'eye' of the storm, it _____ strangely quiet.

4 _____ the storm, we _____ that many houses were damaged.

5 I _____ a letter to my penfriend _____ my English lesson yesterday.

	5

Skills
Reading

Braveheart: the film and the history books

Braveheart's real name was William Wallace and he lived about 700 years ago. We don't know very much about his life. We only know that he was born in Scotland in 1267, that he fought against the English, and that he died about 1305.

King   Queen

In 1995, the Australian actor and producer Mel Gibson decided to make a film about the life of Braveheart. He produced the film, and he also acted in it as Braveheart. The French actor, Sophie Marceau, was the beautiful English Queen, Isabelle. The story takes place in Scotland, and in the film you can see many beautiful places in Scotland. The film-makers wanted to find a lot of places for the many fights, so you can also see places in Ireland in the film.

Many people watched Braveheart at the cinema, and became interested in the story. So, after the film, a lot of people wanted to read history books about Scotland. Readers found that the film tells the story of some of Wallace's life very well. But sometimes the film story and the story of Wallace in history books is very different. For example, in the film King Edward dies before Wallace. But history books tell us that Wallace died in 1305, and that Edward fought against the Scots for another eight years and died in 1313. In the film, Wallace meets and is in love with Isabelle, King Edward's wife. But Isabelle was born in 1296. This means that she was only nine years old at the time the English arrested and killed Braveheart in 1305. In history books, she became King Edward's wife in 1308.

4 a Read the text quickly. Answer the questions.

1 What was Braveheart's real name?
_____

2 When was Braveheart born?
_____

3 Which actor was Braveheart in the film?
_____

4 Why did lots of people read books about Scotland?
_____

5 In the film, who did Braveheart love?
_____

	5

b Read the text again. Decide which of these sentences are true in history (write ✓) and which are only in the film (write ✗).

1 Braveheart was born in Scotland. ☐
2 He fought against the English in Scotland and Ireland. ☐
3 The English killed him. ☐
4 Isabelle was King Edward's wife. ☐
5 King Edward died before Wallace. ☐

	5

Listening

5 📼 Listen to this story about Tim, Joe and Roberto. Write the names for each experience.

1 *Joe and Tim* _____ went to Rome last year.
2 *Roberto* _____ lives in Rome.
3 _____ stayed in his room.
4 _____ went swimming.
5 _____ went to the airport alone.
6 _____ had Joe's passport.
7 _____ went to the wrong airport.
8 _____ missed the flight to London.
9 _____ was very angry.
10 _____ stayed all night at the airport.
11 _____ went to work the next day.
12 _____ telephoned the next evening.

	10
Total	**50**

Test answer key and tapescripts

Test for Unit 1

1 *Here is, What is, I am, that is, name is, We are*

2 *This is Jack. He's in the OK Club. Here's his address and phone number.*

3 **A** *line 1: Japan   line 2: Turkey, Canada   line 3: The United States, Country, Hungary   line 4: Mexico, Britain line 5: Greece, Australia*
B *line 1: students draw 5 dots   line 2: three   line 3: one, eight line 4: Numbers   line 5: students draw 7 dots, two   line 6: six, four   line 7: ten*

4 *2 Sorry!   3 I'm fine, thanks.   4 That's right.   5 Listen. 6 That's wrong!   7 Brazil. And you?*

5 *This, from, in, with, me, my, is, Goodbye*

6 *Peter, 12, University Road, London, SE13 9LB, England*

7 *Dear, Thanks, pizza, coffee, Please, Kerry*

8 *morning, 392, Hi, This, is, Hello, Are, you, I'm, here*

Tapescript
Receptionist Good morning. Grand Hotel. Can I help you?
Peter Oh, hello! Yes, er … room three nine two, please.
Receptionist Sorry? Room three one two?
Peter No, room three nine two, please.
Receptionist Just a moment …
Magda Hello?
Peter Hi, Magda! This is Peter!
Magda Peter! Hello! Are you in Oxford?
Peter What?
Magda Are you in Oxford?
Peter Oh! No. I'm here … in London. Listen, are your free …

Test for Unit 2

1 *1 What's, It's, an, name, that's*
2 Who's, a spy, British, she is

2 *Who's   He's   who are   They're   Are they   they are*

3 *2 Yes, you are.   3 I'm fifteen.   4 Oh! I'm not fifteen. 5 How old are you?   6 Where are you from?*

4 *Animals: bird, fish, shark*
Classroom: chair, desk, pencil, table
People: agent, friend, girl

5 *2 nineteen   3 eighteen   4 twelve   5 twenty   6 thirteen*

6 *2 It's a club for young people.   3 Are you a member of the club? 4 Yes, I am.   5 Are Ricky and Jack members, too? 6 Yes, they are. Come with me this evening!*

7 */i:/ D, E, G, P, T, V*
/e/ L, M, S, X

8 *Here's the shop.   Ah, here it is.   How old are you?   I'm fifteen, and my friend's seventeen.   sorry   eighteen*

Tapescript
Phil Now where … Aha! Steve … Here's the shop. Come on!
Assistant Good morning, boys!
Phil } Hello.
Steve } Good morning.

Phil Now, mmm … Where is it? Aha! Here it is – *Two brothers*.
Assistant Can I help you?
Phil Yes, this video – *Two brothers*, please.
Assistant How old are you?
Phil Pardon?
Assistant How old are you?
Phil Oh. I'm er … I'm fifteen, and my friend's er …
Steve I'm seventeen!
Phil Yes, my friend's seventeen.
Assistant Seventeen, are you? No, sorry. You're not eighteen. But this is a good film … Look here …

Test for Unit 3

1 *1 dogs   2 haven't   3 Have they, a   4 they have 5 Has, got a   6 he hasn't   7 She, got, fish   8 hasn't, a dog 9 Have, got a   10 No, haven't/Yes, have*

2a *2 This animal is from Africa.   3 It has got a yellow and brown/ brown and yellow body …   4 … and a very long neck. 5 It's got a very short tail.*

b *giraffe*

3 *2 African elephants   3 are your brothers   4 have got black bodies   5 old are your friends   6 have got long hair*

4 *2 white   3 blue   4 green   5 black   6 orange*

5 *family   father   grandmother   brothers   sister*

6a *2 a black and white body.   3 it hasn't got any legs. 4 eight legs. It's got a grey body.   5 It has got a small head.*

b *2 penguin   3 snake   4 spider   5 giraffe*

7 *1 B   2 D*

8 *Students should describe one of the characters, following the model, and mention hair, eyes and height. They should give their character a name.*

9 *2 a boy/girl   3 (student's age)   4 fair/dark hair 5 brown/blue/green/grey   6 Yes, I have./No, I haven't.*

Tapescript
1 Are you a student or a teacher?
2 Are you a boy or a girl?
3 How old are you?
4 Have you got fair hair or dark hair?
5 What colour are your eyes?
6 Have you got glasses?

Test for Unit 4

1 *2 are   next   3 is   under   4 is   on   5 are   chair 6 are   in*

2 *2 Are there, No, there aren't.   3 Is there, Yes, there is. 4 Is there, No, there isn't.   5 Are there, Yes, there are. 6 Are there, Yes, there are.*

3 *2 Emma's pen   3 Dave's book   4 Ricky's jeans 5 Jack's bag   6 Carol's computer*

4 *1 shirt   2 jumper   3 trousers   4 jeans   5 trainers*

5 *your, her, isn't, my, 's, his, 's, our, haven't, Their*

6 *Students should describe each room, mentioning which room it is, what it contains, and where the furniture is located.*

Test for Unit 5

1 2 *do* 3 *likes* 4 *'d like* 5 *a* 6 *Would* 7 *like* 8 *some* 9 *any* 10 *you like* 11 *don't* 12 *don't* 13 *doesn't like*

2 2 *U* 3 *U* 4 *C* 5 *U* 6 *C* 7 *U*

3 2 *some food* 3 *money* 4 *sugar* 5 *love* 6 *apple pie*

4 1 *strawberry* 2 *pear (not a vegetable), potatoes* 3 *cheese (not meat), chicken* 4 *milk (not a herb or spice)*

5 1 *menu* 2 *Fish* 3 *Vegetables* 4 *Drinks* 5 *Milk* 6 *juice* 7 *Hot* 8 *Coffee*

6 1 *F* 2 *T* 3 *rice, fish, meat, vegetables* 4 *bread, potatoes, milk, cheese* 5 *T* 6 *F*

7 *Students answer the questions in note form, and use their notes to write a short description of a favourite dish.*

8a 1 *c* 2 *d* 3 *a*

b 1 *£1.20* 2 *£4.80*

c *Can, I'd, like, ice, Would, you, or, you, got, Vanilla*

Tapescript
8a
1
Customer That's a nice shirt
Assistant Yes, it's thirty pounds fifty.
Customer *Thirty* pounds fifty?
Assistant That's right.
Customer Oh, well … thank you.
2
Boy Have *you* got any money?
Girl Mmm … I've got … twelve pounds and … er … sixty pence.
Boy Twelve pounds sixteen?
Girl No, twelve pounds *sixty*.
3
Woman 1 Would you like a coffee?
Woman 2 That would be nice, thank you.
Woman 1 Two coffees, please.
Waiter Two coffees … That's sixty p, please
Woman 1 Twenty … forty, sixty p … Here you are.
Waiter Thank you!
8b
1
Stallholder Good morning. What would you like?
Customer Have you got any oranges?
Stallholder Oh yes, I've got some lovely oranges – and they're only twenty p.
Customer I'll have six, please.
Stallholder That's one pound twenty pence, then.
2
Customer Right, thanks … and I'd like some potatoes.
Stallholder Potatoes are two pounds forty a kilo.
Customer Two pounds forty?
Stallholder That's right. They're from France – they're very nice!
Customer Mmm. OK – I'll have two kilos then, please.
8c
Waiter Hello. Can I help you?
Customer Er … ye-es … I'd like an ice cream, please
Waiter An ice cream. OK … Would you like chocolate or vanilla?
Waiter Sorry?
Waiter Would you like chocolate or vanilla?
Customer Oh! Er … Have you got a strawberry ice cream?
Waiter No, sorry. Chocolate or vanilla.
Customer Er … OK. Vanilla, please.

Test for Consolidation 1

1a *Pleased to meet you.*
Where are you from?

b *Are there other British students here?*
Who is that woman?
Have you got any brothers?

c *is, like, How, old, are, Do, the, Does, is, our*

2 2 *Her eyes are blue* 3 *She's got a French mother and an English father.* 4 *He's got a black moustache.* 5 *There are a lot of French books in her house.* 6 *Her grandmother and grandfather live in London.*

3 2 *hasn't got* 3 *aren't* 4 *doesn't teach* 5 *they haven't got* 6 *there isn't*

4 *Rooms: bathroom, kitchen, cooker*
Food: meat, beef; vegetables, carrots; fruit, lemons; drinks, hot, water
Body: trousers; shoes; head, hat
Countries and languages: China, Spain, Greek, United States

5 2 *They aren't very tidy. Their room's a mess.* 3 *There aren't two chairs in the corner. There's one chair near the bed.*
4 *The computer isn't under the window. It's on the desk.*
5 *There aren't three posters on the door. There's one poster on the door.* 6 *There isn't a cat on the chair. There's a dog.*

6 *Students write a description of their own room, modelling it on the text in Exercise 5.*

7a *The order is: 7, 3, 4, 1, 6, 2, 5*

b *(7) I'm from France, from Paris* *(3) No, sorry!* *(4) Milk, but no sugar, please.* *(6) It's terrible!* *(5) It's great.*

Tapescript
Paula Hello. Are you the new French teacher?
Annette Yes, that's right . My name's Annette.
Paula I'm Paula. I teach English. Ah! the bell! It's break time. Would you like a coffee, Annette?
Annette Oh, yes please! Is there a cafe near the school?
Paula A cafe? Well, no. Sorry! But we've got a kettle in the teacher's room.
Here we are. Come in.
Here's some coffee. Would you like milk and sugar?
Annette Milk, but no sugar, please. Mmmm … lovely. Thanks
Paula So what do you think of our school?
Annette It's great. The students are very nice.
Paula And what do you think of the food in the school dining-room?
Annette Well … it's terrible!
Paula Yes, it is. I usually eat at home. Look! There are two chairs! Let's sit down.
John Hello, Paula!
Paula Hi, John. This is Annette, the new teacher.
John Pleased to meet you, Annette. You're not English. Where are you from?
Annette I'm from France, from Paris. I teach the …

Test for Unit 6

1 *for, before, by, at, in, for, after, with, at, to*

2 2 *What time do you go to work?*
3 *Anna's sister doesn't go swimming every day.*
4 *What does your family usually do for relaxation?*
5 *Do your friends often visit you?*
6 *Why don't you watch TV?*

3 1 *usually* 2 *always* 3 *never* 4 *sometimes* 5 *often*

4a *Verbs: meet, paint, play, read, work*
Adjectives: hopeless, huge, interesting, noisy

b *read play does noisy paint interesting*

5 2 ✓ 3 ✗ 4 ✓ 5 ✗ 6 ✗

6 1 *Tim and Jane* 2 *the new student club* 3 *Fox the cat*
4 *Mrs Black/Jane's grandmother* 5 *colourful old clothes*

7a 1 *7.20* 2 *12.30* 3 *8.50* 4 *9.15* 5 *5.45*

b 1 *1* 2 *spies/007/James Bond* 3 *2* 4 *music, Brazil*
5 *America*

Tapescript

1 *Around Britain* is a programme about travel. Its on Radio 1 at twenty past seven.
2 We've got late night *Spy Stories* on Radio 4. This evening the story is about double–oh–seven. That's right – James Bond! That's late night *Spy Stories* at half past twelve.
3 Are you a film fan? We've got *Top 10 at the Cinema* for you on Radio 2 at ten to nine.
4 At a quarter past nine, please join us for *Carnival Time!* – a programme about music in Brazil. It's on Radio 2. That's at a quarter past nine, after *Top 10 at the Cinema*.
5 *Family and Friends*. Today, we talk to children in America. *Family and Friends* is on Radio five at quarter to six.

Test for Unit 7

1 A *those* B *this* C *These* D *that*

2 1 *is, lot* 2 *are, some* 3 *are, few* 4 *is, some* 5 *are, four*

3 *Countable, singular: apple, table*
Countable, plural: people, knives, plants, women
Uncountable: water, food, orange juice, bread, fruit, cheese

4a 1 *circle* 2 *triangle* 3 *square* 4 *rectangle*

b a *triangle* b *circle* c *square* d *rectangle*

c *square*

5 2 *B* 3 *A* 4 *C* 5 *A* 6 *C*

6a 1 *tin opener* 2 *microphone* 3 *camera* 4 *matches*

b 1 ✗ 2 ✓ 3 ✓

7a *for: taking children to and from school*
shape: rectangular

b *Students use their answers to the questions in Exercise 7a to write a short description of the bus and its purpose.*

Test for Unit 8

1 3 ✗ *Can your brother speak English?* 4 ✗ *I can't swim.*
5 ✓ 6 ✓ 7 ✗ *I must go.* 8 ✗ *You must always do your homework.*

2a 2 *isn't* 3 *about that* 4 *so* 5 *agree* 6 *possible*

b *Student's own answer*

3 1 *at* 2 *on* 3 *in* 4 *in* 5 *at* 6 *on*

4 2 *He can only write Russian.* 3 *The basilicus basilicus lizard is really amazing.* 4 *She can swim for about twenty minutes.*
5 *Athletes must always eat …* 6 *They must also study the techniques of their sport (also).*

5 *Possible answers:*
Sports: play basketball/tennis/badminton/baseball, go swimming, do judo

---

Other activities: ride a bike/horse, cook, play drums/music, do aerobics, walk

6 2 *under* 3 *equipment* 4 *training* 5 *surface* 6 *dangerous*

7a *The order is: 3, 6, 1, 4, 2, 5*

b *The order is: 2, 6, 4, 1, 3, 5*

8a A *4* B *2* C *3* D *1*

b 1 ✓ 2 ✓ 3 ✗ 4 ✓

9 1 *Emma must organize her time.* 2 *She must do her school homework..* 3 *She must learn all the techniques of her sport.*
4 *She must get a lot of sleep.*

Test for Unit 9

1a *having, sitting, dying, causing, killing*

b *are sitting, (are) having, is causing, is killing, are dying*

2 *aren't, is, doesn't, are, isn't, I'm, Don't*

3 *going, Are you, not, Is, is, is he*

4 *comfortably, happily, hard, immediately, miserably, steadily, terribly, warmly*

5 *happily=comfortably, warm, miserable, terrible, steadily/hard, immediately*

6 2 *tour guide* 3 *holiday-maker* 4 *business traveller*
5 *tour company advertisement*

7 1 *reefs* 2 *tourists* 3 *pieces of coral* 4 *taking pieces of coral*

8

Tapescript

Here is the weather. Well, visitors to Lindo on the east coast are having a great time today. It's warm and sunny – perfect weather for swimming and relaxing. In the south of the island it's sunny too, but its also a little bit windy. People are at the beach, but they've got their sweatshirts on. Bad news for the west coast, I'm afraid. It's raining hard there – but that's good for the plants at least! In the north, well, again no sun. It's cloudy again today, but at least it isn't raining … In the centre of the island, up in the mountains, it's good news again today. The skiers are very happy because its snowing. This afternoon we have sun coming, so sun and snow – very good conditions for skiing. That's the end of the weather … now for the news. Farmers are saying …

---

9 *Students write a postcard to a friend or member(s) of their family, using their notes from Exercise 9a. They should write in an informal style.*

Test for Unit 10

1 *says, live, I'm having, is giving, works, goes, eats, I'm eating, I'm getting, Are you having*

2 2 *much pocket money* 3 *many hours* 4 *many students*
5 *much time* 6 *many hours*

3 *13th August, 12th June, the eighth of December, the twentieth of November, 30th March*

4 3 *three pounds, twenty* 4 *a quarters* 5 *a third*
6 *twenty-one thousand, eight hundred and sixty-nine*
7 *two-thirds*

5 2 *April* 3 *May* 4 *seventh* 5 *eighth* 6 *twelfth*

6 *help, looking, present, for, much, I've, got, how about, can*

7 *55 kg, 65 kg weight, 60 kg, 1m 52 cm*

8a *sports 5   healthy food 3   snack food 4   television 1   sleep 2*
b *1 ✓ 2 ✗ 3 ✗ 4 ✓ 5 ✗*

Test for Consolidation 2

1 *1 c, a 2 b, a 3 b, c 4 a, c 5 a, b 6 c, c 7 a, c*

2a *2 I don't go to the cinema on Friday nights.   3 She can't speak English very well.   4 The visitors aren't getting on the bus.*

b *2 Has Dad got a birthday present for me? 3 Do the OK Club members usually meet on Friday evening? 4 Can the Dictionary Man speak and write Chinese?*

3 *2 visitor 3 beach 4 five thousand 5 slowly 6 awful*

4a *2 present 3 music 4 station 5 shape 6 holiday*

b *2 beach holiday 3 birthday present 4 round shape 5 space station 6 noisy music*

5 *tall, grow, height, them, late, run, average, a lot, noise, danger.*

6 *Do you like sports?*
Which sports do you play?
How many times a week do you play basketball?
Where do you play?

7 *Possible answers:*
   2 I spend a little (of my pocket money) on swimming.
   3 I spend half (of my pocket money) on cassettes and CDs.
   4 I spend a third (of my pocket money) on the cinema.
   5 I spend a quarter (of my pocket money) on chocolates and sweets.
   6 I spend two-thirds (of my pocket money) on going out with friends.
   7 I spend seventy-five per cent (of my pocket money) on clothes.

Test for Unit 11

1 *didn't, were, was, was, had, did, had, went, went, did, go, did, have, did, wasn't*

2 *2 well 3 completely 4 violent 5 were 6 damaged*

3a *Adjectives: clear safe violent*
Time phrases: after before during

b *2 Before, clear 3 During, violent 4 After, safe*

4 *freezing enormous terrifying amazing*

5 *A 3 B 5 C 1 E 4*

6 *1 ✓ 2 ✗ 3 ✗ 4 ✓ 5 ✓ 6 ✗*

7a *2 No, it wasn't. 3 No, they didn't. 4 Yes, he was.*

b *1 Three hours. 2 It was cloudy in the morning, but during the race it was very hot and sunny.*

Tapescript
Interviewer Hello … Hello! Excuse me. Can we have a word with you? I'd like to ask a few questions.
Runner Yes, sure.
Interviewer Well first of all congratulations! How do you feel? Are you tired?
Runner Well, yes, I'm very tired, but I feel pretty good.
Interviewer Right, so was this your first marathon?
Runner No, it wasn't. I was in the marathon here for the first time last summer – with some friends from work.
Interviewer I see, and this year, did any friends run with you?
Runner No, this year I was alone … but my husband was here to watch me.

Interviewer Was your husband there at the end?
Runner Yes, he was. It was fantastic to see him!
Interviewer He didn't run with you?
Runner No, my husband doesn't like running – in fact he's hopeless at sports!
Interviewer And can I ask your running time?
Runner Yes. Three hours – not bad at my age!
Interviewer And did you have a good time?
Runner Well yes, but I was a bit stupid. The weather forecast was cloudy, and there was no sun in the morning, so I didn't wear anything on my head, and I didn't put any sun cream on my face. During the race, the sun was very hot, and now you can see that my nose is very red!
Interviewer Yes, I can see! So your message is, runners must wear a cap!
Runner Yes, in hot weather it's a very good idea.

8 *At nine o'clock we had breakfast by/near the pool. Then, at 11 o'clock, we went to the market. In the afternoon, it was sunny, so we went to the beach/swimming. But in the evening, the weather was cold, so we went to the cinema.*

Test for Unit 12

1 *1 b 2 a 3 b 4 c 5 b 6 c 7 b 8 c 9 a 10 b*

2 */d/: closed, moved, opened*
/t/: crashed, helped, jumped, stopped, walked
/ɪd/: waited, wanted

3a *A: arrest   hijackers   passengers*
B: acrobats   show

b *A: arrest, hijackers, airport, passengers, safe*
B: tickets, show, acrobats, miss, seat

4a *Story 1: B, E, A*
Story 2: D, C

b *1 ✗ 2 ✓ 3 ✗ 4 ✗ 5 ✓ 6 ✓*

5a *B*

5b *airport, two, hours, bomb, American, visitor, suitcase, decided, area, wasn't*

Tapescript
Newsreader … and here is a news report from France. Police closed the airport in Paris for nearly two hours yesterday. A French police officer said, 'We had a report about a bomb. In these situations, we must always think about the safety of the public first.' Later, an American visitor talked about the experience. Over to our reporter in Paris. Hello, Anne.
Journalist Hello. I'm here in Paris with Mr Smith. Mr Smith, you were in the airport this afternoon. Tell us what happened.
Mr Smith Yes, my wife reported that there was a suitcase near Customs. The police decided to ask all staff and visitors to leave the area. But when they opened the bag, it was full of clothes. It wasn't a bomb at all! Of course, it was a big problem because …

Test for Unit 13

1a *2 knew 3 said 4 sat 5 told 6 understood*

b *told said understood sat became*

2a *2 win 3 eat 4 write 5 kill 6 give*

b *2 won it 3 ate them 4 wrote, us 5 killed him 6 gave, her*

3 *1 greedy 2 terrible, tidy, annoyed 3 lazy, tired*

4 *2 d doctor 3 e architect 4 f lawyer 5 b farmer 6 g explorer 7 c actor*

5 *a 3 b 2 c 1 d 5 e 4*

6 1 ✗ 2 ✓ 3 ✓ 4 ✗ 5 ✗

7 1 (His family moved to Australia) when he was 12 years old.
2 She sent him to interviews.
3 (They chose him) because he enjoyed fights.
4 (It was important) because it won lots of Oscars.
5 His family is very important to him.

8 paragraph 2: 5   paragraph 3: 6, 2   paragraph 4: 4
paragraph 5: 3

Test for Unit 14

1 2 P 3 F 4 P 5 F 6 P 7 P

2a A *went, walked, was* B *telephoned, found* C *booked, waited*
D *decided, wanted* E *asked, agreed*

b 2 E 3 B 4 C 5 A

c *Three years <u>ago</u>, I decided that I wanted to see the Great Wall of China. <u>First</u>, I asked a friend to come with me, and she agreed. <u>So</u> we telephoned lots of tourist companies and found a good price. <u>Next</u>, we booked a hotel near the Great Wall, and waited excitedly for the summer holidays. <u>Finally</u>, my dream came true. We went to China, and I walked along the famous wall. It was fantastic.*

3 for, at, to, for, on, in, about, to

4a 2 planned 3 booked 4 read 5 pulled 6 trained
7 stayed

b A 3, 4, 7 B 2, 5, 6

5 *Students make plans with suggestions of places to visit and eat, then write a letter giving the plans in detail.*

6 1 b 2 c 3 a 4 c 5 c

7 eggs ✗ lemons ✓ chocolate ✗ sugar ✓ book about plants ✗
flowers ✓ birthday card from me ✓ birthday card from
Gemma ✗ .

Tapescript
Gemma OK then, Steve. What sort of cake shall we make?
Steve How about a chocolate cake? There's a recipe for chocolate cake in this recipe book. It looks fantastic!
Gemma Mmm. No, Mum doesn't like chocolate.
Steve OK then … Let's make a lemon cake.
Gemma … but we haven't got any lemons.
Steve No problem. I'm going shopping this afternoon to get Mum's birthday present and a card. I can get the lemons at the same time. Shall I get some sugar, too?
Gemma Yes, good idea. There isn't much sugar left in the packet. Maybe you should get some eggs, too …
Steve Let's have a look in the fridge … No, it's all right, there are lots of eggs in here.
Gemma Oh, OK then. So, what present are you buying for Mum?
Steve That's easy. She wants a book about plants.
Gemma Oh no! I'm giving her a plant book – I bought it yesterday. You can't buy another book.
Steve Oh Gemma! The plant book was my idea, remember. So what can I get her?
Gemma Why don't you get her some flowers?
Steve That's a great idea. Then we can both give her the book and some flowers … So, when can we cook the cake? …

Test for Unit 15

1 2 Jack's 3 They're 4 girls' 5 Alison's Anna's
6 Anna's 7 Jack's

2 1 caps, one, cap, one 2 caps, ones, ones 3 one, ones, one

---

3 2 Whose 3 hers 4 ours 5 mine

4 1 camera 2 umbrella 3 glasses 4 wallet 5 bracelet

5 unusual, missing, easily, usually, absolutely

6 *Students make notes by answering the questions, then write the dialogue using the information from their notes.*

7 Children: A Don't, I'll B Would C Shall
Mother: A about B please C thank you

Test for Consolidation 3

1 2 b 3 c 4 b 5 d 6 d 7 c 8 b 9 c 10 d 11 c
12 a 13 c 14 a 15 b 16 b 17 d 18 c 19 a 20 b
21 a

2 1 sock, embarrassed 2 dark, frightened 3 wet, miserable
4 expedition, excited 5 noisy, tired

3 1 sank, in 2 found, last 3 During, became 4 After, saw 5 wrote, before

4a 1 William Wallace 2 1267 3 Mel Gibson 4 Because they became interested in the story of Braveheart. 5 Queen Isabelle.

b 1 ✓ 2 ✗ 3 ✓ 4 ✗ 5 ✗

5 3 Tim 4 Joe and Roberto 5 Tim 6 Tim
7 Joe and Roberto 8 Joe and Tim 9 Tim 10 Joe and Tim
11 Tim 12 Roberto

Tapescript
Anne Hi, Joe. I came to say goodbye. I'm going on holiday tomorrow.
Joe Hi, Anne. Where are you going?
Anne I'm going to Rome with some friends.
Joe Really? I went to Rome for a holiday last year.
Anne Did you have a good time?
Joe Yes, I did … but I had a terrible journey home.
Anne Really? What happened?
Joe Well, I went with my brother, Tim. We stayed in a really nice hotel and my Italian friend, Roberto, looked after us, and we had a fantastic time. Then, on the last day Roberto and I decided to go swimming – that was the big mistake!
Anne Why? What happened?
Joe Well, my brother had a headache, so he stayed in his room. Then after Roberto and I went swimming, we met some of his friends, so we stayed talking.
Anne So you got back to the hotel late?
Joe That's right, very late. So Tim decided to leave my bags at the hotel and go to the airport alone. That was OK because Roberto offered to drive me to the airport in his car. The big problem was that I didn't have my passport – Tim had it.
Anne So you were worried about not finding your brother?
Joe Yes. I didn't want to miss my flight, and I didn't want to be in Italy without a passport!
Anne Of course not. So, go on. What happened next?
Joe Well, of course Roberto drove me to the airport, but we were really unlucky. There are two airports and he took me to the wrong one! We drove to the right airport really fast – I was quite frightened – but of course it was very late, so I missed the flight.
Anne That's terrible. Did Tim catch the plane and leave you?
Joe No, he didn't. He waited for me. But he was really angry!
Anne I can imagine. So what did you do next?
Joe We got the next flight to London at eleven o'clock in the evening. Of course, we arrived very late at night … and we had no English money, so we slept in the airport. In the morning Tim took the underground to work, and I went home to bed. Then that evening Roberto telephoned to check that we were all right. He was very sorry about taking me to the wrong airport, but that was my fault too, really.
Anne That's an awful story. I must remember that there are two airports in Rome!